Rev. Everett Diederich, S.J.
Missouri Province Educational Institute
4511 W. Pine Blvd.
St. Louis, MO 63108

D0205375

II

Fundamental Liturgy

THE PONTIFICAL LITURGICAL INSTITUTE

HANDBOOK
FOR LITURGICAL STUDIES

VOLUME II

Fundamental Liturgy

ANSCAR J. CHUPUNGCO, O.S.B.

EDITOR

A PUEBLO BOOK

The Liturgical Press   Collegeville Minnesota

A Pueblo Book published by The Liturgical Press

Design by Frank Kacmarcik, Obl.S.B.

Library of Congress Cataloging-in-Publication Data

Handbook for liturgical studies / Anscar J. Chupungco, editor.
   p. cm.
  "A Pueblo book."
  Includes bibliographical references and index.
  Contents: v. 1. Introduction to the liturgy.
  ISBN 0-8146-6161-0 (vol. I)
  ISBN 0-8146-6162-9 (vol. II)
  1. Liturgics—Study and teaching. 2. Catholic Church—Liturgy-
-Study and teaching. I. Chupungco, Anscar J.
BV176.H234   1997
264—dc21   97-20141
                                             CIP

Contents

PART III: LITURGY AND THE HUMAN SCIENCES

* translated by Paul L. Duggan
** translated by Matthew J. O'Connell
*** translated by David Cotter, O.S.B.

Introduction

This volume, which carries the title *Fundamental Liturgy,* corresponds in some measure to that section of theological study called "Fundamental Theology." Volume I, which is introductory, offers a working definition of the liturgy, reviews its historical development, and presents its sources. The present volume, on the other hand, leads the reader to a deeper understanding of the liturgy by examining the basic concepts that belong to its definition. What concepts must one have in order to understand and explain the nature and purpose, the plan and actualization, and the relational character of the liturgy? This volume addresses these questions under three headings, which develop the foundational concepts of the liturgy, namely epistemology, celebration, and human sciences.

Epistemology discusses the nature of the liturgy from five perspectives. The first deals with the theology of the liturgy. In the past the liturgy was often regarded rather restrictively as a composite of rubrics and ceremonials. Today the liturgy is studied as a theological reality insofar as it is a cultic encounter with God, possesses elements that have a theological bearing, and hence can become the object of a systematic theological examination. This is what is meant by "liturgical theology." The second perspective refers to the symbolic nature of the liturgy. The liturgy not only uses symbols and is composed of various symbols, it is a symbol in itself. Its components, whether they are words, actions, or material elements, reveal through the veil of signs the presence of God, the mystery of Christ, and the community of the Church. The third epistemological perspective treats the question of spirituality. The liturgy is the source and summit of Christian life; indeed, its celebration is the basic form of spirituality. A vibrant spirituality, together with the glorification of God, is the ultimate purpose of liturgical celebrations. The fourth perspective is pastoral liturgy. The liturgy is not celebrated in a vacuum but in the day-to-day reality of the assembly.

Attention to the pastoral needs of the worshiping community stems from the profound realization that the liturgy is for the sake of the people. To be effective the liturgy must be pastoral. Lastly, in order to promote active participation in the liturgy there is no better instrument than catechesis.

From epistemology the volume moves on to consider the liturgical celebration. This section consists also of four perspectives. The first deals with liturgical ecclesiology. The liturgy is an action not only of Christ but also of the Church, which he always associates with himself in the work of redemption. It is the Church, the community of believers, that celebrates the liturgy and in whose behalf ministers preside or assist. Liturgical celebrations are always an ecclesiological fact. The second perspective is the liturgical assembly. The conciliar reform stresses the liturgy's communal character, which the gathered assembly manifests. In the liturgy the assembly becomes the reality, present here and now, of the Church at worship. The third perspective is active participation, which is the chief goal of the conciliar reform. It underlies the use of the vernacular, the revision and simplification of rites, liturgical catechesis, and inculturation. The fourth perspective is liturgical ministry. The assembly must be served by ministers, whether ordained or lay, who express thereby the authentic meaning of hierarchy, order, and Christian service.

The final section of this volume examines the relation of the liturgy to human sciences. Because the liturgy is a ritual action, its study touches on everything that the word "rite" signifies. Rite denotes psycho-sociological and anthropological realities and is regulated by their principles. That is why the liturgy, which falls under the category of rite, needs to be studied in the context of human persons, their cultural genius, and their social traits and traditions. Furthermore, rite is expressed and shaped by human language. Here the word "language" includes not only the spoken or written words but also the symbolism of gestures. Hence the liturgy, being a rite, is a linguistic fact. Rite also vests itself in arts in order to show the beauty and nobility of its content or message. The liturgy has always sought to clothe its divine message in visual and aural beauty, not only because of God but also out of respect for the assembly. Finally, rite is grafted in the cultural values, patterns, and institutions of particular groups. The liturgy as rite is a blending of different cultures that are for the most part foreign to a large number of assemblies in various parts of the world. It is a problem that is addressed by inculturation.

Anscar J. Chupungco, O.S.B.
Editor

Abbreviations

A	*Ambrosius.* Milan, 1925–.
AA	Vatican II, *Apostolicam actuositatem* (Decree on the Apostolate of the Lay People)
AAS	*Acta Apostolicae Sedis.* Rome, 1909–.
AB	*Analecta Bollandiana.* Brussels, 1882–.
ACC	Alcuin Club Collections. London, 1899–.
ACW	Ancient Christian Writers. New York, 1946–.
A.Dmitr	A. Dmitrievskij, *Opisanie liturgiceskich rukopisej hransjascihsja v bibliotekach pravoslavnago Vostoka,* I–II. Kiev, 1895, 1902.
AG	Vatican II, *Ad gentes* (Decree on the Church's Missionary Activity)
AGreg	Analecta Gregoriana. Rome, 1930–.
AL	Analecta liturgica. Rome (see SA).
Anàmnesis	*Anàmnesis: Introduzione storico-teologica alla liturgia.* Edited by the professors at the Pontificio Istituto Liturgico S. Anselmo, Rome, under the direction of S. Marsili and others. Casale Monferrato, 1974ff. Vol. 1, *La liturgia: Momento nella storia della salvezza.* Turin, 1974. Vol. 2, *La liturgia: Panorama storico generale.* Casale, 1978. Vol. 3/1, *La liturgia: I sacramenti. Teologia e storia della celebrazione.* 1986. Vol. 3/2: *La liturgia eucaristica: Teologia e storia della celebrazione.* Casale Monferrato, 1983. Vol. 5, *Liturgia delle ore.* 1990. Vol. 6, *L'anno liturgico: Storia, teologia e celebrazione.* Genoa, 1988. Vol. 7, *I sacramentali e le benedizioni.* 1989.
ASE	*Annali di storia dell'esegesi.* Bologna.
AST	Analecta sacra Tarraconensia. Barcelona, 1925–.
BA	Bibliothèque Augustinienne. Oeuvres de S. Augustin. Paris, 1949–.
BAR	S. Parenti and E. Velkovska, *L'eucologio Barberini gr. 336* (BELS 80). Rome, 1995.
BEL	Bibliotheca Ephemerides liturgicae. Rome, 1932–.
BELS	Bibliotheca Ephemerides liturgicae Subsidia. Rome, 1975–.
Bugnini	A. Bugnini, *The Reform of the Liturgy: 1948–1975.* Collegeville, Minn., 1990.

ButLitEc	*Bulletin de littérature ecclésiastique.* Toulouse, 1899–1936.
CAO	*Corpus antiphonalium officii.* Rome, 1963–1979.
CBL	Collectanea biblica Latina. Rome.
CCL	Corpus Christianorum. Series Latina. Turnhout, 1954–.
CCCM	Corpus Christianorum Continuatio Mediaevalis. Turnhout, 1971–.
CE	*Caerimoniale episcoporum.* Vatican City, 1984.
CL	*Communautés et liturgies.* Ottignies, Belgium.
CLLA	*Codices liturgici Latini antiquiores.* Freiburg/Schweiz, 1968.
Conc	*Concilium.* Edinburgh.
CPG	*Clavis Patrum Graecorum.* Turnhout, 1974–.
CSEL	Corpus scriptorum ecclesiasticorum Latinorum. Vienna, 1886.
CSIC	Consejo superior de investigaciones científicas. Madrid, 1940–1941.
DACL	*Dictionnaire d'archeologie chrétinne et liturgie.* Paris, 1907–1953.
DB	*Rituale Romanum: De benedictionibus* (Kaczynski). Vatican City, 1984.
DMP	*Directorium de Missis cum pueris—Directory for Masses with Children (EDIL1* ##3115-3169, pp. 968–980; *DOL* ##2134-2188, pp. 676–688).
DOE	*De ordinatione episcopi, presbyterorum et diaconorum.* Vatican City, 1989.
DOL	International Commission on English in the Liturgy, *Documents on the Liturgy 1963–1979: Conciliar, Papal and Curial Texts.* Collegeville, Minn., 1982.
DPAC	*Dizionario patristico e di antichità cristiane.* 3 vols. Casale Monferrato, 1983–1988.
DS	H. Denzinger and A. Schönmetzer, *Enchiridion symbolorum.* 32nd ed. Freiburg, 1963.
DSp	*Dictionnaire de spiritualité ascétique et mystique.* Paris, 1932–.
DSPB	*Dizionario di spiritualità biblico-patristica.* Turin, 1993.
DV	Vatican II, *Dei Verbum* (Dogmatic Constitution on Divine Revelation)
EDIL1	*Enchiridion documentorum instaurationis liturgicae 1* (1963–1973). Ed. R. Kaczynski. Turin, 1976.
EDIL2	*Enchiridion documentorum instaurationis liturgicae 2* (1973–1983). Ed. R. Kaczynski. Rome, 1988.
EO	*Ecclesia Orans.* Rome, 1984–.
EP 1961	A.-G. Martimort, *L'Église en prière: Introduction à la liturgie.* Paris, 1961.

EP 1983	*L'Église en prière*, 1983.
EphLit	*Ephemerides liturgicae*. Rome, 1887–.
EstTrin	*Estudios trinitarios*
FCh	Fontes Christiani. Freiburg.
FOP	Faith and Order Papers. Geneva.
FS	Festschrift
GCS	Die griechischen christlichen Schriftsteller der ersten drei Jahrhunderte. Leipzig.
GE	Vatican II, *Gravissimum educationis* (Declaration on Christian Education)
GeV	*Sacramentarium Gelasianum Vetus*
GrH	*Sacramentarium Gregorianum Hadrianum*
GS	Vatican II, *Gaudium et spes* (Pastoral Constitution on the Church in the Modern World)
HBS	Henry Bradshaw Society. London, 1891–.
HDG	*Handbuch der Dogmengeschichte*
HGK	*Handbuch der Kirchengeschichte*
HJ	*Heythrop Journal*. Oxford, 1960–.
HS	*Hispania sacra*. Madrid, 1948–.
IEHE	*Instituto español de historia eclesiástica*. Rome.
IGMR	*Institutio generalis Missalis Romani—General Instruction of the Roman Missal (EDIL1, ##1381–1736, pp. 469–546; DOL ##1376–1731, pp. 465–533).*
IGLH	*Institutio generalis de Liturgia Horarum—General Instruction of the Liturgy of the Hours. (DOL nos. 3431–3714, pp. 1091–1131).*
Irén	*Irénikon*. Chevetogne, 1926–.
Jungmann	J. A. Jungmann, *Missarum sollemnia*. 2 vols. Casale Monferrato, 1963.
JAC	*Jahrbuch für Antike und Christentum*. Münster, 1958–.
JLw	*Jahrbuch für Liturgiewissenschaft*. Münster, 1921–1941, 1973–1979.
JThS	*Journal of Theological Studies*. London, 1900–1905; Oxford, 1906–1949; n.s. Oxford, 1950–.
KB	*Katechetische Blätter*. Munich, 1875–.
LeV	*Lumière et vie*. Lyon, 1951–.
LG	Vatican II, *Lumen gentium* (Dogmatic Constitution on the Church)
Lit	*Liturgia*. Rome, N.S. 1967ff.
LJ	*Liturgisches Jahrbuch*. Münster, 1951–.
LL	A. Nocent, "I libri liturgici." *Anàmnesis* 2: *La liturgia: Panorama storico generale.*

xii

LO	Lex Orandi. Paris, 1944–.
LQF	Liturgie- (until 1957: geschichtliche) wissenschaftliche Quellen und Forschungen. Münster, 1909–1940; 1957–.
LThk	*Lexikon für Theologie und Kirche.* Freiburg, 1957–1965.
LV	*Lumen vitae.* Brussels, 1946–.
MD	*La Maison-Dieu.* Paris, 1945–.
MA1981	*Missale Ambrosianum.* Iuxta ritum sanctae Ecclesiae Mediolanensis. Ex decreto Sacrosancti Oecumenici Concilii Vaticani II instauratum. Milan, 1981; new ed. 1990.
Mansi	J. D. Mansi, *Sacrorum conciliorum nova et amplissima collectio.* 31 vols. Florence–Venice, 1757–1798; reprinted and continued by L. Petit and J. B. Martin, 53 vols. in 60. Paris, 1889–1927; reprinted Graz, 1960–.
MEL	Monumenta Ecclesiae liturgica. Paris, 1890–1912.
MGH	Monumenta Germaniae historica. Berlin, 1826.
MHS	Monumenta Hispaniae sacra. Madrid, 1946–.
ML	C. Vogel, *Medieval Liturgy: An Introduction to the Sources.* Washington, 1986.
MR1570	*Missale Romanum* ex decreto Sacrosancti Concilii Tridentini restitutum Pii V Pont. Max. iussu editum (various editions; here *Missale Romanum* ex decreto Sacrosancti Concilii Tridentini restitutum Summorum Pontificum cura recognitum. Editio XIX iuxta typicam. Turin–Rome, 1961).
MR1975	*Missale Romanum* ex decreto Sacrosancti Oecumenici Concilii Vaticani II instauratum auctoritate Pauli Pp. VI promulgatum. Editio typica altera. Vatican City, 1975.
MS	*Medieval Studies.* Toronto–London, 1938–.
MuS	*Musicam sacram.* EDIL1 ##733-801, pp. 275–291; DOL ##4122-4190, pp. 1293–1306.
NBA	Nuova biblioteca Agostiniana. Rome.
NDL	*Nuovo dizionario di liturgia.* Rome, 1984.
NHL	*Neues Handbuch der Literaturwissenschaft.* Frankfurt-am-Main.
Not	*Notitiae.* Vatican City, 1965–.
NRT	*Nouvelle revue théologique.* Louvain, 1869–.
OB	*Rituale Romanum, Ordo benedictionum.* Vatican City, 1984.
OBP	*Rituale Romanum, Ordo baptismi parvulorum.* Vatican City, 1969,[1] 1973.[2]
OCA	Orientalia christiana analecta. Rome, 1935–.
OCM	*Rituale Romanum, Ordo celebrandi matrimonium.* Vatican City, 1969,[1] 1991.[2]
OCP	*Orientalia christiana periodica.* Rome, 1935–.

ODEA	*Pontificale Romanum, Ordo dedicationis ecclesiae et altaris.* Vatican City, 1977.
OE	Vatican II, *Orientalium Ecclesiarum* (Decree on the Catholic Eastern Churches)
Oe	*Rituale Romanum, Ordo exsequiarum.* Vatican City, 1969.
OICA	*Rituale Romanum, Ordo initiationis christianae adultorum.* Vatican City, 1972,[1] 1974.[2]
OLM	*Ordo lectionum Missae—Lectionary for Mass:* Introduction, 2nd ed. *EDIL2* ##4057-4181, pp. 337–370; *LD*, pp. 135–176.
OP	*Rituale Romanum, Ordo paenitentiae.* Vatican City, 1974.
OPR	*Rituale Romanum, Ordo professionis religiosae.* Vatican City, 1970; rev. ed. 1975.
OUI	*Rituale Romanum, Ordo unctionis infirmorum.* Vatican City, 1972.
PDOC	*Petit dictionnaire de l'Orient chrétien.*
PG	J. P. Migne, Patrologia cursus completus: Series Graeca. Paris, 1857–1866.
Ph	*Phase: Revista de pastoral liturgica.* Barcelona, 1961–.
PL	J. P. Migne, Patrologia cursus completus: Series Latina. Paris, 1844–1855.
PO	Vatican II, *Presbyterorum ordinis* (Decree on the Ministry and Life of Priests)
PRG	*Pontificale Romano-Germanicum*
QL	*Questions liturgiques.* Louvain, 1911–.
RAC	*Reallexikon für Antike und Christentum.* Stuttgart, 1950–.
RB	*Revue biblique.* Paris, 1892–.
RBén	*Revue bénédictine.* Maredsous, 1884–.
RCT	*Revista catalana de teología.* Barcelona, 1976–.
RED	Rerum ecclesiasticarum documenta. Rome, 1954.
RET	*Revista Española de teología.* Madrid, 1940–.
Rev Lit et Monastique	*Revue de liturgie et monastique.* Maredsous, 1911–1940.
RG	*Revue grégorienne.* Paris, 1911–.
RHE	*Revue d'histoire ecclésiastique.* Louvain, 1900–.
Righetti	*Manuale di storia liturgica.* Vol. 1 (2nd ed., 1950); vol. 2 (2nd ed., 1955); vol. 3 (1949); vol. 4 (1953). Milan.
RL	*Rivista liturgica.* Praglia–Finalpia, 1914–.
RPL	*Rivista di pastorale liturgica.* Brescia, 1963.
RSPT	*Revue des sciences philosophiques et théologiques.* Paris, 1907–.
RSR	*Recherches de science religieuse.* Paris, 1910–.
SA	Studia Anselmiana. Rome, 1933–.
SAEMO	*Sancti Ambrosii Episcopi Mediolanensis Opera*

SC	Vatican II, *Sacrosanctum concilium* (Constitution on the Sacred Liturgy)
ScC	*Scuola cattolica.* Milan, 1873–.
SCA	Studies in Christian Antiquity. Washington, 1941–.
SCh	Sources chrétiennes. Paris, 1941–.
SE	*Sacris erudiri.* Steenbruge, 1948–.
SF	Spicilegium Friburgense. Freiburg, 1957.
SFS	Spicilegii Friburgensis Subsidia
SL	*Studia liturgica.* Rotterdam, 1962.
ST	Studi e testi. Vatican City, 1900–.
StudPad	*Studia patavina.* Padua, 1954.
ThS	*Theological Studies.* Woodstock, 1940–.
TQ	*Theologische Quartalschrift.* Tübingen, 1819–.
TRE	*Theologische Realenzyklopädie.* Berlin, 1947–.
TS	*Typologie des sources du moyen âge occidental*
TTZ	*Trierer theologische Zeitschrift.* Trier, 1945–.
TU	Texte und Untersuchungen zur Geschichte der altchristlichen Literatur. Berlin, 1882–.
TuA	Texte und Arbeite. Beuron, 1917–.
UR	Vatican II, *Unitatis redintegratio* (Decree on Ecumenism)
VC	*Vigiliae Christianae.* Amsterdam, 1947–.
Ve	*Sacramentarium Veronense*
ViSpi	*Vie spirituelle.* Paris, 1947–.
WUNT	Wissenschaftliche Untersuchungen zum Neuen Testament. Tübingen, 1950.
Wor	*Worship.* Collegeville, Minn., 1951–. Formerly *Orate Fratres*, 1926–1951.
ZAW	*Zeitschrift für Alttestamentliche Wissenschaft.* Berlin, 1881–.
ZRG RA	*Zeitschrift der Savigny-Stiftung für Rechtsgeschichte (Romantische Abteilung).* Weimar.

Part I

Liturgical Epistemology

1

Theology of the Liturgy

"It is the desire of the Church to carry out a thorough general reform of the liturgy," reads no. 21 of the constitution *Sacrosanctum concilium* of Vatican Council II. With this directive the Church welcomed the growing desire for a reform of worship and the individual efforts of the twentieth-century pontiffs to achieve a general reform of the liturgy. A path had cleared to deepen theological understanding of the liturgy and a concept of the Church's worship that in many points differs from the post-Tridentine period. Such liturgical development inaugurated a new epoch.

A problem arises when we ask what consequences flowed from the council's decision to reform the liturgy and from its concept of liturgy as regards the theological discipline that is termed "liturgiology" or "liturgical science." The purpose of this chapter is to outline the nature and tasks of liturgical science and to situate it in the realm of theological science.

REFLECTIONS ON THE HISTORICAL PATH TOWARD A
THEOLOGY OF THE LITURGY
If we consider the expression "theology of the liturgy" in a technical sense, the history of this part of theology is relatively short and is seen as a problem of modern times. If, however, we consider the expression more widely and understand by "theology of the liturgy" the effort on the part of all Christian generations to reflect on the experience of worship and to grasp the relation between faith and praxis, then its history is quite long and complex.[1]

[1] Some reconstructions of this path prove to be quite useful; cf. S. Marsili, "La liturgia, momento storico della salvezza," *Anàmnesis* 1, 33–156, especially 47–84;

Authors who study the history of the theological understanding of worship usually start with an inquiry about the term "liturgy" in order to grasp its meaning and the evolution of this meaning,[2] especially regarding the Old and New Testaments. The observations that are made with regard to the term, its usage and non-usage in Sacred Scripture, serve to bring out the original notion of worship in the Jewish-Christian experience. The terminological analysis shows that the intention is present in Scripture to rescue ritual moments from an unproductive, externalized, legalistic, and formal interpretation.

In the translation of the Septuagint, the term λειτουργία had taken on a technical sense indicating Levitical worship; thus the dichotomy between spiritual worship and ritual worship was underlined, differing from the original notion that the spiritual component was intrinsic to worship. The New Testament generally leaves out this technical term and recovers the understanding of worship along spiritual lines, the most genuine line of the prophetic tradition.

Some reflections are needed in order to start from the fact of the enduring worship-event in Christian praxis. Without doubt Christ, the sole mediator between God and human beings, renders obsolete and useless all religious mediation (cf. Hebrews 11); but the mystery of the Church, founded and willed by Christ as his body, has provided the value of sacramental mediation over the ages. It follows that the references to worship speak not only of an absolute and irreducible newness with regard to content but also of a continuity with the language and ritual of the Old Testament. We are looking at a process of assimilation and reinterpretation.[3]

Deep within the biblical understanding of the "theological" nature of worship lies the awareness of the unbreakable relationship that links the rite to the event of the covenant. Two consequences flow from this: (1) the rite is never a substitution for life; life is called to be

---

idem, "Teologia liturgica," *NDL*, 1508–25; idem, "La liturgia nel discorso teologico odierno. Per una fondazione della liturgia pastorale: individuazione delle prospettivee degli ambiti specifici," *Una liturgia per l'uomo. La liturgia pastorale e i suoi compiti* (= Caro Salutis Cardo–Studi, 5) Padua, 1986, 17–47; A. Kavanagh, *On Liturgical Theology* (New York, 1984).

[2] To do this, authors accept the conclusions in H. Strathmann and R. Meyer, "Leitourgéo," *Grande Lessico del Nuovo Testamento* (Brescia, 1970) 6:188ff.

[3] Cf. N. Füglister, *Il valore salvifico della Pasqua* (Brescia, 1976) 103, 125, 134, 298, 302.

covenant, the place of encounter with God; (2) the rite refers totally to the reality of the covenant, serving as its memorial; therefore worship is not the performance of a religious person for God but rather is the place of God's self-communication to humans. People are called to accept the newness of God's gift, to open themselves to God in the obedience of faith.

The ritual moment is situated within the existence of the human saved by the Lord. Still, liturgy remains the ritual access to the salvation-event, the expression that gives fullness to a cultural life that is both acceptance and welcome of the salvation-event that has occurred in history — that history marked by the presence of God that the rite itself helps to identify.

The dimensions that constitute every celebration can be reduced to three: (1) historical, namely, the intrinsic connection of the liturgy with salvation history; (2) communitarian, that is, where the covenant is ritualized (and reactualized), the subject is the people (the community); (3) mystery-based, marking the modality of the appearance of the saving event in the celebration. This modality, both in the Old and in the New Testament, is that of the ritual mystery that becomes celebrated where the believer/community, by opening itself to receive the salvific event, lives it in continual tension toward the ἔσχατον.

A second great phase in a theology of the liturgy is one in which symptoms of regression emerged. From a genuinely theological understanding of the connection between faith and worship, between life and worship, that was characteristic of the patristic age, there was a shift to less theological understanding, ever more allegorizing, ascetic, moralistic. Even in the presence of undeniable symptoms of regression, the progressive manifestation of a complex of cultic and ritual elements (rites, prayers, feasts, etc.) was taking shape as a rich and articulate ecclesial praxis and was becoming central to the Christian community's experience of the life and nature of the Church.

The evolution (as well as the regression) seems linked to a double pole: external/cultural[4] and internal/theological-

[4] One thinks in this regard of the evolution of "cultural paradigms": evolving, that is, of the whole "constellation of beliefs, values, techniques, and so forth, shared by the members of a given community" (T. Kuhn, *La struttura delle rivoluzioni scientifiche. Come mutano le idee della scienza*, 7th ed. (= Einaudi Paperbacks, 4) (Turin, 1987) 151; evolving of ideas, models, and institutions. One thinks also, by way of example, of an Augustine, who constantly inquires into the "signified"

pastoral.[5] In any event, the liturgy appears as a manifestation of the faith of a Church that has become part of time and history. The instances of regression are then read by paying attention to the ecclesiological perspective; it is the changing of the Church's "self-understanding" to take into account the evolution (or perhaps regression) in understanding worship. This occurs while resisting the line that would favor the perspective according to which the liturgy is an event that realizes the mystery of Christ, an event that "generates" the Church. We now pose a new question in which the "theology of the liturgy," understood in a technical sense, must reflect on why worship exists and how it has that meaning and that efficacy in the total experience of faith.

SOME MODELS OF "LITURGICAL SCIENCE"
When the liturgy was considered mainly as a collection of norms issued by the ecclesiastical hierarchy for the regulation of rites and public ceremonies, "liturgical science" was understood as the "science of rubrics," that is, the systematic compilation and interpretation of the norms. The manuals of this science were collections in which the external procedure of the rite was minutely described. The sources were, besides the liturgical books, the countless decrees and responses of the Congregation of Rites (more than four thousand decrees). This model, which was viewed as a part of Church law, could be interpreted as a reduction of liturgical science to the study

---

of liturgical practice by reducing the "signifier" to mere deferral, to pure pointing; we can think about the "difficulty" that Thomas had in articulating satisfactorily the descending phase (sanctification) and the ascending phase (worship) of the liturgical experience. Coupling these two great thinkers is not a prejudice against worship or against ritual; they did not thematically explore this element completely simply because it was an integral part of the cultural and religious horizon in which they lived. They were not "challenged" by the problem concerning "why" cultic praxis should exist in the experience of faith.

[5] The progressive distancing of the liturgy from the Christian community, the disappearance of the catechumenate and the old penitential discipline, the multiplication of "private Masses" — all these are factors that enable understanding the reaction that would develop in the modern age. Within the Church this would be marked by radical contraposition to external worship, marked by "interiorism," by "meditative" and ascetical practices. In the world of cultures "suspicions" would arise on this specific human "behavior": it would be called upon more and more to "justify itself" as such.

of grammar and syntax so that rules might be correctly applied, with no interest in the actual theological significance.

Another fundamental aspect of "liturgical science" is evaluating the Church's worship from the viewpoint of its historical development. By "liturgy" we understand here the cultic acts or cultic forms emerging within a specific time under multiple influences. The first great labor completed by scholars who developed the historical aspect was the research and publication of the liturgical sources. This led to the analytical study of the same sources and created the conditions enabling them to produce studies of the history of the liturgy within the broadest context of the Church's historical path. An early phase of these studies is characterized by approaching liturgy as a reality containing enormous riches: the scholar discovers them, studies them, and presents them with suitable commentary so that others also might enjoy this patrimony. Any attempt to interpret the facts of the liturgy is virtually absent, and this absence deprives these studies of their undisputed importance. A second phase could be defined as that of critical approach. The aim is to traverse the evolutionary path of the liturgy, yet also to become aware of the "why" underlying the various changes; moreover, current praxis is to be reviewed.

Methodologically, the shift is important. The history of the liturgy aims at interpreting the forms of worship by making use of different keys such as the relation between liturgy and cultures, the pastoral application, the comparison among the diverse practices of different churches, the relationship between the texts, gestures, and formulation of the faith. Here we must give simultaneous attention to liturgical "signifiers" and "signified." Doing the history of the liturgy more and more takes the shape of a critical inquiry, at times with varying interpretive keys, preferably with a synthetic and unitary hermeneutical tool that succeeds in bringing out the modalities with which liturgical expressions translate the newness of Christian worship that is essentially a remembrance of the paschal covenant.[6]

---

[6] An accurate reconstruction of the two models presented till now is found in F. Brovelli, "Per uno studi della liturgia," *ScC* 104 (1976) 567–635. Cf. also G. Bonaccorso, *Introduzione allo studio della liturgia* (= Caro Salutis Cardo–Sussidi, 1) (Padua, 1990); idem, "Lo studio della liturgia nel dibattito teologico contemporaneo," *Celebrare il mistero di Cristo. I. La celebrazione: introduzione alla liturgia cristiana* (= *BELS* 73 / Studi di liturgia–Nuova serie, 25) (Rome, 1993) 21–44.

Some models explicitly understand "liturgical science" as a genuine theological reflection. Such studies place liturgical signifiers and signified in relation to the salvific work effected by God in Jesus Christ in history. It is a question here of attaining the truth-value of things liturgically signified, that is, their relation to the totality of salvation.

In the liturgical movement, which has been so relevant in our time, we can remember Lambert Beauduin[7] as the initiator of a genuine liturgical line in the study of Christian worship. He recovered the theological aspect of the liturgy by linking it closely to the celebrant subject, namely, the Church; the liturgy is the worship of the Church.

Odo Casel

However, a decisive thrust toward theological comprehension of Christian worship was achieved by Odo Casel.[8] The category this author uses is that of "mystery"; it allows him to hold together (and this is his originality) two aspects that will appear ever more inseparable where the aim is to form a theology of the liturgy — the theological aspect and the anthropological-philosophical aspect. "Mystery," indeed, is the historical unfolding of the salvation worked by God in Christ; in the "meantime" the Church lives in the faith and in the mystery of the worship of Christ.

By making use of the reconstructions of two contemporary scholars,[9] we can say that the central thesis of Casel is that the mysteries are salvific actions of God. Since the mystery surpasses all possible cognition, communication, or participation of a theoretical and abstract sort it cannot engender a pure doctrine but must be realized in symbols, which are necessary modes of expression for mysteries. Since symbols by their nature put into action the event to which they refer, they too are "mysteries." "The difference between the cultic mystery and the real mystery that is Christ lies only in the fact that

[7] Cf. especially his book *La piété de l'Église. Principes et faits* (Louvain, 1914).

[8] Casel's basic work is *The Mystery of Christian Worship* (London, 1962) ed. by B. Neunheuser.

[9] G. Lafont, "Permanence et transformations des intuitions de Dom Casel," *EO* 4 (1987) 261–84; E. Ruffini, "Orientamenti e contenuti della teologia sacramentaria nella riflessione teologica ontemporanea," *"Mysterion" e "sacramentum." La sacramentalità negli scritti dei Padri e nei testi liturgici primitivi*, E. Ruffini and E. Lodi (= Nuovi saggi teologici, 24) (Bologna, 1987) 15–56.

the former is the symbolic representation of the latter; therefore the difference involves only the mode of being, not the essence itself of the mystery."[10]

Casel affirms that "the Lord has given us the mysteries of worship: the sacred actions which we perform, but which, at the same time, the Lord performs upon us by his priests' service in the Church. . . . An act common to God and his human community can only be properly carried out in a symbolic action. . . ."[11] It seems that one can state that even with all the limits that different criticisms have imputed to Casel's reflections, the "theology of the liturgy" that he elaborated succeeds in individuating and holding together in an articulate manner both human cultic being and the concrete reality of the Christian mystery. Indeed, the special synergy between God's action and human action occurring in the liturgical act constitutes the horizon of possibility for worship. And this lesson still seems to be of extraordinary importance.

At this point we wish to examine two models that were influenced by the preceding ones but that followed their own path, an important path since generations of liturgists were trained in their schools. We are referring to Cipriano Vagaggini[12] and Salvatore Marsili.[13]

Cipriano Vagaggini

Vagaggini's main concern lies in placing liturgy within general synthetic theology; here his bent as a systematic theologian is displayed. For Vagaggini, the theological examination of the liturgy is the fundamental presupposition for being able to live it adequately on a spiritual level and to highlight its pastoral value concretely and usefully. It becomes indispensable, then, to consider the liturgical reality

---

[10] E. Ruffini, "*Orientamenti . . .,*" 42.

[11] O. Casel, *The Mystery of Christian Worship*, 15, 22.

[12] Vagaggini's fundamental work is *Theological Dimensions of the Liturgy* (Collegeville, 1976). In line with Vagaggini we can place P. Visentin, "Lo studio della teologia nella liturgia," *Introduzione agli studi liturgici* (= Liturgica, 1) (Rome, 1962) 189–223. The main studies of this author are collected in P. Visentin, *Culmen et Fons. Raccolta di studi di liturgia e spiritualità* (a cura di R. Cecolin e F. Trolese). I: *Mysterium Christi ab Ecclesia celebratum*. II: *Lex orandi e lex credendi* (Caro Salutis Cardo–Studi, 3–4) (Padua, 1987).

[13] Besides the works mentioned in the preceding notes, of importance are the articles "La liturgia nella strutturazione della teologia," *RL* 58 (1971) 153–62, and "Liturgia e teologia. Proposta teoretica," *RL* 59 (1972) 455–73.

in the light of its ultimate principles or else to clarify the fact of the liturgy with the light of reason, and to do that, it is necessary to rethink the whole systematic theological synthesis.

This involves assuming the truly scientific value of the inductive method and applying it to liturgical rites and formulas. "Theological liturgy defines the study of liturgy in a theological context by bringing to the historical inquiry about liturgical action the importance of what has been the subject of prior research, and by introducing the results and consequences thereof into the elaboration of its spiritual, pastoral, and juridic content.

"General theological liturgy, while concentrating on the theological point of view, studies the elements common to the individual parts of the liturgy. Special theological liturgy studies in the same way the elements that are peculiar to these same individual parts: the Mass, the other sacraments, the sacramentals, and the liturgical year."[14]

This "theological liturgy" is theological with respect to the method and also with respect to the referent constituted by revelation as sacred history. "The liturgy, in fact, is nothing but a certain way in which Christ, in the present intermediate time which extends from Pentecost to the parousia, in this eschatological time already going on, communicates the fullness of His divine life to individual souls, reproduces His mystery in them, draws them into His mystery."[15] The theological stature mentioned above allows Vagaggini to employ a "classic" theological method and, at the same time, to open himself in a balanced way to an understanding of revelation as history of which liturgy is a part realized as worship, as cultic action.

Salvatore Marsili

Salvatore Marsili appears as the major Italian specialist on the work of Casel, as an original and personal interpreter of Caselian thought, and as a continuer of that thought with trends of independence.

Marsili's reflection moves decisively toward the construction of a "theology of the liturgy," or rather of a "liturgical theology." To accomplish this, he maintains that it is fundamental to study the "theological nature of the liturgical act," and this, for Marsili, signifies the study of the nature of what is realized in the celebration. The departure point is the individuation in Christ-sacrament of the essential

[14] C. Vagaggini, *Theological Dimensions of the Liturgy*, xxiv.
[15] Ibid., 15–16.

moment of revelation. Consequently, sacramentality is not only the actuation mode of historical revelation but also the primary and essential reality in the light of which the whole content of faith, since it is the first object of experience in the celebration, is the object of intellectual reflection. Liturgical theology is, then, a discourse on God in the light of the sacramentality that is the mode of being of the revelation both in its first historical existence and in its actuation in the liturgy. Underneath lies the comprehension of the liturgy as the actuating moment of salvation history, rather, as the "moment itself of salvation history," a moment that creates the time of the Church, that is, the extension of salvation into the ambit of the human community, just as the incarnation had been the actuating moment of the same history of salvation in Christ.

Marsili also elaborates, on an epistemological level, a viewpoint that makes liturgical science into a constitutive and basic part of theological science. The object of theology is the unique mystery of Christ and the unique history of salvation, which Scripture reveals as a promise and as a fact, which dogmatics illustrates and explains, which moral theology orders toward practical execution, and which in the liturgy is realized and actuated sacramentally. Therefore a theological reflection on the "salvific economy" consists of two basic poles: Scripture and liturgy. Since the liturgy is that in which this same revelation becomes an event of salvation, it appears as a synthesis of the whole of salvation history.

It is difficult to escape the impression of power and completeness in Marsili, even though, approaching it with a critical spirit, one is compelled to point out a kind of "aporia" that runs through the whole system. Just to affirm the theological worth of liturgical science that accrues to it from the incomparable grandeur of its object, Marsili is led to leap over fundamental passages and connections (essential among all of them is the theoretical comparison of the relationship between history and salvation history and that between history and cultic ritual) in order to arrive at an understanding of the liturgy as an absolute value and, given this, to prescind from rite and from worship.

Something of a paradox appears in the theme summarized above. Although starting out to justify and render spiritually beneficial the worship whose cultural obviousness no longer seems to be in evidence, the absoluteness of this value that is the liturgy does not require effort on the theologian's part to reflect on the rite. Rather, there is a kind of non-ritualness (or non-cultualness) of Christian liturgy.[16]

The question of ritualness, insufficiently featured in theological elaborations, has been present in studies of a pastoral character. At first these deal with practical concerns and come finally to think of liturgical reflection as addressing the problem of celebrating, taken in all its anthropological and theological import. These same studies can bring into interaction different viewpoints around the reality of Christian worship, so as "to recognize its original and irreducible status, accessible to different points of view but not capable of being reduced to any of them."[17]

THE TEACHING OF THE CONCILIAR CONSTITUTION
SACROSANCTUM CONCILIUM

In preparing to inquire into *Sacrosanctum concilium (SC)* to find in it a "theology of the liturgy," let us set some premises:

1. *SC* does not contain a speculative theology on the nature of the liturgy.

---

[16] The most recent contributions with the purpose of reflecting on the problem of the "theology of the liturgy" (in general and in Marsilian thought) are by A. M. Triacca, "Teologia della liturgia o teologia liturgica? Contributo di P. Salvatore Marsili per una chiarificazione," *RL* 80 (1993) 267–89, and by S. Maggiani, "La teologia liturgica di S. Marsili come 'opera aperta,'" *RL* 80 (1993) 341–57. Whereas for the first author Marsili's work is incomplete and needs to attain a broadening of the meaning of liturgy that encompasses mystery-action-life (namely, the whole of ecclesial expression), for the second author the Marsilian work contains within itself notable "seeds" that, although they did not yield fruit within it, are now yielding fruit, given that Marsili has been able to renew at least in part his own judgment on the relation between liturgy and rite by reevaluating symbol-ism as the "place" appropriate for living the worship in spirit and truth.

We believe it is necessary to recall some significant works that follow the road of theological reflection on the liturgy by addressing rigorously its dimensions of cult, rite, and symbolic action: L. M. Chauvet, *Du symbolique au symbole. Essai sur les sacrements* (Paris, 1979) idem, *Symbole et sacrement. Une relecture sacramentelle de l'existence chrétienne* (Paris, 1987).

There are useful reviews and reflections on Chauvet's work: cf. the review by G. Lafont in *EO* 5 (1988) 231–35 and the article by A. Grillo, "Ragioni del simbolo e rifiuto del fondamento nella sacramentaria generale di L. M. Chauvet. Spunti per una critica 'in bonam partem,'" *EO* 12 (1995) 173–93.

[17] G. Bonaccorso, *Introduzione allo studio . . .*, 92.

2. *SC* is a reflection on the content of celebrative action so as to grasp, on the basis of patristic and liturgical tradition reelaborated by the liturgical movement, its *nature as mystery*; the theology of *SC* is the doctrine of the liturgical mystery and its celebration.

3. The key points of this doctrine seem to be present in *SC* in two modalities: (a) one that is more synthetic, assertive, and in some way "defining," consisting in situating the liturgy within the economy of salvation (as a particular aspect of that economy); hence the recognition of the liturgical act as being irreplaceable and unsurpassable, since it is the exercise of the work of salvation completed by Christ in the paschal mystery; in virtue of this and under this aspect, the liturgy is *culmen et fons* (summit and source); (b) another modality more descriptive of the same liturgical action, assuming as a basic hermeneutical category that of the *ecclesiology of communion:* a holy people, gathered on the Lord's day around the Word of God; a priestly people, called to offer the sacrifice of Christ and to participate in his paschal banquet. All this is described as participation in the celebration of the Lord's manifold presence.

4. *SC* employs an understanding of Word and sacrament that requires their mutual relationship and a type of reciprocal immanence: the Word is of course sacrament; the sacrament, on the other hand, is an actuation of the Word.

5. Finally, it must be remembered that a correct interpretation of *SC* is impossible unless its reception is taken into consideration: specifically, that particular reception consisting in the liturgical reform (books and ecclesial praxis); *SC* explains the liturgical reform, and the concrete actuation of the liturgical reform interprets *SC*.

This last reflection conditions our way of inquiring into *SC*. We would like now to carry out something of a critical return to the conciliar constitution *SC:* the challenge (theoretical and practical) appears still to be the one set by the need of having to resignify the rite as such (as a moment capable of saying in its particular language the "whole" of Christian existence) and to reconsign it to the communities as a reality that is anthropologically and culturally situated in the now of our history. "The liturgy . . . is the outstanding means whereby the faithful may express in their lives and manifest to others the mystery of Christ and the real nature of the true Church" (*SC* 2). "Liturgical services are not private functions, but are celebrations belonging to the Church, which is a sacrament of unity, namely their holy people united and ordered under their bishops" (SC 26).

Liturgical action is configured here as an aspect of the life of the Church, an apt manifestation of its nature and its mystery. This emphasis on the theological value of the liturgy seems to us to be correctly filtered through a theological-pastoral vision both of the overall praxis of the Church and of liturgical praxis. When SC speaks theologically about the liturgy, it presents it as a praxis capable of expressing the way in which the liturgy is placed within the life of the Church as well as the extent to which it is capable of being shaped as a true sign of the Church. Thus it seems to us that SC, albeit obliquely, has an articulate and unitary vision concerning the theology of the liturgy: it has theological value not only as a memorial of the salvific event but likewise as a qualified manner of the Church presenting itself, or more specifically, "an apt sign of the Church in the world."

Yet when we take into consideration nos. 26–32, 33–36, 37–39 of SC, which give the criteria for liturgical reform, once again it is the unifying category of a pastorally useful liturgical celebration that emerges. The liturgical celebration of the mystery of Christ, of which the Church is the full subject, must be conducted through a system of signs that is concerned with being true and expressive for people today. This means that the liturgical reform — when its criteria are indicated — must open itself to the most properly and rigorously celebrative horizon, and therefore of cultic and ritual praxis.

Finally, in setting norms and concrete application, the liturgical reform postulates a taking charge of its cultic and ritual praxis, since precisely under this aspect it is a qualifying moment for the life of the Church. It seems that we rediscover here that genuinely Caselian sense of profound reciprocity between the cultic character of humans and the concrete reality of the Christian mystery. Therefore we do not regard it as risky to identify one of the fundamental points of SC in this affirmation: the original action of God in Christ (= the salvific mystery) today is given to humankind in the Church through liturgical celebration.

Recent ecclesial experience and reflections on the constitution seem to move in this direction. The peculiarity of liturgical action (*actio liturgica, actio sacra in cui opus nostrae redemptionis exercetur — Missale Romanum, oratio super oblata Feriae V in Coena Domini*) is that of being a *symbolic-ritual action*: thus the ritual core of the liturgy is viewed as inescapable and fundamental.

SC states that Christ is present in liturgical actions (no. 7); that the liturgy is a realization of the mystery of Christ by the power of the Holy Spirit through a shared rite (no. 6); that the liturgy is the exercise of the priesthood of Christ through sensible signs (no. 7); that the liturgy is salvation history in action by means of the sacrifice and of the sacraments (nos. 2, 5, 6, 48). It seems fair to state that the novelty given by the council to the liturgy is precisely the formalization of its nature as an action of Christ and the Church. If one reviews carefully the preconciliar and conciliar phases of the document's genesis, one comes to perceive the progress of an understanding of the liturgy that passes from the simple to the complex, namely, from a restricted and essentialistic concept of rite in the juridical sense to a broadened concept that comprises other elements singularly present in the phenomenological analysis of rite.[18]

Is this not a matter of attributing to the conciliar document, seen in its genesis, in its parts, in its whole, and in its reception, a very complex understanding of the liturgy, that is not reducible to the elements deemed to be *de necessitate,* present *ad decorem vel ad sollemnitatem,* or as *caeremoniae secundariae?* The liturgical action in its complexity seems to take well-defined contours analogous to those of the "ritual phenomenon" as it emerges from anthropological analysis.

In summary, the overall reflection that goes back "critically" to *Sacrosanctum concilium* seems to be the following: the liturgy is the action of the Church in which Christ becomes present, and this action assumes the features of ritual action similar to that described as well in anthropological sciences.

AN OUTLINE OF LITURGICAL THEOLOGY

As the first step toward an authentic liturgical theology, let us ask, "Why does the paschal event of Christ present itself in the liturgy in a ritual manner?" It is a question of uncovering the reason by which

[18] Cf. A. Catella and R. Tagliaferri, "Le domande e le intenzionalità cui risponde l'impianto di 'Sacrosanctum Concilium,'" *RL* 77 (1990) 129–43; R. Tagliaferri, "Quale modello di pastorale liturgica emerge dal Concilio? Riflessione di 'ermeneutica' conciliare," *RL* 79 (1992) 25–38; A. Catella, "Forme dell'iniziativa pastorale recente. L'ambito della celebrazione," *Progetto pastorale e cura della fede* (= Disputatio, 7) (Milan, 1996) 85–99.

we cannot not celebrate, nor skip over ritual mediation if we want to "approach the mystery."

1. "In order to establish and legitimize scientifically liturgical theology, it is first necessary to investigate the possibility of the paschal mystery becoming realized in ritual."[19] This is a very interesting mode of expression, since it explicitly identifies the role of understanding the rite if one wants to understand Christian worship. Room is made, therefore, for the anthropological aspect within a theological inquiry. Yet the anthropological aspect still seems to be thought of as separate from (as preliminary to) the theological.

In reality, once the nature of the object under study (Christian rite in relation to its foundations) is clarified, it is necessary to enter into a long course of a phenomenological-hermeneutical inquiry, the outcome of which must be that of discerning the conditions of possibility for uncovering the ultimate foundation of Christian ritual. This involves overcoming the separation between anthropological and theological, between transcendental and categorical: it involves discerning the fundamental unity between anthropology and theology. For a definition of the tasks of liturgical theology (at least in its methodological aspect), it seems right to point out these objectives: arrive at an understanding of the "horizon of meaning" of the Christian action of celebrating;[20] a theology of the Christian practice of celebrating cannot help but discuss scientifically ritual practice, and this right from the beginning; it cannot expunge the reflection on "why" it is necessary to celebrate the rites in order to enter into contact with God; it cannot fail to resolve the paradox in which Jesus, who demands worship "in spirit and in truth," must ritualize his gift and his testament in order to entrust it to his disciples.[21]

We are well aware of the difficulty and the delicacy of the task that presents itself to liturgical theology in inquiring into the "why" of ritual practice. It seems to us that the relation between rite/cult and

[19] M. Augè in "La teologia liturgica," *Metodologia teologica. Avviamento allo studio e alla ricerca pluridisciplinari* (= Universo teologia, 28) (Cinisello Balsamo, 1994) 240–51.

[20] Note that, in this expression, we mean by "celebrating" the liturgical reality experienced in its varied and concrete modalities; by "horizon of meaning" we mean the questioning extended to include intention; cf. A. N. Terrin, *Leitourgía, Dimensione fenomenologica e aspetti semiotici* (= Le scienze umane) (Brescia, 1988) 16.

[21] A. Catella, "Introduzione generale," *Celebrare il mistero di Cristo . . . .,* 13–8.

Christian liturgy is a serious case within those more general relations that exist between evidence and faith, between the sacred and faith, between religion and faith. And it is truly useful for our task to keep in mind the paths traveled by scholars who surmount separations and dichotomies or, indeed, facile juxtapositions or sanctions in order to demonstrate the theological relevance of the respective categories mentioned above.[22]

In order now to be more explicit and simple, let us go back to a text of *Sacrosanctum concilium:* "Every liturgical celebration, because it is an action of Christ the Priest and of his Body which is the Church, is a sacred action surpassing all others; no other action of the Church can equal its effectiveness by the same title and to the same degree" (no. 7).

As can be seen, here there are present specific realities of Christian faith, and these occur through realities really and fully human, such as relation, action, and the like. It is not said that the two levels are identical or that the one of faith is equivalent to the human. It is stated, however, that in order to gain access to understanding and to attain an authentic "obedience of faith," it is necessary to enter into a comprehensive "horizon of meaning" of those human experiences (in general and, specifically, in their concrete realization of religious experience); "one cannot understand the peculiarity of biblical faith except by showing the way in which it realizes this dimension of the experience that is designated by the sacred."[23] And further: "One cannot establish the truth of the sacred except by starting with faith; yet reciprocally one cannot justify faith as the true form of conscience except by showing the debt that it has with respect to the sacred. Therein lies the theological interest of the problem of the sacred, the reason for which it does not constitute a simple application of theological principles, but rather an aspect of their own intuition."[24]

The consequences of these considerations for liturgical-theological study are evident. Liturgical theology is intrinsically ordered toward the event of revelation *sub specie celebrationis,* under the aspect of

---

[22] Besides some studies mentioned in previous notes, we can point out as fundamental G. Colombo, ed., *L'evidenza e la fede* (= Quaestio) (Milan, 1988); D. Power, *Unsearchable Riches: The Symbolic Nature of Liturgy* (New York, 1984).

[23] A. Bertuletti in "Il sacro e la fede. La pertinenza di una categoria teologica," *ScC* 123 (1995) 665–8; here on pages 675–6 where the author cites P. Beauchamp, *Le récit, la lettre et le corps* (Paris, ²1992).

[24] Ibid., 667.

ritual and symbol, as a modality of the presence and of the history of the mystery. It is therefore inclined to prefer the sacramental immediacy of theological mediation. It looks to the sacramental sign of the thing theologically signified, in the context of the celebrative action; it cannot, therefore, renounce a course that pays constant attention to those philosophical, anthropological, phenomenological sciences that investigate human religious action.

To illustrate, this could consist in following the line of inquiry on *religious experience.* Its polar dynamics, its characteristics of "unconditional," of "self-manifestation," of "gratuity" require a specific language for a specific way of acting: symbolic language and ritual action. This type of inquiry appears to be the right question to bring out intention, that is, the "why" of celebrating. For while celebrative action as symbolic language and symbol in action allows for communication/communion with God, it always preserves its difference, excess and disproportion. This occurs precisely through the innate and characteristic symbolic otherness of ritual action.[25]

We conclude this reflection on the "why" of celebration with an expression of St. Augustine. In Sermon 272 *(Sermo in die Pentecoste ad infantes, de sacramento),* addressed to neophytes who share in the Eucharist, the bishop of Hippo wants to explain the mystery to which they have been introduced: "You are the body of Christ . . . if therefore you are the body of Christ and its members, and your mystery is placed on the Lord's table, then receive your mystery. To that which you are, say Amen."[26]

It seems that Augustine is offering a meaningful understanding of the liturgical action: an experience capable of establishing a singular communicative circle. We find, indeed, a sender who is first, who takes the initiative; yet this does not cancel the addressee who, indeed, is necessarily and completely involved. This is the liturgical action: a communicative circle characterized by a continual increment of meaning based on the Christian community's experience of faith that conforms more and more, throughout history, to a plan that

[25] I draw this "itinerary" and these reflections from R. Tagliaferri, "La via liturgica," *Servitium* 28 (1994), and G. Bonaccorso, *La liturgia: celebrare il mistero* (Padua, 1996).

[26] "Vos estis corpus Christi . . ., si ergo vos estis corpus Christ et membra, mysterium vestrum in mensa Domini positum est: mysterium vestrum accipitis. Ad id quod estis, Amen dicitis." Augustini Sermo 272 = PL 38, 1247.

stands at the beginning and at the same time awaits eschatological fulfillment.

2. Is the core of liturgical theology the reflection on "what" is celebrated, or rather, "What does the Christian community celebrate?" The task is one of inquiring about what the Christian believes and what the Christian celebrates. Nonetheless, this is not to understand the "what does one believe" as a content placed within a container (= the liturgy). It is a matter of studying the concrete liturgical praxis in order to grasp therein "the faith as it is celebrated": the *mysterium* celebrated by the Christian community.

There is need for further reflection that could be expressed in a question: "Does not the statement made by the preceding reflection and articulation of the arguments bring up the doubt that the Christian object of celebrating turns out to be drawn from the human experience of celebration?"

There are two lines of response. A first line is one that looks appropriately at the ritual experience, not relegating it a priori to the midst of human efforts for rising to God. Moreover, it seems necessary to recall that "ritualization . . . brings into expression the recognition on our part of the meaning that is given there; it furthermore fixes that meaning, preventing it from being tied to the uncontrollable precariousness of immediate psychological experience. Consequently, the rite structures the human *conatus* itself, that therefore will no longer be naked need, but will be able to have representation and awareness."[27] Moreover, when the religious experience is correctly analyzed, it is an encounter of the two constitutive poles of this experience (and which remain within the experience, and indeed come revealed in their irreducible diversity): the Transcendent and the appropriation of this encounter/experience. It would be improper and reductive to place this experience exclusively at the level of immanence: in it the gift from on high is constitutively present.[28]

A second line is more exquisitely theological, reaching to gain from one side the methodological relevance of the recourse to religious

[27] G. Angelini, "L'approccio teologico-pratico all'Eucaristia. Impostazione teoretica e problemi emergenti," *Celebrare l'Eucaristia. Significato e problemi della dimensione rituale* (= Collana di telolgia pratica, 3) (Turin [TO], 1983) 113–37; here, p. 135.
[28] Cf. A. N. Terrin, Leitourgía . . ., 32.

experience not only as a preliminary phase surmountable by the affirmation of faith but also as a constitutive and irreplaceable dimension of its intentionality; from the other side, intending to show that the singular regime of christological faith cannot in any way be deduced from that experience.[29] Christological faith does not eliminate human religious experience nor that of the rite and the celebrative action, nor is it its sole content. The christological event is the reality that unveils the religious experience and makes it true.

Let us summarize: the Christian liturgical celebration is the specific point for believing appropriation of the gift of Jesus Christ to the life of the Christian.[30] Now, this gift of Jesus Christ to the life of the Christian can be restated by the term "mystery"; it is beginning with the reflection on this reality that the study of the object of celebration will advance. For the purpose of describing the fundamental steps to take, let us proceed in this manner:

(a) There is, above all, the matter of examining the genuine notion of *mysterium* and *sacramentum* and of grasping two fundamental elements. The "mystery" reality is inseparably expressive of the "salvation event" and of the celebration of this event. The "mystery" reality has a historic-salvific nature and structure.

(b) *Sacrosanctum concilium* in nos. 5, 6, and 7 invites us to take a second step. By investigating salvation history in order to grasp its overall plan and the internal dynamics, we come to discover that the celebration is an integral part of this plan and of these dynamics, that is, the celebration is part of salvation history. The absoluteness and undeducibility of the salvific plan and of its realization in Christ require a word and an action that have those connotations explained where we established the relevance of symbolic language and of the celebrative action to religious experience.

It is helpful to reread the text of *SC* 6 (which is the logical consequence of *SC* 5): "Just as Christ was sent by the Father, so also did he send the Apostles, filled with the Holy Spirit, not only so that by preaching the Gospel to all people they might announce that the Son of God, by his death, freed us from the power of Satan and from death, and brought us into the Father's kingdom, but also so that they might bring into effect, by means of the Sacrifice and the sacra-

[29] A. Bertuletti, *Il sacro e la fede* . . ., 684, 686.
[30] Cf. G. Angelini, *L'approccio teologico-pratico* . . ., 121.

20

ments, on which the whole liturgical life depends, the work of salvation that they announced."

(c) The third step brings us truly into the heart of the theological-liturgical quest: grasping the presence of salvation history in the liturgical celebration. Here, too, a conciliar indication can be employed. Indeed, *SC* 7 takes up the notion of liturgy around the category of the Lord's manifold presence: "In order to achieve this great work, Christ is always present in his Church and, in a special way, in liturgical actions. . . . Therefore every liturgical celebration . . . is a sacred action surpassing all others."

At this point the search for and identification of the dimensions of the liturgical action that make it the Lord's presence can be explained: the anamnetic dimension (memorial), but also the proleptic, doxological, and epicletic dimension. In a theological-liturgical discourse, we regard as important and decisive the thorough study of this category of presence/presences.

It is above all necessary to overcome an objectivistic manner of considering the presence. There is no question that the fact of the objective value of the liturgical memorial gets proclaimed: its non-dependence on one's efforts or on the subject's qualities. However, one must pass to a relational vision, in the sense that in the celebration a presence occurs that is at root a relation connoted by a mediated immediacy, namely, of a personal encounter that is realized through a sign/symbol.

Second, the whole range of the dimensions of the liturgy must count in "telling" the presence. The liturgical act will then appear as a "presence" that cannot be sequestered, that is not to be dismissed, that is always to be invoked and sung, always experienced between the "already" and the "not yet," between memory and expectation. Between times, in the time of the Church, Christ is no longer visible; and yet the Absent One is present in a plurality of ways: he is present in the Church that in his name announces his Word; the Church that in his name repeats his actions; the Church that in his name lives fraternal communion. In these testimonies he takes shape and becomes seen and found.[31]

[31] S. Maggiani, "Un rito per celebrare oggi: valore simbolico e pastorale," *Riuniti per fare memoria del Signore risorto. Senso, arte e prassi della celebrazione liturgica* (= Nuova collana liturgica–2d series, 5) (Milan, 1986) 9–37; C. Rocchetta, "Celebrare

(d) Another phase of the work of theological-liturgical inquiry consists in exploring the relation between faith and liturgy. We should begin with the conviction that the celebration has as its fundamental purpose the act of faith, that is, that the faith is actually expressed as an effective encounter with the mystery of the Lord's pasch. The celebration is correlative to the act of faith; its purpose is to increase the act of faith — it is expressive of the complex and total believing existence and does this in and through a special action capable of placing humans before the salvific event — and at the same time to become an acknowledgment (acceptance/agreement) that salvation is given only in the mystery of the Lord's pasch.

Starting here, we should dwell on the relation between the Word of God and liturgy, between Bible and liturgy. First it is important to stress that the liturgical celebration (texts and gestures) is substantiated by the biblical word, which provides the deep sense of everything that is being carried out. Many parts of the Bible have their source in liturgical situations or else have emerged through them. Moreover, it is a fundamental fact that the Bible when read becomes the Word of God in liturgical proclamation; Word that God says "here and now" to the one who receives it with believing, interpreting, and actualizing attention; Word that engenders celebrative action in which there is acknowledgment, the act of faith mentioned above.

The celebrant assembly expresses its agreement by responding with its word that acknowledges and prays and by participating in a symbolic gesture (rather, by opening itself in the Spirit to the inner appropriation of the mystery that is given and fulfilled in the rite). In the liturgy the Word becomes a sustaining event for faith, for that act of human liberty that welcomes the event and its gift of grace.[32]

---

il mistero di Cristo. Dall'unicità dell'evento alla molteplicità delle formeliturgiche e alla risonanza nella vita," ibid., 38–59; idem, "Liturgia: evento e memoria," *La celebrazione cristiana: dimensioni costitutive dell'agire liturgico* (= Studi di liturgia– Nuova serie, 14) (Genoa, 1986) 45–78; cf. J. J. Von Allmen, *Célébrer le salut. Doctrine et pratique du culte chrétien* (Geneva–Paris, 1984) (Italian translation, *Celebrare la salvezza. Dottrina e prassi del culto cristiano*, Leumann [TO], 1986).

[32] On these themes see G. Lathrop, *Holy Things: A Liturgical Theology* (Minneapolis, 1993); AA.VV., *Bibbia e liturgia. 1. Dall'esegesi all'ermeneutica attraverso la celebrazione. 2. Scriptura crescit cum orante. 3. Dove rinasce la Parola* (= Caro Salutis Cardo–Contributi, 6, 7, 8) (Padova, 1991–1993).

The very understanding of the path of the Word within the liturgical action (from the Word proclaimed and celebrated to the faith that welcomes) identifies another aspect of the relation between faith and liturgy: the liturgical action is a singular *locus theologicus,* a singular *confessio fidei.* This proclaims with authenticity and truth the *mysteria fidei,* yet also says forcefully that the faith cannot help but be given as celebrated, indeed, that celebrating is taken up as constitutive of faith itself.[33]

(e) The reflection on the relation between faith and liturgy presents the fundamental fact that the salvation event celebrated in the liturgy necessarily postulates the response of faith by the celebrant; thus it is the same object of celebration that includes (so to speak) the subject. *SC* 7 and *SC* 26 declare explicitly this constitutive relation between the Church and the celebration: "Liturgical actions are not private actions, but are celebrations of the Church . . . they belong to the whole body of the Church, they manifest it and point to it."

The relation between liturgy and Church is total, and the ecclesiological principle is affirmed that the Church in its totality (and in its evident and necessary articulation) is the "place" where alone the liturgy can be found to be in its proper environment and understood as actual celebration. Moreover, the liturgy is the "place" where the body of Christ reveals itself as Church, rather, in its authentic nature as a means of intimate communion with Christ (cf. *Lumen gentium* 1, 3).

The consequences that flow from these affirmations are extremely important. The liturgy is a communitarian (ecclesial) action in the sense that it is put into being, as by its complete subject, by the Church as it is actually and locally joined in assembly. The Church celebrates in the sign of the assembly, which is the most expressive manifestation of the Church, one of its most qualified "epiphanies." The expression "assembly subject of the celebration" is to be understood in the active, transitive sense: the assembly *agit celebrationem.* And yet the complementary, passive aspect cannot be ignored, namely, that the assembly *fit per celebrationem,* that is, is formally constituted in Church by dint of the celebration and not by dint of the activism of the assembly itself.[34] Yet if this

<hr />

[33] F. Brovelli, "Fede e liturgia," *NDL,* 543–55.

[34] S. Magiani, "Celebrare il mistero di Cristo alla luce della riflessione pneumatologica," *Spirito Santo e liturgia* (= Studi di liturgia–Nuova serie, 12) (Casale Monferrato, 1984) 59–84.

last expression is true, then it must be affirmed that the Church has a liturgical nature (dimension) by its inner constitution. It is born where people are summoned before God to have a part in God's gift of covenant; that "day of holy convocation" is the source of the Church's life. It lives the "holy convocation" as a synthesis moment and as the summit of its life; indeed, there it recognizes God as such and accepts God's word, which becomes a plan of life and a judgment; both this plan and this judgment are Love.

There is one last consequence: if the liturgy is communitarian action, if the Church is community that has as its source and its summit the participation in the covenant, then the liturgical assembly can only be constituted and live by the power of the relation, whether with God or among people. All the dynamism of the *actuosa participatio* is rooted here, and this dynamism assumes a dimension and a *ministerial* form (of service) that takes effect in a plurality and complementarity of charisms and ministries.[35]

In concluding this study about "what" Christian liturgy celebrates, we can underscore the fact that this road, which closely unites the "why" and the "what," also allows us to address correctly some problems that seem to make more difficult and problematic the reception of liturgical experience on the part of the Christian people. Some relations are in need of greater attention: relation of the liturgy to the vision of the cosmos, of humankind, of history, of bodiliness; relation to ethics, to charity; relation to spirituality, devotion, prayer (= objectivity vs. subjectivity? communitarianism vs. individualism?).

3. A third area of study still remains for the theology of the liturgy: that of "how to celebrate." And an answer to this question can be that one celebrates with the "live body," that is, one celebrates with the totality of one's own being and one's own doing situated in time and space.

(a) Liturgical time, generally understood, is the time lived as a celebrative encounter between humans and the salvation event that is historical. Thus the first relation between time and liturgy is given by the historical-salvific nature of the mystery that it celebrates. In this sense the liturgy is an efficacious sacramental moment in salvific time.

[35] For this theme of the relation between Church and liturgy, a fundamental reflection is by S. Marsili, "La liturgia culto della Chiesa," *Anamnesis*, 1:107–36.

Yet the liturgy is also a special time that symbolically suspends the flow of time. Liturgical time generates the time of existence in the sense that it enables humans to grasp the meaning and value of the days on which they are called to work. The term "sabbatical" is the source and summit of industrious time. This inserted time (we could call it the "feast") constitutes the time of human existence and appears capable of transforming time; it is a kind of symbolic modification by which liturgical time is not just "some" other time, but other time: qualitatively different. The Church can and should favor, in the context of all of Christian existence, a day (Sunday) and times (Liturgy of the Hours and liturgical year). Liturgical time, in fact, preaches/celebrates the mystery of Christ in a festive situation, namely, in a situation of absolute and undeducible otherness and newness. And this time judges and undermines any plan opposed to the lordship of God.

Precisely because of this the time of celebration is offered, we stated, as an opening and readiness for the encounter; as a moment capable of showing the structure of the human being as a being who decides. In the time of celebration chronological time is assumed to be occupied by God's appeal and by the responsible and obedient decision of humans.[36]

(b) With regard as well to the relation between space and liturgy, originally this relation is based on the "connaturality" between the structure of salvation and the structure of liturgical celebration. Salvation is a reality that is realized not only in time but also in space: in cosmic space and in the space that humans build and live in. In some way the liturgy is the "environment" of the actual giving of the salvific event, the environment where the possibility is given to humans to find it and welcome it.

Yet the liturgy originates — just as for time — a kind of "other space": churches with their structure and their furnishings are that "well-adorned upper room" that not only contains but also tells the mystery that becomes present there. And this space, insofar as it is "made" (dwelt in) by each one and by the assembly, is capable of telling the nature and the tasks of each person and of the whole

[36] Cf. A. Rizzi, "Categorie culturali odierne nell'interpretazione del tempo," *L'anno liturgico* (= Studi di liturgia–Nuova serie, 11) (Casale Monferrato, 1983) 11–22.

assembly. Indeed, the assembly is the true church, the true space, the true place where the salvation event is sacramentally effected. It is in the light of these observations that all theological reflection on the place of worship finds its basis, all reflection on the celebration of the dedication of churches and altars, all practical directives for the construction and furnishing of churches.

(c) Liturgical actions, as celebrative (symbolic and ritual) actions, consist of different elements: words, gestures, sounds, silences, movements. In their human richness and poverty they are the liturgical way of experiencing and having a share in the mystery of salvation. One element that appears most present in the liturgical celebration is surely the word.[37] We can list various word situations: one person reads from a book in front of everyone, and in turn everyone listens; one addresses to God the prayer in everyone's name, and in turn everyone participates and agrees; all speak a word that can be a response, an agreement, a proclamation, a praise, an invocation.

We observe that words, when they are not analyzed individually but in their interweaving and in their proceeding from silence (or their advance toward silence), in reality are a genuine experience of listening and response: an experience of dialogue. Here we recover what we might call a constant of Christian celebration: every celebrative structure appears as a dialogue between God who speaks and the people who listen and respond; this is affected by the fact that all of salvation history (the covenant) is of a dialogic nature. Moreover, a theological meaning is highlighted that underlies this constant: God alone takes the initiative in salvation; God alone manifests the divine and calls upon human beings to share in this revelation. Indeed, the Christian assembly gathers and exists thanks to this call.

A similar (yet different) mode of "word situation" is found in singing and music.[38] *Sacrosanctum concilium* justifies singing and music in the liturgy by adducing three reasons: to make prayer more pleasing, to foster unanimity, to render rites more solemn (cf. no. 112). It is surprising to observe that these reasons are, in fact, three

[37] P. De Clerck, "Le langage liturgique: sa nécessité et ses traits spécifiques," *QL* 73:1–2 (1992) 15–34.

[38] L. Deiss, *Spirit and Song of the New Liturgy* (Cincinnati, 1970); M. Veuthey, *Music and Liturgy: The Universa Laus Document and Commentary* (Washington, D.C., 1992).

fundamental values present in the human practice of singing and playing music: singing together is an experience that strengthens the unity of a group; the musical and song adornment of the word can lift a text out of its mere informative or conceptual content and uncover and profit from its poetic and affective aspect, which enables anyone singing or listening to penetrate and experience a multilayered resonance; finally, singing and music, as part of the "language of the feast," are a constitutive part of celebrative time and space.

A final word on all those non-verbal elements that we can group under the category of gestures: they are at once action and language, and they make possible connections, relations, and interactions. Through these gestures all the senses and the perceptive capabilities of humans are involved in the liturgical action. An expression seems to be confirmed here: *caro salutis est cardo* [the flesh is the hinge of salvation]. Indeed, liturgical gestures are not some sort of instrumental extensions of the human; they are human bodiliness that approaches, sees, touches, perceives, expresses, "does" the mystery of salvation.

CONCLUSION

"In the time of the Church, Christ is no longer visible. Luke insists on this point: once he is risen, he is the 'Living One,' a divine title (Luke 24:5); he lives in God, he is no longer of this world, as the account of the Ascension is pleased to emphasize. And nevertheless, though absent, he is present. . . . And the Church is obligated, in order to live by the salvation of its Lord, to rediscover the dynamics of the in-carnation and thus to rediscover in its human component those 'keys to the vault' that have sewed up and sealed the encounter with the Word in the flesh: the Word of the Gospels, baptizing with water and spirit (Matt 3:11; 28:19), the breaking of bread . . . (Matt 26:26ff.; Mark 14:22-25; Luke 22:19-20; 1 Cor 11:23-25). If we enter the celebra-tive 'game' with amazement and gratuity, it is not difficult to listen to the Voice, to go in and dine with the Living One. It is in this same encounter that we can get eyedrops for our eyes and recover our sight . . . and get warmth for our heart (cf. Rev 3:14ff.)!"[39]

[39] S. Maggiani, *Un rito per celebrare oggi*, 25.

Bibliography

AA.VV. *Celebrare il mistero di Cristo. Manuale di liturgia*. Vol. 1, *La celebrazione: Introduzione alla liturgia cristiana*. BELS 73. Studi di liturgia, n.s., 25. Rome, 1993.

Bonaccorso, G. *La liturgia: Celebrazione del mistero*. Padua, 1996.

Borobio, D., ed. *La celebración en la iglesia*. Vol. 1, *Liturgia y sacramentología*. Salamanca, 1985.

Fagerberg, W. *What Is Liturgical Theology? A Study in Methodology*. Collegeville, Minn., 1992.

Grillo, A. *Teologia fondamentale e liturgia: Il rapporto tra immediatezza e mediazione nella riflessione teologica*. Caro salutis cardo — Studi 10. Padua, 1995.

Kavanagh, A. *On Liturgical Theology*. New York, 1984.

Lathrop, G. *Holy Things: A Liturgical Theology*. Minneapolis, 1993.

López Martin, J. *"En el Espíritu y la verdad": Introducción a la liturgia*. Agape 5. Salamanca, 1987.

Marsili, S. "La liturgia momento storico della salvezza." *Anàmnesis* 1:33–156.

Power, D. N. *Unsearchable Riches: The Symbolic Nature of Liturgy*. New York, 1984.

Schmemann, A. *Introduction to Liturgical Theology*. New York, 1986.

Vagaggini, C. *Theological Dimensions of the Liturgy*. Trans. L. J. Doyle and W. A. Jurgens. Collegeville, Minn., 1976.

2

Liturgy and Symbolism

As the liturgical movement made the transition from its efforts to achieve renewal to promoting a scholarly study of liturgy, two episte-mological problems emerged. One concerned methodology and the systematic study of liturgy as a division of theology; the other had to do with the adequate understanding of liturgy in relation to spiritual-ity and pastoral studies as practical *loci theologici*.

Two inescapable conclusions followed: first, that the theological study of liturgy, both as to content and method, does not precede but rather follows liturgical action; this shows that theology is in itself an effective undertaking of the Christian body or else it is not Christian theology. The second conclusion has to do with the revitalization of the study of theology, following the work done in the first half of the twentieth century by the liturgical movement and by the biblical and patristic movements that resulted, in the second half of the century, in the guidelines of Vatican II in *Optatam totius* 16, which is the matrix of the epistemological maturing of liturgy, biblical studies, and patristics. In this mature state the pillars of theology, Sacred Scripture and the Fathers, interact with liturgy, spirituality, and pastoral studies.

Within this horizon, which inspires the whole range of Christianity and inspires new structures in theology, the keystone of liturgical studies and the clue to its entire epistemology is liturgical symbol-ism. Now, after the crises of the sixties and seventies, we must again raise the question whether symbolic language is to be exorcised, or whether we should instead inquire if "today's people," because they are up to date, are more cautious in their approach to symbols than in their attitude toward concepts. For fundamental liturgy and liturgical epistemology we acknowledge our acceptance of symbols and their sacramental specificity: we refer to "liturgical symbolism" along with "theological symbolism," the theology of the symbols of faith among the churches as well as the theology of liturgical symbols.

THE SYMBOLIC UNIVERSE AND CHRISTIAN SYMBOLISM

In the symbolic world no one is alien or ignorant. Anyone outside the symbolic world would be outside history, neither situated nor acting in the realm of human existence that is time and space. Nevertheless, symbolism is still a forest that some find difficult or impossible to traverse while others, accepting it as a given, take pains to traverse again and again by multiplying descriptive and interpretive schemes.

Symbol is a linguistic phenomenon because human beings are linguistic beings in their metaphysical structure. Linguistically, then, symbols are signs that not only refer to an indicated reality but make it present in mediated fashion. For example, in the realm of traffic signs a directional arrow is a simple *indicator,* while in the case of the Second Ecumenical Council of Nicea the icon of a salvific event is its *symbol.* The sign mediation of the indicator remains abstractly neutral between us and our affairs, whereas the sign mediation of the symbol involves the concrete; it becomes for us a historical sign of the reality toward which we are to turn. Between indicator and symbol, then, stands an indefinite series of signs that variably combine indicative values with symbolic values and are thus partly indicators and partly symbols.

Linguists attempt to schematize their inventory of indicators and symbols by punctuating the series in somewhat arbitrary fashion. They also insert into the series thus schematized some signs that are otherwise classified as metaphors, metonymies, emblems, coats of arms, and all the other sign forms in the repertory of semiotics. The risk of error arises in the possible confusion between the values proper to one sign and those proper to others. For example, looking at an icon as if it were an indicator and not a symbol has caused error, and has occasioned a horror of "sacred images" that has little or nothing to do with liturgy, worship, and Christian faith, all of which are thus made dependent on an uncontrollably disjointed "imagery" that is more or less "religious." Mistakes also arise from the casual manner in which all sorts of signs are lumped together under the category of symbol.

In speaking of symbols, moreover, it is always possible to err under the pressure of operative aspects of symbolism. This seriously distracts us from the perception of the source of our symbolic system. "Renewing" mystery-based symbols is not a catechetical undertaking, nor is it pedagogical or didactic; what is required is consistency in bringing forth the mystery-based realities themselves, presenting them in terms of signs that uniquely make them present and do not merely allude to them. "Making" liturgical symbols "understood" does not mean adding an explanation to the rites or clothing ritual in discursive ideas that inevitably distort it. Instead, it means directing the celebration and its celebrants in accord with the τάξις by which it is constructed and within which they are active participants, and not providing the liturgy with reasons that accord with one's own tastes. To "hold to" the symbols of the great ecclesial tradition is not to repeat what has been done before just as it was done in the past; it is to make one's own the fullness of ecclesial memory and recreate it in an original manner, not stamping it out of the same mold. This whole subject leads beyond the epistemological category and is open to other issues as well.

The stumbling block of allegory also deserves our attention. In everyday language "allegory," namely telling about one thing by speaking of another, is quite common. In theological language allegory, understood in this general sense, is a figure stimulated by the need to merge varied perspectives in speaking about God and divine realities so as to optimize our human discourse. A greater precision of meaning is attained if we can show the relationship between what we say and the thing we are talking about; indeed, that relationship is established through attention to a varied range of reality and/or conventional expression. Allegory, however, is a genus with multiple species. From the intuitions of Johann Wolfgang von Goethe, who first distinguished allegory from symbol, to the linguistic science of our own time, which has punctiliously investigated the whole range of semiotics, scholars have managed to establish a systematic scheme of allegorical figures. We prefer not to name the genus at all, but to call "allegorical" only those signs that have no real relation, but only a conventional relation to the thing they are intended to express. This kind of systematic scheme is more suitable to the complexity of human language, but it is not universally adopted. Convention still persists in generalizing all semiologic mediations not as "allegory," but as "symbolism."

Two points in particular must be established. The first is that "biblical allegory" is the classic name for a whole series of linguistic mediations that may be based on reality, nature, or events, or on convention, metaphors, or metonymies; thus these mediations in Scripture require specific clarification. The other is that the study of the process of allegorization and of post-Nicene Western symbolization (after the seventh Ecumenical Council) from the Carolingian period to the late Middle Ages documents wide swings between the use and abuse of allegory, a circumstance that had pernicious consequences for genuine symbols. Abused by Amalar of Metz and William Durand to the point of debasement, allegory was exorcised by Florus of Lyons and Albert the Great, yet was used by Thomas Aquinas. Conventional but not strictly biblical allegory cannot be put to serious use unless account is taken of the circumstances that require scientific analysis and of facts scientifically established in different contexts. In the whole array of semiologic mediations, however, the irreplaceable function of symbolic structure is never sufficiently emphasized. Besides describing phenomena — in which case the function of symbol is to present a schema or code of the scientific characteristics common to all phenomena (+; –; √ etc., to use examples from modern logico-mathematical symbolism) — symbol always plays a role in boundary- or limit-experiences, the precious and refined occurrence of what transcends ordinary phenomena.

There is a genuine synchronicity between authentic, meaningful symbolic language and the ontology of the ineffable. In theological language symbolism refines and enhances theological discourse in a manner far beyond the refinement and enhancement it brings to any other type of discourse. This involves the formation of a full theological language, pregnant with every semiological and ontic potential for human discourse about God. It is the formation of mystery-based theological language, itself pregnant with the sacramentality that Christian faith recognizes in the efficacious signs of the theandric relationship established by grace in the history of the covenant between God and humankind.

Moreover, in the absence of an illusion of a fully-realized utopia, the fullness of potential in mystery-based symbolism is the sense of fulfillment to be found in the effort to overcome the gap that can only be achieved through mental and practical ascesis. This ascesis must be applied to heal the four initial schisms: from God, from ourselves, from others, and from the cosmos. Through the schism from ourselves — although there is an anthropological dynamic verifiable in each of the levels and in all four together — flashes something of the myth of the original androgyne: "Each one of us is a symbol of the whole human being because what was one has been divided into two. Therefore each of us is always seeking the symbol of oneself."[1] This echoes a doctrine that considered the male and female human beings as "symbols" of one another.[2]

In the wake of Hugh of St. Victor's *De sacramentis christianae fidei* 1, 9, 3, *STh* III 61 R emphasizes that we are "subjected by sin to corporeal realities" in order to deduce from this that "through the sacraments we may humble ourselves by acknowledging the aid of the same corporeal realities." Still, through the schism with the cosmos — likewise in an anthropological dynamic common to all four levels — we must look, in a way differing from that of the medievals, upon this humiliation: *humi / liare* is "to release / to the ground." This becomes positively exponential if it is considered synchronically with the kenotic-theandric humiliation (Phil 2:7-8). That is, we can here assess the sacramental value that visible nature and the nature of our human existence present after the advent, by the work of the Spirit, of the Son of God (cf. Rom 8:19-23). We Christians find ontological resolution by entering into the universal symbol system of God, which is a virtual circle of every vicariousness of presence, whether schismatic or healed, imperfect or perfect, intramondane and internatural: the human being is the very image of God.

THE SACRAMENTAL SYMBOL OF CHRISTIAN THEOLOGY

The Sacramental Symbol Is the Veil of Revelation

The symbol is the sign that reveals its transcendence, the signifier of its signified, yet it is something that veils its transcendence and is even a troubling object. Thus "the critique of the idol is a condition for conquering the symbol."[3] It is not a matter of simple similarity-dissimilarity between signifier and signified; in one instance the less a symbol has of similarity, the less its frame of reference is valid; in another instance the more similarity, the more risk there is of some

---

[1] Plato, *Convivium*, 191 d.
[2] Aristotle, *Genesis of Animals*, 722 b.
[3] Paul Ricoeur, *De l'interpretation*, 510.

εἴδωλον or "phantom" interposing itself, straying from its transcendence. If dissimilarity were to make them concealing and if similarity were to make them revealing without other complications, there would be no difficulties, because the symbols would themselves function on their own in a scale of revelation according to the gradation of their similarity, and totally dissimilar symbols would be excluded, that is, they would not function at all as symbols. Instead, between the concealing and the revealing of the symbol there develops an asceticism, a dialectic of efficacy between similarity and dissimilarity. "Revealing" is first a matter of referencing and then a matter of transparency of the symbolic veil, first a matter of the symbolizing subject and then a matter of the symbolized object.

Thus would symbol be an obstacle and not a support for mystery? More of an obstacle than a support? Quite the contrary. Christian specificity is not the solution to be radically explained and justified; it is an elementary solution, connatural in the historical theandric economy, that is, in synchronism with the faith, a basic solution. Irenaeus of Lyons notes, "There is nothing that does not signify God."[4] Yet the critique of the aberrant phantom on which the validity of the referring symbol depends should begin by taking into account that sacramental symbolization is a given system, and for its part it should begin by symbolizing in succession through constellations in a single sky. Symbolic activity brings out the significative system of the *uni / versum*, of the "turned to one," and means taking a consistent attitude in the semiologic organization of one's own universe. Maximus the Confessor teaches: "Symbolic theorization of intelligible realities through sensible realities is a spiritual knowledge and wisdom of visible realities through invisible ones."[5] Symbolization achieves an osmosis between the intelligible and the sensible; it is an *admirabile commercium,* a "wondrous exchange," in itself.

Symbols are not nouns, they are verbs; they are not names indicating distance but actions telling of presence. In the symbolic frame of reference the signifier is not there to point out the signified but rather to place us together with it: συμ / βάλλω, "to make into one, together, at the same time, in the same place," and the significance consists in the vicariousness that the signifier assumes with respect to the signified: the absent signified becomes for us vicariously present in the signi-

---

[4] *Adversus haereses,* 4, 18, 2.
[5] *Mystagogia,* 2.

34

fier. The fact remains that unfortunately the symbol is reduced by regarding it merely as a signifier. This would mutilate any sign, but it runs directly into a contradiction of terms in the case of συμ-βάλλειν, of truly "placing together" signifier and signified and significance. The critique of the aberrant phantom may be employed here for applying the value of the symbolic veil, consisting in the mediation of its vicariousness that reveals the immediacy of the revealed presence; through this paradoxical mediation of immediacy the symbol is the sacramental reality itself insofar as it is "epiphany" and "glory."

The Sacramental Symbol Is the Epiphany of Holiness

Iconoclasm, which is no more and no less than symboloclasm in figurative-visual symbols, separates a human from an image just as idolatry separates God from symbol (whether visual or some other kind of perception, it is the same thing). In other words, the subject is correctly placed in the symbolic field if it avoids removal from the mystery provoked by idolatrous separation or by symboloclastic separation, from one or the other equally, since both amount to an offensive separation: separation from God is offensive to God.

The ineffability of the triune God is a Christian mystery, as is the divine economy through Christ in the Spirit, namely, the efficacious sacramentality of the caring and providential God for humans, even to the point of the "wondrous exchange" above every marvel of exchange, the theandric nuptials in the divinizing incarnation of the Word of God: "*O admirabile commercium!* The creator of human nature . . . becomes man and gives us his divinity" (Antiphon of Vespers in the Octave of Christmas). The Second Vatican Council has paraphrased Eph 3:9: ". . . God's saving plan, the mystery of Christ or the sacrament hidden from eternity in God" (*PO* 22). And then there is the reflection referred to by Vatican II's Dogmatic Constitution on Divine Revelation, *DV* 13, in order to illustrate the equality of συν / κατάβασις, "come down / with," the condescension of God both rendering divine speech similar to human words and rendering the divine Word similar to humans:

"God said, 'Let there be light!' and there was light. God saw that the light was good and separated the light from the darkness and called the light day and the darkness night" (Gen 1:3-5). . . . You have seen that the blessed hagiographer and even, through the hagiographer's language, the merciful God has indulged the smallness of human ability. . . . Indeed, through the smallness of those who listened to him, the Holy Spirit inspired the language of the hagiographer so that he might relate everything by adaptation. To understand the ineffable kindness of God and the condescension that he has used in his speech, caring and provident for our human nature, see how the son of thunder (Mark 3:17) does not move with the same steps but, since the human race had advanced in its ability, he leads those who listen to him to a more sublime knowledge. He says: 'In the beginning was the Word, and the Word was with God, and the Word was God,' (John 1:1) and adds: 'The true light came into the world, the light that shines on everyone' (John 1:9). Indeed, just as by the Word of God the sensible light was created and the visible darkness dispelled, so also the intelligible light dispels the darkness of error and guides those astray to the truth (John 1:14). With the greatest thanks we therefore receive from the divine Scriptures."[6]

Thus through this divine coming-down with humans, our mystery-based symbols are, each in its proper order, sacramentals, that is, each by the conditions of its order, revealing and efficacious from on high; they are not magic, the pretended manipulation of the divine captured for the pleasure of the lowly. With the greatest thanks we then accept every condescension of the merciful God by which the Holy Spirit adapts and suits every word for us. "The Spirit of the Lord fills the universe, and by embracing everything it knows every word" (Entrance Antiphon of the Solemnity of Pentecost).

This is an epiphany on high that is the appearing of Holiness: namely, the epiphany of the interpersonal relationship of the triune God with us and of ourselves with our God. A clarification: an epiphany of Holiness, not of the sacred ("sacred" in the sense of the phenomenology of religions, that is, in the now-current sense); being a transcendence "set apart" ("sacred," after R. Otto) it does not lie in our symbolic interconnection, and it stirs up other hermeneutical problems by its modes of presence; although, unfortunately, it is not uncommon that improper forms of the "sacred" substitute for "Holiness." The sole Christian form of the sacred in sacramental symbolism is Holiness: namely, we repeat, the divine Transcendent placed in personal relationship with the immanent human being, not with transcendence set apart. *STh* III, 60, 1 R states: "A thing is called a

[6] John Chrysostom, *Homilies on Genesis,* 3.

36

sacrament both because it has in itself a hidden holiness — in this sense *sacramentum* is the same as the hidden sacred *(sacrum secretum)* and because in itself it is ordered to that holiness."

The Sacramental Symbol Is the Glory of Immanence

The symbolic dynamic of mystery is not something optional; indeed, it thoroughly pervades Christian life in its sacramental heart. While any symbol whatever refers to the order of a transcendence, the sacramental symbol refers to the order of Christian immanence. This is not the usual exclusive polarity of transcendence but rather is the antonomastic characteristic position of our transcendent God in his theandric economy. In contrast to *trans / scandere*, "to go up, to rise / beyond," which is from common matrices, both religious and non-religious, the term itself *in / manere*, "to remain, to dwell, to be in," comes from a biblical, specifically New Testament matrix: John 14:15-17, 19-20, 23; 1 John 4:12-13, 15-16. The immanence of our divine Transcendent is for us a mystery-based experience and sacramental permanence of *Emmanuel*, "God-with-us" (Isa 7:14 / Matt 1:23).

Thus our symbolic dynamic is not so much a scientific methodology as an experiential poetic of the presence of God aesthetically mediated, namely, paradigmatically for every kind of Christian experience of the presence of God, a liturgical mystery-based experience. The indispensable contact, epistemological and hermeneutical, normal and physical, of our liturgy with our theology, with our spirituality, with our pastoral concern, engages here. If in Christian life to attain the divine life and its infinity of Truth, Goodness, and Beauty a synergy is achieved between symbolization and conceptualization, between symbolic logic and logic of the excluded middle, which, while both are logic, do not cancel each other out rationally but are postulated anthropologically, symbol is not rationally "less true" than concept, it is anthropologically "more real" than concept. And just as theological conceptualization has its qualification in the rational mode, so liturgical symbolization has its specific normative qualification: glory of Immanence, namely, epiphany in the beauty of God-with-us. Ποιητική, is derived from "to form artfully, to give being by giving to light, to arouse by celebrating, to fulfill by frequenting" / "to get done creatively"; and αἰσθητική is derived from "sensibly to perceive, to contemplate, to grasp."

All of these are variations of "to do" / "to get done" in sensibly perceptible symbols in which the Christian mystery emblematically acts, in the liturgy, with the liturgy. These variations suit the variegated fullness of συμ-, "with," in Christian mystery-based symbol, in liturgical symbol: συν is "coexistence, equality, completeness, subsidiarity, complementarity, reciprocity; temporal simultaneity, spatial co-presence." Our sym-bol converges with the event of the Son of God appearing for the destruction of all dia-bolicalness (1 John 3:8): δια / βάλλω, "to disunite, cause evil between two parties, upset, strike morally; to accuse, calumniate, discredit, render hateful; to deceive, oppose someone"; δια is "penetration through and consequent division, temporal separation, spatial distancing, rivalry, differentiation by incomplete quality, by surpassing superiority, by strengthened completion, by protracted time, by exacerbated space." And yet the divine economy of the incarnation of the Son by the Spirit — ". . . the word became flesh and lived among us, and we have seen his glory, the glory as of a Father's only son, full of grace and truth" (John 1:14) — is an economy converging with the divine economy of the primordial creation. "He was in the beginning with God. All things came into being through him, and without him no one thing came into being. What has come into being in him was life, and the life was the light of all people" (John 1:2-4), the paschal converging (*SC* 5) of the theandric iconic constitution of creation and of the incarnation, of the theology of humankind and of the theology of grace.

LITURGICAL SYMBOLISM AND THE THEOLOGY OF THE SACRAMENTS

The extension of the sacramental category to all liturgical symbolism should not provoke excessive concern. The hypothesis of "sacramental inflation"[7] has become an unconvincing slogan, although in its time and place it had a different appeal. Attention is to be given more to the method than to the fact; the sacramental symbolic sense is to be cultivated broadly in Christian life, both because for too long it has remained hidden between parentheses and therefore is not usually examined and because its very eclipse has sufficiently and convincingly shown the serious mutilations that result its neglect. Method, we repeat, must be guided by good sense; moreover, methodology should be easily summarized. This involves mental and

[7] G. Colombo, *Dove va la teologia sacramentaria?* 673.

operative attention to the analogous categorization of sacrament. "Sacrament" occurs in a whole analogy of its own, just as "symbol" does. The remark of Irenaeus of Lyons that we have quoted: "There is nothing that does not signify God," taken in the strong sense, has a connection to the comment of Thomas Aquinas: ". . . taking on the name of sacrament not equivocally but analogically, that is, with different reference to the whole."[8] This whole "has in itself a hidden holiness . . . and has in itself an ordering to that holiness," indeed analogically and not equivocally, therefore not with a univocal meaning but with a different reference. The good sense required thus lies in discerning mentally or operatively the diversity of the reference. And just as this good sense is essential, so it would be foolish to avoid its understanding. In other words, it is foolish to equivocate on the sacramental symbol and it is likewise foolish to neglect it in order to stay safe in foolishness, and omission has the same seriousness as commission.

Hence the attitudes that have emerged ever since agreement was reached, under the influence of Vatican II, to revise the extension of the sacramental category to all liturgical symbolism, shifting from the early medieval and Tridentine Sacramentary foundation to a basic epistemology of the resulting *continuum sui generis*. For the liturgy it is the acquisition of a sacramental theology of celebrative ritual action; for systematic theology it is the fundamental revision of general sacramental theology. The judiciously diverse, namely analogical, reference to sacramental symbol postulates the interaction of liturgical science with systematic theology, and of both with the human and theological sciences of anthropology and of language. These are things that in the last thirty years have aroused theoretical attempts that are already classic albeit not definitive, and also processes of interminable in-depth dissection. Obviously the former must occur in the progress of theological and liturgical thought; the latter is inadmissible insofar as it is an idle return to the past (more or less intellectualistic, or positivistic) that would deny the synergy between symbolization and conceptualization in the field of liturgical studies. When we are speaking specifically about symbol, the concept cannot proceed solely along the way of conceptualization. Even more than the bending of the meaning by ritual inadequacies (such as baptismal illumination

[8] *STh* III, 61, 1 ad 3.

by infusion, chrismal confirmation following the Eucharist, eucharistic Communion with the bread alone), the reducing of the comprehension of the constitutive whole to a minimalist validity of the rite has diverted and destroyed the fundamental celebrative consistency.

In analyzing the sacramental symbol of Christian theology, phenomenology should proceed with circumspect caution. Indeed, because of the typically Christian irruption of the divine into the human, despite discontinuities or even impressive points of contact with the symbolization of civilizations and cultures, our liturgical symbolism does not permit a simple ratification of the discontinuities and ruptures. As we reflect on the classic attempts in the last thirty years, two fundamental poles appear: (1) the pole that is the sacramental hinge between liturgical symbolism in its whole complex on one side, and on the other side the septenary resulting from the sacraments of initiation, matrimony, ministry-priesthood, penance in sin, and anointing in sickness; (2) the pole that is that sacrament of the septenary valid for catalyzing the other sacraments of the same septenary and the whole complex taken as one.

Church as Sacrament

What I term sacramental "hinge" and others call sacrament with one or another qualification that may indicate in some way the identity of fundamental mediation is the critical threshold of Vatican II: *SC* 5, 7; *LG* 9, 48; *AG* 1, 5; it is the (symbolic) sacramental constitution of the Church. According to *GS* 45, "every benefit the people of God confer on humanity . . . is rooted in the church's 'being the universal sacrament of salvation,' at once manifesting and actualizing the mystery of God's love for humanity." Church as sacrament therefore completely fulfills the makeup of the sacramental symbol of Christian theology, veil of Revelation, epiphany of Holiness, glory of Immanence. Yet while the sacramental constitution of the Church declares passively its right of full belonging to the universe of Christian symbolism, this does not suffice to identify actively its basic mediation regarding other sacramental symbols and the sacramental septenary. Nor does the inclusion of Christ as sacrament, foundational in its own way, suffice. The critical *admirabile commercium* based the sacramentality of the old covenants from creation to Israel on the original iconicity of humankind to God, because on that, and on the iconicity of God condescending kenotically into history to humans, and on the iconicity of the divinized human in history in Christ Jesus the man-God it bases the sacramentality of the definitive covenant of the pasch to the Church. The basic mediation of the Church ordered to the universe of Christian symbolism — and, reciprocally, of Christ — stems from its unity, as from a common single source, with the basic mediation of Christ himself, "the one who came by water and blood . . . not with the water only but with the water and the blood. And the Spirit is one that testifies. . . . There are three that testify: the Spirit and the water and the blood, and these three agree" (1 John 5:6-8). The Church is manifested as a basic sacrament when it appears as the Spirit's testimony, a testimonial agreement of the Spirit, the water, and the blood; namely, a testimonial agreement on the theandric nuptials of the Cross. "For it was from the side of Christ as he slept the sleep of death upon the cross that there came forth [John 19:34] the wondrous sacrament of the whole church."[9] The Church becomes the fundamental sacrament of the risen one, namely, a nuptial symbol of him, and he in turn of the Church: sacrament-spouse of sacrament-spouse. Through this the Church is time-space conditioning the sacraments and liturgical symbolism in their entirety. The anamnesis of the theandric nuptials of Christ and the Church is fundamental for the sacraments because it is the diastole through the Spirit of the systole that is the epiclesis of the Spirit. "All those, who in faith look towards Jesus, the author of salvation and the source of unity and peace, God has gathered together and established as the church, that it may be for each and everyone the visible sacrament of this saving unity."[10] "Advancing (in history) . . . by God's grace, promised to it by the Lord so that it may not waver . . . but remain the worthy bride of the Lord" (LG 9). "Christ when he was lifted up from the earth drew all humanity to himself [John 12:32]. Rising from the dead (see Rom 6:9) he sent his life-giving Spirit upon his disciples [John 20:22] and through him set up his body which is the church as the universal sacrament of salvation" (LG 48).

The time-space of our epistemology is the Church in its role as bride by the power of the Spirit. The "great mystery of Christ and the Church" (Eph 5:32) is also fundamental for the sacraments, since it is

[9] SC 5; the conciliar text quotes Augustine, *Ennar. in ps.* 138, 2, and the prayer after the second reading of Holy Saturday in the Roman Missal preceding the reform of Holy Week.

[10] LG 9; cf. Cyprian, *Ep.* 69, 6: *inseparabile unitatis sacramentum.*

ecclesiotypical. The referring of the sacraments to the Church as bride should take into account the nuptial dimension of each and every one of them. According to *LG* 35, "the sacraments of the New Law . . . prefigure the new heaven and the new earth [Rev 21:1]," yet Rev 21:2-3 sees that newness realized in the "holy city, the new Jerusalem, . . . prepared as a bride adorned for her husband," and hears that she is called "the home of God . . . among mortals . . . they will be his peoples, and God himself will be with them." This is the ecclesial bridal quality, the theandric *admirabile commercium*, the ultimate "newness" that the sacraments "prefigure."

The Eucharist as "Sacrament of Sacraments"
The sacrament that I call the catalyst of the other sacraments of the septenary itself, and others call sacrament with one or another qualification that indicates some identifying derivation, is the Eucharist as "source and summit" (*LG* 11) of Christian life. ". . . the other sacraments, and indeed all the ecclesiastical ministries and works of the apostolate are bound up with the Eucharist and are directed towards it. For in the most blessed Eucharist is contained the entire spiritual wealth of the church, namely Christ himself our Pasch and our living bread, who gives life to people through his flesh—that flesh which is given life and gives life by the holy Spirit."[11] Rather than to Thomas Aquinas, I would refer to Pseudo-Dionysius, whom *STh* explicitly echoes in its own manner and who makes his own comment:

"The rites of Synaxis. The Eucharist is the sacrament of sacraments. We need to consider it before considering the other sacraments and then, in describing the sacred rites, we need to go back to the divine and hierarchical science according to the Scriptures and through the Holy Spirit to its sacred contemplation. Then let us consider in a holy manner especially why the characteristic common also to the other hierarchical sacraments is attributed in particular to it and not to others, why it alone is called communion and Synaxis while each of the sacramental actions leads our individual life to the one divinization and (each one) gives communion and joining (synaxis) with the One through the union of the divine with individual realities. The participation in the other hierarchical symbols receives its fulfillment from its theandric and perfecting gifts. Indeed, it is not possible for

[11] *PO* 5; the conciliar text quotes *STh* III, 73, 3; 79, 1, and especially 65, 3.

one to be initiated into a hierarchical sacrament without the divine Eucharist effecting the joining (synaxis) to the One of anyone who participates in the sacrament and bringing him into communion with God. . . . Therefore, each hierarchical sacrament does not by itself achieve our communion and joining (synaxis) with the One, given its incompleteness with respect to perfective fulfillment, even though the initiate's participation in the divine mysteries is the purpose and the crowning of each sacrament. Thus the name [of each sacrament: Synaxis—joining—is the name of the Eucharist] is appropriate and adequate to the truth of the real event."[12]

Connecting all the other sacraments with the Eucharist is really not pietistic, nor is it useless. Without its catalytic ability, without the sacraments being situated relative to it, their identification is not possible. "By [the Eucharist] the church continues to live and grow" (*LG* 26) and "the Eucharist . . . gives the church its perfection" (*AG* 39). Thus, between the fundamental sacramentality of the Church-bride-body and the supreme and optimal sacramentality of the Eucharist as "source and summit" of Christian life an osmosis goes on that catalyzes the Church itself. The hermeneutically conditioning ecclesiotype of the "great mystery" of Christ and the Church shows its power in a eucharistic (not ideological!) ecclesiogenesis.

[12] Dionysius the Areopagite, *Celestial and Ecclesiastical Hierarchy*, 3, 1.

Bibliography

AA.VV. *Filosofia e simbolismo*. Rome, 1950.

Alleau, R. *La science des symboles: Contribution à l'étude des principes et des méthodes de la symbolique génerale*. Paris, 1977.

Benoist, L. *Signes symboles et mythes*. 2nd ed. Paris, 1977.

Breton, S., et al. *Le mythe et le symbole: De la connaissance figurative de Dieu*. Paris, 1977.

Castelli, E., et al. *Umanesimo e simbolismo*. Padua, 1958.

Chauvet, L.-M. *Symbol and Sacrament: A Sacramental Reinterpretation of Christian Existence*. Collegeville, Minn., 1995.

_____. *Du symbolique au symbole: Essai sur les sacrements*. Rites et symboles 9. Paris, 1979.

Chenu, M.-D. "Les sacrements dans l'économie chrétienne." *MD* 30 (1952) 7–18.

____. "Foi et sacrement." *MD* 71 (1962) 69–77.

____. "Pour une anthropologie sacramentelle." *MD* 119 (1974) 85–100.

Colombo, G. "Dove va la teologia sacramentaria?" *ScC* 102 (1974) 673–717.

De Lubac, H. "Typologie et allegorisme." *RSR* 34 (1947) 180–224.

Delzaut, A. *Communication de Dieu par-delà utile et inutile: Essai théologique sur l'ordre symbolique.* Paris, 1978.

Naud, G. *Structure et sens du symbole.* Montreal-Tournai, 1971.

Ortigues, E. *Le discours et le symbole.* Paris, 1977.

Rahner, K. *The Church and the Sacraments.* Trans. W. J. O'Hara. Quaestiones disputatae 9. New York, 1963.

____. *Meditations on the Sacraments.* New York, 1977.

Ricoeur, P. *De l'interprétation: Essai sur Freud.* Paris, 1965.

Ubbiali, S. "Liturgia e sacramento." *RL* 75 (1988) 297–320.

____. "Il sacramento nella 'teologia dei misteri.'" *Teologia* 9 (1984) 166–84.

Valenziano, C. "Prospetto per una trattazione antropologica dei simboli nelle nostre culture cristiane." In AA.VV., *Symbolisme et théologie*, 29–44. SA 64. Rome, 1974.

____. "Aspetti antropologici dei simboli nella iniziazione cristiana." In AA.VV., *I simboli della iniziazione cristiana*, 243–57. Rome, 1983.

____. "Narrazione del caos e del cosmos." *Ricerche teologiche* 4 (1993) 397–408.

____. "Narrazione della trascendenza e dell'incanto." *Ricerche teologiche* 5 (1994) 397–402.

Jesús Castellano Cervera, O.C.D.

3

Liturgy and Spirituality

The relationship between liturgy and spirituality has been at the center of attention of the liturgical renewal and is still the object of studies and research by liturgists.[1] Both terms refer to indissociable realities of the life of the faithful and the ecclesial community. One cannot think in a consistent manner about a liturgy that does not express and nourish Christian spirituality. One cannot talk about a true Christian spirituality that does not find in the liturgy as celebrated and lived its source, its summit, its school.

At the level of language and meanings, the terminology that is used is fluid. The pairing can be expressed by the terms "liturgy and spirituality" or "liturgy and spiritual life." In both cases the liturgy is understood as the celebration of the Christian mystery; spirituality or spiritual life means the lived Christian experience in the richness of its manifold aspects. One can also talk about "liturgical spirituality" in the sense of a spiritual experience that in its doctrinal and vital principles and in its style is inspired, nourished, modeled, and expressed starting with the liturgy. These distinctions show that the terminology is fluid and that precision and clarity are necessary for correct theological formulation. In the same way, it is evident that the

---

[1] Cf. some monographic issues of journals: "Ni Jerusalén ni Garizin," *Revista de Espiritualidad* 150 (1979); "Liturgy as a Formative Experience," *Studies in Formative Spirituality* 3 (1982); "Liturgia e spiritualità," *RPL* 3 (1984); "Liturgie et spiritualité," *MD* 154 (1983); "Liturgia: Spiritualità nella Chiesa," *RL* 4 (1986); "Educazione alla preghiera. Istanze del movimento liturgico," *RL* 2 (1988); "Liturgia, Catechesi, Spiritualità," *RPL* 149 (1988) 4; "Eucaristía y experiencia mística," *Revista de Espiritualidad* 213–14 (1995). Since 1993 the Spanish journal *Oración de las horas* has taken the significant title *Liturgia y espiritualidad*.

two realities are close, provided they are understood in the light of the theology of liturgical and spiritual worship in the New Testament.

The importance of the theme and the desire to reach a fruitful theoretical and practical relationship has deep historical roots in the so-called dissociation between theology and holiness, between liturgy and popular piety, and consequently between liturgy and spirituality; or in the distinction, somewhat imprecise in fact, between objective and subjective piety, with the former understood as piety and spirituality rooted in the ecclesial and objective sources of Christian life — Word and sacrament — and the latter as based on more individual and subjective expressions such as personal prayer, contemplation, ascesis, mystical life. In reality, Christian spirituality cannot help but sink roots into the mystery of salvation and cannot prescind from personal response nor, consequently, from subjective involvement, beginning with theological life.

It is not a matter of restating here the long history of the relations between liturgy and spirituality, which in this century has engendered an abundant bibliography. This has involved particularly the beginnings and the period of liturgical renewal up to the threshold of Vatican II and beyond.[2] Today the rediscovered harmony between these two realities, the topicality of the theme, and the desire to orient their relationship in a positive manner is highlighted, for example, by the presence of courses on liturgy and spirituality, and on liturgical spirituality, both in specialized institutes of liturgy and in institutes of spiritual theology. Attempts at unitary schemes are found as well in diverse dictionaries of liturgy, where significant room is given to the term "liturgical spirituality," and in dictionaries of spirituality, where the term "liturgy" is given prominence.[3] The integration still remains

[2] Cf. S. Marsili, "La 'spiritualità liturgica' in clima di polemica," *RL* 61 (1974) 337–54; F. Brovelli, "Liturgia e spiritualità: storia di un problema recente e suoi sviluppi," AA.VV., *Ritorno alla liturgia. Saggi sul Movimento liturgico* (Rome, 1989) 213–78; B. Secondin, "Liturgia e spiritualità: dialoghi incompiuti e imperfetti," *RPL* (1988) 4, 47–54.

[3] "Liturgie et vie spirituelle," *DSp* (1976) 9:873–939; published in separate volumes by the same publisher (Paris, 1977); E. Ruffini, "Celebrazione liturgica," *Nuovo Dizionario di Spiritualità* (Rome, 1979) 154–76; D. Sartore, "Liturgia," *Dizionario di Spiritualità dei laici* (Milan, 1981) 427–42; B. Neunheuser, "Spiritualità liturgica," *NDL* (Rome, 1984) 1419–22; J. Castellano, "Liturgia," *Dizionario Enciclopedico di Spiritualità* (Città Nuova, 1990) 1450–68; K. W. Irwin, "Liturgy," *The New Dictionary of Catholic Spirituality* (Collegeville, 1993) 602–10.

problematical in the realm of treatises and in manuals both of liturgy and of spiritual theology, where a synthesis is hard to achieve when it is not a matter of a real absence of a theme, as if liturgy had nothing relevant to say to spirituality or spirituality to liturgy.[4]

And yet the relation between the two perspectives is logical and necessary. The liturgy draws the attention of spirituality because it is its source on the levels of theological science and life experience. Spirituality emphasizes the need for celebration and for assimilation of the mystery celebrated, guided, and animated by the theological virtues, performed with a contemplation that steers us toward holiness and Christian mysticism. Moreover, the liturgy requires a spirituality, a celebration that can be called "mystagogical" in the full sense and that extends into daily living and our different vocations, with concerns for evangelical life, witness, and mission.

In the area of introductory questions there is a lack of a methodological treatise on the specific task, the characteristic themes, and the suitable method within a systematic course, whether of liturgy or of spiritual theology. Nonetheless, some valid efforts at integration do exist in some recent manuals of liturgy and, in general, in specialized institutes of liturgy and of spirituality.[5]

From scientific study, some essential clarifications must be achieved in order to understand the relations between liturgy and spirituality and, consequently, a notion of liturgical spirituality. These have to do with, first of all and on a theological level, the spiritual nature of the liturgy and the consistent liturgical dimension of Christian spirituality. Second, it can be interesting, in the fields of the history of liturgy and of spirituality, to study the relation between the celebration of the Christian mystery and its expression. Third, in studying the relation between liturgy and spirituality, we should be

[4] In some recent manuals of liturgy the theme has become a specific chapter. Cf. J. López Martín, "*In Spirito e verità." Introduzione alla liturgia* (Cinisello Balsamo, 1989) 457–501; M. Augé, *Liturgia. Storia, celebrazione, teologia, spiritualità* 2d ed. (Cinisello Balsamo, 1994) 301–13.

[5] Cf. A. M. Triacca, "Rilievi critici in vista di una 'epistemologia' della «Spiritualità liturgica»," eds. B. Calati, B. Secondin, and T. Zecca, *Spiritualità: Fisionomia e compiti*, LAS (Rome, 1981) 115–28; idem, "La Spiritualité liturgique est-elle possible? De la méthode à la vie," AA.VV., *Liturgie, Spiritualité, Cultures. Conférences Saint-Serge. XXIX, Sémaine d'Etudes liturgiques*, Paris, 29 juin–2 juillet 1982, ed. A. M. Triacca and A. Pistoia, CLV (Rome, 1983) 317–39.

mindful of the objective and subjective conditions of celebrating, namely, on that necessary personal participation that is open to the celebrated mystery and is expressed in a consistent continuity in daily existence. Finally, it can be useful, for the purpose of formulation, to illustrate the relation of the liturgy with some themes that spirituality has favored as its own: personal prayer, contemplation, mystical life, ascesis, involvement in the world, apostolate, mission, piety, and popular religiosity. The same holds for consistently illustrating the necessary spiritual dimension of some sectors of the liturgy: sacraments, eucharistic celebration, Liturgy of the Hours. All this can converge in the exposition of the legitimacy, notion, and characteristics of liturgical spirituality.

LITURGY AND SPIRITUALITY: THEOLOGICAL ILLUMINATION

These concepts and relationships need to be synthetically clarified from the theological point of view. The liturgy was defined by Paul VI at the very time of the approval of the liturgical constitution *Sacrosanctum concilium* as the "first school of our spiritual life"; moreover, it is "the first and most necessary source of the Christian spirit" (*SC* 14). The term "school" expresses the didactic and pedagogical character of the liturgy in its content and in its celebration: the Word of God, prayers, liturgical texts, rites and gestures, its symbolic universe, the richness of the sacraments and of the liturgical year. Through the liturgy the Church carries out daily a rich spiritual pedagogy of contents and attitudes. The expression "source" indicates the mystagogical character, the initiation into the mystery, the communion with the mysteries of salvation made present in the liturgy. In this sense the liturgy is the source and summit of Christian spirituality as sacramental experience.

With regard to the concept of liturgy and its demands, presupposing adequate specific treatment, here a reference will suffice to the theological precision achieved by the description of the liturgy in *SC* 7 with the needed thorough trinitarian and anthropological grounding of the postconciliar documents and of the *Catechism of the Catholic Church (CCC)*. This notion places the accent on the sanctifying and cultic dimension of the priesthood of Christ and on intimate union with the Church; it indicates clearly the need for an acceptance of the divine life and for an adequate response in liturgical participation and in the existential worship of life; it postulates a "spirituality," a strong theological, personal, and communitarian dimension. Spirituality accentuates the intrinsic necessity of full participation, which welcomes and celebrates the mystery in faith, hope, and love in an experience that is called to grow and mature because it is connatural with the liturgy and with the life that follows it, the dynamism of holiness, the configuration to Christ. The wide range of *CCC* in this regard is exemplary. It has continued broadly with the true meaning and the definition of the liturgy (cf. no. 1070) and has filled out the theology of *SC* with a better formulation of the trinitarian sense: it provides needed space to the figure and the action of the Father (nos. 1077–83); it mentions the presence and action of Christ which culminates in the paschal mystery (nos. 1084–90); and it develops a splendid theology of the action of the Holy Spirit (nos. 1091–109).

Christian spirituality, in its most genuine sense, must be understood as "life in Christ" and "life in the Holy Spirit." It is existence rooted in the sacramental communion with the Lord, with his word, his life, his mysteries; thus it expresses what we call "holiness," both in its fulfillment and in its search and partial realization in the universal call to all and in individual vocations (cf. *LG* 40–42). This is the strongest sense of the christocentric vision of the life of the faithful according to Pauline and Johannine theology. It is life according to the Spirit, actuated and supported by the action of the Spirit of Christ, poured into us by means of the sacraments. Thus we come to the realization of God's design: Christians become true children of the Father, guided by the Spirit, gathered by the Church, present in the world. The richness of the Gospel and of the Spirit's action enables talk about a Christian spirituality and about various aspects of Christian life, which, in the measure that they are authentic and comprehensive syntheses of the Gospel's fundamental wealth, are also designated by the term "spirituality."

The liturgical celebration, in the perspective of salvation history, marks and shapes Christian spirituality with some original characteristics: the trinitarian sense and the fullness of the aspects of the economy of salvation expressed by the Word of God and by the sacraments with all the concrete demands of life and witness. It also indicates the dynamic and progressive sense of holiness, the path of perfection for people's maturity and the growth of the reign of God. It emphasizes the paschal character of Christian holiness, namely the configuration to the mystery of Christ dead and risen, expressed initially in baptismal symbolism as a continual dying and rising. Moreover, it requires the full ecclesial nature of the spiritual life, an essential note of Christian holiness: communitarian spirituality, insertion into the ecclesial body, apostolic and missionary orientation, and full participation in the historical and cultural reality of the Church. Nonetheless, the liturgy is set in the normal context of Christian life as a point of insertion into salvation history, a continual celebration of the mystery of Christ and the Spirit, a path that accompanies the everyday experience of the faithful from baptism until the final moment of the paschal passage from death to life.

The spiritual life is marked by the sacraments of Christian initiation: baptism, confirmation, and Eucharist. Therefore, spirituality in its various expressions, in the supreme demands of contemplation, of virginity, of martyrdom, of charity, is essentially the spirituality of baptism and confirmation, a sharing in the mystery of Easter and Pentecost; a spirituality that the Eucharist confirms, nourishes, and ripens, bringing it to fulfillment, and that the other sacraments and rites (orders, matrimony, and virginal, monastic, and religious consecration) determine. Baptism characterizes Christian life: insofar as it is the source and initial cause, to live in the power of baptism; as the essential content of grace, to act according to its potential with the threefold office of priest, prophet, and king. As a model of Christian living it calls for a continual dynamism of dying and rising, renewed and enriched by the celebration of the Eucharist and prayer in the framework of the liturgical year, according to one's personal vocation.

The CCC confirms this vision of spirituality when it defines Christian life as "life in Christ" and "life according to the Spirit" and describes it in the trinitarian dimension (nos. 1691–96, 1699). In this sense it points to Christian holiness (no. 2012) and Christian mysticism, distinguishing clearly the common vocation to holiness, which is communion with the mystery and the mysteries of Christ. It adds that there exists, besides an essential "sacramental mysticism" open to all, the charism of the mystics who have a particular experience of the mystery of Christ and who witness "for the purpose of making manifest the free gift granted to all" (no. 2014). The liturgy therefore accompanies all of a Christian's spiritual life in its birth and development up to the peaks of holiness and mysticism.

Thus we need to remember the statement that Vatican II made on the relationship between liturgy and spiritual life. In fact, this question did not escape the attention of the council fathers at the time of examining and drafting *SC*. The theme had been debated in the preceding decades and could not be ignored. Pius XII had spoken about it in his encyclical *Mediator Dei;* in the continuity of the magisterium an explicit reference had to be made. Numbers 9–13 of *SC* enlighten some aspects of spirituality with a generic leading statement: relation of the liturgy to other activities of the Church; demand for proper ethical and personal dispositions for active, conscious, and fruitful participation; relation to prayer, ascesis, and devotions.[6]

Source and summit. What the council affirms about the activities of the Church can be applied to Christian spirituality: "The liturgy is the summit toward which the activity of the Church is directed; at the same time it is the fount from which all the Church's power flows" (*SC* 10). The liturgy, and in a special way the celebration of the Eucharist, is the source and summit of all of the Church's activity because it is a realization of holiness (source) and worship (summit). Indeed, "grace flows to us from the liturgy . . . and particularly from the Eucharist as from a wellspring. The sanctification of human beings and the glorification of God in Christ, toward which all other activities of the Church converge as toward their end, are achieved with the greatest efficacy" (*SC* 10).[7]

Indeed, every Christian life begins with baptism and confirmation, is nourished by the Eucharist, is restored by penance. The life of believers matures and grows in contact with Christ. All the other means for growing and expressing the spiritual life (ascesis, prayer, devotions, work, witness) have their source in the liturgy, especially in baptism and confirmation; by the sacramental character they establish believers in the everlasting dimensions of the royal priesthood and of spiritual worship. Outside of the liturgy special graces can be received, and an effective response should be made to the grace

[6] Cf. *Documents on the Liturgy, 1963–1979* (Collegeville: The Liturgical Press, 1982) 7.

[7] R. Falsini and G. Cavagnoli, "La liturgia come «culmen et fons». Genesi e sviluppo di un tema conciliare," AA.VV., *Liturgia e spiritualità* (Rome, 1992) 27–49; 51–70.

received; such acts make explicit the baptismal and eucharistic grace or, in the case of a conversion, tend toward it. The faithful can have strong moments of spiritual experience outside of liturgical actions; in them their response to God reaches a true summit (in martyrdom, in contemplation; in a moment of intense prayer, of self-giving, of love for neighbor, etc.). This response proceeds from the grace of the sacraments and tends toward the cult of glorification rendered to the Father through Christ in the Spirit.

It must be noted that *SC* supports the harmonization of celebrating spiritually and living the celebrated mystery with two expressions of traditional liturgical spirituality: the principle of *The Rule of St. Benedict*, chapter 19: *mens concordet voci* [mind and voice should agree]; and the golden principle of the Easter collect for neophytes: *vivendo teneant quod fide perceperunt* [may they uphold by their lives what they have grasped by faith] (*SC* 11 and 10).

Extraliturgical activities. Together with the council itself we must affirm, "Spiritual life is not exhausted by participation in the liturgy alone" (*SC* 10, 12). Between the "source" and the "summit" there exists a broad margin of the spiritual worship of life. In this are included all of the other activities of the faithful, without which a concrete and committed spirituality would be inconceivable. Of all these activities the council mentions these in particular: the observance of the commandments, the works of charity, of piety, and of apostolate, the evangelization that precedes and follows every liturgical celebration (*SC* 9); the proximate and remote preparation for conscious, active, and fruitful participation in the liturgy, imbued with theological life (*SC* 11); personal prayer and ascesis (*SC* 12); pious exercises (*SC* 13).

The liturgy is the source and summit of the spiritual life; yet it would lack something of its genuine dynamism if it were not lived with the exigencies of theological life and if it did not have a concrete influence in daily existence. The council explicitly states: "The liturgy moves the faithful, nourished by the paschal sacraments, to live in perfect union, and demands that they express in life what they have received through faith" (*SC* 10). It is a demand of the dialogic dimension of salvation history to respond to God's gift, to put it into effect in actual living. Nevertheless, the importance and centrality of the liturgy in spiritual life remains. From it every undertaking of ascesis and apostolate receives light and strength; every exercise of virtue and every work of charity tend toward it. "Indeed, apostolic work is ordered so that all who have become children of God through faith and baptism might gather in assembly, praise God in Church, take part in the sacrifice and at the table of the Lord" (ibid.).

For accepting and assimilating sanctification, for deepening the sense of the true worship of God, personal prayer has decisive importance; it arises from the condition of the children of God received in baptism and effects communion with Christ which is the fruit of the Eucharist. Paying attention to the pairing of prayer and ascesis (*SC* 12), the council synthesizes two great attitudes of spirituality by way of making evident the necessary relation with the whole spiritual life of the faithful. The formulation of the legitimacy of prayer is upheld by the precept and example of Christ; yet in reality every authentic prayer has its root in the gift of the Spirit and in the filial grace of baptism. The mention of Christian ascesis is illustrated by the necessary conformity to the mystery of Christ, rooted in baptism and in the spiritual worship of life that has a true eucharistic character.

Keeping in mind as well the importance that popular piety and its exercises have had and still have for spirituality, especially in some places, the council illustrates this expression of Christian life in its relation to the liturgy. It is known that many pious exercises arose on the edges of the liturgy and often as substitutes for a piety that could not become nourished at its source. The council grants their legitimacy, yet urges, "It is necessary that these exercises, taking into account liturgical periods, be ordered so as to be in harmony with the sacred liturgy, draw inspiration from it in some way, and lead Christian people to it, given that it is by far superior in nature" (*SC* 13).

Some authors maintain that some expressions of *SC* do not bring out completely the unitary relationship between liturgy and spirituality because they lack a full statement of the unity of Christian life and spiritual worship through the priesthood of believers. This doctrinal formulation is found in *LG*, where the sense of the "priesthood of believers" and of "spiritual worship" is recovered at a biblical, liturgical, and theological level, which succeeds in tying the liturgy to believers' entire lives. It is on the basis of the biblical theology of spiritual worship and of the priesthood of believers (*LG* 10 and 11) that the cultic sense of spiritual life should be applied in all its manifestations: prayer, ascesis, charity, apostolate, work, contemplation, mystical life. All is done in the dynamism of charity and in the constant action of the Holy Spirit. In the light of this dynamism, dichotomies are overcome. The whole of Christian life, by the power of baptism, of confirmation, and of the Eucharist, with the grace of the other sacraments and the practice of the virtues, becomes spiritual worship (*LG* 34).

The relation between liturgy and spirituality can be pressed to the point of establishing a kind of equation: "The whole life of the faithful, every hour, day and night, is like a λειτουργία through which they dedicate themselves in service of love to God and to men, joining with Christ's action who, by dwelling among us and by his self-giving, has sanctified the life of all people."[8] The *CCC* joins liturgy and life when it states: "The term 'Liturgia' in the New Testament is used to designate not only the celebration of divine worship but also the proclamation of the Gospel and charity in action. In all these cases, the service of God and of men is involved. In liturgical celebration, the Church is a servant, in the image of its Lord, the sole 'Liturgos,' since it shares in his one priesthood (worship) that is prophetic (proclamation) and royal (service of charity)" (*CCC* 1070). Liturgy and spirituality shine in the unity of the very life of Christ and of Christians, sharers of his priesthood in worship, proclamation, and charity.

THE HISTORICAL PERSPECTIVE

At the historical level different authors have studied the relation between liturgy and spirituality and have provided summary syntheses through the ages. In general, history contrasts the two realities that enjoyed unity at the beginning of the Church. Divergence began in the Middle Ages and became more pronounced in the *devotio moderna*. It crystallized in the modern era when piety and popular religiosity prevailed, and it has moved toward some harmony, not without polemics, through the years of liturgical renewal, to the council, and to the present.[9]

---

[8] Paul VI, Apostolic Constitution *Laudis canticum* (11/1/1970) no. 8.

[9] A. Girolimetto, "Liturgia e vita spirituale: il dibattito sorto negli anni 1913–1914," *Liturgia: temi e autori. Saggi di studio sul movimento liturgico*, ed. F. Brovelli (Rome, 1990) 211–74; A. M. Triacca, "La riscoperta della liturgia," AA.VV., *La spiritualità come teologia* (Rome, 1993) 105–30.

This formulation runs the risk of grand syntheses that can only be partial. The history of the relations between liturgy and spiritual life must be rewritten with a broader and more consistent vision, if not completely then at least partially. The general visions proposed in polemical times are too conditioned by the desire to have one tendency prevail over the other. There are too many distinctions to be made, and there are many commonplaces that do not stand up to serious monographic studies of epochs, authors, and schools of spirituality. The scientific seriousness in this field must now be rigorous; the grand syntheses that encompass centuries of history with summary judgments on the relation between liturgy and spiritual life are to be taken with great caution, whether with regard to the primitive era or to the Middle Ages or, finally, to post-Tridentine spirituality, summarily dismissed as antiliturgical or barely attentive to the liturgy.[10]

There is a need for serious monographic studies that can give an account of the complex interaction between liturgy and spiritual life, keeping in mind that although the liturgy has suffered a long crisis in the people's understanding and in full participation, the sacramental flow of the liturgical life was never interrupted in the great spiritual, personal, and collective experiences of the history of the Church. This vision, completed with scientific rigor, should offer a more impartial panorama of the relation between liturgy and spirituality in the course of history. Thus moments of splendor, evolution, and regression can be brought to light, often due not to the liturgy or to spirituality in themselves but to their diversified praxis, whether in some groups or in the cultural situation of the life of the Church. This involves an analysis of spirituality in its historical development that cannot be separated from the history of the liturgy. An updated history of liturgical spirituality could be important and clarifying.

---

[10] G. Braso, *Liturgy and Spirituality*, 30–55; C. Vagaggini, "Liturgia e storia della spiritualità: un campo d'indagine," AA.VV., *Introduzione agli studi liturgici*, CAL (Rome, 1962) 225–67; W. Witters, "Liturgie et Spiritualité. Esquisse d'une Histoire," *Parole et Pain* 2 (1965) 626–38; S. Marsili, "Spiritualità liturgica," *I segni del mistero di Cristo* (Rome, 1987) 463–503; *Liturgie et vie spirituelle*, DSp, 884–923; A. Caprioli, "Liturgia e spiritualità nella storia. Problemi, sviluppi, tendenze," AA.VV., *Liturgia e spiritualità*, 11–25; B. Petra, "Liturgia e spiritualità nella tradizione orientale," *RPL* 4 (1992) 53–8.

SPIRITUAL AND THEOLOGICAL DIMENSION
OF LITURGICAL LIFE

It is not enough to have a more enlightened theology and a more precise history. From the doctrinal statement that highlights the mutual
interaction between liturgy and spirituality, the liturgical-pastoral exigency flows that should concretely favor the relationship of osmosis
between liturgical celebration and Christian experience, always following the wise observation of an author who had already made an
initial response to the problem: it is celebration that should pass into
lived experience, and not vice versa.[11] Now, despite all the work of
the liturgical renewal, while evaluating positively all the fruits coming from participation in the liturgy, we are still far from having
achieved full interaction. It cannot be affirmed that on a general and
popular level there exists in fact a spirituality consciously modeled
on the liturgy. Perhaps because of this, in practice there is still a lack
today of a strong experience of lived liturgical spirituality, and spiritual experiences abound that are too disconnected from the contents
and the form of the liturgy.

Rather, one observes the need for a liturgical participation that involves the best spiritual energies. This is required by the very nature
of the liturgy that, being an exercise of the priestly office of Christ in
sanctification and in worship, asks of the Church as Bride, intimately
united with Christ in the liturgy, a ritual participation inspired by
theological life, open to contemplation and to liturgical holiness. The
liturgy postulates a spiritual participation, inward and outward, so
that it might express and nourish a noble spirituality.[12]

Thus between liturgy and spirituality there is a necessary dimension of continuity in life, a dynamism of interiorization and of
growth, to be and to live in Christ, to be in total conformity with the
paschal mystery. The key of this unity, according to the *CCC*, is the
work of the Holy Spirit, whose action links celebration and life. The
communion or synergy with the Spirit offers the possibility of a
multiple dynamism of interiorization and continuity: "The desire and
work of the Spirit in the heart of the Church is that we live by the life
of the Risen Christ. When he finds the response of faith in us,

[11] Cf. G. Moioli, "Liturgia e vita spirituale," *RL* 61 (1974) 325–36.

[12] S. Marsili, "La liturgia primaria esperienza spirituale cristiana," T. Goffi and
B. Secondin, *Problemi e prospettive di Spiritualità* (Brescia, 1983) 249–76.

aroused by him, true cooperation is achieved. Thanks to this, the liturgy becomes the common work of the Spirit and of the Church" (no. 1091). Every liturgical celebration should be prepared and conducted in the dynamism of the Spirit: "The assembly should prepare itself for meeting the Lord, to be 'people at the ready.' This preparation of hearts is the work of the Holy Spirit and of the assembly, especially of its ministers. The grace of the Holy Spirit seeks to awaken faith, conversion of heart and adherence to the Father's will. These dispositions are the condition for accepting other graces offered in the celebration itself and for the fruits of the new life that it is intended to produce thereafter" (no. 1098).

The royal road of a renewed interaction between celebration and Christian experience cannot fail to be an intensification of liturgical mystagogy in its three articulated demands: the mystagogy of initiation into the understanding and structuring of the spiritual life, beginning with the Word, the sacraments, the liturgical year; the mystagogy of participation in the celebration of the mystery and mysteries of Christ, with all of the best spiritual energies, on a path of persevering faithfulness; the mystagogy of assimilation, for perfect conformity to Christ in doing and in suffering, to the point of reliving in one's own existence, the paschal mystery which is the fundamental baptismal and eucharistic archetype of Christian ascesis and mysticism, and this by following the rhythm of the daily, weekly, and yearly liturgy of the Church.[13]

FIELDS OF RESEARCH AND FUNDAMENTAL THEMES
The breadth of the themes of liturgy and spirituality offers the chance for broad study and research to handle in systematic treatises not only the great principles or periods of history but also the different aspects and the theological and practical sectors. The complexity of theology and of liturgical celebration opens the horizon to a broad treatment that could comprise not only the relation between liturgy and spirituality in general but also with each of the great chapters of liturgical theology (paschal mystery, action of the Spirit, church — assembly, Word of God, prayer) and consequently of a spirituality of

---

[13] N. Fantini and D. Castanetto, "Ritualità: autentica esperienza spirituale," AA.VV., *Liturgia e spiritualità*, 117–67; D. Sartore, "La mistagogia, modello e sorgente della spiritualità cristiana," *RL* 73 (1986) 508–21; J. Castellano, "Celebrazione liturgica ed esperienza spirituale," *RPL* 4 (1988) 55–66.

the eucharistic celebration, of baptism and of the other sacraments, of the Liturgy of the Hours, of the liturgical year, of the sacramentals, of the sanctifying and cultic dynamism, and in the theological-spiritual contents of the liturgical texts. The methodological key of this treatment requires a special sensitivity in grasping in each of these sectors the demands that nourish, express, and ask for a personal and communitarian response, with precise concerns for celebration and for life.[14]

From the viewpoint of spirituality, the path can be taken of examining the sacramental foundations of Christian life and of some themes of particular importance: personal prayer, ascesis, contemplation, mystical experience, apostolate, involvement in the world, popular piety. It is appropriate to dwell on these themes, which cannot fail to have a relationship with the liturgy as source, summit, and school, as the light that comes from theology and from life. The themes most studied in this regard have been, in line with emphases peculiar to our times, before and after Vatican II, those linked to the prevalence of some tendencies of spirituality. Many treatises have concentrated on the axis of prayer and devotions.[15]

Later other interests prevailed concerning themes such as the apostolate, liberation, popular religiosity; or else specific sectors of spirituality in some categories: consecrated life, laity, family, new religious movements.[16] There is always interest in the thorough study of the theology of mysticism in its sacramental foundation, in historical experiences, and in spiritual orientation and discernment.[17]

[14] This way is traced by B. Neunheuser, "Spiritualità liturgica," *NDL*, 1419–42, and by J. López Martín, *"In Spirito e verità," Introduzione alla liturgia*, 475–500.

[15] C. Koser, "Pietà liturgica e «pia exercitia»," *La liturgia rinnovata dal Concilio* (Turin, 1964) 229–77; J. Castellano, "Religiosità popolare e liturgia II," *NDL* (Rome, 1984) 1176–87. On personal prayer, idem, "Preghiera e liturgia," ibid., 1095–111; idem, "Luoghi odierni di educazione alla preghiera," AA.VV., *Liturgia e spiritualità*, 71–116; B. Baroffio, *Liturgia e preghiera* (Turin, 1981); "Meditazione e liturgia," monographic issue of *RL*, 6 (1990).

[16] Many of these themes have good summaries of theological, pastoral, and spiritual character in their respective entries in the dictionaries, such as in the *NDL*. Cf. A. Favale, "Movimenti di risveglio religioso e vita liturgica," *RL* 73 (1986) 449–68.

[17] O. Clément, *Sources. Les mystiques chrétiens des origines* (Paris, 1982); B. Baroffio, "La mistica della Parola," AA.VV., *La mistica. Fenomenologia e riflessione teologica* (Città Nuova, Rome, 1984) 31–46; C. Rocchetta, "La mistica del segno sacramentale,"

LITURGICAL SPIRITUALITY:
NOTIONS AND CHARACTERISTICS

Some authors not only establish the relation between liturgy and spirituality but also center their discourse on the specific category of liturgical spirituality. The attempt is to grasp liturgy in a vital synthesis insofar as it demands a personal and communitarian mode of celebrating and living the celebrated mystery. Or else, following another perspective, it is Christian spirituality itself that is studied, ordered, and lived, according to the values, rhythms, and form of the Church's liturgy. Nonetheless, it is good to avoid the risk of carrying on a generic discourse on liturgical spirituality, as if a Christian spirituality were possible that was not essentially liturgical, or as if liturgical spirituality were a form alongside other ecclesial spiritualities, forgetting that it is Christian and ecclesial spirituality par excellence. Indeed, it possesses characteristics that place it at the peak of all other Christian spiritualities. It is a spirituality valid for everyone, an expression of salvation in Christ; it contains all the aspects of spirituality and is objectively superior to every other one.[18]

Some authors have sought to express in a brief definition the content of liturgical spirituality. One can be quoted as excelling in its completeness:

"Liturgical spirituality is the perfect practice (as far as possible) of Christian life by which a person, regenerated in baptism, full of the Holy Spirit received in confirmation, and participating in the celebration of the Eucharist, draws all of his or her life from these sacraments, for the purpose, within the framework of the recurrent celebrations of the liturgical year, of continual prayer — specifically, the liturgy of the hours — and of the activities of daily life, of growing in sanctification through conformity to Christ, crucified and risen, in hope of the final eschatological fulfillment, to the praise of his glory."[19]

---

ibid., 47–76; J. Castellano Cervera, "La mistica dei sacramenti dell'iniziazione cristiana," ibid., 77–111; "Mystère . . . Mystique," *DSp* 10 (1861–1874, 1889–1984); G. Rapisarda, "La liturgia propedeutica alla esperienza mistica," AA.VV., *Mistica e Scienze umane* (Naples, 1983) 83–99.

[18] Cf. S. Marsili, "Spiritualità liturgica," *I segni del mistero di Cristo*, 509; A. M. Triacca, "Per una definizione di «spiritualità cristiana» dall'ambiente liturgico," *Not* 25 (1989) 7–18.

[19] B. Neunheuser, "Spiritualità liturgica," 1420. Another, more synthetic definition is found in C. Vagaggini, *Theological Dimensions of the Liturgy*, 661–5.

Other authors describe liturgical spirituality by illustrating some of its characteristics. The method is apt, as long as one takes into account what has been expressed regarding the concept of liturgical spirituality. Since it is the Church's spirituality, it brings out some notes that should be found in every other Christian spirituality. S. Marsili was first to highlight some notes: spirituality that is christocentric, paschal, biblical, sacramental, cyclical. Others add its historical, prophetic, mystagogical, and dynamic nature.

Liturgical spirituality is trinitarian and theocentric, because it acknowledges the primacy of God's salvific action and gratuitous initiative, and everything in the end refers to God in an attitude where praise, thanksgiving, and gratuitousness prevail. It acknowledges the Father as source and end of every action and sets the paschal mystery in the center; it celebrates in the sacraments and especially in the Eucharist the active and real presence of Christ, who communicates his grace in its manifold richness and leads the faithful to a communion of life with him, dead and risen; in prayer and in praise it joins in his priesthood. It is pneumatological spirituality, because in all of its aspects of sanctification and worship, in its components — Word, sacraments, signs — the Spirit of the Father and of Christ pervades the liturgy, in order to share the divine Presence with the Church and with individual believers, and fulfills in the Mystical Body the mystery of unity in one Spirit and the perfect configuration to Christ. Through Christ and in the Spirit the ultimate source and the definitive end of liturgical actions always remains the Father, whom Christ has revealed to us and whom the Spirit impels us to invoke: Abba, Father!

It is ecclesial and communitarian; it emphasizes the communitarian aspect of the salvific plan, the union and solidarity of all in sin and salvation, the unity of the people of God present in all legitimate local assemblies throughout the earth, the necessary communion of Saints, and communion in holy things. From the spiritual viewpoint it reaffirms the need for mutual charity in Christ and the interdependence of everyone in the common growth toward holiness. Liturgical spirituality is also ecclesial, inasmuch as its expressions of worship and sanctification are regulated and established by legitimate ecclesial authorities, who watch over, with respect for the traditions and culture of distinct local churches, the purity and orthodoxy of the formulas and the forms of worship, and sanctification in the unity of the same apostolic faith.

With regard to its constitutive elements, it is above all biblical. The Word of God occupies an eminent place in the liturgy as an essential component of liturgical acts, inspiring the meaning of all sacraments and prayers; indeed, the liturgy is the realization of salvation history today, proclaimed by the Word, and realized in the sacraments.

It is mystery-based, insofar as the liturgical spiritual experience passes through the liturgical mysteries and signs; faith and catechesis help in perceiving the significance of liturgical symbols. In their variety they confer an inexhaustible richness of meaning to the mystery of Christ in sanctification and worship. Through them the whole person is taken up into participation in the divine life, and the cosmos itself becomes a means and expression of communion of humanity with God. It remains open to cultural adaptation and to a spirituality that is the legitimate expression of the variety of cultures.

Spirituality, inspired by the liturgy insofar as it is marked by the temporal rhythm of the Church's celebrations, is cyclical, without remaining imprisoned in a circle but rather in a growing line somewhat "spiral," oriented toward definitive fulfillment. In different liturgical cycles (daily, weekly, yearly) with their own specific commemorative celebrations the faithful immerse their own existence into the mystery of Christ. Daily prayer with the sanctification and offering of time, with its culminating point in the Eucharist, sets fleeting human time with its efforts and labor into God's salvific time and into eternity; every week the Lord's day renews, in feast and rest, the mystery of creation and of the new creation in the expectation of the Lord's definitive coming. In the yearly cycle, the faithful are placed into contact with the salvific reality of the mysteries of Christ's life and of his glorious death, to which they must conform their own lives.

Liturgical spirituality is also personal, while still communitarian. The community, indeed the liturgical assembly, is made up of living persons in whom the plan of salvation is accomplished in each person with particular gifts and missions. Liturgical spirituality is as rich as it is personal, as it is personally lived and assimilated into each one's concrete circumstances in the Christian community with each one's own gifts of nature and grace (character, mentality, talents, charism, involvement in the world). Thus liturgy realizes the mystery of unity in the Spirit and in the variety of the Spirit's charisms.

By its dynamism, it is missionary: it strives to manifest the received grace to the world; after having involved the world in its intercession, the Church, which in the liturgy manifests itself as a convened community (ἐκκλησία), tends to become an ἐπιφανέια, a manifestation of the mystery of Christ to the world by word and deed. The λειτουργία tends toward διακονία, toward service of brethren in charity, toward missionary proclamation, toward dialogue.

Liturgical spirituality is eschatological: it tends toward its full realization in glory. Sanctification and worship tend toward their perfect final expression in the heavenly Jerusalem. Every liturgical celebration, although a foretaste of the ultimate realities, remains marked by hope and expectation; every encounter with Christ in the Church refers, in hope, to the definitive encounter with him and the full realization of God's reign. The liturgy arouses and celebrates the "blessed hope"; the liturgical texts often return to this expectation, which is the partially realized promise; every celebration is a *maranatha* of the Church and of the cosmos, reaching in hope toward final consummation.

Finally, liturgical spirituality, in the light of *Marialis cultus,* is also essentially Marian. The Church, in its "Marian profile," while celebrating the mysteries makes use of the same attitudes by which the virgin Mary associated herself with the mystery of Christ: as virgin in listening and prayer, offering as virgin and virgin mother, model and teacher of spiritual life for all Christians, when she teaches them to make of their own lives a worship pleasing to God.[20]

CONCLUSION

The relation between liturgy and spirituality are so close that they merit particular attention and consistent development, especially in our time, when nostalgia is felt for authentic spiritual experience. It is a challenge for study and liturgical celebration and is also a stimulus for every expression of Christian spirituality.

Still, as S. Marsili hopes, everything should start with a renewed mystagogical celebration of the liturgy:

"So that the liturgy might become a source and reality of spiritual experience, everyone who does the liturgy is required to become

[20] Apostolic exhortation *Marialis cultus,* nos. 16–21; cf. I. M. Calabuig, "Spiritualità mariana e spiritualità liturgica," AA.VV., *La Madonna nel culto della Chiesa* (Brescia, 1966) 219–40.

capable of having this experience. . . . The celebration itself cannot be just any kind. It must be conducted at such a level of faith and of consequent interior attention that it allows the discovery both of Christ's operative presence and of one's own opening to this divine presence and action. Under these conditions the liturgy can and surely will become once and for all an absolutely valid spiritual experience, and therefore capable of giving to the mystery of Christ, this knowledge-union of love that is not reduced to a fleeting sensation of the presence of Christ, outside of us, but becomes every day, within ourselves, the exigency for progressive insertion into the reality of Christ. This must be the way of conformity and configuration to Christ: through the celebration."[21]

[21] S. Marsili, "La liturgia primaria esperienza spirituale cristiana," AA.VV., *Problemi e prospettive di spiritualità*, 276.

Bibliography

AA.VV. *Liturgie et vie spirituelle.* Congress of Angers, 1962. *MD* 69 (1963); 72 (1963).

AA.VV. *Liturgia, soglia dell'esperienza di Dio?* Padua, 1982.

AA.VV. *Liturgia e spiritualità. Atti della XX Settimana di Studio dell'Associazione Professori di Liturgia.* Rome, 1992.

AA.VV. *Liturgia y vida espiritual.* Cuadernos Phase 52. Barcelona, 1994.

Braso, G. *Liturgy and Spirituality.* Trans. L. J. Doyle. Collegeville, Minn., 1960.

Castellano, J. *Liturgia y vida espiritual.* Madrid, 1984.

Corbon, J. *The Wellspring of Worship.* Trans. M. J. O'Connell. New York, 1988.

Irwin, K. *Liturgy, Prayer and Spirituality.* New York, 1984.

Lang, O. *Spiritualità liturgica: Questioni e problemi scelti di spiritualità liturgica.* Einsiedeln, 1977.

Marsili, S. *Spiritualità liturgica.* In *I segni del mistero di Cristo: Teologia liturgica dei sacramenti*, 463–516. Rome, 1987.

Schmidt, H. *Introductio in liturgiam occidentalem*, 88–97. Rome, 1960.

Triacca, A. M., and A. Pistoia, eds. *Liturgie, spiritualité, cultures.* Conférences Saint-Serge: XXIXe Semaine d'etudes liturgiques, Paris, June 29–July 2, 1982. BELS 29. Rome, 1983.

Vagaggini, C. *Problemi e orientamenti di spiritualità monastica, biblica e liturgica*, 501–84. Rome, 1961.

_____. *Theological Dimensions of the Liturgy*. Trans. L. J. Doyle and W. A. Jurgens. Collegeville, Minn., 1976.

Domenico Sartore, C.S.J.

4

Pastoral Liturgy

Vatican Council II expressed, through *Sacrasanctum concilium* 1, the conviction of achieving through the liturgical reform the first and principal aim that John XXIII had assigned to it: "to enable the Christian life of the faithful to grow more and more every day." The entire Constitution displays this fundamental pastoral intent, marvelously expressed in one of the council's most prophetic passages: "Zeal for the promotion and restoration of the liturgy is rightly held to be a sign of the providential dispositions of God in our time, a movement of the Holy Spirit in his Church. Today it is a distinguishing mark of the Church's life, indeed of the whole tenor of contemporary religious thought and action" (*SC* 43).[1]

In the years immediately following the promulgation of *SC* (1963) intense work was carried out at all levels "to develop more and more this liturgical pastoral action in the Church," as *SC* 43 had asked. Yet everywhere the guidance authoritatively provided by John Paul II to all members of the people of God still carries urgency: "While the reform of the Liturgy, intended by Vatican Council II, has already been put into effect, liturgical pastoral ministry still constitutes a permanent involvement in order to draw ever more abundantly from the richness of the Liturgy the vital power that from Christ spreads out to all members of his body, which is the Church."[2]

---

[1] *SC* 43 constitutes a solemn acknowledgment of the importance of liturgical pastoral action. The text, as is known, reflects almost to the letter two passages from the discourse given by Pius XII on September 22, 1956, to the participants of the International Liturgical Congress of Assisi: cf. *AAS* 48 (1956) 718.724.

[2] John Paul II, apostolic letter *Vigesimus quintus annus*, 10: *Not* 25 (1989) 412–13.

LESSONS OF THE ANCIENT TRADITION

The theoretical-practical reflection on the relations between pastoral activity and liturgy, initiated by the liturgical movement, has succeeded in drawing significant lessons from the ancient Church.

A Pastoral Celebration

In a famous conference held at the Congress of Assisi (1958) J. A. Jungmann, in analyzing the development of liturgical forms, asked: "What attitudes of mind lay behind the creation of these forms? Where do we find the key to the mystery of these varied and often enigmatic forms of words, to this alteration of reading, hymns, and prayers, to this wealth of movement and ceremony? Why, in general, this multiplicity of forms?" The Austrian scholar finds the answer to these questions "in the care of the hierarchy for the Church as the community of the faithful, for the Church as the *plebs sancta* who, led by its pastors and even during its sojourn on this earth, are able to offer worthy service to God and so to become sanctified. This care was decisive in the shaping of public worship."[3] This continual evolution of the liturgy, so that it might remain a vital reality, expresses the Church's conviction that the liturgy itself must be pastoral and must be able to adapt to the needs of the people: differentiated forms of eucharistic celebration are introduced within the bounds of the same locality; the prayer of the Church reflects keenly the events of the times; various pagan popular customs become Christianized, and so forth.[4]

Complete Pastoral Care

A second lesson from the Church of the Fathers underscores the fact that the liturgy always postulates pastoral care, before, during, and after the celebration. Even in times when the liturgical language was understood and the rites were simple and intuitive, the ancient Church was concerned that the people should be prepared for the celebration, particularly by catechetical instructions, which were addressed above all to neophytes yet also constituted valuable instances of permanent formation for the faithful. Theodore of Mopsuestia

---

[3] J. A. Jungmann, "Pastoral Care — Key to the History of the Liturgy," *Pastoral Liturgy* (London, 1962) 369.

[4] Cf. A. G. Martimort, "La pastorale liturgica nell'esperienza storica," *Introduzione agli studi liturgici* (CAL, Rome, 1962) 149–73; cf. also B. Neunheuser, "Leçons du passé pour la participation à la Messe," *QL* 42 (1962) 109–27.

writes: "If this involved only material realities, it would be superfluous to explain them, because just the sight of them would be enough to show us each one of the things that take place. But since in the sacrament there are signs of what will come to pass and of what has already happened, a discourse is needed to explain the meaning of the signs and of the mysteries."[5]

A Celebrant Pastor
A third lesson from the ancient Church refers to the celebrant: the presider should carry out his office of pastor in the course of the liturgical action so that the people might be introduced and guided into conscious and active participation: for example, the appeals of the celebrant that invite the assembly to attentive and fruitful involvement; the dialogues; the instructions of the celebrant (or of the deacon); and all the various efforts at overcoming the difficulty of language incomprehension: for example, the multilinguism attested by Egeria.[6]

LITURGICAL PASTORAL ACTION AND STUDIES
In the years that preceded and followed Vatican II, alongside a liturgical pastoral action ever more intense and organized some efforts were developed also for systematic reflection in order to define better the basis, the purpose, the method, the formal object, and the constitutive elements of liturgical pastoral studies and their specific placement in the broadest range of liturgical science and pastoral theology. These theoretical-practical plans are not formulated according to a unitary method but display different formulations, terminologies, and interests.

Liturgical Pastoral Action
In France, some years after the foundation of the Centre de pastorale liturgique in Paris (1943), A. M. Roguet defined liturgical pastoral activity as "that part of the Church that tends to enable the people to participate in an active and conscious way in worship, so that they might draw from its sources the true Christian spirit."[7] The founda-

[5] Theodorus Mopsuest., *Hom.* XII, 2, R. Tonneau and R. Devresse, *Les homélies catéchètiques de Théodore de Mopsueste,* ST 145 (Vatican City, 1949) 325.
[6] *Itinerarium Egeriae* 47, 2–3; cf. Egérie, *Journal de voyage* (Itinéraire), ed. P. Maraval, Schr 298 (Paris, 1983) 314–5.
[7] Cf. A. M. Roguet, "La pastorale liturgique," A. G. Martimort, *L'Eglise en prière. Introduction à la Liturgie* (Tournai, 1961). This treatment is also found in the 2d ed., yet it is no longer provided nor replaced in the ed. of 1984.

tion of liturgical pastoral action is seen by Roguet in the double movement of the liturgy (cult and sanctification) and in its destination *propter homines* (for the sake of humans).

Yet what place does liturgical pastoral action hold in the mission of the Church? This does not exhaust all of its pastoral action (with regard to Christian celebrations, there is a before, an after, and an at-the-same-time), but it is the very function of the liturgy in ecclesial life that assigns to liturgical pastoral action its principal and unifying task.

There are, in our view, three limitations to be pointed out in this classic concept of liturgical pastoral action that we have summarized: it appears a bit too isolated from the whole of the Church's activity; there is very limited attention to the anthropological dimension of the liturgy; and its responsibility is too exclusively clerical and hierarchical.

In the same French environment, in the sixties, J. Gelineau's concept of liturgical pastoral activity matured, putting more sharply the accent on the function of the signs, in which the faith of the Church recognizes the operative presence of Christ: the task of liturgical pastoral action is the realization of effective communication through the signs, favoring the creation of "a specific cultural environment" and emphasizing the need for suitable biblical-liturgical formation.[8]

The responsibility for liturgical pastoral action is found on the various levels of the people of God, all of whom together are the subject of the celebration; yet it especially belongs to the pastors, with whom lay ministers collaborate, as well as to various study, consulting, and leadership groups, who require differing levels of specific formation.

In Italy, where C. Vagaggini even before the council had shown the necessary "union between pastoral and liturgical action,"[9] L. Della Torre recognizes the foundation of liturgical pastoral activity in the three *munera* (offices) of the Church, which he prefers to call practices: the practice of the Word, the practice of the Christian celebration, the practice of ecclesial planning and verification. This distinction certainly has its usefulness, notes L. Della Torre, but liturgical pastoral

[8] Cf. J. Gelineau, "La pastorale liturgica," *Nelle vostre assemblee. Teologia pastorale delle celebrazioni liturgiche* (Brescia, 1970) 26–41; cf. also in the Italian ed. of 1986.

[9] Cf. L. della Torre, "Prospettive ed esigenze per una pastorale liturgica," P. Visentin, A. N. Terrin, and R. Cecolin, *Una liturgia per l'uomo* (Padua, 1986) 83–105; ibid., "Pastorale liturgica," *NDL*, 1039–61.

action, just as catechetical and organizational, has in the concrete a specific competence that crosses all three practices, having, for each of them, needs to bring out and initiatives to propose. The basic perspective of liturgical pastoral activity is that of favoring the passage from ritual practice to ecclesial practice, understanding by "ritual practice" not just the ritual "plan," but also "the operative models" that flow from it with reference to the context of the celebration, which makes it existentially effective and culturally meaningful. The Spanish pastoralist (and liturgist) Casiano Floristán regards as a basis of liturgical pastoral action the fact that the liturgy is action.[10] Yet the author prefers to talk about praxis, a term that connotes diligence, a critical attitude, concreteness, and in the end a revolution or radical change in the depths of the human being and in society, with specific reference to Marxism. The liturgy is pastoral action insofar as it requires the practice of pastoral activity even though it does not exhaust it: as has already been seen, regarding the time of celebration there is a "before" (the time of evangelization and of catechesis) and an "after" (the time of community and of service to the world).

The purpose of liturgical pastoral action consists in fostering the full, conscious, and active participation of the Christian people, but this perspective is specified by the author's annotations on the sociocultural context of the current liturgy: the persistence of a certain sacral emphasis (a timeless, clerical, interclassist ritualism), the process of secularization, the political dimension, and so on.

Finally, the discourse dwells on the style of celebration in relation to the communitarian dimension of the assembly, to the prophetic proclamation of the Christian message, to the meaning of the symbolic action, to the liturgy-commitment relationship, to the presidential function, and to the exercise of the ministries.

Liturgical Pastoral Studies
In the German-speaking countries a debate began in the twenties on the concept of liturgical pastoral studies (*Pastoralliturgik*), which thereafter developed from several viewpoints: in relation to liturgical studies, to practical theology, to an appreciation of human sciences, to the demands of liturgical reform, and so on. The most enlightening

[10] Cf. C. Floristán, "Pastorale liturgica," *La celebrazione nella Chiesa. 1. Liturgia e sacramentaria fondamentale,* ed. D. Borobio (Turin, 1992) 565–614.

contribution on this complex inquiry seems to us to be that of
B. Jeggle-Merz,[11] which appears as a rereading of a debated essay by
A. Wintersig going back to 1924.[12]

B. Jeggle-Merz does not regard as a current issue the question
whether liturgical pastoral studies are a component of liturgical studies in the context of pastoral theology or whether it assumes a purely
practical function or is a simple aid to praxis. Wintersig attributed to
liturgical pastoral studies the rank of a proper science, that engaged
in the scientific treatment of the liturgy alongside the history and the
theology of Christian worship. B. Jeggle-Merz identifies two main
tasks for liturgical pastoral studies: (1) the analysis of a given liturgical pastoral situation, showing the deficiencies that characterize it in
comparison with an ideal model; and (2) a well-motivated guide for
undertaking correction and renewal.

Yet pastoral liturgy that claims its own place in the work area of
liturgical science should make use of methodological principles that
inspire its research, particularly in relation to human sciences. A specific theological interpretation of a given liturgical situation should
be verifiable and perfectible through interpretive contributions and
models from the various human sciences that engage the problem
under study. The need for an "integrative method" that evaluates the
contributions of anthropological research no longer poses a problem.
Still, an uncritical acceptance of the methods and results of human
sciences would not adequately establish liturgical pastoral studies as
a branch of liturgical science but would lead to pure pragmatism,
which would reduce it to the task of a practical function.

Among the American scholars who have faced the problem of
pastoral liturgy understood as a new academic discipline, we find
particular interest in the contribution of M. Searle, who prefers to talk

---

[11] B. Jeggle-Merz, "Pastoralliturgik: Eigenberechtigter Zweig oder
Anwendungsdisziplin der Liturgiewissenschaft," *ALW* 29 (1987) 352–70; cf.
German bibliography. For an attempt at epistemological reflection beginning with
the contemporary debate on pastoral theology, cf. D. Sartore, "Concetto di pastorale liturgica," *RL* 79 (1992) 9–24. A solid contemporary Italian inquiry is taken
as a point of comparison: M. Midali, *Teologia pastorale pratica. Cammino storico di
una riflessione fondante e scientifica*, 2d ed. (Rome, 1991).

[12] A. Wintersig, "Pastoralliturgik. Ein Versuch über Wesen, Weg, Einleitung und
Abgrenzung einer seelsorgwissenschaftlichen Behandlung der Liturgie," *JLW* 4
(1924) 153–67.

about "pastoral liturgical studies" insofar as the term "pastoral liturgy" indicates too unilaterally an affiliation with pastoral or practical theology with prevailing reference to the work of supervision and guidance for the Church's liturgical celebrations on the part of pastors.[13]

This discipline assumes, however, as a departure point the worship activity of the whole community gathered in assembly and has as its formal object the actual liturgical life of contemporary churches. It carries out a threefold task: (1) an empirical task: a phenomenological description of the event of celebration, explanation of the meaning of words and deeds that constitute the rite, liturgical attitudes, and the specific assembly's receptiveness; (2) a hermeneutic task: how symbols work and how symbolic language communicates, and whether our contemporaries effectively engage in communication with them; (3) a critical task: comparison with the results of other disciplines, critical evaluation of the various forms of religious imagination in the various churches, and identification of the various forms in which contemporary liturgy can be alienated and alienating.

Searle completes the picture of this plan of pastoral liturgy with some methodological notes: the interdisciplinarity and multidisciplinarity of liturgical pastoral research draws from the very characteristics of the liturgical event; the application to the liturgical datum of the methods of human sciences should respect the primacy of the mystery of grace professed and celebrated in the liturgy; the formal object of "pastoral liturgical studies" is the actual worship of the Church that makes present the mystery of grace and the human response to this mystery; the synchronous approach to the liturgy that this discipline represents poses new problems for the historians and theologians of Christian worship; it stimulates the research that is already being done on the relation between the human sciences and the liturgy; the number of scholars is growing who are broadening the horizon of their studies to the ritual experience of Christian communities.

We have thus summarized a series of models of epistemological reflection concerning pastoral liturgy, which open up to different points of view: (1) the three contributions from the Latin area delineate

---

[13] M. Searle, "New Tasks, New Methods: The Emergence of Pastoral Liturgical Studies," *Wor* 57 (1983) 291–308 (cf. American bibliography).

some operative plans of pastoral liturgy, understood as an action of the Church: those of the German and American area treat rather of the concept of pastoral liturgy in relation to liturgical science and pastoral theology; (2) the basis of pastoral liturgy is comprised, with different emphases, in the twofold human-divine component of the liturgy, in the three *munera* of the Church, and in the liturgy as "praxis"; (3) the formal object of pastoral liturgy can be identified, it seems to us, in the study of how the actions and words of the liturgy work and how they can be received in the environment of a particular assembly; (4) the specific purpose of pastoral liturgy is indicated mainly in the conscious and active participation of the entire Christian people in liturgical actions, specifying that it requires effective communication through the signs and a real passage from ritual practice to ecclesial practice; (5) others speak of the tasks of pastoral liturgy, recognizing its threefold function as empirical, hermeneutical, and critical; they also emphasize the interdisciplinarity of this discipline.[14]

A CONCRETE PROGRAM OF PASTORAL LITURGY

Regarding a specific liturgical situation, verified with the help of human sciences and compared to the fundamental principles of Christian worship, we think that a complete and effective program of pastoral liturgy needs to be articulated in four phases: (1) a serious undertaking of liturgical formation, based especially on catechesis; (2) an enlightened and effective conduct of liturgical actions; (3) constant attention to genuine celebration, especially relative to the presidential role; (4) the good functioning of training centers for the liturgy at the various levels of the Church's responsibilities.

Liturgical Formation

All the socioreligious research that has attempted to profile the liturgical situation in various ecclesial environments, the conclusions of experts, the documents of the hierarchy, and our own pastoral experience lead us to stress the need and urgency for more thorough liturgical formation at all levels of the people of God. Moreover, Vatican II had already strongly stated:

"It is the ardent desire of Mother Church that everyone should be formed in this full, conscious and active participation in liturgical

[14] Cf. W. Durig, *Die Zukunft der liturgischen Erneuerung* (Mainz, 1962) 9.

actions. . . . Very special effort is made for this full and active participation of the whole people in the context of the reform and of the fostering of the liturgy. For it is the first and indispensable source from which the faithful can draw the genuine Christian spirit, and therefore pastors of souls in all their pastoral activity should strive to gain it through adequate formation" (*SC* 14).

These well-founded concerns for the future explain historically how *Sacrosanctum concilium*, along with the clear dispositions for a *generalis instauratio* of the liturgy, manifests its interest in promoting suitable liturgical formation at all levels of the People of God. This document, after stating the fundamental principles of the liturgy and before presenting the guidelines for the liturgical reform and its specific modalities, insists on the primary necessity of a solid formation of clergy and people, devoting a series of articles (*SC* 14–19) to them, of which "the importance could not be exaggerated."[15]

The instruction *Inter oecumenici* (1964), in its turn, presents in summary the explicit formative purpose of the whole reform: "It is above all necessary that everyone be convinced that the purpose of the Constitution on the Liturgy is not so much to change the liturgical rites and texts, but rather to foster formation of the faithful and to promote pastoral action that has the sacred liturgy as its summit and source" (no. 5). This text, of the greatest importance, furnishes a key for interpreting not just *SC* but also all of the ensuing reformative course which defines the substantive and hermeneutical criterion of the whole postconciliar liturgical history and synthesizes it in the *fidelium institutio*.[16]

The complexity of liturgical formation also appears in the richness of the terms used in the cited conciliar texts (*institutio, eruditio, instructio, formatio, educatio, manuductio*), linked to verbs such as *adpetere, adquirere, excitare, prosequi, consulere.* However, it seems preferable to us to use the term "formation" because it lends itself to indicate a more specific and intense period in Christian education, seen in its entirety, along the lines of the conciliar declaration *Gravis-*

[15] P. Gy, "2. Concile du Vatican II. La Constitution sur la Liturgie. Commentaire complet: n. 14," *MD* 77 (1964) 32.
[16] G. Genero, "Per una promozione della liturgia: la formazione dei celebranti," AA.VV., *Riforma liturgica tra passato e futuro*, Studi di liturgia /NS, 13 (Casale Monferrato, 1985) 112–3.

simum educationis 2. Among the fundamental objectives of Christian education, this document states that "the faithful should learn to adore God the Father in spirit and in truth (John 4:23), especially through liturgical actions." At the same time, the term "formation" is recommended for its pedagogical overtones, valuable in this context.

A Significant Model of the Liturgical Movement:
Romano Guardini
In view of these formative demands with regard to various aspects of the liturgical movement and cultural changes in progress, it can still be very useful to return to the great models that the liturgical movement has provided us, especially to Romano Guardini (1885–1968). Although Guardini's work proves now to be "dated" with regard to cultural sensitivity and to problems of his times, his guidelines for liturgical formation are still significant, particularly in his book *Liturgische Bildung* published in 1923, which arose in the same cultural and spiritual environment of the two works that preceded it: *The Spirit of the Liturgy* and *Sacred Signs* (1919).[17] Guardini's interest in the liturgy signifies not only the rediscovery of communitarian prayer beyond an individualistic-bourgeois piety but also the overcoming of a purely notional or sentimental religiosity so as to attain a religiousness solidly anchored in the reality of life and of the world.

Starting with the spiritual circumstances of his times, the author proposes "to create the real premises for a living liturgical formation."[18] He understands the term "formation" in its most essential meaning: "It is necessary that individuals and communities be educated to that special mode of spiritual conduct that is required by the very nature of the liturgy."[19] On one side the question is posed: "In what does the essence of the liturgical action consist?" And on the other: "What should the person do, what should the community do, if we want to have appropriate liturgical conduct?"[20] This brings out the specific formative tasks of the liturgy itself.

[17] R. Guardini, *Formazione liturgica* (Brescia, 1988). There is no English translation of *Liturgische Bildung*. The author uses the Italian edition in his Italian contribution to the Handbook. The other two fundamental works are *Sacred Signs* (St. Louis, 1956) and *The Spirit of the Liturgy* (New York, 1935). The first German editions of the two works are from 1919.

[18] R. Guardini, *Formazione liturgica*, 17.

[19] Ibid., 18.

[20] Ibid.

The first perspective to which Guardini's reflection introduces us is the overcoming of the soul-body dualism: "It is the whole person who carries out liturgical activity."[21] The liturgy, from beginning to end, assumes that the human person is the vehicle of liturgical action, becoming ever more human in the deepest sense. This means that in liturgical activity, human bodiliness becomes ever more animated, spiritualized, transfigured.

The profound recovery of this "manifested interiority," of this "full outward manifestation of deep interiority," leads to the reunderstanding of the "human composite" in the sense of symbolic-active and symbolic-receptive.

Thus appears "the first task of an authentic liturgical formation: that of leading to a truly unitary perception of the human composite, so that people might become again 'capable of symbols.'" In particular, then, it is a matter of developing this formative undertaking, in the sense of an "education in suitable symbolic conduct of body and soul." Starting with the most elementary liturgical actions, progress can be made to the most complex actions, leading children from infancy to know and to experience varieties of liturgical conduct, in which they will achieve a complete human experience.[22]

In order to manifest human spiritual richness, the expressive abilities of the body (parts, lines, movements) are not enough, because the person broadens them by assuming into the sphere of his or her own body the things of the world around: clothings, actions, and attitudes of the body with relation to objects, to the setting, with all of its aspects tied to space and time. Guardini discovered in the youth of his times a reawakening of the perception of a deep relationship among things, a kind of kinship, of familiarity, that enabled him to discover the capacity for symbolic perception. Modern culture had led human beings away from a real understanding and experience of their most authentic humanity as well as from a full perception of nature.

The second of the main purposes of liturgical formation is that of enabling the essence of things to be seen and experienced through words and sensible signs, to see how this essence is adapted to the bodily expression of the soul's interior process, and, finally, to see

[21] Ibid., 21.
[22] Ibid., 30.

how these material realities become bearers of full supernatural meaning. It is not a question of imposing artificially concepts and similes or of tying something signified to an exterior form but rather of sharing with children the experience of a transformation of things in symbols, through which the material realities become for humans means for expressing their own religious interiority and grasping that of others.[23]

We have seen that the subject of liturgical behavior is the whole human being, capable of utilizing things in the expression of individual spirituality. Yet the whole of the person involves another aspect of fundamental importance for liturgical life: the insertion of the individual into the life of the community. A Christian person realizes himself or herself only where Church and person live in a reciprocal relationship. Guardini injects at that point a clarification that has gained great significance in recent ecclesiology: we must see and perceive the Church in its universality, yet through the experience of its most concrete dimension, which we find and live in an immediate way within the diocesan and parish community. It is this Church that lives the liturgy. A truly liturgical conduct results only if one has a watchful and full awareness of the Church; one can pray with the liturgy if one does it with this intense and lively communitarian awareness.

Thus a third task is marked for appropriate liturgical formation: education to a communitarian and ecclesial awareness. "By overcoming every kind of individualistic isolation and of romantic-sentimental subjectivism in prayer, in sacrifice and in sacramental action, the believer must place himself or herself totally within the great community of the Church. One should be led to broaden one's heart for the life of the ecclesial community: from communion with those present out to the parish, to the universal Church, to all of humanity, called to enter the Church, putting oneself in harmony with those who are being purified and with those who are already singing the praises of the Lord in the Father's house."[24]

The aspects that until now we have shown in liturgical conduct are found on the level of expression, yet this could stay in the realm of the subjective. It is only by starting with the objective that the con-

[23] Ibid., 39–42.
[24] Ibid., 44–9.

duct gains its full significance. Guardini urges young people to connect their quest for new experiences, a strong personality, and exceptional sentiments, with the objective realities that demand discipline and obedience. The liturgy itself represents this kind of religious experience, which proves to be the most intensely objective kind. The various aspects of liturgical life that we have examined have an objective basis: the whole human being, his or her relationship to nature, the individual in community. The liturgy has an objective character because it is faithful to God and people, it depends on a history and on a positive law, it is constituted by specific words and actions, it involves actual communities, and it is inserted into a tradition and a culture.

From all this there proceeds a fifth task for liturgical formation: to go from the narrow confines of the subjective out to the breadth and order of the objective, living the joy of strong obedience and committed discipline that leads us to cling firmly to the Church with our whole person. We will then comprehend that we must lift ourselves up in order to make our own the Church's great style of prayer, to participate fully in the sublime forms of its liturgy.

Finally, "liturgical formation . . . is an education to *sentire cum Ecclesia*, to unite our heart and our voice to the *Ecclesia orans*."[25]

The cultural context by now has decisively changed, and emphases of a contingent character are continually encountered in pages by Guardini. Nevertheless, it seems to us that the attention to the cultural context, on which Guardini greatly insists in the conclusion of the book *Liturgische Bildung*, and the perennial validity of the guidelines that he offers us, can even today be fruitfully revisited in connection with other anthropological and theological perspectives that have come more recently to enrich our reflection on the liturgy of the Church and therefore on the implementation of an enlightened and effective liturgical formation. We can note as examples the perspectives opened by secularization-desacralization; the evangelization-sacraments relationship; the emphasized attention to the concrete celebration (leadership and participation; presidency and ministries; adaptation and inculturation); the symbolism-feast coupling; the involving and sociopolitical dimension; various aspects of postmodern culture.

[25] Ibid., 61–4.

A Concrete Program for Liturgical Formation

In the light of especially enlightening pedagogical considerations in our sector, by liturgical formation we can understand not just a state of acquired formation but also a fostering action that involves the whole human person and his or her own social experience, in order to aid self-development in a harmonious and unitary manner and to adopt specific behaviors following a program of life.

Since we are talking about liturgical formation, we should understand a specific and fundamental aspect of integral Christian education, both in relation to the whole human person and to the mystery of Christ in its entirety. This educational involvement will surely tend to involve individuals, yet by liturgy's very nature it cannot help referring to the whole community, called to become the subject of the liturgical celebration; indeed, liturgical actions "belong to the whole body of the Church, making it manifest and involving it" (*SC* 28). The specificity of the liturgical experience leads us again to highlight both the cyclical and permanent character of this formation.[26]

FORMATION FOR THE LITURGY AND THROUGH THE LITURGY

A plan of liturgical formation, whether it deals with early initiation or with deepening an already acquired experience, should be divided into two phases:

(1) Forming for the liturgy and for the liturgical celebration: as a point of departure, considerations can be used of biblical character (salvation history as a pedagogy of signs) or of anthropological character (the significance of rituals in human life) in order to introduce Christian liturgy as the presence of Christ through the signs of the Church. The necessary information on the different phases and the different celebrative elements should lead to the mystery of Christ, so that faith might be enlightened and Christian life nourished as we take appropriate advantage of the liturgical experience already in progress and still to be perfected.

(2) Forming through the liturgy: benefit will be drawn from the pedagogical effectiveness that the liturgical actions have in themselves, already at the level of a symbolical-ritual experience, and through the special richness of the language of celebration, but above

[26] We draw this terminology and the phrasing of the following paragraph from M. L. Pedrazzini, "Formazione liturgica," *NDL*, 582–601.

all through the efficacy of grace, which is specific to Christian liturgy, in which salvation is given to us through modalities that help us understand and participate more intensely.

THE ROLE OF LITURGICAL CATECHESIS

Vatican II stated that among the means the Church can employ in its educational task the first is catechesis, "which enlightens and strengthens faith, nourishes life according to the Spirit of Christ, leads to sharing consciously and actively in the liturgical mystery and is a stimulus to apostolic action" (*GE* 4). The deepening of the "liturgy-catechesis" relation in the light of the great patristic tradition and of the Rite of Christian Initiation of Adults should lead us to dwell on a whole series of perspectives that are current in the life of the Church today: the primacy of evangelization and formation of true Christian communities, the contribution of the Bible in the whole formative process, the complex contents of the catechumenal method, the perennial need for mystagogy, and the liturgy-life relation.

We will confine ourselves to outlining three specific aspects on the function of liturgical catechesis for deepening Christian formation:

(1) catechesis as initiation into the liturgy both in the most general sense of a Christian proclamation open to the function of liturgical actions in salvation history, in the life of the Church, and in individual Christians and as initiation into individual liturgical "signs" and their meaning of faith and life;

(2) liturgy as catechesis in action involving the complex contents of Christian celebration, the resources of its symbolism and language, its elegantly pedagogical laws of cyclical nature and permanent formation, and especially its efficacy in "mysteries";

(3) liturgy as a wellspring of catechesis; the complex of signs that constitute the liturgy as an inexhaustible fountain of symbolic elements that explain individual aspects of the mystery of Christ and the Church (these signs promote faith and Christian life, offering psychological approaches and supportive structures for Christian reflection that enhance the ecclesial experience and nourish hope).[27]

---

[27] Cf. D. Sartore, "Catechesi e liturgia," *NDL*, 219–59.

Those responsible for Christian communities are mandated by Vatican Council II "to provide zealously and patiently for the liturgical formation as well as for the active participation of the faithful, both internally and externally, according to their age, condition, type of life and religious culture, thereby achieving the fulfillment of one of the principal duties of the faithful dispenser of the mysteries of God" (*SC* 29).

Here we are examining only the two earliest phases of this age: children and youths. We have underscored the reference to age because this directive of the council obliges Christian pastors and educators to a formation of children beginning in infancy to enable them to grow as adults in the faith, initiate them integrally into the mystery of Christ, and introduce them gradually into the early experiences of ecclesial life, for which the signs and attitudes of the liturgy have primary importance.

The first contact of a child (1–6 years old) with the liturgy is spontaneous and occasional in character (family, church, signs, places, images, actions, especially in the various phases of the liturgical year); later (ages 7–9) the liturgical formation of children becomes more complete and systematic in relation to the intense sacramentalization that generally characterizes this age through an increasingly conscious participation in Christian celebrations. This liturgical maturation is favored, even on a psychological level, by the progressive development of symbolic perception (active and passive) and by the acquisition of the historical-interpretive function that enables the children to link a rite with its past and future. The fullness of participation in the liturgy will grow by the interaction of educative processes and development in the personality.[28]

A pedagogy of the liturgy for children passes through two aspects: (1) initiation into the meaning of the organized and differentiated liturgical community, a privileged place for the encounter with Christ; and (2) the initiation into the language of God and humans in the liturgy, which includes a veneration for the book of the Word and

---

[28] Cf. M. Aletti, "Fanciulli e liturgia. Note di psicologia della religione," *RL* 61 (1974) 615–33; A. Godin and Sr. Marthe, "Mentalité magique et vie sacramentelle chez des enfants de 8–14 ans," *LeV* 25 (1960) 268–88; M. Amman-Gainotti, "La genesi della funzione simbolica nel bambino," *RL* 67 (1980) 317–27; A. Godin, "La fonction historique. Pour une psycopédagogie du chrétien dans le temps," *LeV* 14 (1959) 229–50.

a gradual introduction to biblical language, initiation into liturgical signs and symbols, and introduction to the bodily expressions typical of liturgical action.[29]

In order to avert children from undergoing ritual experiences harmful to their spiritual growth and to favor their correct liturgical formation, especially the first initiation to the Eucharist, the Church promulgated in 1973 the *Directory for Masses with Children (DMP)*, a document of historic importance not only in the liturgical reform but in Christian pedagogy as well.[30] The first educational task that the *DMP* entrusts to parents and educators is that of setting children on their way so that

"they may also experience in proportion to their age and personal development the human values that are present in the eucharistic celebration. These values include the community activity, exchange of greetings, capacity to listen and to seek and grant pardon, expression of gratitude, experience of symbolic actions, a meal of friendship, and festive celebration.

"Eucharistic catechesis, dealth with in no. 12, should develop such human values. Then, depending on their age and their psychological and social situation, children will gradually open their minds to the perception of Christian values and the celebration of the mystery of Christ" (nos. 9–10).

On a concrete level, "for the liturgical formation of children, and in their preparation for liturgical life in the Church," the *DMP* maintains that various celebrations of the Word can have great importance, arranged for the purpose of facilitating for children the perception and meaning of some elements and aspects of liturgical life, which could be summarized under the following perspectives: communitarian action, symbolic experience, gesturing and bodily expression, attitudes of silence-listening-response; fundamental attitudes of prayer: praise, thanksgiving, offering, petition, pardon (cf. no. 13).[31] Finally, the *DMP* sees a great means for deepening children's liturgical formation in eucharistic celebrations suitably adapted to children's psychology and led by prepared and attentive people (nos. 20–54).

[29] Comm. nat. "Liturgie-enfance," *Les enfants à la messe* (Paris, 1968) 34–45.
[30] SC Divine Worship: *Directory for Masses with Children*, Not 10 (1974) 5–21.
[31] Cf. M. L. Pedrazzini, "Formazione liturgica," 591.

In order to complete this "little liturgical reform" for children, in 1974 three Eucharistic Prayers were promulgated that present simpler language and broader possibilities of adaptation, some structural modifications, and especially a greater number of acclamations in order to make children's liturgical participation "more intense and vivid."[32] In some nations Lectionaries have been produced that are better adapted to children, something provided for by the *DMP*.[33]

The attitude of young people toward the liturgy is inscribed in the broadest frame of reference to the condition of youth in recent decades, in particular by the pastorally problematic presence of young people in the Church, of which they are the "hope" yet also the restless "present." Immediately after Vatican II, in different countries, fervid and courageous liturgical initiatives became widespread, which proved to be a great attractive force on the new generations; at a remove their risks can be measured (a certain onesidedness, especially in musical forms, verbal inflation, isolation from a true path of faith of the Christian community, new formalisms, etc.) but also the positive aspects (communitarian preparation, dynamic and festive style, atmosphere of brotherhood and communion, life-liturgy relation, strong influence on young people and adults, etc.).[34]

The reflection on the theme of young people and liturgy developed more recently from a pastoral and liturgical standpoint as well as from that of education into faith. The awareness is growing that young people, even within the confines of the same country, no longer constitute a homogeneous and stable world; new orientations are thriving that touch the religiousness of young people (symbolic claims, sense of feast, attention to the aesthetic and contemplative dimension, etc.). We should note that youthful experiences of intense Christian life are multiplying; in such situations the liturgical problem seems to become less dramatic or else is posed in different terms.

---

[32] The three texts have not been published officially in Latin but have been distributed in multicopied form to those engaged in the work of translation into various languages. For the Italian edition, cf. "La messa dei fanciulli," Libreria editrice vaticana, 1976; cf. D. Sartore, "Preghiere eucharistiche per la messa con i fanciulli," *RL* 65 (1978) 241–8.

[33] D. Sartore, "Lezionari per le messe con i fanciulli," *RL* 73 (1986) 558–69.

[34] Cf. L. della Torre and G. Stefani, *La messa nelle comunità giovanili* (Brescia, 1968); L. Zenetti, *Zeitansage. Anregungen für den Gottesdienst einer neuen Generation* (Munich, 1969).

Moreover, in many Christian communities young people are predominantly the ones who take on the task of liturgical leadership in community celebrations; young people of this sort also seem to surmount the liturgical problem that we have discussed.

However, if our attention is turned toward more general tendencies among the majority of youths, we have to note that their religious difficulties and their disaffection toward the liturgy have probably become prominent, whereas a certain disarray is evident in pastoral care for youth, and silence surrounds the possibility of some liturgical adaptation that might foster young people's participation. The "religious crisis" of young people is often translated into a rejection of the Church's ritual symbols. Yet upon close examination this aloofness from the liturgy is simply an aspect of a more general phenomenon, one that involves adults as well. Their longings basically find their place in the context of the claims of Vatican II and of widespread expectations within the Church, especially regarding adaptation, participation, and communion. Although in a context that is anything but homogeneous, young people seem, often with little balance, to claim celebrative values that are among the objectives of the liturgical reform and that are broadly shared at various levels of the People of God. Instead of excessive repetitiveness, they tend toward greater creativity; instead of a certain rigidity, they seek greater interpretive freedom; instead of rites that are too exclusively traditional, they favor the search for new symbols; instead of an atmosphere of non-involvement, they want to create a festive atmosphere; instead of cold and impersonal liturgies, which seem foreign to our times, they want celebrations that engender courageous choices; instead of massive assemblies, they prefer small groups capable of significant relationships and intense sharing.

These demands, often shared by the most sensitive adults, bring out aspects that are proper to the Christian liturgy, but in their onesidedness they comprise a range of difficult relations between young people and the Church and, even further back, of problems of communication among people of different ages. Young people do indeed experience a special situation of faith, characterized by a weak sense of Christian identity and an often problematic ecclesial membership.

Therefore we believe that the aspirations of young people, their partial intuitions, might be able to be reshaped and rebalanced through a serious and dispassionate confrontation with the liturgy itself and with its indispensable principles. A higher level of attention to young people cannot translate into a lack of respect toward the paschal mystery of Christ, celebrated in his Church. Young people can ask that the liturgy turn toward them only if they themselves can turn toward the liturgy, toward its signs, its content, and its fundamental laws.

More sharply than adults, young people pose for themselves the radical problem of liturgical actions in Christian life: why celebrate the liturgy, why participate in the Eucharist? Why go to confession? Why is it necessary to have celebrations at fixed times? The need becomes evident for gradual reflection on the anthropological and biblical-sacramental foundations of the Christian liturgy and on the ecclesial character of these rites, which make manifest and involve the whole People of God. Christian celebrations cannot be understood just as human celebration, or as a form of conscientization, or as a strong anthropological experience: they are always a living memory of Christ's mystery of salvation, a sharing in his death and resurrection, an expression and gift of his love that frees and saves. Therefore our demands on the Christian liturgy cannot claim total freedom of action; their special relationship with Christ and the Church are explained by their biblical roots, their sacramental character, their ecclesial dimension, their universality, and the like.

The movement of secularization and desacralization that has spread through the Western world in recent decades, yet which imperceptibly is penetrating other cultural areas too, has created difficulties for Christian ritual practice. Yet it is still able to preserve its opportunities for various reasons in which the young are very interested: its symbolic characterization, the openness of Christian celebrations to ideals of liberation and justice, the portion of hope that the Christian liturgy bears.

One of the most commonly heard requests of young people with regard to the liturgy is its insertion into an overall plan of Christian commitment. Even at an anthropological level we experience a whole "human liturgy" that is linked with the most intense moments of our daily experience, while Christian rites, especially the sacraments, are understood as acts that individual believers and the Christian community carry out to an extent not possible with other languages and activities. The young have to be helped to live this tension between life and liturgy, a tension that lends a special power of relevance to Christian celebration and makes it incisive and efficacious.

Liturgical actions, particularly the Eucharist, are the summit and wellspring of Christian life. Authentic celebration is not just a parenthesis in Christian existence; it is a moment of conversion, of validation, of reconfirmed commitment, of assumption of renewed responsibility, of intense communion with God, and of more generous openness to our sisters and brothers. Liturgical celebration thus becomes a saving event for this person, for this specific community: an encounter with Christ through the signs of the Church that can transform our life and lead us into deeper interpersonal relations.

For young people also and especially, liturgical formation is formation through the liturgy. The particular path of faith and the liturgical sensitivity that characterize it must never translate into a "ghetto experience" but should be carried out through two phases divided between them, with both open to the broader Christian community. The first is a phase of group experience, possibly with the presence and collaboration of some adults, which can be structured according to models that favor the participation of the young: explicit stress on the liturgy-commitment relation, dialogue, relevance of the Word, particular forms of festive expression, music and songs adapted to the young, openness to humankind's great problems, proposals for varying liturgical celebrations that can correspond to a differentiated faith situation and can make an articulate path possible. The second is a phase of responsible participation in the community's liturgy, in the preparation and leadership of which young people can become active, in close collaboration with adults, in order to enliven celebrations that they will become real expressions of the community, of its encounter with the risen Christ.

Without taking anything away from the significance of small and homogeneous groups, in order to favor a more intense experience of Church and to promote a participation better felt by young people, Christian liturgy calls attention to the whole gathered community. This might involve less creative celebrations, but it shows a fuller image of the great Church and a more complete practice of the priesthood of believers that is carried out by all — laypeople and ministers — with different functions in the ambit of the Christian assembly. Liturgy therefore educates us to welcome all of our brothers and sisters, young or old, in lesser or greater agreement with us, and it opens our horizons toward a more universal and more authentic ecclesial experience.[35] John Paul II has indicated one of the problems in the liturgy for young people not yet resolved by the postconciliar liturgical renewal:[36] in the service of this complex pedagogical perspective the time has come on the part of the Holy See to publish a directory for the liturgical formation of young people so that new generations can live intensely the liturgy of the Church and become protagonists in effective liturgical leadership in their communities.

LITURGICAL LEADERSHIP

We have seen that the Church of the Fathers expected the presider at the liturgical action to be a pastor so that the people might be brought into and guided in the liturgy and gain an authentic understanding of it. In today's Church this engaging and complex ecclesial activity carried out by the celebrant and his collaborators is often indicated by the noun "leadership" or the verb "to lead." These terms are much used by modern sociology in reference to promotional activities for the action, participation, and self-expression of human groups and communities. For some years now there has been much talk in the Church about leadership, especially in the liturgical perspective, so as to make Christian celebrations truly experienced in their fullest form and significance.[37]

But what does it mean to "lead" a celebration? To lead a celebration means two closely interrelated things. In the first instance, to lead in the sense of "to animate" is to give spirit, vitality, expression, and authentic realization to an action. Second, it means to promote the involvement of a "community" with all of its members so that it might become the conscious and active subject of this action.

[35] R. Sauer, "Jugend und Liturgie. Grundsätzliche Überlegungen zu einem pastoralen Notstand," KB 98 (1973) 397–409; D. Borobio, "Posreforma litúrgica en los Jóvenes frente a la reforma litúrgica de la Iglesia," Ph 97 (1977) 33–51; D. Sartore, "Giovani e liturgia, vent'anni di riflessioni e di esperienze," RL 75 (1988) 221–45; RL 79 (1992); M. Klockener, "Les jeunes et la liturgie: un rapport d'aliénation," MD 179 (1989) 111–44; cf. also in English SL 20 (1990) 137–61.

[36] John Paul II, Apostolic letter Vigesimus quintus annus, 19–21: Not 25 (1989) 419–22.

[37] Cf. L. Brandolini, "Animazione," NDL, 52–65; G. Genero, "Il presidente dell'assemblea e l'animatore della comunità," RPL 168 (1991) 31–33; Segretariado Nacional Español de Liturgia, Equipo de animación. Directorio liturgico-pastoral. Plan de formación (Madrid, 1989).

Indeed, a celebration is always an action of an assembly, in which there are different gifts and tasks; a "symbolic" action, realized through a complex of words, gestures, and things that have not just a functional character but that signify the communion between God and humans effected in Christ by means of the Spirit. It is a complex and articulate action with its own rhythm of parts, its own laws and its own internal logic.

A team that wants to lead a liturgical action, especially a eucharistic celebration, in collaboration with the presider, must take on at least four tasks:

(1) Learn thoroughly the meaning, the purposes, the texts, and the rite of a liturgical action; become aware of the plan that the Church offers us for a specific celebration, with intelligent diligence for interiorization and hermeneutical interpretation.

(2) Prearrange a specific program for a celebration, making necessary choices (e.g., which penitential act, which universal prayer, which eucharistic prayer) with due attention to the rhythm of parts, to persons, and to the elements of the celebration.

(3) Arrange and put into effect with skillful direction the various contributions and roles, namely, besides the service of the presidency, services assigned to various types of ministers or to the assembly. These are: *the welcoming service,* which can include: preparation of the setting; arrangement of the assembly; welcome of strangers, children, and the elderly; the distribution of aids; the setup of various technical services and the like; *the service of the Word:* introduction (overall, or for each reading); choice of readers; technical preparation (pronunciation: articulation, use of microphone, projection of voice, volume, tone, rhythms, key words, pauses); *the service of prayer:* preparation of the universal prayer; stress on communitarian thanksgiving, etc.; *service of song:* use of music and instruments; choice of songs; discernment (artistic level, musical genre, content, liturgical function); preparation (brief mystagogical introduction, performance, direction, review); *service of the altar:* tasks of acolytes and of extraordinary ministers of Communion; Sunday Communion for the sick; *service of charity:* collection of offerings and their eventual destination; presentation of the gifts; offertory procession.

(4) Review at least periodically the celebration in each of its elements — as an organic whole (as an overall action and as a unitary

experience of faith) and in its various aspects, in its link to the life of the community.

Always in close collaboration with the service of the presidency, the liturgical leadership group can be called to two other tasks: prepare and suggest the admonitions (especially at the beginning, at the readings, at the dismissal) keeping in mind the special difficulties of this literary genre (short yet effective; elevated yet familiar style); make suggestions for the homily itself: preparation with the priest, exceptional assistance of a technical type or life testimonies (periodic review of the "state of preaching" in the community, particularly regarding the homily; testing the comprehension of language, expectations, themes used, reactions of the assembly, local problems).

Everything we have said with regard to liturgical leadership referred in a particular way to the exercise of the presidency, which nonetheless has some things peculiar to itself and requires a specific formation, including a technical one. We are not getting into theological clarifications or into exact ministerial distinctions here, but we are referring above all to the eucharistic presidency and then, by analogy, to that of all ecclesial celebrations, including Sunday celebrations in the absence of a priest.[38] The renewed concept of the liturgy, the development of the liturgical reform, ecclesial maturation, and the contribution of human sciences have given more importance and more significant dimensions to this ecclesial ministry.[39]

At one time the role of the celebrant absorbed practically all of the aspects of the celebration, yet it was a less demanding task, more executive and individual, almost self-standing in relation to the community. Nowadays, while the demand for faith and personal partici-

[38] For doctrinal foundations and appropriate theological distinctions, cf. R. Gantoy, *Le ministère du célébrant dans la liturgie nouvelle* (Paris, 1978); B. D. Marliangeas, *Clés pour une théologie des ministères: In persona Christi — In persona Ecclesiae* (Paris, 1978); A. G. Martimort, "In persona Christi," *Mens concordet voci* (Paris, 1983) 330–7; cf. various possibilities of lay presidency in P. Marini, "L'eventuale presidenza liturgica dei laici in assenza del presbitero," *Lit* 10 (1986) 538–56; cf. Spanish translation in *Ph* 158 (1987) 113–38; cf. also Congr. pro Cultu Divino, *Directorium de celebrationibus dominicalibus absente presbytero, Not* 24 (1988) 366–78.

[39] Cf. G. Genero, "Il presidente dell'assemblea. . . ." art. cit. 31–5; D. Mosso, "La formazione dei futuri preti alla presidenza liturgica," *RPL* 168 (1991) 70–7; A. Santantoni, "Arte del celebrare: uno stile per comunicare," *Celebrare oggi* (CEI, Rome, 1988) 76–90.

pation remains fundamental, the presider must continually foster the awareness of the celebrated mystery and the "sense" of the assembly that one presides, for which one is called to be guide, interpreter, and leader. The exercise of the presidency should aim at achieving a celebration that gives to rites and texts all their power of expression and of communion, animated by the dynamism of differentiated roles, alternating between special and ordinary times and with different and complementary forms of participation.

Two mistaken attitudes can be taken toward the liturgical books of Vatican II when their purpose or spirit is not understood: material faithfulness by one who limits oneself to substituting new for old rubrics; and the superficiality of one who presumes to rely upon one's own creativity in disregard for the celebrated mystery, for the assembly present, and for the ecclesial communion.

Pastoral study and practice should lead future priests to recognize the concept of celebration the liturgical book presents; to enable them to enliven the texts, signs, and materials it offers to us; to take advantage of the room for adaptation and creativity provided by the liturgical reform. The deepened and enlightened knowledge of the new liturgical books and especially of their valuable introductions can become an effective school for living and creative celebration.[40]

The effectiveness of the presidential function will depend upon a whole series of spiritual and human qualities, toward which all formation of the presider tends: a strong faith awareness in one's role; capacity for internal assimilation of the various components of a celebration, of living it and of making its organic character experienced; the attitude of symbolic action as well as the effort to personalize and interpret the rites; a profound sense of sharing and participation.

Yet there are other specific aspects of the presidential function that should be patiently taught and reviewed: a style of comportment that is sober, confident, measured, inspired and sustained from within, conscious and sure, far from any sloppiness or arrogance; gesturing that does not seem cold, mechanical, or theatrical and emphatic but spontaneous and meaningful; and a skilled modulation of the voice: always clear and warm, without being artificial or declamatory, more elevated and solemn in proclamations (readings, euchology), more

---

[40] J. Aldazabal, "El libro litúrgico como pedagogía de la celebración," *Ph* 116 (1980) 111–24.

simple and familiar in homilies and instructions. Human sciences can provide useful suggestions to celebrants regarding the diverse function of a small and homogeneous assembly in comparison with that of a large and heterogeneous assembly, which requires a greater formalization of roles, a less creative celebrative style, and a more active presidency.

LITURGICAL ORGANIZATION

In the various assessments that have been drawn up at a more or less official level on the liturgical reform, emphasis is often placed on the inadequacy of promotional entities or centers for the liturgical renewal and on the urgency of their vigorous operational relaunching. It is a discussion set within the vast theological, juridical, and pastoral problem of the "reception" of Vatican Council II in the Church of today.[41] We are not referring so much to the specific tasks of entities or persons who have hierarchical responsibility for carrying out the liturgical reform: the Congregation for Divine Worship and the Discipline of the Sacraments, episcopal conferences, and the diocesan bishop, in their respective jurisdictions.[42]

We limit ourselves to consultative and promotional centers for the liturgical renewal with special attention to national, regional, and diocesan liturgical commissions and to parish liturgical groups (or teams). These liturgical entities that we have mentioned, the last of which has no official standing, have had very distinctive growth. We refer only to the documents of Vatican II and later.[43]

The constitution *Sacrosanctum concilium* (1963) considers diocesan commissions to be important instruments for "developing further the Church's liturgical pastoral action" (no. 43) and completes the institutional picture, asking that national and diocesan liturgical commissions be constituted (cf. *SC* 44) and suggesting regional commissions in order to promote collaboration among more dioceses (*SC* 45). Furthermore, it establishes that, as much as possible, in every diocese there should also be constituted commissions of sacred music and

[41] John Paul II, Apostolic letter *Vigesimus quintus annus*, 17; *Not* 25 (1989) 418–9.
[42] Cf. Y. M. Congar, "La 'réception' comme réalité ecclésiologique," *RSPT* 56 (1972) 369–403; D. Borobio, "La 'recepción' de la reforma litúrgica," *Ph* 56 (1983) 377–401.
[43] John Paul II, Apostolic letter *Vigesimus quintus annus*, 19–21: *Not* 25 (1989) 419–22.

sacred art, affirming clearly the need that "these three commissions collaborate with each other; indeed, it may sometimes be good for them to form a single commission" (*SC* 46). The discussion was continued and clarified by various applicative documents of the council and in particular for the diocesan commissions by the instruction *Inter oecumenici* (1964) and by various documents of episcopal conferences.

Availing ourselves of the conciliar and postconciliar documents, we give a rapid presentation of the structure and the purposes of these operative entities, set at various levels of responsibility:

(1) *National liturgical commission.* This can be a commission composed entirely of bishops and supplemented by an executive body (secretariat, office, or center), or else it can be formed by a "committee" of bishops and a body of consultors made up of priests, religious, and laity expert in the liturgy.

The tasks of this national liturgical commission, in the light of *SC* 44 and of *IO* 45, can be summarized as follows: propose studies and experiments on the basis of *SC* 40, 1–2; organize initiatives of liturgical life throughout the national territory; prepare studies and aids for implementing the bishops' decisions; promote meetings and other initiatives in common with biblical, catechetical, pastoral, musical, and artistic associations and with various lay church groups.[44]

(2) *Diocesan (or regional) level.* Diocesan commissions for the liturgy, sacred art, and sacred music had been introduced even before the council, and their closer collaboration had been wished for. Yet in a large number of local churches everything stayed on paper, and often the three commissions ran into difficulties because of differences in mentality and orientation; even after clear indications given by the council and by postconciliar documents, many differences remained in structure and arrangement.

---

[44] In Italy in 1973, for example, the General Secretariat of the Italian Episcopal Conference instituted as its permanent executive organ the National Liturgical Office, to which was added a consulting board composed of the regional delegates for the liturgy, of directors of liturgical journals, and of officers of associations, centers, and liturgical institutes. This office was assigned the following tasks: coordinate and promote the implementation of pastoral liturgy in Italy; produce the translation and editing (and more recently the updating) of liturgical books; maintain contact with various liturgical entities, also at European level; place itself at the service of the corresponding diocesan and regional offices.

Inter oecumenici attributes to the diocesan liturgical commission the following tasks, which we summarize: review the situation of pastoral liturgy in the diocese; diligently put into effect the provisions from competent authority in liturgical matters and make use of studies and initiatives done elsewhere; suggest and promote every initiative that fosters the progress of the liturgy in the diocese, especially in help for pastors; establish for the various parishes of the diocese a pastoral liturgical plan, identifying and calling upon experts who can propose modalities and aids for systematic and fruitful pastoral work; stimulate agreement and collaboration among liturgical initiatives and other activities of an ecclesial character.

For collaboration at an intermediate level among dioceses and episcopal conferences, on the basis of *SC* 45 regional commissions have also been instituted, less specified in their tasks by official documents and exposed to various difficulties common to other sectors of the Church's life at a regional level. The regional commission is presided by the regional delegate bishop and is composed of diocesan liturgical directors or by presidents of the diocesan commissions, by representatives of men and women religious, and by various experts. The regional commissions have proven useful in various ways: coordination of pastoral activity among various churches; common preparation of aids (e.g., liturgical calendars or guides; books of song or prayer); formation and exchange of experts; formation programs, especially for intermediate leaders.

(3) *The level of parishes and local Christian communities.* As a result of a real need of pastoral liturgy, liturgical teams in Christian communities have emerged nearly everywhere. They involve all those who perform a liturgical ministry as well as representatives from the assemblies. Their tasks are specific and valuable for the purpose of the celebration of all liturgical actions (plan-program-direction) and in a special way for the eucharistic celebration (service of welcome, service of the Word, service of charity, service of the altar, service of prayer, etc.).

A liturgical team is stimulated to grow in its awareness and organizational competence both through times of reflection and study and through participation in the community's liturgy with an active and responsible attitude. This team must open itself to the local church and must stay in contact with the diocesan liturgical commission, from which it must get help in the form of aids and useful directives and to which it must offer the contributions of experience.

CONCLUSION

Even though positive aspects of the acceptance and implementation of the liturgical reform can be noted almost everywhere, the complaint often is made about a scarcity of promotional centers at the various levels of responsibility. This problematic fact can be attributed to various causes: the negative weight of a centuries-old praxis that in its ecclesiological foundations and liturgical articulations was very remote from the new orientation of Vatican II. The ritual changes, even when accepted with faithfulness and obedience, were not always accepted with a deep change of mentality and a proportionate interior renewal. At the level of specific organization there was often a lack of coordination, unity of intentions, experience, constant and patient commitment, drive and mediation. Lastly, the doctrinal and technical formation of liturgical ministers and intermediate functionaries was not always adequately provided.

The deficiencies we have brought out should not lead us into pessimism or discouragement but should lead our Christian communities to a courageous relaunching of pastoral liturgical activity with more thorough use of operative entities, a more accurate preparation of those responsible for our celebrations, and a deeper and more vital formation of all of the faithful.

"It appears that the time has come," writes John Paul II, "to rediscover the great breath that drove the Church at the time when the Constitution *Sacrosanctum concilium* was prepared, discussed, voted upon and promulgated, and saw its first measures of application. The grain was sown: it has felt the rigor of winter, but the seed has sprouted and has become a tree. Indeed, we have here the organic growth of a tree, ever more vigorous the more deeply it sets its roots into the soil of tradition."[45]

Nonetheless, it must be acknowledged that in reality not many years have passed since those fervid and contested beginnings. The liturgical renewal of Vatican II has already yielded valuable and lasting fruits, "responding to those realities that the liturgical movement had prepared, the fulfillment of those expectations, for which so

[45] Ibid., no 23; *Not* 25 (1989) 422–3.

many people of the Church and so many scholars had worked and prayed."[46] Only in the third millennium will these already remarkable developments display all their potential, so that the Church might celebrate ever more consciously the mystery of Christ and live it ever more faithfully in charity and in hope.

[46] Cf. "Insegnamenti di Paolo VI," XV (1977) 662.

Bibliography

A. Pastoral Liturgy

Della Torre, L. "Prospettive ed esigenze per una pastorale liturgica." In P. Visentin, A. N. Terrin, R. Cecolin, *Una liturgia per l'uomo*, 83–105. Padua, 1986.

____. "Pastorale liturgica." *NDL* 1039–61.

Gelineau, J. "La pastorale liturgica." *Nelle vostre assemblee: Teologia pastorale delle celebrazioni liturgiche*, 26–41. Brescia, 1970.

Jeggle-Merz, B. "'Pastoralliturgik': Eigenberechtigter Zweig oder Anwendungsdiziplin der Liturgiewissenschaft." *ALW* 29 (1987) 352–70.

Roguet, A.-M. "La pastoral liturgique." In A.-G. Martimort, *L'Église en prière: Introduction à la liturgie*. Tournai, 1961.

Sartore, D. "Concetto di pastorale liturgica." *RL* 79 (1992) 9–24.

Searle, M. "New Tasks, New Methods: The Emergence of Pastoral Liturgical Studies." *Wor* 57 (1983) 291–308.

B. Liturgical Formation and Catechesis

Chavasse, A. "Histoire de l'initiation chrétienne des enfants de l'antiquité à nos jours." *MD* 28 (1951) 26–44.

Formare alla liturgia (theme). *RL* 68, no. 5 (1981).

Klöckener, M. "Les jeunes et la liturgie: Un rapport d'aliénation." *MD* 179 (1989) 111–44; see also in English: *SL* 20 (1990) 137–61.

La educación litúrgica (theme). *Ph* 146 (1985).

Liturgia e catechesi (theme). *RL* 75, no. 1 (1985).

Matthews, E. *Celebrating Mass with Children*. New York, 1978.

Mazza, E. "Fanciulli." *NDL* 536–43.

Pedrazzini, M. L. "Formazione liturgica." *NDL* 581–601.

Sacred Congregation for Divine Worship. *Directory for Masses with Children* (November 1, 1973). Trans. International Committee on English in the Liturgy. Washington, 1974.

Sartore, D. "Catechesi e liturgia." *NDL* 219–331.

_____. "Giovani e liturgia, vent'anni di riflessioni e di esperienze." *RL* 75 (1988) 221–45; also *RL* 79 (1992).

C. Formation of Ministers — Liturgical Leadership

Brandolini, L. "Animazione." *NDL* 52–65.

Centre National de Pastorale Liturgique. "Fiches pour la formation des animateurs de célébration." Paris, 1975–1977.

Genero, G. "Per una promozione della liturgia: La formazione dei celebranti." In AA. VV., *Riforma liturgica tra passato e futuro*, 112–13. Studi di liturgia, n.s., 13. Casale Monferrato, 1985.

D. Liturgical Presidency

Aldazabal, J. "El libro litúrgico como pedagogía de la celebración." *Ph* 116 (1980) 111–24.

Gantoy, R. *Le ministère du célébrant dans la liturgie nouvelle*. Vivante liturgie 85. Paris, 1970.

La formación liturgica del sacerdote (theme). *Ph* 106 (1990).

"Liturgiewissenschaft in der Priesterausbildung." *LJ* 47 (1992) 79–80.

Marliangeas, B. D. *Clés pour une théologie du ministère: In persona Christi, in persona Ecclesiae*. Théologie historique 51. Paris, 1978.

Sartore, D. "La formazione del presbitero presidente." *RL* 68 (1981) 623–37; see also *NDL* 601–8.

Szafranki, R. T. "The One Who Presides at Eucharist." *Wor* 63 (1989) 300–16.

Domenico Sartore, C.S.J.

5

Catechesis and Liturgy

In the years preceding and following the Second Vatican Council there was much discussion on the relation between catechesis and liturgy;[1] there is often talk about a "difficult dialogue," an "insufficient debate," a "problematic encounter," and so forth.[2]

Based on a large inquiry sent to all the episcopal conferences in the world on the part of the Congregation for Divine Worship, it turns out that in many nations notable efforts have been made in the search for a more enlightened and constructive relation between these two aspects of the life of the Church in the perspective of a more unitary and organic pastoral practice; but there are still complaints about attitudes of mutual mistrust, due also to the lack of catechetical formation in ordained ministers and of liturgical formation in catechists.[3]

We will attempt to show the various aspects of this problematic theory and practice, listening to the respective viewpoints of liturgists and catechists as they address questions to each other and raise issues, which often are not answered in a balanced or thorough manner.[4]

---

[1] Besides the contributions indicated in the bibliography, cf. G. Venturi, "Liturgia e catechesi; prassi e riflessione di un decennio," *RL* 77 (1985) 7–38; E. Alberich, "Catechesi e liturgia," *Dizionario di catechetica,* ed. J. Gevaert (Turin, 1986) 387–98.

[2] Cf. M. L. Petrazzini, "Liturgia e catechesi: un incontro possibile?" *RL* 66 (1979) 498–511; A. Rouet, "Catéchèse et liturgie: radiographie d'un débat insuffisant," *MD* no. 140 (1979) 7–23.

[3] Cf. G. Fontaine, "La pastorale liturgique," Congr. del Culto Divino, *Convegno Commissioni Nazionali di Liturgia* (Padua, 1986) 873.

[4] E. Alberich, "Catechesi e liturgia: punto di vista di un catecheta," *RPL* no. 149 (1988) 11–20; L. della Torre, "Catechesi e liturgia: punto di vista di un liturgista," ibid., 21–39.

RECIPROCAL QUESTIONS

Problems Posed from the Side of Liturgy

In reviewing writings, catechisms, programs, and various aids, the overall impression is given that current catechesis does not yet give proper emphasis to the liturgy, to what it represents in the history of salvation, in the life of the Church, and in the concrete experience of individual believers.

Catechesis, so open to the values of the most recent Church renewal, does not yet seem to be penetrated in depth by the principles and guidelines of the liturgical reform. Concerned with the proclamation and with its translation into concrete living, it seems less sensitive toward the celebrative event, which is situated as the summit of the proclamation and the source of Christian existence. Should catechesis only teach belief for living and not for celebrating? Who will take on the delicate task of a "mystagogy" of the celebration? Who will introduce people to the great religious attitudes necessary for celebrating? Who will initiate people into an affective knowledge of the "signs" and into a progressive and cyclical experience of liturgical time?

Liturgy is sometimes exploited as a function of catechetical objectives or of objectives not otherwise respecting the nature of the liturgy itself: we are referring not only to the classical topic of confirmation with all the problems that it holds but also to certain celebrations stuffed with commentaries or with audiovisual inserts, as well as to a certain improper use of liturgical "signs," which make one think that "allegorism" is back.

One frequently observes an incorrect treatment of the liturgy by catechisms: there is an insufficiency of the salvation-history perspective; little attention is given to the memorial aspect of the celebration in relation to the theme of the covenant; the "typological" meaning of the Bible and the "celebrative" dimension of the Word are not shown; the liturgical year is undervalued as an itinerary of faith and life and never presented in its theological dimension; regarding the sacraments, recourse is made to various liturgical fragments but there is no real interpretation *per ritus et preces;* and a meager relation is often found between liturgical books and catechetical aids. There is great limitation in the liturgical formation of catechists and in their low interest in the liturgy.[5]

---

[5] L. della Torre, "Catechesi e liturgia: punto di vista di un liturgista"; cf. also J. Aldazabal, "Preguntas a la catequesis desde la liturgia," *Ph* no. 118 (1980) 255–66.

Problems Posed from the Side of Catechesis

In their turn, catechetical experts and pastoral workers in the field raise some questions. Liturgists tend to absolutize the liturgy as if it were the exclusive place for the actuation of Christ's salvific work, and they do not give sufficient importance to evangelization, to catechesis, to Christian life, or even to God's sovereign freedom in the divine interventions of salvation. The same complaint is advanced when the liturgy is considered as the *culmen et fons* (source and summit) of catechesis and as its "structural norm." Thus when we speak of the liturgical dimension of catechesis, of the need for a "liturgical bent" in catechetics, we sometimes forget the centrality of the "liturgy of life," of worship "in spirit and truth."[6]

In substance, we can state that, despite the rediscovery of the convergence in principle between liturgy and catechesis and a greater effort for a thorough and constructive dialogue, there are still difficulties and tensions both on the theoretical and on the pastoral level. Catechesis seems to have advanced too far without the liturgy and sometimes finds it hard to assimilate proposals, contents, and methodological suggestions that could come to it from the liturgical tradition and from the current liturgical renewal. In their turn, some liturgical scholars tend to identify in liturgical actions, in a too exclusive fashion, the "today" of salvation, with excessive insensitivity toward the cultural and pedagogical concerns of catechetics, toward the path that it has made in all the Church in recent decades.

Differing Sensitivity

As a complement to these contrasting and sometimes polemic questions, here we wish to add some points that focus on the differing sensitivity that contradistinguishes liturgy and catechesis:[7]

The conviction is certainly better matured that catechesis and liturgy are two aspects of the one mission of the Church, but one finds between them a notable and perhaps inevitable diversity of mentality and sensitivity. One can consider, for example, the different ways of relating to time: catechesis is more synchronic and attentive to the cultural situation; liturgy is more diachronic and more anchored in tradition. Thus the liturgy proclaims the Word and believes

---

[6] E. Alberich, "Catechesi e liturgia: punto di vista di un catecheta."
[7] A. Rouet, "Catéchèse et liturgie: radiographie . . ."

in its vitality and efficacy in virtue of a special presence of Christ, while catechesis is more sensitive to its human conditioning and to what surrounds its proclamation in the Church.

Catechesis and liturgy have carried forward in recent years an exceptional power of adaptation while relating in different ways to tradition. Liturgy seems to some to be still too bound to sources while current catechesis still has much to learn from old models; but the one and the other notice now more acutely the risks of an all-out change and suffer together the burden of some unresolved knots in the life of the Church; for example, the persistent disjunction of Christian initiation and the insufficiency of pastoral arrangements that often are uncritically introduced.

At the center of common interests there is without doubt rituality, or rather, Christian sacramentality. A certain unease is evident for catechesis in facing the task of situating and interpreting sacramentality, while liturgy does not always succeed in achieving an authentic symbolic-ritual experience and especially does not succeed in evangelizing rituality fully.

Sometimes catechesis and liturgy become problematic precisely in their concrete relation and in the experienced dialogue: catechesis strives to be linked with the liturgy, taking its rhythm from the liturgical year and assuming celebrative dimensions; the liturgy, in its turn, aware of its ability to be "catechesis in action," sometimes accentuates this aspect with an excess of admonitions, explanations, visual elements, and the like. Out of this can arise a confusion of genres, which compromises the symbolic effectiveness proper to a celebration and ends by taking catechesis away from its specific method and from its real tasks.

Finally, catechesis and liturgy find themselves faced with an upstream problem, which they experience in different ways: the meager level of faith of Christian communities — which increases the responsibility and the difficulty of catechesis to the point of threatening its identity and which dramatically accentuates the disharmony between the rites and the community — and the limits and pluralism of specific Christian assemblies.

FOUNDATIONS OF A RELATION
In order to launch a more thorough dialogue between catechesis and liturgy, overcoming the distress of contrasts and polemics, and

in order to achieve a greater mutual interaction, it seems necessary to appeal to at least three foundations: the lessons of a common past; the guidelines of the most recent documents of the ecclesiastical magisterium; and a thorough theological study of this relation in the horizon of a more global consideration of the mission of the Church.

A Revisitation of Patristic Catechesis

A renewed awareness of the deep relation that unites catechesis and liturgy passes through a rediscovery of patristic catechesis, "which remains most alive and least marked by time in the work of the Fathers."[8] The great patristic catecheses display the formative method the Church put into action for Christian initiation, especially for those who submitted their names for baptism at the beginning of Lent for the following Easter, becoming *competentes* or *electi*. In this formative process the celebrations themselves carried out a fundamental role, not only the rites that characterized the catechumenal path but especially the sacraments celebrated at the Easter Vigil. This liturgical experience assumed particular efficacy through the authenticity of the celebrations, through the connection to Easter, but especially through the intensely shared mystery on the level of faith and grace. These were the premises for later mystagogical catechesis. We note the fundamental aspects of this itinerary of Christian formation:

— it was presented as a complete pastoral program, an integral initiation into Christian existence in the Church (faith, prayer, morals, liturgy, community life, Christian hope, etc.);

— it was structured according to a chronological development oriented toward a process of maturation and of growth, through various degrees;

— it was not limited to verbal proclamation (albeit systematic and thorough) but was enhanced by various ritual elements;

— it had a typically ecclesial character: the community would welcome, participate, and collaborate, especially through the institution of sponsorship and the exercise of the ministries;

[8] J. Danielou and R. du Charlat, *La catechesi dei primi secoli* (Leumann, Turin, 1967) 5; O. Pasquato, "Rapporto tra catechesi e liturgia nella tradizione patristica," *RL* 62 (1985) 39–73.

— the profoundly spiritual dimension of this process of initiation can be underscored: it was a path of enlightenment and of maturation of faith, of progressive incorporation into Christ and the Church.

This patristic catechesis maintained a close rapport with the liturgy. It was a catechesis that found in the liturgy its fullest expression, its continuous wellspring, and a constant frame of reference in accordance with a law of cyclicalness and of integral and permanent formation.

Guidelines Arising from the Most Recent Documents of the Magisterium

In some conciliar and postconciliar documents we find the second foundation for examining thoroughly the catechesis-liturgy relationship. We confine ourselves to these:

Vatican II spoke of catechesis as "the first of all the means that the Church can employ to carry out its educational mission" (*GE* 4). The council repeatedly affirmed the catechetical-pedagogical function of the liturgy: it is "the first and indispensable source from which the faithful can draw the genuine Christian spirit" (*SC* 14); it is a "rich font of instruction for the faithful" (*SC* 33); "A catechesis that is more directly liturgical should be inculcated in every manner" (*SC* 39).

The various *Ordines*, besides introducing celebrative forms that make easier the understanding and participation of the faithful, insist greatly on the preparatory catechesis and tend to involve the families more and more in the Christian initiation of children.

With reliance on the patristic model that we have recalled, the *Ordo Initiationis Christianae Adultorum* (1972) takes on profound significance in today's Church,[9] since "the gradual and progressive course of evangelization, catechesis and mystagogy is presented by the *Ordo* as typical form for Christian formation."[10] From this emerges the primacy of evangelization, the function of the Christian community, the relevance of the liturgical year in permanent catechesis, the close and organic connection of the three sacraments that make a Christian, and the role of a mystagogical type of catechesis for the sacraments already received in view of a fuller experience of their divine efficacy. This is an experience that finds its place in participating in the life of

[9] Cf. *Rite of Christian Initiation of Adults*, Introduction, 1–63.
[10] Cf. *Rito dell'iniziazione degli adulti: Premessa della CEI.*

the ecclesial community by means of catechesis, liturgical celebration, and the testimony of a new life.

Postconciliar Documents

The *General Catechetical Directory* (1972), outlining the various forms and tasks of catechesis, brings out the relationship that catechesis should have with liturgical life: "Catechesis should be at the service of an active, conscious and authentic participation in the liturgy of the Church: not only by illustrating the significance of the rites but by educating the faithful in prayer, in thanksgiving, in penance, in trusting petition, all necessary for a true liturgical life" (no. 25).

In the apostolic exhortation *Evangelii nuntiandi* (1975) of Paul VI, the purposes of catechesis are set on the broadest horizon of evangelization, understood as "a complex process of different elements: renewal of unity, witness, explicit proclamation, heartfelt assent, entrance into the community, acceptance of signs, initiation into the apostolate" (no. 24).

In the 1977 Synod of Bishops on catechesis the liturgical dimension emerged vigorously.[11] The apostolic exhortation *Catechesi tradendae* (1979) of John Paul II echoes this: "Catechesis is intrinsically linked with every liturgical and sacramental action, because it is in the sacraments, and especially in the Eucharist, that Christ acts in fullness for the transformation of humans." In this document the horizon of catechesis is extended in the "threefold dimension of Word, remembrance and witness, namely of doctrine, celebration, and witnessing," which is carried out especially by catechesis that is done in the liturgical context and in particular during the liturgical assembly. Respecting the rhythm proper to this context, "the homily takes up the path of faith proposed by catechesis and carries it to its natural fulfillment" (no. 48).

Among the documents issued by particular churches, the most significant seems to us to be the *Rinnovamento della catechesi* [renewal of catechesis] 1970, by the Italian bishops, translated into several languages and recently reconfirmed as an authoritative guide for further catechetical renewal in Italy. In it an organic and complete vision is found on the relation between catechesis and liturgy. We note some qualifying points:

[11] Cf. *QL* 1979/1–2: *Liturgie et catéchèse à marge du Synode des évèques de 1977*; A. Cuva, "La liturgia al Sinodo dei vescovi sulla catechesi," *Not* no. 139 (1978) 90–118; no. 140 (1978) 131–43.

The prophetic mission of the Church is carried out "by the Word, by the liturgical celebration, and by the witness of living" (no. 19); indeed, "the preaching of the Word and the path of faith reach their peak in the liturgical celebration" (no. 27). Catechesis prepares the faithful for liturgical participation: "it initiates the faithful in apprehending the value of the signs by which God reveals and communicates himself: it prepares them for the profession of faith, which they express especially in the eucharistic action, and makes them ready to fulfill with Christ the offering pleasing to the Father." Yet catechesis goes on to address the participants themselves in the liturgical action: "thus, the liturgical experience, which touches each person in a singular way, strengthens the catechetical action: the faithful grow in the knowledge of the Christian mystery, nourished by the paschal sacraments" (no. 32).

The liturgical perspective emerges correctly in relation to the purpose of catechesis but becomes more explicit in relation to the sources of the catechesis. The liturgy is the "inexhaustible source of catechesis" because it is a "living expression of the mystery of Christ." The liturgy is thus a "valuable catechesis in action" (no. 114), especially because "it achieves what it signifies" (no. 115). In particular, in the liturgical year there is "a fabric that offers the widest range of basic themes for every form of catechesis" (no. 116).

Theological Foundations
The complaint is often heard that the theological reflection on the catechesis-liturgy relation has remained at a casual and fragmentary level. We note some points:

The catechesis-liturgy relation is set in the full ecclesial context beginning with the fundamental functions or mediations of the Church, whether they refer to the four distinctive marks of the early Christian community (κήρυγμα, λειτουργία, κοινωνία, διακονία), or to the three offices that characterize the mission of the Church, continuing the salvific work of Christ: the formation of the Christian and the building of the ecclesial community. A relation arises here of interaction and complementarity, which should be brought to an operative level in a strong commitment of mutual collaboration and integration.[12]

[12] Cf. E. Alberich, "Catechesi e liturgia; punto di vista di un catecheta"; A.-M. Triacca, "Catechesi e Liturgia: singolarità . . ."; P. Sorci, "Liturgia e catechesi: per un chiarimento. . . ."

104

Yet catechesis and liturgy carry out the mission of the Church in different modalities: catechesis is expressed according to the laws of science and education; liturgy, according to the laws of celebration. Catechesis is teaching and formation; liturgy is symbolic-ritual experience.

Nevertheless we must be careful not to impoverish unilaterally either the concept of liturgy or the concept of integral catechesis of Christ and of the Church. Catechesis is not just a form of teaching and verbal communication but rather an exercise of the prophetic ministry of the Church and an ecclesial mediation of maturation in faith.[13]

The very search for an ecclesiological foundation in the catechesis-liturgy relation leads us to frame these problems in the mission of the Church, especially with respect to its commitment to charity and service, into which both liturgical celebration and catechesis issue.

SPECIFIC FORMS OF THE CATECHESIS-LITURGY RELATION

The Liturgy, Catechesis in Action
The significance of the liturgical celebration for catechesis, as for theological reflection, depends first of all on the sacramental condition of the Church, on the fact that it builds itself in the most existential manner wherever the community celebrates the liturgy, the summit and source of the Church's life. This theological principle has an anthropological foundation in that every human experience, individual or communitarian, gains its full stature through the way of symbolic experience, which confers full form to inner sentiments and dispositions, involves a person with all his or her faculties, and achieves the most complete communion.[14]

The Liturgy of the Word, first of all, has an effective catechetical function; it is celebrated in close connection with the sacramental rite with the help of the homily, which takes on an evident mystagogical function. What in ordinary catechesis is only recalled and explained acquires in the liturgy a truly unique power of actuality. Yet so that a liturgical celebration might really be an experience of faith and Christian life and therefore intensely formative, it is necessary that it be

[13] Cf. E. Alberich, "Catechesi e liturgia; punto di vista di un catecheta," 13–4.
[14] Ibid., 13–4.

truly rooted in the existential fabric of the community, that it be
authentic in word and rite and open to Christian commitment.

Contribution of Catechesis to Liturgy
Liturgy continually is in need of catechesis not only for pastoral
reasons, more or less contingent, but because Christian worship constitutes a mystery accessible only in faith, which requires an always-
renewed initiation.

The task of catechesis with regard to liturgy begins by showing the
meaning of liturgical actions in salvation history and the life of the
Church and by shedding light on the anthropological and sociological foundations of Christian rites, with their deep roots in human
nature and in community life. More specifically, catechesis initiates
into liturgical signs, in their fourfold dimension: memorial, representative, prophetic, and promissory, in the awareness that they are in
continuity with the divine teaching attested throughout the Bible.
Catechesis moves from their natural symbolism in order to reach the
expressive value they have assumed in biblical revelation and in the
Church's tradition.

In relation to the celebration itself, the task of catechesis is even
more demanding on the attitudes and conduct that are constitutive of
Christian celebration.[15] Catechesis should become, then, mystagogy,
in the highest meaning of the term: starting with the signs, in the
light of biblical typology, it should lead the faithful to live the mystery of Christ, to base and foster their commitment in the world, and
to reawaken continually their eschatological hope.[16]

Contribution of Liturgy to Catechesis
Many points that we have seen emerging in the preceding pages
were already tending in the direction of the contribution the liturgy
can give to catechesis, with its "total" language, which has a meaning
and power particularly effective for the expression of and education
in faith. Thus we want to take up and present anew the function of
the liturgical year as a path of faith and grace, as a promotional pic-

---

[15] G. Lukken, "La liturgie comme lieu théologique irremplaçable," *QL* 56 (1973)
97–112.

[16] Cf. J. Gelineau, ed., "Assemblea santa," *Manuale di liturgia pastorale*, I. parte:
La celebrazione del culto cristiano (Bologna, 1990) 60–175; G. Venturi, "Celebrazione
catechista e celebrazione liturgica. Riflessioni e prospettive," *RL* 77 (1985) 111–30.

ture of Christian experience, and as a celebrative context of the sacraments and of the various Christian rites. In this perspective the liturgy is inserted as the "source of catechesis." The liturgy, indeed, can become for catechesis an inexhaustible source of symbolic elements and concrete starting points to introduce the individual aspects of the mystery of Christ and the Church and for cultivating faith and Christian life: sacramental celebrations, principal and secondary signs, gestures, postures, words, things, places, and temporal determinations. For catechesis as well as for the homily all these become illuminating and stimulating realities as psychological contact points and as experiential data already familiar to the faithful. They will remain thereafter as a supporting structure and a lasting remembrance of a proclamation of faith and a message of life. Thus, for example, the sign of the cross in its various forms introduces us into the two main mysteries of our faith; the use of holy water becomes a remembrance of baptism; the gathered assembly and the very building that welcomes it guide us into the mystery of the Church; the gestures of reverence, prayer, forgiveness, and communion speak to our Christian existence; the Amen and the Alleluia, as St. Augustine comments on them, suggest a whole program of living for Christians gathered in the name of the Lord,[17] and so on.

From many points of view, even apparently marginal, the liturgy can be a source of catechesis, capable of nourishing faith and calling to conversion, of building community day by day, of continually proposing effective referrals to Christian hope and to a generous ecclesial commitment.

CONCLUSION

A profound and vital dialogue between catechesis and liturgy can further perfect the mutual enrichment that is already one of the most abundant fruits of the liturgical movement and of the current ecclesial renewal. Catechesis can rediscover more effectively an ancient tradition that it has in common with the liturgy, recovering the primacy of evangelization, the historical salvific horizon, the catechumenal method, and the suggestions of mystagogy. The liturgy can become more sensitive to the cultural and pedagogical problems of

---

[17] D. Sartore, "Mistagogia ieri e oggi: alcune pubblicazioni recenti," *EO* XI (1994) 181–99.

catechesis and more attentive to the real situation of the community's faith. The still problematic relationship between catechesis and liturgy can become less dramatic and more thoroughly probed if placed in the broader perspective of a Church in a state of mission, called to generous service of human advancement and evangelical charity.

Bibliography

Sources and Documents

The Catechetical Documents: A Parish Resource. Chicago, 1996.

John Paul II. *On Catechesis in Our Time.* Apostolic exhortation *Catechesi tradendae.* Washington, 1979.

Paul VI. *On Evangelization in the Modern World.* Apostolic exhortation *Evangelii nuntiandi.* Washington, 1976.

Rite of Christian Initiation of Adults. Prepared by the International Commission on English in the Liturgy and the Bishops' Committee on the Liturgy. Washington, 1988.

Sacred Congregation for the Clergy. *General Catechetical Directory.* Washington, 1971.

Studies

AA.VV. *Liturgia e catechesi.* Atti XII Settimana APL. Rome, 1993.

Alberich, E. "Liturgia e catechesi: La sintesi del mistero cristiano offerta dalla liturgia." *Orientamenti pedagogici* 13 (1966) 691–713.

Costa, E. "La celebrazione, come catechesi integrale." *RL* 60 (1973) 33–7.

Dreissen, J. *La linea liturgica della nuova catechesi.* Turin, 1969.

Sartore, D. "Catechesi e liturgia." *NDL* 219–30.

Sorci, P. "Liturgia e catechesi: Per un chiarimento teologico-pastorale." In *Liturgia e catechesi dell'iniziazione cristiana.* Ed. R. Falsini. Milan, 1985.

Triacca, A. M. "Catechesi e liturgia: singolarità, rapporti, confronti." *RL* 63 (1985) 74–96.

_____. "Il rapporto 'liturgia-catechesi' nella dinamica eccleiale: Parallelismo o convergenza?" *Not* 239 (1988) 322–46.

Vagaggini, C. "Catechism and Liturgy." In *Theological Dimensions of the Liturgy,* 887–98. Trans. L. J. Doyle and W. A. Jurgens. Collegeville, Minn., 1976.

Venturi, G. "Liturgia e catechesi." *RL* 77 (1985) 7–38.

Monographs

Catéchèse et liturgie. *MD* 140 (1979).

Liturgie et catéchèse dans le renouveau pastoral. *NPL* 123.

Liturgia y catechesis. *Ph* 118 (1980).

Liturgia e catechesi. *RL* (1973) no. 5.

A quando la svolta liturgica nella catechesi? *RL* (1982) no. 2.

Liturgia e catechesi. *RL* (1985) no. 1.

Part II

Liturgical Celebration

Nathan Mitchell

6

Liturgy and Ecclesiology

NEW DIRECTIONS FOR ECCLESIOLOGY

For many Catholics Vatican II is remembered chiefly for the dramatic changes mandated by the Constitution on the Sacred Liturgy, promulgated in the typical edition of liturgical books and subsequently embodied in a host of vernacular translations and cultural "adaptations." These liturgical changes cannot, of course, be isolated from the theological and pastoral principles that accompanied them. For the council did not simply decree a new way of doing liturgy; it proposed a new way of being church.

Prior to Vatican II the theological images that dominated twentieth-century ecclesiology were those of "the church militant" (*ecclesia militans*) and "the Mystical Body of Christ" (*corpus Christi mysticum*). This latter image, derived from Col 1:24, provided the inspiration for Pope Pius XII's famous encyclical *Mystici Corporis*. In it, the pope wrote: "If we would define and describe this true Church of Jesus Christ — which is the One, Holy, Catholic, Apostolic Roman Church — we shall find nothing more noble, more sublime, or more divine than the expression 'the Mystical Body of Jesus Christ.'"[1]

The first draft of the council's own schema *De Ecclesia* reiterated this view, asserting that the Roman Catholic Church and the Mystical Body of Christ are identical.[2] This image of the body — where some

---

[1] *Mystici Corporis* 13; English translation in Claudia Carlen, ed., *The Papal Encyclicals 1939–1958* (Wilmington, N.C., 1981) 39.

[2] "*Ecclesia Catholica Romana est Mysticum Christi Corpus.*" Schema 1962, p. 12, n. 7, as cited (with discussion) in Einar Sigurbjornsson, *Ministry Within the People of God*, Studia Theologica Lundensia 34 (Lund, 1974) 31.

members are inherently inferior to others and *all* are subordinate to the head — emphasized the rational, juridical, hierarchical, and magisterial qualities of the Church, especially its structures of authority and obedience.

As the council's deliberations unfolded, however, it became clear to a majority of the world's bishops that such an ecclesiology offers an incomplete, imperfect understanding of the Church. While the theology of the Mystical Body was not totally abandoned, its centrality was replaced by another biblical image — that of the pilgrim People of God. Moreover, as the council's ecclesiology evolved, *ecclesia militans* gave way to *ecclesiae mysterium*. To see the Church merely as a militant, monarchic institution in which the threefold offices of Christ — teacher *(potestas docendi)*, priest *(potestas sanctificandi)*, and king *(potestas regendi)* — are concentrated in the hands of a few is a reductionist view. For the Church is not, ultimately, a monarchy but a mystery, a "sacrament — a sign and instrument of communion with God and of unity among all people" *(Lumen gentium* 1). Thus the Church cannot be reduced to the hierarchy. On the contrary, so richly diverse and complex is this graced mystery of the Church that its greatness exceeds even the holiness of its most eminent member, as St. Augustine once observed:

"Holy is Mary; blessed is Mary — and yet the Church is greater than she. The Virgin Mary is part of the Church, a member of the Church, a distinguished, eminent — indeed the *most* eminent — member. But still, she is only a member of the entire body. The body undoubtedly is greater than she, one of its members. For the Lord is its head; head and body together form the whole Christ. In other words, our head is divine — our head is God.

". . . So too, all of you whom I address are members of Christ. And who bore you? I can hear the voice of your hearts saying 'Mother Church.' This mother of yours is holy, esteemed; and like Mary, she is both mother and virgin. The proof of her motherhood lies in all of you! By giving *you* birth, she gives birth to Christ, for you are Christ's members."[3]

For Augustine, the Church's "virginity" and "motherhood" are not pious abstractions. They are "real-life" characteristics of the Church's

---

[3] Augustine, *Sermo* 25.7; Latin text in PL 46:238. Translation mine.

114

own members, men and women who, holding faith fast in their "virgin" hearts, become *mothers* at the baptismal font.

"Let Christ's members bear in their hearts what the Virgin Mary bore in her body — namely, Christ himself! Thus *you also will be mothers of Christ!* Don't shrink back! It's not remote; it's not beyond your strength! You have already become children; now become mothers. . . . Bring to the bath of baptism whomever you can . . . and thus you will become 'mothers of Christ,' bringing neophytes to birth."[4]

For Augustine, every member of the Church is both God's child and God-bearer, virgin and mother. *All* the baptized thus share responsibility for that new life the Church celebrates in the Easter sacraments.

So the Church is "like a stranger in a strange land, pressing ahead on its pilgrimage amid the persecutions of the world and the consolations of God."[5] Its life arises from the same deeply mysterious design through which God sustains the entire universe in wisdom and goodness — and bestows divine life on a fallen humanity (*LG* 2). In sum, the Church is pilgrim, sacrament, mystery, People of God. It is a "holy, priestly nation" that has been "purchased at a great price," "washed in the blood of the Lamb" (See 1 Pet 2:5, 9; Rev 12:11).

This new way to understand and to be Church was adumbrated in *Sacrosanctum concilium* (with its emphasis, in paragraph 14, on "full, conscious, active participation" in the liturgy) and developed more fully in the first two chapters of *Lumen gentium* ("The Mystery of the Church" and "The People of God"). It is rooted in three fundamental convictions: (1) that salvation is a social reality; (2) that the Church is not only "essentially hierarchical" but also "essentially charismatic and sacramental"; and (3) that the local liturgical assembly is truly an "altar community," and thus truly a "church."

Salvation: A Social Reality
In the second chapter of *Lumen gentium*, the council vigorously affirmed that the mystery of salvation is essentially corporate and social, not private and individualistic. As a visible communion of persons among whom the eschatological (i.e., the "full, final, definitive") grace of

---

[4] Augustine, *Sermo* 25.8; Latin text in PL 46:239–40. Translation mine.
[5] Augustine, *De Civitate Dei*, bk. 18, ch. 51; 2. Cited in *LG*, 8.

God in Christ is revealed and expressed, the Church is intimately linked to the whole history of God's relations with the cosmos — the deeds of creation (Genesis 1–2); the covenant with earth and its creatures (see Gen 9:12-13); the Sinai covenant with Israel (see Exodus 19); the "new and everlasting covenant" in Jesus' blood. Moreover, as "a chosen race . . . a holy nation," all the baptized together share a single identity as priestly "People of God" (1 Pet 2:9-10).

"At all times and in every race, anyone who fears God and does what is right has been acceptable to him (cf. Acts 10.35). He has, however, willed to make men holy and save them, not as individuals without any bond or link between them, but rather to make them into a people who might acknowledge him and serve him in holiness. He therefore chose the Israelite race to be his own people and established a covenant with it. He gradually instructed this people — in its history manifesting both himself and the decree of his will — and made it holy unto himself. All these things, however, happened as a preparation and figure of that new and perfect covenant which was to be ratified in Christ. . . . Christ instituted this new covenant . . . in his blood (cf. 1 Cor 11.25); he called a race made up of Jews and Gentiles which would be one, not according to the flesh, but in the Spirit, and this race would be the new People of God . . . reborn . . . through the word of the living God . . . from water and the Holy Spirit."[6]

The Church: Not Only Hierarchical, But Sacramental, Charismatic
Lumen gentium goes on to speak of the Church as a community in which both "the common priesthood of the faithful" and "the ministerial or hierarchical priesthood" are "ordered to one another," each of them "sharing in the one priesthood of Christ" *(LG 10–11)*. Thus this organic priestly community called "Church" is not only hierarchical, but charismatic and sacramental:

"Taking part in the eucharistic sacrifice, the source and summit of the Christian life, *they* [i.e., all the faithful] *offer the divine victim to God* and themselves along with it. And so it is that, *both in the offering and in Holy Communion*, each in his own way, though not of course indiscriminately, has his own part to play in the liturgical action. Then,

[6] *LG* 9.

116

strengthened by the body of Christ in the eucharistic communion, they manifest in a concrete way that unity of the People of God which this holy sacrament aptly signifies and admirably realizes."[7]

In the council's teaching the hierarchical nature of the Church is clearly not meant to be or to become the symbol of a "divided" liturgical assembly. What unites presiders and people (one faith, one baptism, a share in one priesthood of Christ) is always greater than what separates or distinguishes them. The eucharistic assembly is thus a united company whose members embody in their diverse gifts, roles, and ministries all the Spirit-filled dimensions of ecclesial life and service — hierarchical, charismatic, sacramental. In a profound sense, the Church is defined by what it does at worship.

Local Liturgical Assembly as "Church"
It comes as no surprise, then, that *Sacrosanctum concilium* understands the liturgy not merely as another "duty" or "obligation" the Church is compelled to "perform" but as the very action that signifies and enacts the Church's authentic nature and identity:

"[I]t is through the liturgy, especially, that the faithful are enabled to express in their lives and manifest to others the mystery of Christ and *the real nature of the true Church*. The Church is essentially both human and divine, visible but endowed with invisible realities, zealous in action and dedicated to contemplation, present in the world, but as a pilgrim."[8]

The Church and its liturgy are inextricably intertwined; one cannot be imagined without the other. For this reason *Lumen gentium* asserts that each local "altar community," no matter how small, poor, or insignificant, constitutes an authentic experience of the Church's presence and purpose:

"This Church of Christ *is really present in all legitimately organized local groups of the faithful*, which, insofar as they are united to their pastors, are also quite appropriately called Churches in the New Testament. In them the faithful are gathered together through the preaching of the Gospel of Christ, and the mystery of the Lord's Supper is cele-

[7] *LG* 11, emphasis added.
[8] *SC* 2, emphasis added.

brated. . . . In each *altar community,* under the sacred ministry of the bishop, a manifest symbol is to be seen of that charity and 'unity of the mystical body, without which there can be no salvation.' In these communities, though they may often be small and poor, or existing in the diaspora, Christ is present through whose power and influence the One, Holy, Catholic and Apostolic Church is constituted. For 'the sharing in the body and blood of Christ has no other effect than to accomplish our transformation into that which we receive.'"[9]

AN ECCLESIOLOGY SHAPED BY DOXOLOGY

The challenge of Vatican II, therefore, was not simply to find a new way of worshiping but to find a new way of being church in and for the world. Significantly, the council approved not only a dogmatic constitution on the Church *(Lumen gentium)* but also a pastoral constitution on the Church in the modern world *(Gaudium et spes).* The opening words of this latter document boldly redefined the Church's relation to the world and are worth quoting here:

"The joy and hope, the grief and anguish of the people of our time, especially of those who are poor or afflicted in any way, are the joy and hope, the grief and anguish of the followers of Christ as well. Nothing that is genuinely human fails to find an echo in their hearts. For theirs is a community composed of men and women, of people who, united in Christ and guided by the Holy Spirit, press onwards towards the kingdom of God and are bearers of a message of salvation intended for all."[10]

Here there is no emphasis on hierarchy and power, no insistence on the Church's "rights" and "privileges." Instead there is a humble openness to the Spirit's promptings and a recognition that Church and humanity have much to learn from each other:

"The people of God believes that it is led by the Spirit of the Lord who fills the whole world. Moved by that faith, it tries to discern in the events, the needs, and the longings which it shares with other people of our time, what may be genuine signs of the presence or of the purpose of God. . . .

[9] *LG* 26, emphasis added.
[10] *GS* 1.

118

". . . [I]t will be increasingly clear that *the people of God, and the human race which is its setting, render service to each other;* and the mission of the Church will show itself to be supremely human by the very fact of being religious."[11]

The Church is thus not so much a body of beliefs as a way of life. This way is patterned on Christ, led by the Spirit, embodied in the Gospels, and enacted in the liturgy. According to the famous axiom attributed to Prosper of Aquitaine, *legem credendi lex statuat supplicandi.*[12] The Church's common worship, its public prayer, is the "norm" of belief. Note that the word "norm," used here, refers not to fashionable trends and customs or to "statistical frequency" but to the God-given pattern or standard according to which something is to be done. This is the sense in which, as Fr. Aidan Kavanagh has noted, the liturgy may be described as "normative" or "canonical":

"The *lex credendi* is subordinated to the *lex supplicandi* because both standards exist and function only within the worshipping assembly's own subordination of itself to its ever-present Judge, Savior, and unifying Spirit.
". . . The law of belief does not constitute the law of worship. Thus the creeds and the reasoning which produced them are not the forces which produced baptism. Baptism gave rise to the trinitarian creeds. So too the eucharist produced, but was not produced by, a scriptural text, the eucharistic prayer, or all the various scholarly theories concerning the eucharistic real presence . . ."[13]

Above all, then, *doctrine arises from doxology* — from the prayerful, believing Church engaged in ritual word and deed. As Father Kavanagh says, Christians do not worship because they believe, but because in the liturgy they encounter the Lord who promises to be

[11] *GS* 11; emphasis added.
[12] "Let the rule of prayer lay down the rule of faith." The fuller passage outlines the conditions Prosper attaches to this axiom: "Let us next look also at the sacred prayers which in keeping with the apostolic tradition our priests offer after one norm the world over in every Catholic church. Let the rule of prayer lay down the rule of faith." English translation in P. de Letter, *Prosper of Aquitaine: Defense of St. Augustine* (= Ancient Christian Writers 32) (Westminster, Md., 1963) 183. For the Latin text of this passage, see *PL* 51:209.
[13] *On Liturgical Theology* (New York, 1984) 91, 92.

with his faithful people "always, until the end of the age" (Matt 28:20). The normative rules for Christian belief and behavior are thus derived from that same Jesus Christ who

"is always *present* in his Church, especially in her liturgical celebrations . . . *present* in the Sacrifice of the Mass not only in the person of the minister . . . but especially in the eucharistic species . . . *present* in the sacraments . . . *present* in the Word . . . *present* when the Church prays and sings, for he has promised 'where two or three are gathered together in my name there am I in the midst of them.'"[14]

Though each one is distinctive, all these modes of Christ's presence are genuine, real, and effective. Through them the Christian assembly rehearses — *practices* — the presence of God's kingdom in and for the world. For this reason liturgy is the privileged place where the Church discovers and actualizes its own deepest identity. That identity, as Fr. Juan Mateos has pointed out, consists in being — or becoming — nothing less than "a new human community."[15] For *this* was the heart of Jesus' revolutionary message. Faith and salvation are not simply about gaining "eternal life"; they are also about transforming human society. They are about feeding the hungry, clothing the naked, visiting the sick and imprisoned, sheltering the homeless, providing care for widows and orphans, welcoming the stranger (See Matt 25:31-46). In short, faith is about action, mercy, and justice. It means taking a bold stand against injustice; acting on behalf of the weakest and most vulnerable members of society. As Jesus understood it, humanity's trouble lies

"in the very foundations of the institutions it has created: in the striving for money, desire for prestige and thirst for power; in the threefold ambition of 'holding,' 'climbing,' and 'commanding' that spurs people on to rivalry, hatred, and violence."[16]

For this reason, Father Mateos notes, Jesus regarded the major religious institutions of his time — temple, priesthood, monarchy — as largely irrelevant. He proposed, instead,

[14] Matt 18:20; *SC* 7, emphasis added.
[15] "The Message of Jesus," translated by Kathleen England, *Sojourners* 6:7 (July 1977) 8–16.
[16] Mateos, "The Message of Jesus," 12.

"to create a new society in which people could be free and happy (Mt 5:3-10). To attain this people had to voluntarily renounce the three false values: money (thirst for riches), glory (ambition for recognition), and power (desire to dominate). Instead of hoarding, sharing; instead of ambition, equality; instead of domination, solidarity and humble, voluntary service. Where there was rivalry, hatred, and violence, there should be fraternity, love and life."[17]

The community that Jesus aimed to create was thus a gathering of disciples from whom these voluntary renunciations were required (and not simply "recommended"): (1) the *renunciation of riches* — because it is essential for believers to break away from unjust economic systems and from the false prestige and power they promote; (2) the *renunciation of privilege* — for the community of Jesus is meant to be a "discipleship of equals" rather than an elitist coterie based on ambition and self-interest; and (3) the *renunciation of false values* — for salvation comes from God's initiative rather than from human achievement.

Such a community is the one "rehearsed" in the Christian liturgy. In the words of the proper preface for the feast of Christ the King,

[Christ] claims dominion over all creation, that he may present to you, his almighty Father, an eternal and universal kingdom: a kingdom of truth and life, a kingdom of holiness and grace, a kingdom of justice, love, and peace.[18]

Here we see that Jesus is precisely the kind of king who doesn't act like one! His is the crucified "kingship" of a humble shepherd who comes not to command, destroy, and kill but to give his own life for his own. Jesus is "king" of a new humanity whose relationships are characterized by mutual love, joy, peace, tolerance, kindness, generosity, loyalty, simplicity (See Gal 5:22-23; cf. Col 3:12-13). It is a community without "privileges" based on race, ethnic identity, national origin, social class, or gender; a community in which all social,

---

[17] Mateos, "The Message of Jesus," 12.

[18] English translation is that of the International Commission on English in the Liturgy (ICEL), in *The Sacramentary,* approved for use in the dioceses of the United States of America by the National Conference of Catholic Bishops and confirmed by the Apostolic See (New York, 1985) 475.

economic, racial, and sexual barriers have fallen — for among Christians there can be "neither 'Jew' nor 'Greek,' neither 'slave' nor 'free person,' neither 'male' nor 'female,' for all are one in Christ Jesus" (Gal 3:28). Through the cross and blood of Jesus, our king, a new humanity is created,

"in which there is no one on top or beneath, but *all* are last and first at the same time (Mt 19:30), children with one father and mother, servants with one Lord, disciples with one teacher, poor people whose only riches and security are God (Mt 6:19-21; 19:21). Here there is not 'mine' or 'thine' (Acts 4:32). It is a group filled with perfect joy (Jn 15:11; 16:24), mutual affection (Rom 12:10; Col 3:12), swift and unlimited pardon (Mt 18:21-22; Col 3:13); where no rivalry or partisanship exists but all are united in love (Col 3:14) and reciprocal support (Mt 5:7). Each one shoulders the burden of the others (Gal 6:2), the gifts of each are at the service of all (Rom 12:3-8; 1 Cor 12:4-11; Eph 4:11-13), and authority means greater service, not superiority (Lk 22:26-27).[19]

This is the ecclesiology that the liturgy rehearses and promotes. It offers not only an ideal icon of who and what the Church should be but a lively sacrament of the whole world's future. For the liturgy embodies not only Jesus' vision of Church but God's plan for all humanity — for the world, the cosmos. That plan is not merely to redeem the universe, but to transform it. The destiny that awaits us is a resurrection-destiny.

Liturgical ecclesiology is, simultaneously, this-worldly and otherworldly. On the one hand, it *transforms* eschatology into ethics, by insisting that Jesus' disciples must live and work for justice, peace and charity in *this* world if a "new humanity" is ever to emerge. On the other hand, it *restores* eschatology to ethics by insisting that our destiny — as a species, as a planet — is intimately bound up with the destiny of the whole material cosmos, which will be transfigured by "the Spirit of that One who raised Jesus from the dead and now dwells in you," the same Spirit who "will set creation itself free from slavery . . . to share in the glorious freedom of the children of God" (Rom 8:11, 21-23).

[19] Mateos, "The Message of Jesus," 15; slightly altered.

CHARACTERISTICS OF A LITURGICAL ECCLESIOLOGY

A "liturgical ecclesiology" is thus characterized not only by an emphasis on the Church's cultic activity but also — and more importantly — by its emphasis on the Church as a body of disciples who enflesh Jesus' vision of a new human community based upon justice, mercy, and compassion. The Church is neither "doctrine" simply, nor "doxology" simply; it is a new way of living together. We may summarize some salient aspects of this "new way of living" in the following three points:

The Meaning of "Church"

In most modern European languages, the word "church" refers either to a building or to the people gathered in faith, prayer, and worship. Tradition suggests, however, that church properly — and in the first instance — means the living assembly of believers, while *domus ecclesiae* ("house of the church") is the proper architectural term for the structure within which such an assembly worships. Thus, Paul sends greetings to "Prisca and Aquila, my co-workers in Christ Jesus" and "the church [that meets] at their house" (Rom 16:3-35). Clearly, Paul is not speaking here of some abstract "universal" church — or even of a diocese or parish in the modern sense. He is referring to a relatively small group of believers who gather regularly for instruction, worship, mutual support, and encouragement in the private home of a (probably prosperous) local patron.

These "household churches," as L. Michael White has noted, are crucial for understanding both the nature of Paul's mission to Gentile communities and the nature of the Christian assembly itself.[20] In major cities, White writes, "there were probably several such house church cells loosely tied together. There may have been six or more at Corinth during Paul's time."[21] Moreover, the basic social fabric of Christian life as well as the travel demanded by missionary activity

"depended upon the hospitality of these house church owners. A number of important social conventions developed around the practice of household hospitality which came to apply equally well to groups as to individuals. Some of these social conventions can still be

---

[20] L. Michael White, *Building God's House in the Roman World: Architectural Adaptation Among Pagans, Jews, and Christians* (Baltimore, 1990) 105.

[21] Ibid.

glimpsed in [Paul's] letters in terms of 'extending the right hand of fellowship' or 'greeting with a holy kiss' (Gal 2:9; Rom 16:16)."[22]

These household churches probably did not have, in Paul's day, any distinctive architectural features. The assembly gathered in a private, domestic setting — very likely in a *triclinium*, or dining room, since this was often the largest space for accommodating guests in a Greco-Roman house.

"In dealing with the circumstances of worship, Paul presupposes that the gathering was held around the common table. Thus, dining in individual house church groups was fundamental. At Corinth, in the context of communal dining, a lack of discernment regarding the meal as a sign of fellowship among the members of the group was creating dissension. Still, the communal meal was the center of fellowship *(koinonia)*, as eating was a sign of social relations with others. *The extension of hospitality through the meal setting was the central act that served to define the worshiping community,* the church *(ekklesia)* in household assembly."[23]

Eucharistic hospitality is key to Christian identity, a sine qua non of any community's existence as "church." The church is defined by its dining, by how it behaves when it gathers for "the Lord's Supper." Paul understood — as did other and later Christian writers — that when celebrating Eucharist, the Body of Christ is not only *on* the table, it is also *at* the table. Perhaps the most graphic description of this reality comes from a sermon to the newly baptized, attributed to St. Augustine:

"If you want to understand the body of Christ, listen to what the apostle Paul says to the faithful: 'You are the body of Christ, member for member' (1 Cor 12:27; Rom 12:5). *You* are Christ's own body, his members; thus, *it is your own mystery which is placed on the Lord's table. It is your own mystery that you receive.* For at communion, the priest says 'The body of Christ,' and you reply 'Amen!' When you say 'Amen,' you are saying yes to what you are. Be a member of Christ's body, then, so that your 'Amen' may be true. For here, we bring nothing of our own. Let us listen to the very same apostle as he

[22] Ibid., 106.
[23] Ibid., 107, 109, emphasis added.

speaks about this sacrament: 'Because the loaf of bread is one, we, though many, are one body' (1 Cor 10:17). Understand, and rejoice! Unity, truth, faithfulness, love — all are present. 'One loaf of bread.' What is this one bread? 'We, though many, are one body.' Recall that bread is not made from a single grain, but from many. When you were exorcised, you were ground like wheat. When you were baptized, you were leavened. When you received the fire of the Holy Spirit, you were baked. *Be* what you *see; receive* what you *are.*"[24]

Obviously, over two millennia geographic expansion and the increasing complexity of ecclesial organization have produced enormous changes in our liturgical practice and even in our eucharistic theology. But one central fact remains firmly implanted in Catholic tradition: Without the full celebration of Eucharist by the assembly and its ministers, there is no church. For in a very fundamental sense, the Eucharist *creates* the church, brings it into being as the visible sacrament "of communion with God and of unity among all people" (*LG* 1).

The "Liturgy of the World"
Prior to Vatican II sacraments were often thought of as splendidly isolated individual encounters with God. They were seen as privileged "dispensaries" of grace that could then be applied to daily life in order to sanctify or sacramentalize it. A sacrament was thus a kind of "sacred space" to which Christians could retreat from the secular world in order to commune with God and to find the moral strength for living lives of faith. The world itself, in this view, remains utterly deprived of grace, devoid of any real relation to God. Only through sacraments does God's presence have any chance of penetrating the world or its history.

But a different model of sacraments and their meaning has emerged since the council. In this model God's grace is always, already, creating salvation at the very roots of human existence. Karl Rahner summarized the importance of this new model very well:

"The world is permeated by the grace of God. The sacraments are specific events of God's grace as forgiving, sanctifying, and imparting the divine nature. But while they have this significance this does

---

[24] *Sermon* 272; Latin text in PL 38:1247–8; my translation.

not mean that it is solely in the moment of the sacramental act that the grace of God impinges upon a world that is secular. . . . [Rather,] the world [itself] is constantly and ceaselessly possessed by grace from its innermost roots, from the innermost personal center of the spiritual subject [i.e., the human person]. It is constantly and ceaselessly sustained and moved by God's self-bestowal."[25]

The world itself thus constitutes, for Rahner, a "terrible and sublime liturgy, breathing of death and sacrifice, which God celebrates . . . in and through human history in its freedom."[26] It is within this grace-filled history, this "liturgy of the world," that God's ultimate, saving act occurred in the liturgy Jesus celebrated on his cross. As a real event in space and time, Christ's sacrifice belongs to this "liturgy of the world," even as it is the source of that liturgy's continuing power, grace, and holiness. Sacraments are thus not invitations to abandon a wicked world; rather, they "constitute the manifestation of the holiness and the redeemed state of the secular dimension of human life and of the world."[27] Christian sacraments are thus humble landmarks, small (though indispensable) signs that the whole world belongs to God, that everywhere God is adored and experienced as the One who has "set all things free" to receive the divine life. Within "the infinitude of the world as permeated by God," the sacrament is a beacon reminding us of the "limitlessness of the presence of divine grace."[28]

Thus in Eucharist the Christian assembly offers through its bread and wine the world itself, which "is already ceaselessly offering itself up into the inconceivability of God in rejoicing, tears and blood."[29] Celebrating the Lord's Supper, the church stands revealed as *the* basic sacrament of salvation for the world. Gathered in communion around the holy table, Christians become the visible, effective sign of the whole world's destiny, the place where God's grace is both historically present and "eschatologically triumphant" (cf. 1 Cor 15:28).

[25] "Considerations on the Active Role of the Person in the Sacramental Event," *Theological Investigations* (New York, 1976) 14:166.

[26] Ibid., 169.

[27] Ibid.

[28] Ibid.

[29] Ibid., 172.

Becoming Present to the Mystery of Christ
For centuries Catholic theology has been obsessed by the question
How does Christ become present in the sacraments, especially in the
eucharistic bread and wine? In the New Testament, however, the
primary question is not How is *Jesus* present? but rather, How do *we
Christians* become present to and participate in the mystery of Christ?

Bibliography

Chupungco, A. *Liturgical Inculturation: Sacramentals, Religiosity, and Catechesis.*
Collegeville, Minn., 1992.

Kavanagh, A. *On Liturgical Theology.* New York, 1984.

Lathrop, G. *Holy Things: Foundations for Liturgical Theology.* Minneapolis, 1993.

Power, D. N. *Unsearchable Riches: The Symbolic Nature of Liturgy.* New York,
1984.

Rahner, K. *The Church and the Sacraments.* Trans. W. J. O'Hara. Westminster,
Md., 1974.

Schillebeeckx, E. *Christ: The Experience of Jesus as Lord.* Trans. J. Bowden. New
York, 1980.

Skelley, M. *The Liturgy of the World: Karl Rahner's Theology of Worship.* Collegeville, Minn., 1991.

Mark Francis, C.S.V.

7

The Liturgical Assembly

It would not be an exaggeration to maintain that the single most important accomplishment of the liturgical reform promoted by the Second Vatican Council was the restoration of the active assembly in the
Church's worship.[1] In fact, the entire program of renewal ultimately
centers around such a restoration. The faithful's "full, conscious and
active participation in liturgical celebration" announced in article 14
of *Sacrosanctum concilium* sums up the council's overarching goal:
that the assembly of the baptized be once again the principal agent in
the liturgical event. This recovery of the importance of the liturgical
assembly and the assembly's closer theological connection to a more
broadly based ecclesiology was made possible because of the
groundwork laid by biblical and historical scholarship prior to the
council.[2] Papal pronouncements on the liturgy during the first half of
the twentieth century also helped to spur research on the nature and
function of the assembly.

---

[1] See the principle reflected in the articles of the following conciliar documents:
SC 6, 10, 26, 41, 42, 106; *LG* 11, 26; *PO* 5, 6.

[2] Concern with the assembly occupied many of the French language scholars
during the first part of the century. See, for example, the paper from the Sixteenth
Liturgical Week in Louvain (1933); *La participation active des fidèles au culte,* Cours
et conférence des Semaines liturgiques 11 (Louvain, 1934), with papers by B.
Capelle, B. Botte, P. Charlier and others; Henri Chirat, *L'assemblée chrétienne á l'âge
apostolique* (Paris, 1949); A.-G. Martimort, "L'Assemblée liturgique," *MD* 20 (1949)
153–75; also see a review of the contribution of scholars to studies on the liturgical
assembly before the council, especially in light of ecclesiological concerns: Y. Congar, "Réflexions et recherches actuelles sur l'assemblée liturgique," *MD* 115 (1973)
7–29.

In 1903 St. Pius X in his motu proprio *Tra le sollecitudini* declared what was to become the battle cry for the twentieth-century liturgical movement. He maintained that active participation in the holy mysteries and in the public and solemn prayer of the Church is "the first and indispensable source of the true Christian spirit."[3] This concern was echoed by Pius XI, who deplored the fact that so many of the faithful attended Mass as "silent spectators."[4] But it was Pope Pius XII in his encyclicals *Mystici Corporis* (1943) and *Mediator Dei* (1947) who legitimated much of the research on the history and theology of the liturgy carried out during the reigns of his two predecessors. This research did much to lay the foundation for a reappraisal of the relationship of the faithful to Christ in the liturgical event and for regarding the liturgical assembly itself as an "epiphany" of the Church. It was in this context that Pius XII in *Mediator Dei* affirmed that the liturgy is "the priestly action of Christ continued in the Church"[5] and defined it as "the worship of the entire mystical body."[6] The encyclical, however, was limited by a canonical and clerical understanding of the nature of the Church inherited from the Counter-Reformation. It defined the Church primarily as "a visible and hierarchically constituted society."[7] Following from this understanding it was logical to posit that the liturgy belonged first of all to priests because they act "in the name of the Church."[8] Despite this limitation, *Mediator Dei*

---

[3] (November 22, 1903); see A. Bugnini, *Documenta pontificia ad instaurationem liturgicam spectantia* (Rome, 1953) 12–3.

[4] Apostolic constitution *Divini cultus* (December 20, 1928) 9: *AAS* 21 (1929) 40.

[5] "Itaque animus satius aptiusque ad Deum erigitur; ac Iesu Christi sacerdotium per omnem saeculorum decursum nullo non tempore viget, cum sacra Liturgia nihil aliud sit, nisi huius sacerdotalis muneris exercitatio," *AAS* 39 (1947) 529, see also 521.

[6] "Sacra igitur Liturgia . . ., integrum constituit publicum cultum mystici Iesu Christi Corporis, Capitis nempe membrorumque eius," ibid., 528; also 532.

[7] "Ecclesia nempe societas est, atque adeo propriam postulat auctoritatem ac Hierarchiam," ibid., 538. Interestingly, in the same paragraph the pope alludes to the concept that the earthly organization of the Church reflects in some fashion the heavenly hierarchy — a concept advanced by the Pseudo-Dionysius in the fifth century and which has often given warrant to ecclesiastical structures throughout the history of the Church.

[8] "Quoniam igitur sacra Liturgia imprimis a sacerdotibus Ecclesiae nomine absolvitur, idcirco eius ordinatio, moderatio ac forma ab Ecclesiae auctoritate non pendere non potest," ibid., 539.

did much to foster the restoration of the liturgy to the assembly. Scholars who promoted such a restoration used as their warrant the history of the assembly's participation in the liturgy both in Judaism and the early Church. It is to this history that we now turn.

A BRIEF HISTORY OF THE LITURGICAL ASSEMBLY IN JUDEO-CHRISTIAN TRADITION

Assembly in the Old Testament

"Assembly" translates the term ἐκκλησία used in the Septuagint to render the Hebrew word *qahal*. It is instructive to look at examples of *qahal* in the Old Testament, since it is the *qahal* that is the principal point of reference for the early Christian understanding of ἐκκλησία / assembly. *Qahal* signifies both the call that convokes the gathering and those who respond to the call and constitute the assembly. Thus the term evokes both the gathered people and the event of gathering as well. In Israel the *qahal* was convoked to hear the words of the king and to give an "official" communal response to these words. In the case of a *qahal Yahweh*, of course, this solemn assembly assumed more than civic importance — it directly dealt with the relationship between God and Israel. The *qahal Yahweh* was the privileged place and time for the people of Israel to celebrate their identity as God's chosen people. This choice was acknowledged and the covenant with God ratified by the people in *qahal* after hearing God's word. It is for this reason that the Greek ἐκκλησία, with its connotation of a duly summoned assembly, was such an appropriate rendering of *qahal*. Unlike another Hebrew term for assembly, *'edah* — used to describe liturgical assemblies that take place on fixed dates — *qahal* usually connotes a special, "extraordinary" convocation of the people at a decisive moment in the history of Israel.[9]

There are several examples of *qahal* in the Old Testament. The primary example is found in Exodus 19 — the first assembly of the people after their liberation from Egypt. After the people have prepared themselves through fasting and purification, Moses, acting on God's command, calls the people of Israel together at Mount Sinai to hear the word of God. It is Israel's affirmative response to God's word that makes them a people. It also serves as the basis for the

[9] See H. Cazelles, "The Old Testament Liturgical Assembly and the Various Roles Played in It," *Roles in the Liturgical Assembly* (New York, 1977) 101–13.

covenant (Exod 24:3). This covenant is in turn ratified by a solemn sacrifice during which the blood of the sacrificial victims is splashed on the altar and on the people, thereby uniting God and the assembly (Exod 24:6-8). While there was an evolution in the solemn *qahal* over the centuries, its basic four elements were: (1) a gathering of the people convoked by God; (2) an event during which God is present in a special way to the people; (3) a moment of solemn proclamation of God's word that is in turn received and acknowledged by those gathered; (4) a solemn ratification of the relationship (covenant) between God and the people, usually by means of sacrifice.

There are other examples of solemn assemblies in the Old Testament, but they are all ultimately related to the first covenant assembly described in Exodus, such as the renewal of the covenant before the people of Israel take possession of the land (Deuteronomy 5) or the *qahal* convoked to renew the Mosaic covenant and purify the Temple under King Josiah, described in 2 Kings 23. Perhaps the most instructive later example is found in Nehemiah 8–10. This passage describes the reading and interpretation of the Bible to the people by Ezra the priest after the Babylonian Exile. In response to the reading of the word, Ezra offers a solemn prayer of thanksgiving that recalls God's merciful dealings with Israel in the past and also asks for God's continued help in the future (Nehemiah 9). Instead of ending with a sacrifice (which was an impossibility since the Temple had not yet been rebuilt), the assembly ratified the renewed covenant by pledging to offer sacrifices and support to the future Temple (Nehemiah 10). Many scholars see in this liturgy the prototype of the liturgy of the synagogue: the form of Jewish worship that was to survive the destruction of the Second Temple in A.D. 70 by the Romans.

Liturgical Assembly in the Early Church
While New Testament authors sometimes employ general words such as πλῆθος (crowd)[10] and even συναγωγή (synagogue)[11] to refer to an assembly or purposeful gathering, in addition to verbs that speak of assembling — e.g., σύναγεῖν, συνέρχομαι, ἀθροίζομαι — the preferred term for the gathered Christian community is ἐκκλησία / assembly; undoubtedly because of its association with the Old Testament *qahal*.

---

[10] For example, Acts 17:5; 15:12; 22:7.
[11] For example, Jas 2:2.

In the Acts of the Apostles this word was first used in reference to the local community of believers in Jerusalem, the mother church (Acts 8:1). The use of the term quickly becomes more broad to encompass not only a local grouping of believers at Jerusalem, Antioch, or "throughout Judea, Galilee and Samaria" (Acts 9:11) but the universal Church as well — all those throughout the world who believe in Jesus Christ (Acts 15). The Synoptics use the term ἐκκλησία twice in describing the community of disciples formed by Jesus (Matt 16:18; 18:18). Paul, who is the first to use the term ἐκκλησία in the New Testament corpus, employs it sixty-five times, mainly in reference to the local communities of Christian believers to whom he is writing. In 1 Cor 11:18, however, Paul uses the word in a way that speaks of the action of forming the assembly: the ἐκκλησία "when you come together as a church" (NRSV) (συνερχομένων ὑμῶν ἐν ἐκκλησίᾳ). Paul's consistent identification of ἐκκλησία with the body of Christ informs his understanding of the eucharistic action of sharing in the one bread (1 Cor 10:17) which constitutes the church as the body of Christ in a shared life of profound communion and cooperation characterized by the term κοινωνία.[12] Those who are baptized into Christ Jesus and make up the assembly enjoy absolute equality regardless of social status because having put on Christ in baptism they no longer belong to the former structures of the world — they have become a new creation (2 Cor 5:17). Paul therefore declares to the Galatians that having been baptized, "there is no longer Jew or Greek, there is no longer slave or free, there is no longer male and female; for all of you are one in Christ Jesus" (Gal 3:28). This image of church as the body of Christ is most fully developed in the letters to the Ephesians and Colossians, where Christ is declared the head of the body, the Church (Col 1:18, 24), and the Church itself is called the fullness (πλήρωμα) of the body of Christ (Eph 1:23). In the Pauline tradition, then, the Church as body of Christ, the eucharistic assembly, and the sacramental presence of Christ are so closely identified as to be inseparable.

While not all of the New Testament authors use the metaphor of the body in reference to the ἐκκλησία, the identification of the assembly of baptized with the very presence of the risen Lord becomes a matter of faith for the early Church. Jesus' promise in Matt 18:20, that

[12] See also 1 Corinthians 12; Romans 12.

"where two or three are gathered (συνηγμένοι) in my name, I am there among them," reflects the experience of the early Christian community at prayer. It is this presence of the risen Lord that renders Christian prayer efficacious, since it is Christ himself praying with the assembly who is the means of salvation and grace for humanity in the presence of the Father. The regular meetings of the ἐκκλησία thus constitute the ongoing presence of this source of salvation. For this reason it is not surprising to see that the early Church has left a very consistent record emphasizing the importance of the assembly. An exhortation in the letter to the Hebrews expresses well the conviction of the first Christians that linked the assembly to the whole of the Christian life lived in expectation of the final coming of Christ. "And let us consider how to provoke one another to love and good deeds, not neglecting to meet together, as is the habit of some, but encouraging one another, and all the more as you see the Day approaching" (Heb 10:24-25).

The significance of the assembly for primitive Christianity is also reflected in extrabiblical sources. Even non-Christians witnessed to the regular meetings of the Christian faithful. In the famous letter to the emperor Trajan describing his interrogations of Christians as governor of Bythnia, written around the year 111, Pliny the Younger comments that "their custom had been to gather before dawn on a fixed day *(stato die)* and to sing a hymn to Christ as if to a god."[13] The text then goes on to describe an oath *(sacramentum)* taken by those present to avoid sinful deeds and refer to a communal meal that ends the gathering. Pliny's account parallels the exhortation found in a contemporary document, the *Didache* 14:1, that calls upon Christians to "come together (συναχθέντες) on the Lord's Day and break bread." Justin Martyr, writing several decades later (around the year 150) says, "On the day named after the sun, all who live in city or country-side assemble (συνέλευσις γίνεται). The memoirs of the apostles or the writings of the prophets are read for as long as time allows. When the lector has finished, the president (προεστὼς) addresses us and exhorts us to imitate the splendid things we have heard" (1 Apol. 67:3). Justin goes on to describe intercessory prayer, the presentation of the gifts of bread and wine over which the presider proclaims a prayer of

[13] ". . . quod essent soliti stato die ante lucem convenire carmenque Christo quasi deo dicere secum invicem . . ." (*Ep.*, 10, 96).

134

thanksgiving, and the sharing of the eucharistized gifts. Justin's is one of the earliest accounts of the eucharistic celebration. While he describes the specialized ministries of presider and lector he also clearly emphasizes the active involvement of all those assembled for worship.

While the obligation of Christians to gather together on the Lord's Day is mentioned by many of the early patristic writers, perhaps no better exposition of the importance of the assembly to the early Church can be found than that of the *Didascalia of the Apostles*. This document, dating probably from the first half of the third century, was a practical guide for the use of bishops leading Christian communities in Syria.[14] After describing a detailed arrangement of priests, deacons, men, women, and children in the liturgical assembly, the author advises his fellow bishops: "When you are teaching, command and exhort the people to be faithful to the assembly of the church. Let them not fail to attend, but let them gather faithfully together. Let no one deprive the Church by staying away; if they do, they deprive the body of Christ of one of its members!"[15]

Of all the patristic writers of the period after Nicaea, John Chrysostom returns most consistently in his homilies to the importance of the assembly for the individual and corporate Christian life. In commenting on those who fail to see the need to assemble with the wider Church since they can pray at home, he answers: "Do not say, 'Can I not pray in my own home?' Of course you can pray at home, but your prayer has more power when you are united to other members, when the whole body of the Church raises its prayer to heaven with a single heart, the priests being there to offer the vows of the gathered multitude."[16] While Chrysostom places great emphasis on the actions and presence of the priest, he also maintains that the assembly is an integral part of the liturgical action — especially during the Eucharistic Prayer, which the priest proclaims in the name of all.

[14] See R. Hugh Connolly, *Didascalia Apostolorum* (Oxford, 1929, 1969) xxvii; for partial but modern English translation see Lucien Deiss, *The Springtime of the Liturgy* (Collegeville, 1979) 176–7.

[15] ". . . et minus membrum facere corpus Christi," *Didascalia*, ed., Connolly, ch. 13, 5.

[16] John Chrysostom, *On the Obscurity of the Prophets*, hom. 2, n. 4, trans. M. Jeannin, vol. 6, 467.

"The Eucharistic Prayer is common; the priest does not give thanks alone, but the people with him, for he begins it only after having received the accord of the faithful. . . . If I say that, it is so that we learn that we are a single body. Therefore let us not rely on the priests for everything, but let us, too, care for the Church."[17]

The Assembly During the Middle Ages and Counter-Reformation
Despite the emphasis placed on the importance of the assembly in the patristic Church, the period just after the sixth century and continuing into the High Middle Ages witnessed its gradual eclipse in the West. There were several reasons for this development, many of which date from the patristic period itself. While the liturgical assembly was an essential part of the definition and practice of the early Church — there could be no Church without assembly — extrinsic factors intervened that weakened the link between assembly and local church. The growing numbers of the faithful militated against maintaining a strong link between local community and the liturgical assembly. The urban church of Rome, for example, which had grown too large for a single eucharistic celebration on Sunday, developed strategies such as the *fermentum* and stational liturgies to maintain a link between local communities and the bishop. In less populated areas, however, apart from *martyria*, or shrines marking the resting places of martyrs and holy men and women, it was the bishop's church that was the obligatory site of the gathering of the local community during the Merovingian period. In fact, clergy as well as laypeople were urged by ecclesiastical legislation to come together with the bishop every Sunday. The tenth canon of the Council of Macon held in A.D. 583, for example, stipulates: "The priests, deacons and the clerics of all ranks should submit to their bishop with an obedient devotion, and they should not be permitted to spend or celebrate a Sunday elsewhere than in the service of their bishop."[18]

In rural areas, however, the establishment of private chapels to accommodate smaller gatherings of the faithful who could not easily attend the bishop's Mass in the city tended to obscure the relationship between local church and assembly, despite attempts to limit celebrations in these chapels. The popularity of the Mendicant orders

[17] 2 Cor. hom. 18, 3 PG 61, 527.
[18] F. Maasen, *Concilia aevi Merovingici* (Hannover, 1893) (MGH) 157; quoted in A. G. Martimort, "Dimanche, assemblée et paroisse," *MD* 57 (1959) 75.

in the thirteenth century later tended to fragment the local assemblies in urban areas, since these orders often built churches in close proximity to parish churches and drew away worshipers even on Sundays and feast days. While local church councils throughout the Middle Ages would enact draconian measures to try to maintain the integrity of the local assembly,[19] by the time of the Council of Trent, the commitment to the assembly was reduced to a mere exhortation that the faithful attend Sundays and feast days at their parish church.[20]

The gradual loss of importance of the assembly also came about because of a shift in the theological understanding of the nature of Christian worship. Since liturgy was celebrated in a language that was becoming increasingly incomprehensible to the faithful, this heightened the role of a growing cadre of clerical "experts" deputed to pray for the rest of the Church. This development tended to throw lay participation in the liturgical event into a very passive and individualistic mode. The construction of churches in the Middle Ages with chancels set apart from the nave by rood screens simply gave physical expression to the gulf that had opened between clergy and laity in the liturgical celebration. The growth of "private Masses" encouraged in part by the commutation of penances, coupled with the rise of the "Mass priests" — those ordained without any pastoral responsibility other than to celebrate the Mass — also tended to make the worship event something done by the priest and merely watched by the laity. Finally, the tendency toward an exaggerated objectification and sensualist understanding of the presence of Christ in the eucharistic elements stemming from the eucharistic controversies beginning in the ninth century also tended to distract theological attention from the equally traditional notion of Christ's presence in the assembly.

Prior to the Council of Trent, however, the official descriptions of the Mass liturgy still included some mention of the assembly. In one of the more representative *Ordines missae*, written in 1502 by Alexander VI's master of ceremonies, Burchard of Strasbourg, it is supposed that the faithful participate passively but devoutly since they are

[19] See Martimort, ibid., 81.
[20] See Session XXII of the Council of Trent, *Decretum de observandis et evitandis in celebratione missae.*

137

mentioned from time to time.[21] Among other actions, the faithful are directed to stand on Sundays and during Eastertide, answer the prayers at the foot of the altar with the servers, and bring up their own offering. It is instructive to contrast the attenuated but real inclusion of the faithful in Burchard's *ordo* with the *Rubricae generales missalis* and the *Ritus servandus in celebratione Missae* of the Missal of Pius V (1570). Direct references to assembly have been omitted. The rubrics concern only the celebrant priest; the assembly is mentioned only in an oblique and secondary way. Thus for the period after the Council of Trent to the reform of the *Ordo Missae* promoted by Vatican II, the assembly was clearly deemphasized to the point of being an incidental part of the rite.

LITURGICAL AND THEOLOGICAL PRINCIPLES OF THE ASSEMBLY IN THE REFORM OF VATICAN II

In the period just prior to Vatican II the ferment caused by the liturgical movement and by papal encyclicals such as *Mediator Dei* led to the adoption of various strategies by some in the avant-garde to restore an active liturgical assembly. Even within the possibilities allowed by the Tridentine rubrics, promoters of liturgical renewal sought to involve the faithful in an active way through dialogue Masses (at which the assembly would respond with the acolytes) and offertory processions (in which the gifts of bread and wine would be brought to the priest by members of the assembly). But it was the Second Vatican Council that affirmed the importance of the assembly by offering a systematic presentation of principles supporting its central role in the worship event. The assembly's right and duty to participate in the prayer of the Church is essentially based on the reestablishment of the link between the nature of the Church as the People of God and the celebration of the liturgy. *Sacrosanctum concilium* declares that "the Church . . . earnestly desires that Christ's faithful when present at this mystery of faith, should not be there as strangers or silent spectators. On the contrary . . . they should take part in the sacred action, conscious of what they are doing, with devotion and

---

[21] *Ordo servandus per sacerdotem in celebratione Missae since cantu et sine ministris secundum ritum S. Romanae Ecclesiae;* see B. Neunheuser, "The Liturgies of Pius V and Paul VI," *Roles in the Liturgical Assembly* (New York, 1977) 208; J. K. Leonard and N. D. Mitchell, *The Postures of the Assembly During the Eucharistic Prayer* (Chicago, 1994) 72–4.

full collaboration" (*SC* 48). The council also reaffirmed the communal nature of all Christian worship — a characteristic that had been severely compromised since the Middle Ages due to the excessive emphasis placed on the role of the priest. "Whenever rites, according to their specific nature, make provision for communal celebration involving the presence and active participation of the faithful, it is to be stressed that this way of celebrating them is to be preferred, as far as possible, to a celebration that is individual and, so to speak, private" (*SC* 27). Following from these principles, three main theological orientations of the Christian assembly can be highlighted: (1) the liturgical assembly is convoked by God; (2) the liturgical assembly is an epiphany of the Church itself; (3) the liturgical assembly is an anticipation of the reign of God.

The Liturgical Assembly as a
Gathering of the Baptized Convoked by God
Just as the *qahal* of old was convoked by God, so today the assembly of the baptized is called together by the action of the Spirit. Just as God's saving grace is unmerited and prevenient in our lives (see Eph 2:4-10; 1 John 4:10-19), God's initiative needs always to be acknowledged as the ultimate foundation of the Christian assembly. The 1994 instruction *Inculturation and the Roman Liturgy* describes well this important characteristic of the Christian assembly.

"Now the Church has specific characteristics which distinguish it from every other assembly and community. It is not gathered together by a human decision, but is called by God in the Holy Spirit and responds in faith to his gratuitous call (*ekklesia* derives from *klesis* 'call'). This singular characteristic of the Church is revealed by its coming together as a priestly people, especially on the Lord's day, by the Word which God addresses to his people and by the ministry of the priest who through the Sacrament of Orders acts in the person of Christ the Head."[22]

The Liturgical Assembly as the Epiphany of the Church
The Constitution on the Sacred Liturgy states clearly that the liturgy is the "outstanding means whereby the faithful may express in their

---

[22] Congregation for Divine Worship and Discipline of the Sacraments, "The Roman Liturgy and Inculturation: IVth Instruction for the Right Application of

lives and manifest to others the mystery of Christ and the real nature of the true Church" (SC 2). Thus the gathering of God's people in liturgical assembly can be rightly called a "sacrament" because God's grace and presence are manifested in a unique way in the context of the liturgical gathering of the baptized. Paradoxically, this presence is incarnated and made apparent in communities composed of sinful and fallible human beings — some of whom obscure this presence and render the "sacrament" of the assembly less apparent. The assembly is indeed a sign, an epiphany of the Church, but one that also reflects its struggles and failures, a sign of Christ and his presence that will only be perfectly transparent and fulfilled at the end of time.

It is, of course, only by virtue of the mystery of Christ's leading the assembly that the liturgy has power. *Sacrosanctum concilium* affirms that "the liturgy, then, is rightly seen as an exercise of the priestly office of Jesus Christ. It involves the presentation of the people's sanctification under the guise of signs perceptible by the senses and its accomplishment in ways appropriate to each of these signs. In it full public worship is performed by the Mystical Body of Jesus Christ, that is, by the head and its members" (SC 7). The ecclesial grounding of the liturgy is rooted in the union of Christians with Christ. "From this it follows that every liturgical celebration, because it is an action of Christ the Priest and of his body, which is the church, is a sacred action surpassing all others. No other action of the church can equal its efficacy by the same title and to the same degree" (SC 7).

As a kind of sacrament, the assembly as the "epiphany of the Church" is never an abstraction but takes place at a particular time and in a particular place. As *Lumen gentium* points out:

"The Church of Christ is present in all legitimate local congregations of the faithful, which, united with their pastors, are themselves called churches in the New Testament. . . . In any community existing around an altar, under the sacred ministry of the bishop, there is manifested a symbol of that charity and 'unity of the Mystical Body, without which there can be no salvation.' In these communities, though frequently small and poor, or living far from any other, Christ

---

the Conciliar Constitution on the Liturgy (nn. 37–40)," 22. (hereafter RLI). For the English language text see *Origins* 23:43 (April 14, 1994) 746–56.

is present. By virtue of Him the one, holy, catholic, and apostolic Church gathers together" (LG 26).

The most complete manifestation of the Church, then, consists in the full, active participation of all God's holy people in the same liturgical celebration, especially in the same Eucharist, in one prayer, at one altar, at which the bishop presides, surrounded by the college of his priests and by his ministers (cf. SC 41). It is in these celebrations that the Church is most manifest, since it reflects the fullness of the local church.

The Liturgical Assembly as an Anticipation of the Reign of God
While the assembly is a real but imperfect sign of God's presence, it points the way to the fulfillment of the world in Christ at the end of time. The liturgy, especially the eucharistic celebration, is the joyful foretaste of the banquet of God's reign, when God will be all in all. The exultant praise of the risen Lord, the Lamb who has been slain whose blood has purchased for God "those of every tribe and tongue, every people and nation" (Rev 5:9), is a characteristic of our earthly liturgy as well as the eternal heavenly worship. The gathering of the baptized as brothers and sisters regardless of culture, social class, and gender serves as sign of the banquet at the end of time that will gather all of God's children around the same table. The sacramental presence of Christ in the liturgy is also a pledge that he will indeed return in a definitive manner. In proclaiming that "Christ will come again" in the context of the eucharistic celebration, the Church at prayer echoes the intense eschatological expectations voiced from the beginning of Christianity.

CULTURAL CHALLENGES
The rediscovery of the assembly as the principal agent in the liturgical event and the principal minister to which the other liturgical ministries are ordered has also led to a new appreciation for the role played by the culture of the people gathered to worship in Christ's name. The foundational document of the liturgical reform, *Sacrosanctum concilium*, expressed a marked sensitivity to the impact of the assembly's culture on the liturgy. Attention to the cultural context of the celebration is especially important when the assembly is composed of members who are not of a Western cultural tradition. Articles 37–40 expressly treat of the legitimate variations in the liturgy occasioned

by the "genius and talents of various races and peoples" (SC 37–39) that must be both allowed and encouraged in order for the members of a given culture to participate in the liturgy with mind and heart. Article 40 of the constitution allows for even more radical departure from the *editio typica* in cultural contexts that are largely removed from the sober "Roman genius" that informs much of the renewed liturgy. The constitution as well as the subsequent liturgical documents are cognizant that it is not sufficient to employ liturgical forms from another age and culture without modification. For the assembly to make the Church's prayer its own, its culture must be reflected in the liturgy.

The 1994 instruction *Inculturation and the Roman Liturgy* interprets articles 37–40 of the Constitution on the Sacred Liturgy and specifies among other areas that the language of prayer, music, movement (gestures), and the liturgical year itself are all aspects of the liturgy that need to reflect the cultural context of the local assembly.[23] This instruction is complemented by the instruction *Comme le prévoit*[24] (On the Translation of Liturgical Texts for Celebration with a Congregation). This Roman document significantly advanced the discussion on inculturation by describing the liturgical act as one of communication. Hence the cultural specificity of the assembly will affect the way in which the assembly interprets the liturgical celebration. For this reason *Comme le prévoit* emphasizes the method of dynamic equivalence in translation rather than a slavish (and ultimately unfaithful) literal translation of liturgical texts. It also opens the door for the creativity of the local church, stating that "texts translated from another language (Latin) are clearly not sufficient for the celebration of a renewed liturgy," and calls for the composition of new prayers written in the language of the people — informed by the euchological tradition of the Church.[25]

CONCLUSION
The restoration of a conscious and active liturgical assembly is a paradigm of the entire program of ecclesial *aggiornamento* promoted by the Second Vatican Council. The faithful of a local church assem-

---

[23] See RLI 52–61.

[24] Consilium, *Comme le prévoit* on the translation of liturgical texts for celebration with a congregation, January 25, 1969: *Not* 5 (1969) 3–12; DOL 123.

[25] Ibid., 43.

bled by Christ and in his name constitute a sacramental sign of his continuing presence in the world. Their participation in the liturgy, conditioned as it is by local conditions, foreshadows the heavenly worship described by the author of the book of Revelation:

"After this I looked, and there was a great multitude that no one could count, from every nation, from all tribes and peoples and languages, standing before the throne and before the Lamb, robed in white, with palm branches in their hands. They cried out in a loud voice, saying, 'Salvation belongs to our God who is seated on the throne, and to the Lamb!'" (*NRSV* Rev 7:9-10).

Bibliography

Congar, Y. "Réflexions et recherches actuelles sur l'assemblée liturgique." *MD* 115 (1973) 7–29.

Gallen, J. "Assembly." In *The New Dictionary of Sacramental Worship*. Ed. P. Fink. Collegeville, Minn., 1990.

Gy, P.-M. "'Eucharistie' et 'Ecclesia' dans le premier vocabulaire de la liturgie chrétienne." *MD* 130 (1977) 19–34.

Hurd, B. "Liturgy and Empowerment: The Restoration of the Liturgical Assembly." In *That They Might Live: Power, Empowerment, and Leadership in the Church*, ed. M. Downey, 130–44. New York, 1991.

Marsili, S. "La liturgia culto della Chiesa." *Anàmnesis* 1:107–136.

Martimort, A.-G. "The Assembly." *The Church at Prayer*. Vol. 1, *Principles of the Liturgy*, 89–111. Collegeville, Minn., 1987.

Roles in the Liturgical Assembly. Papers of the Twenty-third Liturgical Conference at the Saint-Serge Institute in Paris, June 28 to July 1, 1976. Trans. M. J. O'Connell. New York, 1981.

Vincie, C. "The Liturgical Assembly: Review and Reassessment," *Wor* 67 (1993) 123–44.

8

Participation in the Liturgy

I. THE HISTORICAL PICTURE

THE EARLY CENTURIES

The early centuries were decisive for the study of the participation of the faithful in the liturgical life of the Church. Many patristic writings of these times reveal to us that the faithful have always had a very active part in liturgical celebrations. To see how true this statement is, it helps to examine briefly some excerpts from the ancient writers of the early centuries. Particular attention is given to the eucharistic celebration.

We place our attention immediately on the Liturgy of the Word. For the preliminary rites, namely those before the readings, we have no specific notice at our disposition. Thus we begin with the readings. From what we have been able to learn from the patristic writings that we studied, it is certain that in the ancient Church the faithful participated with great attention and devotion in this first part of the Eucharist.

From Chromatius of Aquileia, it is known that the faithful would sing the *Alleluia* during the Liturgy of the Word. It is a chant that invites one to render praise to God and to confess the true faith; it is the acknowledgment of the power of God as the Creator of heaven, of earth, and of human beings and as the Savior of the world. It is to be noted here that for Chromatius, the chant of the *Alleluia* is addressed to God the Father. Still according to Chromatius, this is a sign of unity among believers and, at the same time, a sign of each believer belonging to the one Church.[1]

---

[1] Chromatius of Aquileia, *Sermo XXXIII* 1–3 = Étaix-Lemarié, CCL IXA, 150–3; see also Augustine, *Sermo CCXLIII*, 9 = PL 38, 1147.

The fact that the faithful have sung during liturgical celebrations ever since antiquity is demonstrated historically by a non-Christian writer, Pliny the Younger. We know from a letter of his to the emperor Trajan that at the beginning of the second century Christians had the custom of gathering together on a set day before sunrise and of singing in alternation between themselves a hymn to Christ as to a God.[2] This mode of performing chants during ritual celebrations is also confirmed by St. Augustine: in his times, during ritual functions the psalms would be sung in alternate choirs with the participation of the people.[3] After the readings comes the universal prayer, and all those present pray fervently both for themselves and for all others wherever they may be, as Justin writes in his *I Apologia*.[4]

Now we move to the second part of the eucharistic celebration. When the preparatory rites are finished, the great prayer of thanksgiving is started. To help the faithful participate in this part with the greatest attention and devotion the preface begins with the word of the celebrant addressed to the faithful, inviting them to lift up their hearts to the Lord, thus freeing their spirit from material thoughts and stimulating their attention to what is said in the Eucharistic Prayer. To this appeal the faithful respond: "We have turned them toward the Lord," as St. Cyprian and St. Cyril of Jerusalem attest.[5] The celebrant continues and says: "Let us give thanks to the Lord," and all respond: "It is fitting and just."[6] After this dialogue, the whole assembly sings the *Sanctus* to join with the heavenly choir of angels in praising God.[7] When the priest finishes the prayer of thanksgiving, all the people present acclaim by saying *"Amen."*[8]

The rite of Communion follows, which begins with two rituals: the exchange of the kiss of peace among the faithful and the recitation of the Our Father by the faithful. For the kiss of peace, the most signifi-

[2] *C. Plinius Traiano Imperatori*, Liber X, 96 (97) 1 = Durry, 74: "Quod essent soliti stato die ante lucem conuenire carmenque Christo quasi deo dicere secum inuicem."

[3] Augustine, *Enarrationes in Psalmos XLVI*, 1 = Dekkers, CCL XXXVIII, 529, 4–8.

[4] Justin, *I Apologia* LXV = Otto, 176–8.

[5] Cyprian, *De dominica oratione* 31 = Moreschini, CCL IIIA/2, 109, 562–9; Cyril of Jerusalem, *Catéchèses mystagogiques V*, 5 = Piédagnel, SCh 126, 150–2.

[6] Cyril of Jerusalem, *Catéchèses mystagogiques V*, 5, 152.

[7] Ibid., 152–4; Eusebius of Caesarea, *Histoire ecclésiastique*, X 4 = Baroy, SCh 55, 103.

[8] Justin, *I Apologia* LXV = Otto, 178.

cant text that speaks of this rite in the eucharistic celebration is certainly the *De oratione* by Tertullian: he considers it as a seal of our prayer, and therefore no sacrifice can be celebrated without the peace.[9] Nonetheless, the meaning that another ancient author attributes to this rite cannot be neglected. According to Cyril of Jerusalem, this kiss is not of the same kind as those that common friends give to one another in the street. This kiss unites the souls of the faithful by removing all ill feeling from them.[10] Before approaching the altar to receive the bread and the chalice, the faithful recite the Our Father.[11]

When the time comes for Communion, the faithful communicate under both species. It is interesting to note the rite of Communion described by Cyril. It begins with a formula proclaimed by the celebrant, which reads in this way: "Holy things to the holy." The people answer: "Alone Holy, alone Lord, Jesus Christ."[12] After this, the faithful approach the altar to receive the holy mysteries. When a believer reaches the altar, he or she extends the hands with the fingers held together, places the left hand in the form of a throne on the right, and receives the consecrated host in the palm of the hand. At the words of the celebrant, "The body of Christ," the believer responds: "Amen."[13] After having communed with the body of Christ, he or she also approaches the chalice. This time, the hands are not extended, but, bowing in an attitude of adoration and respect and saying "Amen," the believer takes the blood of Christ. The holy bishop continues and invites the person who has communed, while the lips are still moist, to brush them with the hands, and with them to bless the eyes and forehead and other senses. Then, while awaiting the prayer and having been judged worthy to receive this grand mystery, the believer gives thanks to God.[14]

---

[9] Tertullian, *De oratione* XVIII 1–5 = Diercks, CCL I, 267, 1–9.

[10] Cyril of Jerusalem, *Catéchèses mystagogiques V*, 3, 148.

[11] Idem., *Catéchèses mystagogiques V*, 11, 160. In the West, however, this prayer is recited by the celebrant, and the faithful listen: Augustine, *Sermo LVIII*, 12 = Verbraken, *EO* 1984/1, 131, 233–5.

[12] Cyril of Jerusalem, *Catéchèses mystagogiques V*, 19, 168. Similar expressions are also found in *Les Constitutions Apostoliques*, Livre VIII, 13, 11–3 = Metzger, SCh 336, 208, 42–6.

[13] Cyril of Jerusalem, *Catéchèses mystagogiques V*, 21, 170–2.

[14] Idem., *Catéchèses mystagogiques V*, 22, 172. With regard to this last exhortation, see also John Chrysostom, *Hom. XLVII* = PG 63, 898.

What is the meaning of this "Amen" pronounced by the person communing? This "Amen," says Ambrose, is the acknowledgment on the part of the faithful that what they receive is truly the body of Christ.[15] In other words, it is our confession of faith in the eucharistic Christ. However, Augustine understands it as our insertion into the body of Christ, which makes us become members of the body of Christ, which is the Church. In other words, according to Augustine, the Eucharist is what makes the Church.[16]

FROM THE MIDDLE AGES TO *MEDIATOR DEI*
Unfortunately, over the course of time this living and conscious participation of the faithful in the liturgy diminished even to its total disappearance. The faithful were participating ever less attentively in liturgical celebrations. They shifted from the role of active protagonists, as we have seen in the early Church, to that of totally silent and passive spectators in a solely clerical liturgy, such as the one being celebrated before Vatican II. Certainly many factors contributed to the emergence of this situation: political and sociocultural factors, theological currents and notions of every epoch, and so on. Before continuing on to the liturgical movement, a word on the Council of Trent is appropriate. Having as its chief purpose the overcoming of erroneous doctrines and the chaotic state of the liturgy of those times, the council set itself in the tendency of unity and control. As a consequence, it was unable to deal with the part regarding the participation of the faithful.

The liturgical movement of the nineteenth century, which prepared the ground for the liturgical reform of Vatican II, had as its objective the liturgical participation of the faithful. Some scholars maintain that the first decisive step of this movement had its start in France, at Solesmes, with Prosper Guéranger. Then, by his writings[17] and with the collaboration of his followers, the movement spread into every other country. After 1840 the concern emerged more and more for the

---

[15] Ambrose, *De sacramentis*, IV 25 = Botte, SCh 25 bis, 116: "Ergo non otiose dicis tu: Amen, iam in spiritu confitens quod accipias corpus Christi. Cum ergo tu petieris, dicit tibi sacerdos: CORPVS CHRISTI, et tu dicis: AMEN, hoc est, uerum. Quod confitetur lingua, teneat adfectus."

[16] Augustine, *Sermo CCLXXII* = PL 38, 1247. See also no. II of the Second Part.

[17] The two best-known works of Guéranger are the *Institutions liturgiques* and *L'Année liturgique*.

problem of the participation of the faithful in the liturgy. Here we shall see what are the most significant events of the last hundred years of this movement up to Vatican II. We open our discourse with the pontificate of Pope Leo XIII.

During the twenty-five years of the pontificate of Leo XIII (1878–1903), although the liturgical movement still had need to mature before it could produce ideas capable of influencing the Church's liturgical life, the study of sacred music developed. In this period, the liturgical movement was still only the work of individuals who also tried to involve Church authorities. They succeeded in this purpose when Pius X was elected (1903–1914).

With Pius X the movement finally became the work of the whole Church, which involved the supreme authority. The liturgical work of great importance by Pius X is distinguished above all by three documents: the motu proprio *Tra le sollecitudini* of 1903, the apostolic constitution *Divino afflatu* of 1911, and the motu proprio *Ab hinc duos annos* of 1913. Our interest lies especially with the first, *Tra le sollecitudini*, in order to document the problem of the participation of the People of God in the liturgy. By this intervention Pius X gave a decisive thrust to the liturgical movement. For the pope, the Church and worship are two fundamental means for the sanctification of the faithful. The liturgy for him is "active participation in the holy mysteries and in the public and solemn prayer of the Church"; as such, the liturgy is the "first and indispensable source" of Christian life.

Benedict XV (1914–1922) became pope in 1914, the year in which the First World War broke out. Despite that, he sought to advance the reformative work begun by his predecessors; he continued to insist on the necessity of active participation on the part of the faithful in liturgical celebrations. The process of the liturgical movement went on with ever more intense rhythm. From this period there is an amazing literary production for the study of the liturgy: diocesan bulletins, weekly and monthly periodicals, magazines, and many other works of great importance, for example, the *Liber Sacramentorum* of I. Schuster. Moreover, numerous courses, weeks, and congresses of liturgical studies were conducted open to everyone. The dialogue Mass spread especially among young people. In 1922 in St. Peter's a large group of young people participated in the Mass of Benedict XV, reciting the *Credo* and the *Pater Noster* along with him.

The Missal became more commonly used among the faithful and, little by little, replaced devotional books.

Benedict XV died in 1922, and Pius XI (1922–1939) succeeded him. During the years of his pontificate all ecclesiastical life was centered on the task for the reform of the liturgy. From 1922 onward numerous congresses and gatherings were held everywhere, and almost all had as their central theme liturgical participation at Mass on the part of the people.

From 1939, the year in which Pius XII was elected successor to Pius XI, until 1943, some pressing theological-liturgical problems that were awaiting responses by the new pontiff became research topics. The request was widely made for thoroughly studying and explaining the doctrine of the Mystical Body regarding the relations between liturgical piety and extraliturgical devotions or practices, regarding the necessity to introduce the common language in ritual celebrations, and so on. It was in this climate of expectation that the encyclical *Mediator Dei* (November 20, 1947) was issued, the most important document about the liturgy before Vatican II.

Above all, the encyclical describes the liturgy as the public worship of the whole body of Christ, head and members. This worship has as its special effect the sanctification of the faithful. It then speaks of the nature of active participation in the rites by virtue of the priesthood common to all believers. The principal contribution of this encyclical consists in having provided a clear explanation of the concept of liturgy. It is seen as "summit and source" *(culmen et fons)*. It is the summit because all of the Church's life, whether liturgical or extraliturgical, tends toward it; it is the source because all grace derives from it. Therefore the liturgy is the privileged place of the encounter between God and humans in Christ the Mediator. The liturgical reform under Pius XII especially stimulated the pastoral sector, which aimed at making the liturgy more intelligible at the level of the faithful.

Mediator Dei was followed by numerous other reforms desired by Pius XII, such as the use of local languages in liturgical functions, granted to several countries of Europe and Latin America; the permission to celebrate afternoon Masses under certain specific conditions; the mitigation of the laws concerning eucharistic fast; and the directives for a renewal of sacred music for the purpose of assuring a more active and conscious participation of the faithful in the liturgy, especially at Mass. As scholars note, after *Mediator Dei* the liturgy followed the definitive path of pastoral concerns, and the reforms that followed from 1951 to 1960 always aimed principally at this aspect.

THE TURN OF VATICAN II:
THE LITURGICAL CONSTITUTION

After Pius XII, John XXIII was elected pope. The new pontiff continued the task of reform and included liturgical reform in the program of the council. John XXIII thus sowed the seed for the birth of the most important liturgical document: the Constitution on the Sacred Liturgy (= SC). In the history of the liturgy the reform of Vatican II stands out from all other reforms by its pastoral character. The ultimate purpose of the council is the conscious participation and active insertion of the people of God in the worship life of the Church (SC 10–12, 19, 21, 30–31, 36, 38, 40, 54, 63, 78–79, 101, 104). If we define the liturgical reform of Vatican II as a *Vatican turn* because of its pastoral character, we believe that we are not far from the right path. Indeed, both during and after the council, the active participation of the faithful was always the dominant idea in the area of the liturgy and was studied always under the pastoral aspect. SC was solemnly promulgated by Pope Paul VI on December 4, 1963. Here we provide a summary of this document.

The Public, Social, Integral, and
Communitarian Character of the Liturgy
SC elaborated a whole series of articles to illustrate the public, social, integral, and communitarian character of the liturgy (SC 26–32). We quote an excerpt that clearly expresses this idea:

"Liturgical actions are not private actions, but are celebrations of the Church, which is the 'sacrament of unity,' that is, the holy people gathered and ordered under the leadership of the bishops. Therefore these actions belong to the whole Body of the Church, manifest it and point towards it; individual members are involved in different ways, according to the diversity of their states, their duties and their effective participation" (26).

Active Participation in the Liturgy on the Part of the Faithful
While it is true that the liturgy is the public worship of the Church, it is a worship collectively performed in the name of its totality. In order to be this, it requires the active participation of the faithful.

Aware of this fact, *SC* dwells several times on this theme both at the level of generic formulation and at the level of concrete application in the various parts of the liturgy (*SC* 11, 19, 21, 26–31, 48, 50, 114, 124). No. 14 shows "that it is the ardent desire of Mother Church that all the faithful should be formed in the full, conscious, active participation in liturgical celebrations, which is required by the very nature of the liturgy, and for which the Christian people, 'a chosen race, a royal priesthood, a holy nation, a redeemed people' (1 Pet 2:9; cf. 2:4-5), has the right and duty by the power of baptism." Special care for the liturgy, however, is necessary to make such participation possible. It is thus the duty of pastors to secure this fruitful participation of the faithful in liturgical actions (*SC* 11 and 19). *SC* insists further that the active participation of the faithful must be the principle that guides the reform of the Mass and the revision of its ritual ordering (*SC* 48 and 50), the revision of the sacraments (*SC* 79), the singing of the whole assembly in liturgical actions (*SC* 114), and the construction of sacred buildings (*SC* 124).

The Primacy of the Word of God in the Liturgy
Another point is the reaffirmation of the primacy of the Word of God in the liturgy (*SC* 24). This primacy is founded especially on the didactic character of the Word of God (*SC* 33). Therefore *SC* requires that this close tie between the liturgy and the Word of God be evident (*SC* 35). Finally, the document insists that in the celebration of the Word of God, it be prepared for the faithful with greater abundance: that within a set number of years the greater part of sacred Scripture be read to the people (*SC* 35 and 51). The homily is highly recommended, which is a part of the liturgical action in Sunday Masses and on feast days with the participation of the faithful (*SC* 52).

Use of the Vernacular
The other new feature of *SC* is the use of the vernacular. Among the questions of liturgical reform, that of language has always been considered the most important. Indeed, it plays an absolute role in assuring the active participation of the faithful in the liturgy. Besides giving a basic guideline for the use of the vernacular in ritual celebrations (*SC* 36), *SC* provides other "fixed norms" to regulate individual cases.[18]

[18] No. 54 for the Mass; no. 63 for the sacraments in general; no. 101 for the Divine Office.

Adaptation and the Liturgy

If the liturgy is truly the worship of the People of God, there should be nothing in it that hampers the active participation of believers who stem from different cultures. Therefore *SC* affirms that in the liturgy, while preserving the substantial unity of the Roman Rite, allowance should be made for legitimate diversity and legitimate adaptations for various ethnic groups, regions, and peoples, especially in the missions (*SC* 37).[19]

Thus, with Vatican II the long process of restoring the liturgy to the people was finished. After many centuries the faithful have returned to being active protagonists of the Church's liturgical life.

II. THEOLOGICAL READING

After this historical overview, we move on to another problem of no less importance, the theological foundation of the liturgical participation of the faithful. Beyond what is emphasized by *SC*, is it possible to delineate more specifically the reasons for which the faithful should participate in the liturgy? Based on what can be gleaned from the patristic writings that we have examined, it seems that the main reasons are the following:

THE FAITHFUL ARE CHILDREN OF GOD AND CHILDREN OF MOTHER CHURCH

Why should the faithful participate in the liturgy of the Church, especially in the eucharistic liturgy? To this question, a classic one in theological-liturgical reflection, we respond with some texts of Augustine, Chromatius, and Leo the Great. In his *Sermo LVI* Augustine, with very suggestive and impressive images, explains to the candidates for baptism the deep relationship that binds them by baptism to God and to the Church. He describes their birth into the life of the children of God in terms of physical and biological birth, which happens every day in human society: before being born, they were conceived with the seed of God the Father and thereafter must be given birth in the baptismal font, which is nothing else but the womb of the Church. Briefly, we state that according to Augustine's understanding, the

[19] The fundamental norms of adaptation are found in nos. 37–40. Also useful are nos. 4, 21, 23, and 34 as related norms. Other principles that deal with the various specific arguments: no. 65 for baptism; no. 77 for marriage; no. 81 for funerals; no. 119 for sacred music, and no. 123 for art.

bond that unites the faithful to God and to the Church is a bond of relationship, similar to the biological bond that unites parents to their natural children.[20]

A similar idea can be traced as well in the sermons of Chromatius of Aquileia. Chromatius states that the faithful are called children of God the Father because each of them is conceived as a fetus of justice (*foetus iustitiae*) and given birth by the Church their mother as the fruit of salvation. Chromatius explains that before the coming of Christ the Church was sterile because she had not received the seed of justice; after the coming of Christ she then received the seed of the divine Word by which she became fruitful and fertile and was able to conceive and give birth every day to numerous children of God throughout the world.[21] This whole process happens when we come to the faith. It is to be noted that while according to Augustine, the faithful are conceived with *the seed of God the Father*, Chromatius uses instead two different terms: *the seed of justice and the seed of the divine Word.*

Also interesting are some homilies of St. Leo the Great. In his Fourth Homily for the feast of the Nativity Leo compares the baptismal font to the virginal womb of Mary, because, he says, the same Holy Spirit who overshadowed the Virgin has filled this font. As a consequence the sin that was taken away at the holy conception is here in this font cancelled by the mystical ablution.[22] This perspective of generational and biological relationship points to the participation of the faithful in the Church's liturgical life as a dutiful act of the faithful toward God their Father.

The question now arises: is it possible to trace the theological approach, from which this consistent thread of thought derives, in the Fathers who speak of biological link between God and the faithful? It seems that an answer radiates from a homily of Leo the Great, the Fifth Homily, which the saint delivered on the occasion of the feast of the Nativity. The text follows.[23]

---

[20] Augustine, *Sermo LVI*, 5 = Verbraken, RBén 68, 28, 70 — 29, 73.

[21] Chromatius of Aquileia, *Sermo XXXIII*, 4 = Étaix-Lemarié, CCL IXA, 153, 101–222; see also *Serm. XVIII*, 3 = Étaix-Lemarié, CCL IXA, 84, 64–7.

[22] Leo the Great, *In nativitate Domini Serm. IV*, 3 = Dolle, SCh 22 bis, 114.

[23] Leo the Great, *In nativitate Domini Serm. V*, 5 = Dolle, SCh 22 bis, 132: "Factus est homo nostri generis, ut nos divinae naturae possimus esse consortes. Originem quam sumpsit in utero Virginis, posuit in fonte baptismatis; dedit aquae,

"He became a man of our race so that we might be sharers in the divine nature. He has placed the origin that he took in the womb of the Virgin into the baptismal font; he gave to the water what he gave to his mother; for the power of the Most High and the overshadowing of the Holy Spirit, which enabled Mary to bear the Savior, also enables the water to regenerate the believer."

The explanation by St. Leo is valuable because it brings into open light the close connection between the womb of the Virgin, from which Christ was born, and the baptismal font, the womb of the Church, from which the faithful are born. The pope explains that Christ has become one of our kind so that we might be sharers of the divine nature. He has placed in the baptismal font the origin of the life that he took on in the womb of the Virgin; thus he has given to the water what he has given to his mother, namely, the power of the Most High and the overshadowing of the Holy Spirit that enabled Mary to give birth to the Savior; this power does the same to regenerate the believer in the water.

THE EUCHARIST MAKES THE CHURCH

On this theme, chapter 18 of *De dominica oratione* by Cyprian is important. He explains the meaning of the petition, "Give us this day our daily bread," stating that Christ is indeed the bread of life and that this bread is ours, but not everybody's. We call Christ our bread because he is the bread of those who join his body. For this reason we ask that every day we be given *our bread*, namely Christ, because by remaining and living in him we do not separate ourselves from his sanctification and his body.[24]

Both on the existential-vital level and on the theological-historical level, the body of Christ is the Church.[25] Thus the faithful, by participating in the eucharistic celebration and by receiving the Body of Christ, join at the same time with the Church, the Mystical Body of Christ, and constitute its fullness. In other words, according to Cyprian the

---

quod dedit matri; virtus enim Altissimi et obumbratio Spiritus sancti, quae fecit ut Maria pareret Salvatorem, eadem facit ut regeneret unda credentem."

[24] Cyprian, *De dominica oratione*, 18 = Moreschini, CCL IIIA/2, 101, 331–5.

[25] Very significant is Acts 9:1-6, the famous text of Paul's journey to Damascus, in which Christ identifies himself with the Christians, namely the nascent Church, whom Paul is persecuting.

Eucharist makes the Church. Therefore we comprehend the importance of the participation of the faithful in the eucharistic celebration.

THE WORD OF GOD AND THE EUCHARIST ARE THE FOOD NEEDED BY THE FAITHFUL

As a pastor responsible for the formation of the new members of his community, St. Augustine strives to make understood to the candidates for baptism that they, once they are regenerated into the life of the children of God through the washing, have need of a special food that comprises two things: the Word of God and the Body of Christ.

It is necessary for the faithful to participate in liturgical celebrations because they need a special bread: the Word of God that is read during these functions. It is a daily bread, says St. Augustine, which only the children ask for. It is the bread which does not feed the belly but the mind.[26] Augustine goes on to say that not only the readings that the faithful listen to every day in the churches is daily bread, but also the sermons and the hymns that they listen to and sing are for them daily bread, because these are necessary for their earthly pilgrimage.[27]

From this perspective one understands why, according to St. Leo the Great, preaching is a duty for the one who has that office, since it helps in edifying the faithful, and it would be a mistake to think that there is no need to repeat anew things already explained.[28]

Similarly, the Body of Christ is food. It is the Eucharist. There is a twofold reason for the faithful having need of this food, as Tertullian points out: to live eternally in Christ and to have our personhood from his very Body.[29]

On this point, *Sermo XXXII* of Chromatius of Aquileia, given on the feast of the Nativity, is of interest.[30] With very attractive and figurative language, Chromatius explains to the assembly that Christ

[26] Augustine, *Sermo LVI,* 10 = Verbraken, *RBén* 68, 32, 170–2; ibid., *Serm. 59, 6* = Poque, SCh 116, 192, 76–8.

[27] Idem., *Serm. LVII,* 7 = PL 38, 389–90.

[28] Leo the Great, *In nativitate Domini Serm. V,* 1 = Dolle, SCh 22 bis, 122.

[29] Tertullian, *De oratione VI,* 2 = Diercks, CCL I, 261, 11–2. Cf. also Cyprian, *De dominica oratione,* 18 = Moreschini, CCL IIIA/2, 102, 345–7; Augustine, *Serm. LVI,* 10 = Verbraken, *RBén* 68, 32, 177–80; ibid., *Serm. LVIII,* 5 = Verbraken, *EO* (1984/1), 123, 80–7; ibid., *Serm. 59, 6* = Poque, SCh 116, 192, 68–75; etc.

[30] Cf. Chromatius of Aquileia, *Sermo XXXII,* 3 = Étaix-Lemarié, CCL IXA, 145, 65–72.

is born because he wants to become our bread, bread for our salvation.

According to Chromatius, the fact that Christ was placed in the manger after his birth is a message in which he reveals to us that he will become the bread of the faithful. Indeed, the manger is the place where animals come to get their food. Since we are rational animals, we too also need a manger that we can approach to get our food. Our manger is the altar of Christ, which we approach every day to gain the food of salvation from the Body of Christ.

THE MYSTERY OF OUR SALVATION IS RENEWED IN THE RECURRENT ANNUAL CYCLE

The God of Christianity is not a dead God but rather a living God who can be heard and touched by people of every time. This God is born for humans because he wants to be in them in order to save them, by causing them to enter into the paschal mystery that God had designed. This is the fundamental revelation that the sacred Scriptures offer us. This God whom the human must encounter is found especially by the participation of each believer in the liturgical life. Believers, as individuals and as community, every time they participate in the liturgical celebrations encounter God and renew the mystery of their own salvation promised to them by God. The mystery of our salvation, as St. Leo says, promised at the beginning of the world and achieved at the established time, lasts without end and is renewed for us in the recurrent annual cycle.[31] From the reading of these texts we learn the truly vital requirement of the participation of the faithful in the liturgy of the Church.

CONCLUSION

In reviewing the liturgical history of these twenty centuries, no one can deny that the participation in the liturgy pertains not only to the ministers who celebrate the rite but also involves every baptized individual. Ever since antiquity the participation in the liturgy is considered by the Fathers not just as a manifestation of the personal adherence of each believer to God and to the Church but above all as an indispensable food for their own existence as children of God. In other words, the deep theology of the liturgical participation of the faithful is that of attaining the secure pledge of one's salvation. The

[31] Leo the Great, *In nativitate Domini Serm. II*, 1 = Dolle, SCh 22 bis. 74–6.

grace of God is communicated to humans in a special manner in the sacraments and in other liturgical celebrations. And it is through the active participation of the faithful in these that they become sharers in the paschal mystery. This liturgical participation of the faithful risked disappearing completely were it not for the liturgical movement of the nineteenth century and, above all, for the turn of Vatican II. Today, thirty years after the liturgical reform of Vatican II, we ask ourselves how we have experienced this reform and what are the problems that emerge.

First of all, it seems that the affirmation of the necessity and importance of the liturgical participation of the faithful as explained by Vatican II, unfortunately, is not always understood correctly. In some countries the liturgy has lost its nature of the worship of the Church, in which not only each of its parts has a specific significance, but also each of the participants, ministers and faithful, has his or her very precise function and role. Today, based on a poor interpretation of the proposal of Vatican II to foster the participation of the faithful, in many churches the mode of performing the various parts of the liturgy is easily changed without studying matters well in depth. People are given roles and parts of liturgical celebrations that do not belong to them.

In order to promote the liturgical participation of the faithful, two things are especially necessary: a serious liturgical formation of priests and a solid liturgical catechesis of the faithful.

The priests are the ones who must organize and normally preside over liturgical celebrations; it is also their task to instruct the faithful, by which they should be adequately trained and brought up to date in a timely fashion. They should have good awareness of the meanings and the nature of the sacraments, especially the eucharistic celebration, and also the other ritual functions. Only in this way can they avoid errors of this kind.

With regard to the faithful, a liturgical catechesis is required. The objective of this catechesis is to enable the faithful to understand that their participation in ritual celebrations is not just something optional. It is in the faith in the triune God that every believer finds the ultimate meaning of his or her own existence. And this faith is the grace of God offered and received in the liturgical celebration of the Church, the Mystical Body of Christ. To reach this goal, the faithful must be suitably instructed. Here arises the problem of the method to be used in this catechesis: we have found it in these catechetical-liturgical writings of the Fathers. It is a method that has the liturgy not only as its departure point and arrival point but is always situated in the liturgical context. We can say without hesitation that in these patristic-liturgical writings the main lines are contained for the path of maturation of the liturgical life of every believer in the Church.

Bibliography

AA.VV. *Assisi 1956–1986: Il movimento liturgico tra riforma conciliare e attese del popolo di Dio.* Assisi, 1987.

AA.VV. *La Costituzione sulla sacra liturgia.* Turin, 1967.

Bugnini, A. *Documenta pontificia ad instaurationem liturgicam spectantia (1903–1953).* Parts 1–2. Rome, 1962.

____. *The Reform of the Liturgy (1948–1975).* Collegeville, Minn., 1990.

____. "Restaurare la linea 'autentica' del Concilio?" *Not* 10 (1974) 217–21.

Chedozeau, B. "Le missel des fidèles et la participation à la messe." *MD* 191 (1992) 69–82.

Hameline, J.-Y. "Les 'origines du culte chrétien' et le mouvement liturgique." *MD* 181 (1990) 51–97.

Haquin, A. "Histoire de la liturgie et renouveau liturgique." *MD* 181 (1990) 99–118.

Neunheuser, B. "Movimento liturgico." *NDL* 904–18.

Rousseau, O. *Storia del movimento liturgico: Lineamenti storici dagli inizi del sec. fino ad oggi.* Rome, 1961.

Thomas A. Krosnicki, S.V.D.

9

Liturgical Ministries

The theological foundation for Christian liturgical ministry is found in christology and ecclesiology.[1] In the divine economy of salvation the paschal mystery of Christ, the salvific death and resurrection of the Savior, was to be made present and effective in the world beyond Christ's ascension, until the end of time. This is possible insofar as Jesus willed that the objective mystery of redemption be made present within his community of believers, the Church. Obviously that redemptive, operative presence was not to be extended by the continued visible presence of Christ, the incarnate Word, in a physical manner but in a sacramental mode by which the function of the Christ-event (i.e., the glorification of God and the salvific redemption of creation) is extended in the Church, the body of Christ, through Word and sacrament. As stated by Ignatius of Antioch, "In Christ the perfect achievement of our reconciliation came forth and the fullness of divine worship was given to us."[2] The Constitution on the Sacred Liturgy underscores the christological and ecclesial dimensions of the liturgy when it states, "Christ, indeed, always associates the Church with himself in this great work in which God is perfectly glorified and persons are sanctified" (no. 7).

Although it is in the liturgy of the Church that the once-for-all salvific mystery of Christ is actualized in a given time and space, it

---

[1] For two classical texts that address indirectly the christological and ecclesiological foundations of liturgical ministry, see E. Schillebeeckx, *Christ, the Sacrament of Encounter with God* (New York, 1963), and A. Dulles, *Models of the Church* (New York, 1974).

[2] *Ad Ephesios,* 7:2.

must be noted that this presence of Christ, presence-in-mystery, is not a reenactment of the salvific event with all of its historical ramifications. Rather, the presence of Christ's passion, death, and resurrection is rendered present and effective in a supraspatial, supratemporal, sacramental manner.[3]

Ministers in liturgical celebration, in the widest sense, are all who gather united in faith to celebrate the saving mystery of Christ by actively participating in the liturgical event. Thus all the members of the celebrating assembly by their very presence exercise a ministerial function within the liturgical act. It is precisely through the sacraments of initiation that the members of the assembly have been anointed into the priesthood of all the baptized. This common priesthood gives the faithful both the right and the responsibility of active participation in the liturgy.

But as is evident in Scripture (see Rom 12:4) and from the tradition of the Church, all initiated members do not have the same role or exercise the same ministry within the Church. This is evident in a clear and particular way within the actual celebration of the Church's liturgy. The Constitution on the Sacred Liturgy of Vatican II affirms this explicitly: "In liturgical celebrations each person, minister, or layperson, who has an office to perform, should carry out all and only those parts which pertain to one's office by the nature of the rite and the norms of the liturgy" (no. 28). In brief, it is clear that within the liturgy there are a variety of ministries to be exercised in an ordered fashion for the good of the worshiping assembly.

ORDAINED LITURGICAL MINISTERS
In the proper ordering of liturgical ministries, the first to be considered are those ministries that have been divinely instituted, conferred, and recognized by the sacrament of ordination given to certain members of the faith community.[4] Since apostolic times bishops, presbyters, and deacons have been ordained with the laying-on of hands within and for the well-being of the community of the faithful (see Acts 6:6;

[3] See "The Sacramental Plan of Salvation," J. P. Schanz, *Introduction to the Sacraments* (New York, 1983) 25–39, which follows the tradition of Odo Casel in *The Mystery of Christian Worship* (Westminster, Md., 1962).

[4] The emphasis on historical continuity in the ordained ministry is outlined by F. Hawkins, "Orders and Ordination in the New Testament," *The Shape of the Liturgy*, ed. C. Jones and others (New York, 1978) 290–7.

13:3; 2 Tim 1:6). Tradition notes that during the second century the threefold orders of the episcopacy, the presbyterate, and the diaconate had already achieved universal recognition and import for the Church. Furthermore, each of these ordained offices has its own proper liturgical ministerial dimension.

By episcopal ordination, a bishop becomes the principal liturgist within the local church. It is the bishop who promotes the liturgy; the liturgical life of the diocese centers around the bishop in terms of both leadership and presidency. As the Constitution on the Sacred Liturgy states:

"The bishop is to be considered as the High Priest of his flock from whom the life in Christ of his faithful is in some way derived and upon whom it some way depends. Therefore all should hold in the greatest esteem the liturgical life of the diocese centered around the bishop, especially in his cathedral church. They must be convinced that the principal manifestation of the Church consists in the full, active participation of all God's holy people in the same liturgical celebrations, especially the Eucharist, in one prayer, at one altar, at which the bishop presides, surrounded by his college of presbyters and by his ministers" (no. 41).

The central and primary liturgical ministry of the episcopacy has been codified in the 1984 *Ceremonial for Bishops,* which serves as the normative guide for the liturgical ministry of bishops within the Church.

As it is impossible for any bishop as principal liturgist to be present to his entire diocesan community at the same time, for sacramental as well as administrative reasons his presence is manifest in the local parish by the ministerial leadership of an ordained presbyter (see *SC* 42). The need and the right of the faith community to access to the presence of Christ in the sacraments necessitate this extension of the episcopal service by means of the New Testament priesthood. Among the complex and multiple services of a presbyter, liturgical leadership holds a primary place. In the rite of ordination each *ordinandus* is questioned: "Are you resolved to celebrate the mysteries of Christ faithfully and religiously as the Church has handed them down to us, for the glory of God and the sanctification of Christ's people?" (*Ordination of a Priest,* no. 15). This significant and central ministry of the presbyterate places a grave responsibility upon each presbyter in terms of liturgical availability as well as professional competency. At the same time, presbyters recognize the primary role of the bishops in the liturgy, for, as stated by Vatican II, the bishops "are the principal dispensers of the mysteries of God, and it is their function to control, promote and protect the entire liturgical life of the Church entrusted to them" (*Christus Dominus*, no. 15). Ordination confers on a presbyter a broad liturgical, sacramental ministry within the local church, always exercised in relation to that of the local bishop.[5]

The third order of ordained liturgical ministers within the Church is that of the diaconate. Like the episcopacy and the presbyterate, the diaconate has a liturgical dimension, albeit subordinate to the broader diaconal ministry of service, that is to be manifest within the local community at prayer and exercised in union with the bishop and his priests. In terms of liturgical ministry, the deacon assists the bishop and presbyters in liturgical celebrations, especially the Eucharist, but he is also directed to proclaim the Gospel, preach and baptize, bless marriages, and preside at funerals. The reintroduction of the permanent diaconate in modern times has provided a large and stable group of liturgical ministers in the contemporary Church with its own criteria of selection, program of formation, and guidelines for proper service within the community, including that within the liturgy.

INSTITUTED LITURGICAL MINISTRIES
In 1972 Pope Paul VI reformed the ministries within the Church and opened them to laypeople.[6] The ancient practice of tonsure was dropped with the directive that henceforth entrance into the clerical state was joined with the diaconate, not the tonsure. More significant, however, was the declaration that the ministerial role of the subdeacon, prior to Vatican II a major order leading toward the diaconate and presbyterate, was also suppressed. However, the service of that former major order was to be entrusted to the ministries of reader and acolyte, two of the former minor orders (along with doorkeeper and exorcist) that served as steps leading to priestly ordination within the Church.

---

[5] The relationship between priest and bishop is treated at length in the work of R. Brown, *Priest and Bishop, Biblical Reflections* (London, 1971).

[6] See A. Bugnini, *The Reform of the Liturgy 1948–1975* (Collegeville, 1990) 727–62. Bugnini offers a history of the Vatican revision of orders after Vatican II, beginning with the Consilium revisions.

The formally recognized ministries of reader and acolyte, no longer to be associated with grades toward priesthood or limited exclusively to presbyteral candidates, would be conferred on the candidate not by ordination but by an approved liturgical rite of institution. Hence the term "instituted" reader and acolyte. According to present Church discipline, only men can be formally instituted as lay readers and acolytes. At the same time, all candidates for the diaconate and presbyterate must be instituted as reader and acolyte and exercise these ministries in liturgical assemblies in a competent manner prior to ordination to the diaconate.

In the 1972 apostolic letter *Ministeria quaedam*, by which the discipline of the orders in the Church were reformed, Pope Paul VI outlined the liturgical ministry of the instituted reader:

"The reader is appointed for a function proper to him, that of reading the word of God in the liturgical assembly. Accordingly, he is to read the lessons from sacred Scripture, except the Gospel, in the Mass and other sacred celebrations; he is to recite the psalm between the readings where there is no psalmist; he is to present the intentions of the general intercessions in the absence of a deacon or cantor; he is to direct the singing and the participation of the faithful; he is to instruct the faithful for the worthy reception of the sacraments. He may also, insofar as necessary, take care of preparing other faithful who by a temporary appointment are to read the Scriptures in liturgical celebrations. That he may more fittingly and perfectly fulfill these functions, let him meditate assiduously on sacred Scripture" (no. 5).

It is significant to note that the ministry of the instituted reader is operative within the formal liturgical settings and outside of it as well.

The instituted acolyte assists the deacon and the presbyter within the liturgy, according to the approved rites. "It is therefore his duty to attend to the service of the altar and to assist the deacon and the presbyter in liturgical celebrations, especially in the celebration of Mass" (*Ministeria quaedam*, no. 6). When the ordinary minister of Communion is not present or hindered by ill health, age, or another pastoral ministry, or when the number of communicants is so great that the celebration would be unduly prolonged, the instituted acolyte may distribute Holy Communion. He is not, however, to replace the ordinary ministers of Communion, presbyters and deacons, who might be present and able to exercise their proper ministry.

It should be noted that the category of instituted lay liturgical ministries is theoretically not limited to that of reader and acolyte. *Ministeria quaedam* permits conferences of bishops to request from the Holy See the formal installation of other ministries, liturgical or otherwise, not associated with holy orders, if there is a pastoral necessity or usefulness.[7]

This option has not been acted upon, although in principle there is the possibility of a host of possible instituted liturgical ministries open to men and women within the Church today. In some places this avenue has not been pursued because according to present norms, the instituted ministries of reader and acolyte would still remain limited to men. For this same reason there has not been great interest on the part of some local churches to formally institute men as readers and acolytes. Limiting these instituted ministries to men appears to be too discriminatory. In other places there is no felt need to request additional instituted liturgical ministries as it is evident that the appropriate ministries are being fulfilled without formal installation by both men and women for the pastoral good of the worshiping community.

DEPUTIZED LITURGICAL MINISTRIES

In addition to instituted ministries there is a second category of liturgical ministries that falls under the title of "deputized" ministries. Pope Paul VI in the instruction *Immensae caritatis* (1973) permitted the authorization of special ministers to give Communion to themselves and others of the faithful under specified conditions, having been so deputized by the local ordinary or one so delegated by him. After careful selection and preparation, these Communion ministers are to be formally commissioned for a limited time period according to the approved liturgical rite of the Church.[8]

[7] In 1984 at the gathering of national liturgical commissions, one of the areas addressed was the role of the laity in the liturgy. A synthesis of the interventions has not been made but would prove historically interesting. See Congregazione per il Culto Divino, *Convegno Commissioni Nazionali di Liturgia, 1984* (Rome, 1986) in light of subsequent developments.

[8] The historical, pastoral, and theological significance of the Communion minister has been treated by N. Mitchell, "Special Ministers of Communion," *Cult and Controversy: The Worship of the Eucharist Outside of Mass* (New York, 1982) 268–309. See also Bishops' Committee on the Liturgy (USA), *Study Text 1, Holy Communion* (Washington, D.C., 1973).

The liturgical function of the special minister of Communion is to assist in the distribution of Communion within the Eucharist and to bring Communion to those who are sick, shut-in, or dying when they cannot be a part of the ordinary gathering of the community of faith, especially that of the eucharistic assembly on the Lord's Day. Thus the liturgical ministry of the special minister goes beyond that of the formal liturgical celebration; in a sense it continues it and makes it present to those who, through no fault of their own, cannot be present at the eucharistic gathering.

Furthermore, when there is a genuine pastoral need, a person may be authorized to distribute Communion at Mass on a single occasion *(ad hoc)* without any previous deputation. After the "Lamb of God" the presbyter deputizes the person to fulfill this *ad hoc* ministry, using the Church's approved rite of deputation included in some sacramentaries.

In addition to providing exposition of the Blessed Sacrament, when there is true pastoral need (without giving the final blessing), the special minister of Communion, if properly prepared, may also lead the assembly in the absence of a presbyter in a Communion service. In such cases (e.g., Sunday assemblies without a priest) the minister must observe the approved rite for the distribution of Communion outside of Mass and follow the liturgical directives of both the universal and local Church. Such Communion services, however, are always to be viewed in relation to the celebration of the Eucharist by a presbyter or bishop, from which they draw their proper significance. Again, present Church norms regulate that the special minister of Communion is not to supplant the service of an ordinary minister of the Eucharist (bishop, presbyter, deacon), or even an instituted acolyte, when they are present and capable of fulfilling their ministry within the liturgical act.

RECOGNIZED LITURGICAL MINISTRIES

In place of the present instituted liturgical ministries of reader and acolyte and any additional instituted ministries that might have been recognized formally by institution or deputation, in most local churches men and women are invited to minister in a host of liturgical roles. At most, what is involved is an "informal recognition" that the person is qualified and worthy to fulfill the ministry in a manner appropriate to the sacredness of the act and the needs of the community of the faithful.

Thus men, women, and in certain circumstances children minister as readers during the Liturgy of the Word in both sacramental and non-sacramental liturgical settings. For the most part this implies no formal deputation but rather informal recognition and/or invitation, explicit or implicit, by the local pastor. As a matter of fact, these persons generally undertake the function of the so-called instituted reader without any formal rite of recognition.

In 1992 the Congregation for Divine Worship and the Discipline of the Sacraments promulgated the decision of the Pontifical Council for the Interpretation of Legislative Texts, confirmed by John Paul II, that local Ordinaries could permit, depending on circumstances (e.g., cultural considerations), the ministry of acolyte, in the limited sense of altar server, to be fulfilled by women. This clarification of Canon 202.2 formally approved this liturgical ministry for all members of the faithful regardless of gender. Again, no formal ritual act of institution or deputation is required; this ministry falls within the category of recognized liturgical ministries. At the same time, authorization to serve at the altar does not permit the individual to perform all of the responsibilities of the instituted acolyte (e.g., the right to distribute Communion). The role of the altar server, in some places referred to as "acolyte," is limited and quite distinct from that of the minister properly referred to as an instituted acolyte.

A number of new ministries within the liturgy have emerged with the post-Vatican II liturgical reform, in particular, the introduction of the vernacular liturgy in the revised liturgical rites of the Church. Here we will consider only the more obvious ones: the ministries of music, commentator, hospitality, and environment.

The call for greater participation by all of the faithful in the liturgical action necessitated the introduction of music ministries, which include among others the ministry of the psalmist, the cantor, the leader of song, the organist and other musicians, and the choir to support the community in its own proper and active role in worship. All of these ministries remain recognized as important within the full liturgical context but without any necessary formal institution or deputation. Each ministry, nevertheless, requires its own preparation and set of competencies.[9]

[9] See E. McKenna, "Music Ministries" *The New Dictionary of Sacramental Worship*, ed. P. E. Fink (Collegeville, 1990) 852–4. Bishops' Committee on the Liturgy

The General Instruction of the Roman Missal acknowledges the value of the ministry of liturgical commentator: "This minister provides explanations and commentaries with the purpose of introducing the faithful to the celebration and preparing them to understand it" (no. 68a). In fulfilling this ministry the commentator is, in fact, attending to one of the roles of the deacon within worship. With the growing familiarity with the ordinary liturgical rites, the function of commentator has diminished in importance. Indeed, a certain pastoral caution must be taken when the commentator is present at the liturgy lest his or her remarks appear to be too obvious and therefore unnecessary, even patronizing, or too didactic and thereby intrusive, given the level of understanding on the part of the assembly and the natural rhythm of the liturgical action.

In some churches the ancient order of porter has been transformed and reintroduced as the ministry of hospitality (i.e., usher). To welcome the faithful, especially new members or visitors, is the primary function of this ministry. But it is also within the scope of the ministry to oversee the good order of the assembly (e.g., processions, collection, Communion) and, depending on circumstances, even to exclude those who have, for serious reasons, been banned from the liturgical gathering (e.g., the excommunicated).

Ever more aware of the need for proper environment to facilitate the prayer of the assembly, the ministry of environment has been introduced in some places to both recognize the important contribution of this dimension of prayer and to acknowledge the service rendered by persons within this area of pastoral concern. This ministry might be exercised by the one who traditionally has been referred to as sacristan, although the scope of work is considerably broader and the person who attends to it should possess a certain artistic talent and training to fulfill it properly, alone or in consort with other members of the local community.[10]

FORMATION OF LITURGICAL MINISTERS
The Constitution on the Sacred Liturgy has made several important points that pertain to a consideration of all the liturgical ministers in

(USA), *Music in Catholic Worship,* (Washington, D.C., 1982 ed.) offers pastoral directives for the minister of music.

[10] Various national conferences of bishops have published guidelines for those engaged in the ministry of environment. See Bishops' Committee on the Liturgy (USA), *Environment and Art in Catholic Worship* (Washington, D.C., 1978).

the Church. (1) The nature of the liturgy itself underscores the fact that "liturgical services are not private functions but are celebrations of the Church which is 'the sacrament of unity,' namely, 'the holy people united and arranged under their bishops'" (no. 26). (2) There exists a variety of ministries within the liturgical act so that "each person, minister, or layman who has an office to perform, should carry out all and only those parts which pertain to that office by the nature of the rite and the norms of the liturgy" (no. 28). (3) All ministers, in the exercise of their genuine liturgical ministry, "ought, therefore, to discharge their offices with the sincere piety and decorum demanded by so exalted a ministry and rightly expected of them by God's people." (4) To fulfill a ministry, all must "be deeply imbued with the spirit of the liturgy, in the measure proper to each one and they must be trained to perform their functions in a correct and orderly manner" (no. 29).

It is clear, therefore, that good will alone on the part of a person is not an adequate criterion for the selection of either lay or ordained liturgical ministers. Natural aptitudes and proper formation along with a quality of Christian life consonant with ecclesial ministry are demands and expectations on the part of the Church for all who aspire to or are already engaged in liturgical ministry.

The proper formation of all liturgical ministers cannot be overstressed. Not only is it a matter of learning about the liturgy, but one must know the function of one's particular ministry in terms of both its limits and its demands. Each minister must also come to know how to handle the particular "tools" of the ministry with a degree of style and presence that enhances the liturgical act. Presbyters are to familiarize themselves with the rituals, just as deacons need to grow in their understanding and love for the book of the Gospels. Readers are to be trained in the basics of public reading as they work with the sacred texts included in the Lectionary. The musicians are told not to neglect the Psalter as they select the corpus and assemble the collection of liturgical music for the local Church. And special ministers of Communion need to be sensitized to the sacredness of their activity, for example, in bringing Communion to the sick and elderly.

PURPOSE OF LITURGICAL MINISTRIES
Although the liturgy, which reflects the nature of the Church, is hierarchically structured, this does not mean that it is by its nature cleri-

170

cal, that is, that those in orders (bishop, presbyter, deacon) celebrate the liturgy in a manner that is exclusive or oblivious of the legitimate active role of the baptized laity within it. Rather, given the nature of the assembly, the body of Christ, its inherent richness, and the participatory nature of liturgy, a variety of ministries are to be present and working in supportive harmony for the sake of the fruitfulness of the liturgical action.

This variety of ministers reflects the nature and richness of the Church itself with its diversity of gifts. It is true that there is a distinction of ministries within any given liturgical action, but this should not be interpreted as a source of divisiveness or competition; rather, it should be recognized as a true richness present within the gathered assembly. There is, furthermore, an ecclesial unity in ministerial diversity when all accept the obvious ministerial differences within the community and do not interpret this diversity in terms of ecclesial or social inequality. Liturgical ministries are different, but each — ordained, deputed, or recognized — has its significant function within the assembly gathered in liturgical prayer.

All who minister within the liturgy are ultimately servants of the members of the community with whom they gather, although their designated functions need to differ considerably. The common end or purpose of all ministerial activity is to facilitate the community's worship of God and the sanctification of God's people.

Bibliography

Henderson, J. F. "Lay Ministry, Liturgical." In *The New Dictionary of Sacramental Worship*, ed. P. Fink, 670–73. Collegeville, Minn., 1990.

Lodi, E. "Ministero/Ministeri." *NDL* 838–55.

Martimort, A.-G. "The Assembly." *The Church at Prayer*. Vol. 1, *Principles of the Liturgy*, 89–111. Collegeville, Minn., 1987.

Part III

Liturgy and the Human Sciences

10

The Psychosociological Aspect of the Liturgy

An indispensable condition for a human group to be able above all to survive and then to attain its own full identity is that it be able to live a faith and thus induce it in others. By the term "faith" is understood here a psychological process by which a person or a community places unreserved trust in some ideals judged to be absolute. To do this, the person or community must be in a position to recall a meaningful story constituted by the series of events through which the ideals emerged and the corresponding values were imposed. Indeed, a community that loses the ideal horizons or that does not have in its history sufficient vital references begins a decline that finishes inevitably in self-destruction. Therefore, there is no society that does not realize the urgency of transmitting its own ideals to the following generations and that does not put in motion processes of socialization through which it communicates the reasons of life and the values that emerge from its own tradition. Since the realities that nourish the evolution of a community and contribute to the formation and the development of the personal structure of its members are so rich and complex that they cannot be expressed or grasped or communicated with adequate gestures, the process of socialization uses symbolic language, which allows for different and richer levels of communication. When faith has God as its object, the complex of its iconic, verbal, and ritual symbologies constitutes a religion. Religion represents a specific ambit that allows the human individual as well as the group to experience in an adequate context the need of meaning and even more the need of transcendence that characterizes the human person at the species-specific level. In the case of Christianity the reference is not directed toward a transcendence understood in a generic and not even an absolute way but toward a specific modality of God's self-manifestation through the incarnation, namely in Jesus Christ, who therefore comes to constitute the founding reference of Christian religious experience. Indeed, it is from the life of Jesus and from the tradition arisen around and after him that the ecclesial community draws its own spiritual horizon and lifeblood. On these premises, the Catholic liturgy[1] is considered as a complex process by which the ecclesial community constantly calls to mind the salvific experiences contained in the revelation,[2] in view of salvation, namely, of the full self-realization in Christ of its members and of its historical continuity through successive generations.

BASIC ASSUMPTIONS

To facilitate an interdisciplinary reading of this article, it helps to explain the psychological and theological models to which we refer.

Psychology. The present work is based on dynamic psychology, which focuses on the motivational and symbolical aspects of experience, whether conscious or unconscious, of the personality, making use in particular of the theory of C. G. Jung, because we believe that it is the most functional for the understanding of religious experience.[3]

Theology. In this context the interpretive model of God's action in history is fundamental. The model chosen here is the one that sets as a hermeneutic principle the law of the incarnation and the autonomy of the creaturely and divine spheres. In this theological perspective the formula has been attained of a *dynamic* vision of reality, linked on the one side to biblical and traditional data, on the other to the sciences. By all of these, the relation between a human person (= creaturely reality) and divine action, or grace (= supercreaturely reality), is considered in the perspective of a reciprocal autonomy, considering that historical reality is dependent constantly on the divine action that nourishes it but that can be accepted only gradually. This cannot occur, however, before an attitude of sufficient faith is formed in the person, in order to receive the gift in its complexity and fullness.[4]

---

[1] In the present article, the term "liturgy" — except for a different context — always refers to that of the Catholic Church.

[2] Cf. *Dei Verbum*, 1, 4, 9.

[3] G. Jervis, *Fondamenti di psicologia dinamica* (Milan, 1993); L. Pinkus, "Contributo della psicologia junghiana alla comprensione della vita spirituale," *Il revival dell'irrazionale*, ed. L. Ancona (Milan, 1983) 253–66.

[4] C. Molari, "Considerazioni teologiche," in: A.T.I.-Studio Teologico Fiorentino (eds.) *Creazione e male del cosmo*, ed. Messagero (Padua, 1995).

Thus theological models based on a static concept of nature or, at least implicitly, on magic, such as the miracle-oriented models, lack suitability.

LITURGY AND SOCIALIZATION

Therefore we can define the liturgy, from a psychological viewpoint, as that process of socialization constituted by a sequence of complex ritual units through which the ecclesial community calls to mind the founding events of its own faith, clarifies them, and reformulates them in constant comparison with its own culture. In this process a symbolic liturgy is predominantly used, whether verbal, iconic, or gestural. The community therefore celebrates its own faith through vital symbols whose dynamics are constitutive of individual believers and of the whole community, building links that unite its members, making them grow through shared experiences, and transmitting them to others. It is important, however, to note that the liturgy as a process of socialization is realized fully only when the symbols utilized are adequate for transmitting the same faith without reservations in the ideals and practice of Jesus Christ. In other words, the efficacy of the communication of faith in the liturgical context depends on the authenticity of the experience and the cultural harmony of the symbologies used.

BASIC PSYCHOLOGICAL CONDITIONS FOR "CELEBRATING" THE LITURGY

The purpose of the liturgy is to permit living and interpreting the different tonalities of the human condition so as to succeed in whatever way in bringing out a meaning that enables living all historical situations in a peaceable way by directing them toward the paschal mystery. Some basic psychological conditions, which cannot be renounced if one is to have full self-realization, are its fundamental premise:

The consciousness of human creatureliness. This deals with the dramatic experience of the maturing process: that we have in ourselves neither the reasons for our existence nor sufficient forces for becoming persons completely.

Existential precariousness. Another evolving task that cannot be renounced is that of accepting plainly that our historical form of existence is marked by a deep tendency toward death. It is in dying that we set in a definitive way our personal identity, and paradoxically, learning to die is the only developmental possibility adequate for living in fullness.

Need for transcendence. Finally, full human maturation implies the consciousness that the interweave of tensions — desires, plans, ethical dimensions — that each person experiences cannot find an exhaustive answer in historical reality. Hence the need for a transcendent referral of values.

The value of Christian liturgy does not reside primarily in its doctrinal aspects, namely in the interpretations that it offers on the present and future of the human person, but in the values by which it induces the faith and in the efficacy of its rites. These indeed communicate an experiential truth that is endowed with a transformative power of experience and that therefore assumes a catalyst role for self-realization in a mature sense. The basic reference to the paschal mystery opens one's consciousness to a different reading of reality. Under the appearance, often misleading, of deeds and words despite the painful discovery of one's own precariousness and personal insufficiency, the believer perceives the grand dignity of the call to life as a gift that is concretized in the ecclesial community, through which come vital provisions. These then enable one to discover the possibility of becoming a channel of gifts of life for others. This experience makes one aware that an ambit exists where everything human has meaning, and this meaning witnesses to the continual possibility offered by the faith in Jesus Christ for turning all historical circumstances into constructive opportunities of love. It establishes as well that particular language, dense with the reasons of the heart, that we call "piety." This allows a feeling of authentic solidarity among people, imbuing them with hope and trust, because it is regarded as a reflection of God listening to humanity and as a lofty expression of God's creative fatherhood, according to the revelation of Jesus of Nazareth.

RITE

A rite is a sequence of gestures regulated by rigorously codified norms. The importance of this behavioral scheme becomes ever clearer from the moment it performs, beginning with the animal world, a series of functions that surpass the utilitarian aspect in order to gain cognitive

178

and communicative functions, as can be observed in the rituals of dance or courtship among some animal species.[5]

It is known that the scientific categorization of rite is even more problematic. Here we present a reflection on rite of a strictly psychological order and limited to religious rite. We can consider rite as the basic unit of the liturgical process (of the liturgical celebration). We can hypothesize that the human person notices with differing modalities and intensities the need for transcendence. From the experiential-behavioral viewpoint this is translated into an attraction toward mystery, observed as a strong presence of emotional nature (numinosum),[6] which nonetheless has incisive repercussions on the whole personality. From the cognitive point of view rite stimulates projective tendencies, and since this presents itself as a set of signs without offering a code allowing for an exhaustive interpretation of it, rite tends to exalt whatever is contradictory or even apparently meaningless, whether in experience relating to the outside world or to within the subject.

Contextually, rite presents itself also as a formal series of procedures of a symbolic nature that involve a code of social communication based on the belief that it possesses a specific efficacy by which, if performed and experienced in the provided conditions, has a transformative power on all who celebrate it. The diversification of the roles of all who are involved in the ritual action not only expresses in a clear manner the social structure of the group but also builds its protective capacity, both with regard to upset feelings and — a regrettably less-studied aspect — with regard to the fear and risk that can be inherent in mystical exaltation. Moreover, in religious rite some elements enable the celebrating community to maintain always clearly the transcendent and universal nature of the religious event. For example, the fact that specific roles have corresponding specific vestments serves to indicate not only what is the role and status of the person but also shows in an immediate manner its derivation from a transpersonal authority. Religious rite finds in psychological structure the premises for its celebrations and for being able to understand, in a symbolic sense, the meaning.

[5] K. Lorenz, L'etologia. Fondamenti e metodi (Turin, 1980).
[6] U. Galimberti, La terra senza il male (Milan, 1984).

From a personal point of view, ritual ability develops from early childhood, where the experienced vital range in relation to significant figures and the environment overcomes the functionality of behaviors to give them an experience and a symbolic value. But it is later, with the progress of maturing functions, that one can become aware of some instances of the collective unconscious that stimulate one to achieve a full and ever more authentic identity. Jung, for example, postulates a specific atemporal structure of the human unconscious, namely the archetype of transformation, which stimulates the individual to become consciously inserted into the continually changeable rhythm of existence. The intensity and at the same time the ambiguity of this stimulus can, if accepted, make the person aware that this process of transformation and its demands cannot be satisfied only by remaining on the level of the ego, but they require a qualitative leap, namely the activation of the "transcendent function,"[7] both on the sphere of one's own selfhood and the ambit of whatever is empirical and contingent. It is thus that the individual searches for a suitable setting for the process of individuation, which can indeed be a religion with its own rites.

From the psychodynamic viewpoint I maintain that religious rite is linked to myth in its original etymon and in the value it had in that cultural ambit, namely of proclamation. This proclamation has the aim of explaining the reality through a symbolical narration in which the subjectification of external reality and the objectification of the interior world are verified. By the effect of this bonding, in the ambit of myth there is no world that is not resolved in a collective vision of the world; in every myth, then, a specific phase of the development of collective social conscience shines through that nonetheless is not historicized but rather is atemporal.

Christian rite, by bearing the basic reference to the Logos, modifies the quality of the myth: on one side it historicizes it — indeed, it is based on the historical life of Jesus of Nazareth — on the other it redefines the experience of time through the passage from without-time to beyond-time. The complex of Christian rites as well as each single rite are therefore based on the "myth" of Jesus Christ following two symbolic itineraries: the first sacralizes the five great rites of passage in the life of each person (birth, passage into adulthood,

---

[7] C. G. Jung (1957/1958), *La funzione transcendente, Opere* (Turin, 1980).

marriage, sickness leading to death, and death itself), endowing them with a meaning that is referred to the Christian proclamation. Still following this vector, the liturgical calendar is structured through the transitional moments of the life of Jesus Christ (from birth to the ascension), inserting consciously through a symbolic translation the celebrant community and, in some sense, all of humanity into the awareness of the divine creative action. In the second symbolic itinerary the "divine liturgy," namely the Eucharist, source and summit of all of Christian life, by symbolically ritualizing the culminating moment of the transition-initiation of Jesus Christ, constantly stimulates, at regular intervals, the activation of the process of Christian individuation, which is identification with him. Therefore Christian rite presupposes and establishes a bond between two different orders of reality: the supercreatural and the creatural, which are bonded in the divinized humanity of Jesus Christ. The constant appeal to his "myth" — historical events and ideal values of the tradition associated with him — communicates to the celebrant assembly the transforming power that, by rendering him symbolically present, allows accepting gradually God's transforming action until the attainment of the fullness of life (salvation). Under this aspect rite expresses the faith a community holds toward the ideals preserved in the tradition, accepted and verified by whole generations (memories of the saints). At the same time, rite always anticipates the ideals and the promises not yet effected by appealing to the future as a horizon by which to measure the historical pledge. Finally rite, by appealing to Christ, constitutes the cognizance and at the same time the striving that the community, on one side, experience a cosmic dimension that might free it from esoteric temptations and, on the other, express concretely, through expressions of abiding accord, those relational modalities and vital offerings that anticipate and prepare in history the fullness of time.

BODY AND RITE
The most significant symbolic unity of rite is the body. Its gestures (laying on of hands, blessing), its relation to the concrete, and its historicity communicate constantly and in a perceptible manner the transformative action of rite. Since the body is the repository of memory — without which there would be no possibility of liturgy — and therefore of affection and motivation, only through the body does rite

express and effect the transformation of the person, establish communion among all those who celebrate in communication with the same supercreatural reality, and train them in expressing the cosmic dimension of the sacred. It is in the body that rite inscribes the premonition of the victory over death; it is in the body that it inscribes the sign of a supernatural identity. The gestures allow us to unveil latent meanings and transform them into newness. The body is also the symbolic place of the composition of the conflict between self-realization/salvation and self-destruction/sin. The reference to the body of Jesus Christ is the sole possibility granted to us to experience in a unitary way the separations that lacerate existence: particularly spirit-matter, God-world. The intimate contact that occurs in the eucharistic incorporation is an immediate memory of the law of the incarnation, which means not to evade things human but to enter into them deeply by surpassing habitual human responses. It is in the body and with the body that rite invites us to take on the task of not removing the breadth and depth of human desire but to experience it with great awareness in order to be carried more and more toward the sources of desire rather than toward its outlet, toward the radicalness of the question rather than toward the persistence of the answer. It is only corporally that we can live the experience of the unification of life, which in liturgical symbolism does not end with the lacerating spirit-body split but with the intuition, always shadowy and mysterious, of a harmonious transformation into a "heavenly body," until attaining the perfect stature of sons and daughters of God.

MEMORY

Memory, the chain of remembrances, builds the fabric that allows the person identity and ideation. To remember — the primary undertaking and task of rite — is first of all a process of recall that engenders unity from dispersion. It is indeed only in unity that our subjectivity succeeds in effecting the differentiation between self and outer reality that allows one to build and stabilize identity. If there were not the process of activating memory that builds and rebuilds the sphere of belonging that enables us to recognize our own thoughts, sentiments, and gestures, and at the same time would not link the succession of events and scenes presented to our vision, there would be no identity or reality that could be perceived as a sequence of appearances related to one another. By recall, one becomes aware of one's own peculiarity, that is, the tragic dimension of one's own existence: that of being open to the fullness of meaning that is happiness and at the same time to the implosion of all meaning, which is death. From the personal point of view, this dynamic offers a clear perception of the ephemeral character of all action so as to render necessary a projection that provides continuity and is precisely a search for meaning. Destroying memory is the same as destroying the basis of one's own identity and of the very continuity of time; memory is not a snapshot of the past, since it is not passive but constructive. In the very moment in which a community recalls a memory, it rebuilds, selects, chooses, transforms, searches, in a word, "makes history" and opens the continuity of the future. The past is always with us; its efficacy and influence depend on the decision of the present to remove it or to assume it. Banalizing it, disregarding it, lapsing into custom, imply the temptation to forget and deactivate the creative-transformative potential of memory. Reminiscence, that is, recalling a memory, prefigures the future and creates history, which requires memory, so that the newness that emerges is decipherable and above all free from whatever of the past is dead, that is, bound to cultural backwardness, so as to liberate energies that are perceptible and efficacious and capable of giving form consistent with the present culture. This means actualizing salvific experiences that are transmitted to us by the tradition and that we recall in memory, because only in this way can we take decisions adequate to the demands of life in our time and continue to make historically present the ideals, values, and behavioral models lived and proposed by Jesus Christ.

EMOTIONS

The transformative action of rite sinks even into the emotions that it channels, making them constructively incisive factors in the orientation of life. None of the fundamental emotions is passed over by the liturgy: for example, joy, with its spatial-temporal correlative which is feast, is taken up to a level that, by avoiding reducing it to entertainment — namely an artificial and passing evasion — drives it to the roots of desire to generate a constant attitude of joyous pacification. But the potentiality of liturgical celebration to support personal and group identity and to guide toward recovery of meaning is especially evident in the rites that bedeck the Liturgy of the Dead. In them we see that one who has found death on his or her own path, and therefore the interruption of affective bonds, can express emotions without the fear of losing self, of losing identity. The ecclesial community, while on the one hand deals with the emotive resonance connected to empathic understanding, on the other hand, by the faith that pervades it, acts as a container, thus hindering the overflow of emotions into despair or into disintegration of identity. This cathartic and reconstructive function of liturgical celebration stands out eminently in the Eucharist through the constant reference to the paschal mystery of death-resurrection; in it the priest plays a role of activating and monitoring a composite whole, for which the ritual structure serves as the organizer.[8]

SACRIFICE

While the statement is true that the Eucharist is the liturgical celebration par excellence of Christianity, it is likewise true that it constitutes one of the problematic knots of contemporary religious experience. The eucharistic rite hinges on the pair banquet-sacrifice, where the first of these elements is something easy for us to experience, but the second is remote from the categories of contemporary experience. Indeed, the path of historical explanation is usually too rational, while the psychological understanding of sacrifice can provide some help. Psychology allows us to grasp that the psychodynamic essence of sacrifice is destruction,[9] not of things (first fruits, animals) but rather of the relation with these things and with their affective and symbolic content, whether personal or collective. By destroying the relation sacrifice upsets an order, not to create another out of it but rather to create a void that, by separating us from the bonds that daily experience of the real shows us to be ineluctable or unmodifiable, creates the conditions so that the newness of life might emerge. Sacrifice, by representing the extreme destruction that is death, imposes potentially a kind of virginal uselessness on the values that are the basis for reality and therefore for their meaning for us. Our habitual reality

[8] With this term, taken from embryology, psychoanalysis indicates the capability of a structure to guide the development of more forces by effecting quantitative differences, and by integrating them into a new evolutionary level; cf. R. Spitz, *A Genetic Field Theory of Ego Formation* (New York, 1959); E. H. Erikson, *Childhood and Society*, 2d ed. (New York, 1963).

[9] U. Galimberti, "Il simbolismo del sacrificio in una lettura psicoanalitica," *Servitium* 98 (marzo–aprile 1995) 21–30.

is the one that causes the need to derive from a different order, specifically the symbolic one. In this regard cultural change is important; on the basis of it, projecting ourselves onto the sacrificial victim is not what is suggested for us to do but rather sacrifice as separation and annulment of the ego and of its habitual world.

This is what allows us to pass from one order to another where the other order is not the contrary of the sacrificial order but rather something else altogether, the one and the other together. This dynamic, which at a certain level generates a confusion of meaning, indicates the effective readiness for sacrifice of that order that the ego and its reasons have historically displayed on earth. Freed from the representations and the words of an already written reality, room is made for something that is no longer the repetition of a past but the unsuspected and unexpected source of a new meaning, which one can attain only if ready each time to lose one's life.

So that this experience, if lived in depth and authenticity, might not resolve itself in madness, it is necessary that this renunciation of one's own role identity not abolish a constant reference that helps to understand what happens in the acceptation of the terms "understanding" and "containing." This is possible in the eucharistic experience when the community, entering into the symbolic dimension, experiences a passage toward a transcendent level where one learns to live no longer for oneself but for Christ who has died for us. Only with this constant exercise of demolition of old structures is it possible for the ego to become suitable for hosting this perennial newness that life provides and that is offered in communion with Christ.

CONCLUSION

Although aware that we have outlined only some essential elements for a psychosociology of the liturgy, we intend to provide some reflections regarding its prospects. The most important undertaking seems to us to be a more coherent confrontation with the epochal changes that characterize today's cultural horizon. Difficulties often emerge with regard to the liturgy both as a ritual complex and as a symbolic language held to be now obsolete. Hence the tendency to favor a kind of simplification of the liturgy by reducing its expressive ambit and by taking up a concrete language (words, sounds, objects) that make the celebration immediately usable, as happens, for example, with television.

It seems useful to clarify immediately an ambiguity that is still present today, according to which authentic testimony of the believer or of the ecclesial community would be enough to pass on the faith, and therefore the ritual dimension would be, so to speak, superfluous. Now, if it is true that the transmittal of faith is achieved in the authenticity of the daily life of believers and the communities as an immediate expression in concrete symbologies, nevertheless this aspect is neither complete nor sufficient. Indeed, Christian ideals and values cannot always be translated into consistent and adequate historical choices. Some Christian ideals embrace the past — for example, the testimonies of tradition or historical accomplishments — while others appeal to the future, namely objectives to attain. Therefore they cannot be presented except through ritual structures that recall the memory of the past and anticipate the future: memory and utopia can be mediated only through symbologies that are adequate to present as yet unrealized forms of the possible and desired ideals and at the same time to recall their historical roots. Furthermore, there are also situations and values of the present that do not allow their immediate representation but that can be experienced only through symbolic ritual acts. The analytical reflection confirms in its turn the prudence with which liturgical symbolism is treated: below a certain threshold of concreteness and immediacy the rite is no longer in a position to effect transformative processes because it does not involve deep motivational and emotional dynamics. Besides, there is the risk that, having overcome a certain limit, the concrete element might forcibly impose itself by absorbing the symbol, which therefore ceases to exercise its function of stimulating developmental activity, thus making still weaker the differentiation between "sacred" and "profane." In the final analysis it must always be kept in mind that a symbolism may be too abstract, almost metaphysical, and may allude to an absolute spiritualism (in practice, a kind of renunciation of rituality), or it may be a concreteness of little interest. But the one that can be considered the most qualifying note of the liturgy is: celebrate the mystery of the God who became flesh.

Bibliography

Beirnaert, L. *Esperienza cristiana e psicologia*. Turin, 1970.

Brown, L. B., ed. *Advances in the Psychology of Religion*. Vol. 2. International Series in Experimental Social Psychology 11. Oxford, 1987.

Carotenuto, A., ed. *Trattato di psicologia analitica*. 2 vols. Turin, 1992.

Frijda, N. H. *The Emotions*. Studies in Emotion and Social Interaction. Cambridge, 1987.

Godin, A. *The Psychological Dynamics of Religious Experience*. Birmingham, Ala., 1985.

Jacobi, J. *The Way of Individuation*. Trans. R.F.C. Hull. New York, 1967.

Jedlowski, P., and M. Rampazi. *Il senso del passato: Per una sociologia della memoria*. Milan, 1991.

Jung, C. G. "Psychology and Religion." In *Psychology and Religion: West and East*. 2nd ed. The Collected Works of C. G. Jung 11:3–105. Bollingen Series 20. Ed. H. Read, M. Fordham, G. Adler. Trans. R.F.C. Hull. Princeton, 1969.

_____. *Symbols of Transformation: An Analysis of the Prelude to a Case of Schizophrenia*. The Collected Works of C. G. Jung 5. Bollingen Series 20. 2nd ed. Ed. H. Read, M. Fordham, G. Adler. Trans. R.F.C. Hull. Princeton, 1967.

_____. "Transformation Symbolism in the Mass." In *Psychology and Religion: West and East*. The Collected Works of C. G. Jung 11:201–296. 2nd ed. Bollingen Series 20. Ed. H. Read, M. Fordham, G. Adler. Trans. R.F.C. Hull. Princeton, 1969.

_____. "Christ, A Symbol of the Self." In *Aion: Researches into Phenomenology of the Self*. The Collected Works of C. G. Jung 9/2:36–71. 2nd ed. Bollingen Series 20. Ed. H. Read, M. Fordham, G. Adler. Trans. R.F.C. Hull. New York, 1959.

_____, and K. Kerényi. *Essays on a Science of Mythology: The Myth of the Divine Child and the Divine Maiden*. Trans. R.F.C. Hull. Princeton, N.J., 1969.

Namer, G. *Memoire et societé*. Paris, 1987.

Pinkus, L. "La polarità del lutto." In *Celebrare l'agape nella malattia e nel lutto*. 1993.

_____. "Psicologia e religione." In B. Bernardi, G. Filoramo, E. Pace, L. Pinkus, G. Riconda, and A. N. Terrin, *Introduzione allo studio della religione*. Turin, 1991.

_____. "Psicologia e vita spirituale." In AA.VV., *Esistenza Cristiana*, 107–25. Rome, 1990.

Vergote, A. *Religone, fede, incredulità*. Cinisello (Milan), 1985.

Crispino Valenziano

11

Liturgy and Anthropology:
The Meaning of the Question
and the Method for Answering it

My goal here is to establish an epistemological foundation. I am therefore careful, in the present context, not to leap the gap between the science of liturgy and the science of anthropology, and between the act that is the celebration of the liturgical rite and the act that is hominization and belongs to the anthropology of the person. The usual difficulties which a liturgist encounters when he or she tackles our question are due, admittedly, to the professional biases found in the cultivators of the sciences that use a primarily deductive methodology or to the lack of technical preparation in the field of the human sciences. But such difficulties are greatly increased by the more or less pragmatic haste accompanying a "human celebration" of rites (I am using "human" in a positive and balanced sense).

The care of which I speak is a care not to mistake the anthropological structures of liturgical activity for an immediate application of the anthropological phenomenologies useful and necessary for liturgical action, nor to mistake the epistemological foundation of the question with an interactive meshing of the disciplines or even with the scientific basis of discourse. In dealing with liturgy, there is need in anthropology of what is needed analogously in spirituality and in pastoral practice: as far as epistemology is concerned, there must be a "fundamental" frame of reference, one that is foundational without distracting and distorting digressions and confusing contaminations. The reason? In order that there may emerge, in a manner beyond criticism, the phenomenological outline which brings to light the intrinsic constitution, including the anthropological, of every rite in and of itself, of every celebration in and of itself, and not some "human" interpretation from outside.

I. ORIGIN AND DEVELOPMENT OF THE QUESTION

1. What Is the Question?

Let us observe how two positions of M.-D. Chenu, one based on intuitive projections, the other representing a balance sheet drawn up in the course of work, articulate successive juxtapositions of liturgy and anthropology.

The first of these two belongs to the critical years of the liturgical movement when, after the cataclysm of war with its enormous cultural breakdowns, agitated expectations of a reform led to the encyclical letter of Pius XII and the same pope's plan involving the Curia, as well as to everything that accompanied both, to the point of finally inducing John XXIII to plan a council. It was back then, on the eve of *Mediator Dei*, that Chenu had his insight into the question as such.[1] For the first time, he used the word "anthropology" in the context of liturgical theology, thus inciting liturgical science (the last of the sciences to take this step) to the "anthropological turn" (the history of which, however, does not usually dwell on its influence on our discipline).

Chenu's insight was a generic one but descended to details: it is in itself, and not through a juxtaposition with grace, that human nature is consecrated according to the integral realism of the sacramental symbols, while the absolute gratuitousness of grace does not mean any discounting of the laws or human behaviors proper to the subject, namely, the human being. Moreover, the liturgy is essentially communitarian because it expresses the social nature of the human being in the body of Christ, head and members. By the fact, then, that the liturgy adopts the postulates and resources of the human being, it implies, confirms, and consecrates anthropology (p. 53).

In this circle of interwoven ecclesiological, Christological, and pneumatological implications that were required by the spiritual and pastoral needs of the liturgical movement (p. 54), Chenu then identified three polarities in the interactive dialectic between liturgy and anthropology. The liturgy brings into balance, first of all, the supra-

---

[1] M.-D. Chenu, "Anthropologie et liturgie," *MD* no. 12 (1947) 53–65.

rational and the infrarational because it itself comes into being through the union of "mystery" (the suprarational) and "symbol" (infrarational), two potentialities of the human being that are so difficult to codify that they are often confused with each other in the kind of purely rational balancing of factors by an intellectual theology or a formalist liturgy (pp. 54ff.). The liturgy also brings into balance the individual and the group; the issue here is the role of the "community" in the development of the "person," a perennial problem that in our age is causing a communitarian revolution, in the full sense of this term, which in turn is evidently invading the realm of Christianity: Christian life will be reborn to the extent that authentic communities emerge once again and, with them, an active liturgy (pp. 59–62). Finally, the liturgy brings into balance "inspiration" and "discipline" (pp. 63f.).

Chenu sees the bringing together of liturgy and anthropology as a spiritual and pastoral duty of the liturgical movement, the aim being to activate in a balanced way the potentialities for mutual assistance that exist "dialectically" between the suprarational element of the liturgy (the mystery) and the infrarational element of anthropology (symbol): there is insight here into the new anthropological and linguistic power of symbols to overcome, with the aid of anthropology, the various kinds of theological intellectualism and liturgical formalism. Secondly, the potentialities that exist "dialectically" between the group aspect of the liturgy (the community) and the individual of anthropology (the person): there is an insight here into the new liturgical and ecclesiological power of the community to promote, with the help of anthropology, a liturgical reform and an active liturgy. Thirdly, there are the potentialities that exist "dialectically" between the discipline proper to liturgy and the inspiration provided by anthropology: there is an insight here into the anthropological and ecclesiological power of an evolving liturgical dynamic to achieve, with the aid of anthropology, the intelligibility that resides in the ritual celebration (p. 64).

Chenu's second position was taken during the postconciliar years when, in the eventful implementation of the liturgical reform that had finally gotten underway, our question made its full seriousness felt within the horizon of an "anthropological turn" that was now widely at work in general theological thought and of a turn to inclusiveness that had now been accepted in the form of the interdisciplinarity now characteristic of the general methodologies of the sciences. It was there, right after the gains made and the virtualities revealed by the Council or, if one prefers, after the seeds sown by Vatican II, that Chenu, an expert who had recently worked on the development of *Gaudium et spes,* drew up an assessment of the subject, in terms both of past work and of what needed to be done.[2]

In the twenty years that had passed, the *and* of juxtaposition ("anthropology *and* liturgy," 1947) had become the *of the* of interaction ("anthropology *of the* liturgy," 1967). Chenu now said that the human being provides liturgy with its proper subject, its proper matter, its proper norm, and even its very being, and that this claim is utterly obvious. However, he continues, a minimum of reflection, or a consideration of the history of liturgy or even of the forms of religious worship generally, makes it clear that this obviousness spring from a global perception, which when then subjected to detailed analysis proves to flow from complex sources and motivations. The discernment of these sources and the conscious grasp of these motivations is urgently necessary for the real authenticity and good health of the liturgy, especially when the latter, like art or poetry, must regain its inventive power and its creative insights. The time had come for this. That was one side of the coin. On the other, Chenu notes that Vatican II did not have at its disposal a conscious and developed anthropology.

Two or three centuries of theological thought that had turned away from the human sciences are a sufficient explanation of this lack. It is not that the conciliar debates and documents were lacking in an idea of the human being, but any organized science of the nature, conditions, structures, and dynamism of the human being remained implicit there, though with the special effectiveness of implications. This amounts to saying that for the subject, the matter, the norm, and the very being of the liturgy it was necessary to establish the lines of a "liturgical anthropology," to define and reflect on a *homo liturgicus* (p. 159).

Here again we have, for the first time, a symptomatic lexicon. For one instance, "liturgical anthropology," corresponding to "liturgical theology" and equivalent to an inherent interaction: "anthropology *of the* liturgy," or, if one prefers, equivalent to "liturgy *and* anthropol-

[2] Idem., "Anthropologie de la liturgie," in *La liturgie après Vatican II. Bilan, études, prospective,* ed. J.-P. Jossua and Y.-M. Congar (Paris, 1967) 159–77.

ogy," where the *and* is disjunctive but at the same time says that the two terms are to interpret each other. Another instance: *homo liturgicus,* a consideration of "human beings" that defines them as "liturgical," not so much by their nature (as in the case of *homo sciens* or *homo faber*) as by reason of a gift given which, in certain specific circumstances, makes them capable of turning the matter and norm of the liturgy into an inherent *potentia oboedientialis* insofar as human beings are the subject of the being of the liturgy (but I say this according to the mind of that time). The fact is, Chenu said, that we need to discern the sources and make ourselves aware of the motivations that are available to easy general observation; we need to discern them for the sake of the real authenticity and good health of the liturgy.

This is especially true of the third polarity in the interactive dialectic that was mentioned above, namely, the dialectic between liturgical discipline and anthropological inspiration, a dialectic which could not be more closely investigated prior to Vatican II but which now, after *Sacrosanctum Concilium* and *Gaudium et spes* must be clarified in theory and in practice. Like Chenu's intuitive projections of 1947, so his assessments of work in progress in 1967 were not formulated in generic terms. The emphases now were four in number and were no longer presented in dialectical terms. Two of the emphases repeat earlier preconciliar calls: the emphasis on symbol and the emphasis on community (see pp. 171–77), but with a postconciliar note from *Gaudium et spes,* no. 32, regarding the community of the incarnate Word who entered into the anthropological interplay of human socialization (p. 176).

The other two emphases open up a new path for a conscious and developed anthropology. Here Chenu has a note: "Anthropology. We take the word here in its general and strong sense of 'conception of the human being'" (p. 167, note 10). The reference is to the many anthropological disciplines: philosophical anthropology, regarding which Chenu points out that every philosophy implies an anthropology; biblical anthropology, in connection with which Chenu emphasizes the Pauline conception of σάρξ/ψυχή/νοῦς; theological anthropology (implicitly), but not cultural anthropology (see pp. 165–70). At this point he introduces us at last to the problem of culture. It is therefore not without profit for us if I give an account of the decisive passages (pp. 160–65). The following points are made in these five or six central pages of the essay.

Forms of worship are the products of the temperaments, mentalities, passions, and needs of human beings, depending on the cycles of civilization. Cultic aspirations and activities are permeated and changed by a continual "transfer" in the direction of something "beyond" the human condition. These dynamisms are normal, because religion is of its nature a reference to divinity, but it is also an ambiguous attitude inasmuch as it tends to make these actions of human beings in the world transcend their proper worldly condition. Religious phenomenology analyzes this innate ambiguity. With application to us Christians: some of us are fascinated by the human reality of the Christ in the God-man, while others prefer to contemplate, in the human nature completely assumed by the divine Person, the Word who manifests himself therein. Therefore, while Christology is one and the same amid the various theological balances represented by these outlooks, spirituality (for example) will usually emphasize this or that aspect according to the wisdom the Spirit gives, according to personal or communal charisms, or *according to variations in cultural contexts.*

It seems indeed that in our age theology in general and the theology of the liturgy in particular see in Christ the God-*man* who is a catalyst for our faith-inspired sensibilities, entirely to the profit of a liturgy that is engaged in the history of salvation rather than in more or less allegorical speculations. Moreover, the subject of the celebration is not the human being in general but the human being as marked by the values peculiar to the civilization upon which we have entered. How is it possible, then, that the reference to the divinity, which is constitutive of religion and therefore of worship, or, to put it in real terms, how is it possible that the Christian mystery, which is the divinization of the human being by God's becoming man, should not be renewed by the kind of human renewal proper to the civilization upon which we have entered?

Chenu, who, among other things, does not regard as static the forms of worship of the natural man, which we often deceive ourselves into thinking of as a constant element of religious humanity and as at a constant temperature, cites *Gaudium et spes,* no. 58, on this point: "The Church has existed through the centuries in varying circumstances and has utilized the resources of different cultures . . . to explain the message of Christ . . . and to express it more perfectly in the liturgy and in various aspects of the life of the faithful." Emphasizing the cultural dynamics at work, Chenu adds in a note that this sensitivity to the development of cultures is one of the points on which the work of the postconciliar Church will have to include a new interpretation of *Sacrosanctum Concilium,* which was composed at the beginning of Vatican II, and therefore to plumb its full inspiration in the light of the later conciliar texts (p. 162, note 2).

All this turns his attention to the specific character of the divine economy as understood in Christianity. A redefinition of our liturgy requires that we become aware of this specific character, which is accessible not only to the believing Christian but to any historian or phenomenologist of religion. For there are in fact two kinds of religion, and therefore two kinds of worship can be observed.

There is religion that flows from the nature of human beings when they place themselves in relation to a divinity. The worship which this religion in turn produces is in danger of becoming a mechanism for gaining the favor of the divinity (magic), escaping the hostile forces of nature (superstition), and respecting taboos. In any case, it is a worship that sacralizes things and persons. There is also religion that is based on a hearing of the word of God, who reveals himself and, in the extreme case, becomes himself a human being; this is religion that does not mount up to the divinity but believes in God's descent to humanity. The worship proper to it is of a different order than "religion" (in the first sense); it is of the order of the remembrance and re-presentation of the events of the salvation that has been revealed in and come in history. In short, the cult of the "sacred" tends to the archaic, the hieratic, and the esoteric, while the worship of "mystery" is historical and is, out of fidelity to itself, involved in the developments of history. The ultimate heart or hinge of discourse on religion is this definitive impossibility of reducing to a human "sacral" religion the divine economy of "mystery," the worship of which in the world and in history has the human being as its subject, its matter, its norm, and, in short, its very being.

R. Guardini[3] is the source, which still cannot be ignored, of our question. At bottom, the dehistoricization of the mystery and the antianthropological or even antinatural outlook, for which I consider O. Casel responsible,[4] despite the debt owed him for his

[3] R. Guardini, *The Spirit of the Liturgy,* trans. Ada Lane (New York: Benziger, 1931).
[4] O. Casel, *The Mystery of Christian Worship and Other Writings,* ed. B. Neunheuser (Westminster, Md., 1962).

formulation of a liturgical theology and even because of that liturgical theology — these things were the core of the inevitable disagreement between the first two co-directors of the *Jahrbuch für Liturgiewissenschaft*.

Guardini's forecast at the end of the 1915–1918 war was like that of Chenu after the 1939–1945 war. As a result of the cataclysmic war at the beginning of the century, he had already come to the insight that the liturgy is based on "bipolar oppositions": between nature and culture (in the human being), between the corporeal and the spiritual (in symbols), and between person and community (in the liturgical assembly). In my opinion, we cannot ignore the fact that the riches which he purified for the liturgy in the crucible of his Christian world-view, in his prophecy of the Church, and in his spiritual and pastoral commitment to Quickborn — the riches of popular piety, sensitivity, play, art, architecture, and so on — that all these are load-bearing constituents of anthropological culture (of cultural anthropology). At the time, however, this cultural anthropology did not succeed in reaching mature formulations of its own gains. This, I say, is something we cannot ignore, because to speak of liturgy and anthropology (and even the liturgical theology that flowed from Casel himself cannot fail to speak of them) will prove an impossible undertaking if we ignore symbols, on which Chenu focusses his attention, without ignoring the other "dialectical polarities," or if we ignore culture, on which Guardini focussed his attention, without ignoring the other "bipolar oppositions."

2. Three Approaches to the Question

In the postconciliar period there have emerged three ways of relating anthropology to the liturgy.

Anthropology as "ancillary." This approach is useless, given our epistemological viewpoint, because it is not to be regarded as a scientific approach. I mention it because some people still think of making use of it in too many cases of practical need. Yet, I would say, it is precisely in such cases that it is to be deeply distrusted. For example, to have recourse, in the lived experience of spirituality or pastoral practice, to the services of an anthropology that acts as an obliging handmaid is to chain thought and action to mechanical prescriptions that lack inspiration and effectiveness, and to set up a hopeless vicious circle of failures that are connected with impromptu dips into social psychology, communications theory, and other things. The "ancillary" approach is to be absolutely excluded.

The "phenomenological" approach is to be used with caution. On the one hand, and de jure, religious phenomenology permeates the liturgical journey, so that it must be taken as a paradigm, proper to humanity, for the situation of the liturgy when the latter uses human ritual. On the other hand, and as a matter of fact, religious phenomenology can take possession of the field to such an extent that it monopolizes the dynamics of liturgical ritual and leads to a real gnosis that is at times apologetical, at times irenicist, at times naturalist, but is, in one way or other, reductive of a phenomenon that is by its nature theandric, global, and universalizing.

As a type of religious psychology and sociology, of the comparative history and analysis of the religions, whatever the setting in which it develops, even if this be the philosophy or even the theology of religions, and whatever the theory that is worked out in these settings — this is a phenomenology that does not instill meaning but rather calls for it, a phenomenology that roughs out a meaning but does not replace meaning. To lose sight of this epistemological structure of religious phenomenology in its relation to the practice of Christian worship amounts to supposing that the liturgy — a liturgy — has an epistemological status completely analogous to, if not identical with, the ritual practice of religions established unilaterally by human beings. It amounts also to trapping the worship of the Christian human being — and the Christian human being himself or herself — in that realm of the sacred from which the "one mediator between God and humankind, Christ Jesus" (1 Tim 2:5) has delivered us (see Col 2:8-23).

The regime of this "religious" sacrality neither corresponds to nor is suited to Christian "mystery" symbolism. Nor does the specific character of the liturgy seem to be safeguarded if one hypothesizes a twofold regime: on the one hand, the liturgical celebration, to which is entrusted the mystery of Christians, and, on the other, religious experience, in which the sacredness of the human can take refuge. More concretely, the twofold regime of popular ritualism and liturgical ritualism, of theistic mysticism and sacramental mysticism, of private prayer and communal prayer. Such a dissociation in the liturgy would result in an incurable schizophrenia in Christians, whereas in fact when they celebrate the mystery, they experience it, within the one economy established by their God, as a gift by which it is granted to them to connect themselves with him. This "phenomenological" approach is one that is to be included in our question as a useful and necessary phase of interpretive reduplication.

The "hermeneutical" approach is the approach we are trying. In his last conference, in 1983, Marsili said:

"There is a liturgical theology that can be given that name with greater justice because it builds its discourse about God directly on the categories of the liturgy itself . . . : the sacramental nature of revelation, the presence of the whole of revelation in Christ the sacrament who is repeatedly experienced, the economic aspect of revelation as history of salvation — the presence of the mystery of Christ in the liturgical event, the word of God being made actual — . . . . Some may think that the human sciences provide a special context for a pastoral liturgy. Agreed. But not as a context peculiar to pastoral liturgy. If the liturgy is an actuation of the mystery of Christ in the human dimension, that is, in time and space, then the human sciences always and necessarily have a place in liturgical theology, and not only when this is qualified as 'pastoral' . . . the human sciences [have their place in the liturgical liturgy] not in order to understand and explain the liturgy, but to understand the ways by which human beings may more adequately enter into the mystery of Christ through the liturgy."[5]

No more, no less, indeed, but referring more specifically to anthropology instead of to the human sciences generally, and for the reasons he indicates at the beginning of the citation. It appears that the coherence between this pregnant conception of liturgical theology and the stimulating multiplicity of anthropological disciplines, both those that remain within the bounds of the human sciences (cultural anthropology) and those that go beyond the human sciences (philosophical anthropology and theological anthropology), leads to a hermeneutic of the human element in a liturgy that is theandric and of the liturgical element in human beings when and where, as well as how, they are theandric. There is then an exchange of meaning which

[5] S. Marsili, "La liturgia nel discorso teologico odierno, Per una fondazione della liturgia pastorale: individuazione delle prospettive e degli ambiti specifici," *Una liturgia per l'uomo,* ed. P. Visentin, A. N. Terrin, and R. Cicolin (Padua, 1986) 43, 46–47.

takes into account both what liturgy and anthropology have in common, synergically, and what each of them has that is irreducible.

II. CULTURE AND CULTURAL ANALYSIS

1. Anthropologies . . .

In the presence of "liturgy" that is solidly grounded in its own claims, despite the weight placed on it by its reform in the 60s and the specters of secularization affecting it in the 70s or the weight of its self-enclosed theological systematization in both the preconciliar and the postconciliar periods, "anthropology" becomes a harbor in which theses and hypotheses put in, as well as goals that unite and divisions that fragment. "Liturgy" can count on archaic foundations that persist in one or other way; it was on these that the liturgical movement counted when it noted the afflictions of the liturgy and transmitted its deposits. "Anthropology" must take into account the irreversible breakdown of old ways that opens up new paths still to be explored; and, of course, there are countless dialectics in every anthropology.

Let me start on the morrow of the world war fought at mid-twentieth century:

"The author of this work is aware of breaking new ground. Anthropology, whether philosophical or positive, has not thus far been an autonomous discipline: if philosophical, it has depended on a metaphysics of being (as in antiquity) or on a theological metaphysics (as in the Middle Ages) or on a critique of consciousness (as in the modern age) or on a sociology (as in the present age); if positive, it is included in psychology or in the medical disciplines or, most recently, in depth psychology. . . . The present work, entitled *Man,* seeks to recover from all the images of the human being, however different, a *universal man (homo universalis),* as it were, the human εἶδος (in Plato's sense), the human *forma* (in Aristotle's sense), the 'idea' of the human being (as understood in contemporary phenomenology), the 'fundamental human being' (as understood in contemporary ethnology, both psycho-sociological and mythological). This work has as its subtitle, *Typological Anthropology,* because it consciously develops an anthropology that looks for the meaning of the human person in its existential, concrete 'kinds' or 'stamps' (τύπος = impression, model). General anthropology and typological anthropology intertwine: a general anthropology that is typological in its method seeks to reach an 'essence of the human being' through the variety of historical anthropologies and the variety of systems of thought about the human being; a typological anthropology that is properly such seeks to grasp this 'essence of the human being,' in all its existential breadth, through the variety of concrete 'kinds' of human being."[6]

E. Pryzwara's essay, which is perhaps the only one of its kind, offers us a path that must not be neglected. It is obvious that in anthropology as elsewhere the decades that have passed since Pryzwara wrote have developed scientific and epistemological structures. The deductive anthropologies of philosophy and theology have been given practical applications. Inductive anthropology that adopts various "angles," that is, the "human sciences" such as psychology and sociology, communication and futurology, has established criteria and norms. Inductive anthropology that has a "global" perspective, that is, the human science called "anthropology" in the strong sense (human science/anthropology), declares its claim to be all embracing and is called "cultural" in order to specify its field and method ("culture" here is not ideological but existential, does not serve as a "mould" and yet is a τύπος, and does not look for an essence of the human being but, by means of a sufficient analysis of organized and autonomous collectivities of human beings, does attain to their existence as human). All these anthropologies are "inventions" with disruptive effects. It is precisely in their polyvalence that present-day operational knowledge of the human beings comes into play. And it is in "typology," within the precise lines established by an anthropologically global "culture," that the human apprenticeship to the present state of the sciences takes place.

With regard to our question, the problem concerns the human being as subject of theandric liturgical action, the human being as subject, precisely inasmuch as he or she is a human being. We are not concerned, therefore, with the human being as subject insofar as in the liturgical action (which is a human-divine action/action of the God-man/action of the human being and God) he or she is co-subject with Christ and the Spirit (on this matter the reader must relate *Sacrosanctum Concilium* to the mystery ecclesiology of *Lumen gentium*).

[6] E. Pryzwara, *Mensch. Typologische Anthropologie* (Nürnberg, 1958); Italian trans.: *L'uomo* (Milan, 1968) 37–9 passim.

200

Again, this is a delicate and difficult problem because in our culture, but not only in it, as soon as the emphasis is placed on the human being as such, this human being is, in and of himself or herself, a "theomorphic" subject (even more so than according to M. Scheler)[7] and a "theanthropic" subject" (much more so than according to L. Feuerbach)[8] (on this matter the reader must relate *Sacrosanctum Concilium* to the dynamic anthropology of *Gaudium et spes*).

Moreover, with regard to our question, the problem has to do with the object "liturgy and anthropology," tackling this not by way of a *coincidentia oppositorum*, but rather by way of a reprise of cultural experiences that have recurred in the history of Christianity. Recall, for example, the experience of connecting theology and philosophy at the beginning of the second millennium. In like manner, as we pass from the second to the third millennium, thinkers will, when dealing with the sacraments (for example), use the anthropological category of symbol, this understood as a linguistic kind of sign, just as earlier thinkers used the philosophical category of causality.

2. . . . and Cultural Anthropology

It is in the field of culture[9] that my thoughts here are being roughed out. In other words, in addition to being one of the disciplines contributing to our question, cultural anthropology is also the launching pad for our hermeneutic. Such is the privileged position enjoyed by "culture" in our question, but "culture" in the sense and with the fullness of meaning peculiar to cultural anthropology. "Cultural analysis," for its part, adds the power of induction to the results of deduction; the two together provide an organized and coordinated approach to the many interdisciplinary values of anthropology. Therefore, no existential philosophy of the human being nor the existential aspects of a theology of the person will find the "typological" acquisitions of an anthropology based on a cultural existentiality to be useless or superfluous.

[7] M. Scheler, *On the Eternal in Man*, trans. B. Noble (New York, 1960).

[8] L. Feuerbach, *The Essence of Christianity*, trans. G. Eliot (New York: Harper Torchbooks, 1957).

[9] It is necessary to work with the tools provided by cultural anthropology, and we must suppose the reader to be familiar with this as with philosophical anthropology and theological anthropology. For some of the ideas in my article, however, I refer the reader to my essay, "Per l' 'adattamento' culturale della liturgia dopo il Vaticano II. Appunti metodologici," *Ho Theologos*, n.s. 3 (1985, no. 2) 179–202.

In addition, the rewording, in virtue of the analysis of this or that culture, of what the human being says deductively about itself and its cults, places the human being and its cults in the determinative habitat in which every perspective, even that of purely intellectual reflection, acquires a synergic liberation that is proper to it and gives it an increased value. The inductive contribution of a cultural analysis of the religious phenomenon is not to be a substitute for a philosophy of the ritual that springs from nature or for a theology of the Christian celebration, but, in addition to being a straightforward addition of objective phenomena, it will provide us with the phenomenological detail that is henceforth indispensable in the epochal cultural change upon which we have entered.

Culture means the cultivation of the human being. In order to draw rightful attention to its significance as the most privileged "locus" and "occasion" of anthropology, I have used a neologism that refers both to culture as the effect wrought by the human being and to the human being as the effect of culture: the cultivation *of the* human being, the genitive being subjective and at the same time objective. This is the meaning of "the anthropogenetic circle," itself a neologism that has come into use precisely to express this twofold relation.

I said earlier that in order to reach our goal we must move beyond the intellectual and the pragmatic conception of culture. If *homo* is understood solely as *sciens* or solely as *faber,* culture will be understood as the cultivation either of a rational *humanitas* or of an efficiency-minded *humanitas.* But if *homo* is understood synergically as *sciens* and *faber* and *ludens* and *artifex* and . . . , then culture will be understood as the cultivation of his all-embracing *humanitas:* cultivation/hominization.

But we must also include the symbiosis of "action" and "agent." If we consider that in our case we want to include the symbiosis of the action that is "worship" (liturgy) and the agent that is "culture" (the cultivating/cultivated human being), we immediately realize how the identification of the lexical root of *colere* takes us beyond the elementary words it suggests: *colere* (cultivate) is "to deal with, to take care of, to practice, to dwell"; therefore it means "to cultivate, foster" and also "to venerate, honor," because it means "to deal respectfully, to take due care, to practice in conformity with, to dwell with affection." The need is to grasp the value of the cultic in the cultural and the value of the cultural in the cultic. Because of all this, our subject,

202

the relation between liturgy and anthropology, cult and culture, is a symbolic instance of anthropological analysis and synthesis. It is even the originating core of the anthropogenetic circle. It is the happy focal point of what the jargon calls "synchrony," that is, of juxtapositions that make possible complete overlaps even between realities that may be distant from each other even in the time of their existence. Ours is a hermeneutic of "connaturality" between cult (liturgy) and culture (the cultivating/cultivated human being).

A culture is the organic "form" of any autonomous human collectivity. Without a culture, the identity of a human group does not initially become organically autonomous and in the end breaks down and becomes blurred. It is within this horizon that culture shows the human being in its existential concreteness; since the individual human being is not capable of existential organization and autonomy, it could not successfully manifest or actuate the "total quality" of its identity. And it is within this horizon that culture manifests the coherence of its themes, models, and institutions, its vital, open-ended coherence that is essentially nonrepeatable and multiple in the organic character of its varied autonomies; since individual values are fragile due to their one-sidedness and since individual cultures are self-sufficient due to their nonrepeatability, they could not successfully manifest or actuate the "total quality" of their potentialities.

There is no monoculture in the sense that its themes, models, and institutions are homogenized; there are no subcultures in the sense that there are themes, models, and institutions that are inferior in their organization and autonomy to others that are superior in their organization and autonomy; there is no opposition between culture and nature, except for the bipolar, dialectical opposition of themes, models, and institutions. Therefore, since cultural analysis throws into relief the themes, models, and institutions of individual cultures in the autonomous organization of each individual culture, and throws into relief their constants and variants amid the pluriform and multiple cultures, cultural analysis in our case will throw into stubborn relief the themes, models, and institutions of the liturgy in the autonomous organization that is "Christian culture," along with their constants and variants relative to the cultic themes, models, and institutions of other autonomous cultural organizations.

Christian culture is, of course, a transversal culture; cutting across countless cultures in fact, it is in a position to cut across them de jure, as the jargon has it. It is a "horizontal" culture; that is, its autonomous organization is established in an anthropological habitat which is what it is because of its metaspatiotemporal situation. It is a horizontal culture that cuts across other equally horizontal cultures as well as "vertical" cultures, that is, cultures whose autonomous organization takes shape in an anthropological habitat that is identified and identifiable in particular settings in space and time. I am here touching on problems of acculturation, that is, of intercultural reciprocity in which themes and/or models and/or institutions are interchanged, and on problems of inculturation, that is, of the incorporation of a human being into a given cultural group. These are the main dynamics among the cultural dynamics that demand attention in our question.

All this, in accordance with now approved scientific criteria and standards. Failure to attend to these leads to a lack of intellectual and operational honesty and to unavoidable forms of unproductivity.

III. THE HUMAN BEING AND WORSHIP

Now that we have reached this point, our prospect must include a true and proper cultural analysis, even if only in the form of references, of the two terms of the question. On the basis of cultural analyses of the components of the liturgy (initiation, sacrifice, marriage and states of life, the modes, times, and spaces of biological development . . . all the elements that go into the liturgical totality), it must give in outline a cultural analysis of anthropology itself and of liturgy itself, providing interpretative references and methodological examples. Let us begin with the "constants" of the human being and of worship that are found in *all* cultures.

1. The human being of worship (objective genitive): The human being who produces worship because it is homo symbolicus/(σύμβολον).
It is a cultural constant that the human being speaks of itself and utters itself; that is, a conception of the human being about the human being is a cultural constant, and any variants are (only) this or that anthropological idea, this or that modality and value of the particular anthropological conception. Always and everywhere the human being has tried to produce such a conception, by means of poetry and art, philosophy and the sciences, religion and beliefs, and all these in countless models. The attempt means that the human being explicitly or implicitly identifies itself through an expectant scanning of sets of defining adjectives. Thus, in the jargon of the culture of our times but

also with the recapitulative constancy marking each of the predicates, the human being describes itself as *sciens, loquens, faber, politicus, artifex, ludens, religiosus . . .*, referring respectively to scientific knowledge, autonomous language, organized operation, socialization that personalizes, development of the world at the cosmic level, esthetic poiesis, deliberate alienation, meta-immanent intentionality. . . .

These identifying characteristics have a doubly univocal composition: "human being" is the equivalent of all and each of these predicates / all and each of these predicates are the equivalent of "human being." Wherever and whenever there is a human being, there and then there is a constant process of personalization, and each of the above characteristic predicates / wherever and whenever there is meta-immanent intentionality and each of the characteristic predications, there and then there is always a human being.

The list given is, of course, open-ended, in the sense that it remains possible for cultural analysis to find further anthropologically defining characteristics. A basic cultural anthropology is built up precisely by systematizing anthropological finds of this kind. It is an established fact, however, that constant cultural goods, that is, the products of value that are found always and everywhere in cultures, lead us back compellingly to anthropological predications of the kind I have described. The list given above already shows this process: the human being is *loquens* / language is a cultural constant (product, good); the human being is *artifex* / art is a cultural constant (product, good). . . . I may add: the human being is *mythicus* / myth is a constant cultural product; the human being is *ritualis* / ritual is a constant cultural product (the list is still open-ended).

A basic cultural anthropology gives a privileged place to two characteristics beyond all the other constants: meta-immanent intentionality and the use of symbols, for the human being is recognized as being *symbolicus* (I am not going to give a privileged place to either *religiosus* or *symbolicus*, either in an apologetical effort to persuade or by a choice to be argued).

Meta-immanent intentionality is expressed by the adjective *religiosus*. Note now that "religion" is to be taken in its broadest sense, as accepted in all cultures and acceptable even to atheists, that is, in the etymologically clear meaning of *religare*, "to bind closely," but also "to unbind" (for in compound verbs the prefix *re-* can mean either verbal intensification or an action contrary to the meaning of the verb).

In our case, we are concerned with the action of an immanence that tends to something beyond *(trans)* itself, to a transcendence that is suited, or suitable, to this immanence; a *trans*, therefore, that is seen as something to be joined closely with the self and/or from which to separate the self. Such is the ambiguity of the natural relationship between immanence and transcendence, both in the "believing" human being and in the "atheistic" human being. This relationship is, in fact, quick to take refuge in the allied ambiguity of the "sacred." With regard to the human being and its identification, being "religious" means something fairly close to recognizing the human being as theomorphic (as in Scheler and others) or theanthrophic (as in Feuerbach and others), because whether or not it is psychologically and sociologically religious, the human being shows itself constantly convinced, both in theory and in behavior, of a self-transcendence (the literature on the subject is very abundant and very widely circulated).

But, leaving aside the known and unknown contradictory readings of this *trans* (meta-immanence is a personal God, an impersonal divine, fate, chaos, nothingness, and a thousand other real or ideal "entities"), the distinction of this *trans* from nature is not an option, if we are to grasp without equivocation the reality which makes up the divinity of the human being (the *theo*/morphic, *the*/anthropic human being). This is admittedly a burden which the cultural variants take upon themselves; but the indetermination is only something symptomatic of the real or ideal identity of the human being, and must be entered in the record as such.

However it is understood, whether as a determination or a non-determination, this meta-immanent intentionality, or religion, of the human being is in any case joined to the anthropological capacity for symbol through the significational consistency of mediation through symbols. Mediation through symbols, which cannot be replaced by a simple demonstrative mediation, is in fact the only mediation in the genre of signs that can successfully signal the relation of immanence to transcendence with the vicarial consistency given by the presence of what is absent. This is to say that the constant recognition of anthropological symbolism is equivalent to the constant recognition of the human being as aspiration and project toward an all-embracing self-transcendence.

However the theanthropic and theomorphic human being is understood, it proves to be always symbolic in two directions: symbolic because it is productive of symbols, and symbolic because it is itself a symbol. It is this being-itself-a-symbol that grounds the privileged condition of *homo symbolicus* and *homo religiosus*. Without stopping here to reflect on the human being as producer of symbols (again, the literature is very abundant and very widely circulated), my interest here is in gathering evidence about the human being as itself a symbol (see the citation from Pryzwara above, and the literature he has collected).

"Even in primitive traditions, the human being is described as a synthesis of the world, a universe in miniature, a microcosm. It is the center of the symbolic universe. The wise men of the *Upanishads*, the enthusiastic devotees of alchemy, and the theologians of Christianity have pointed out analogies and correspondences between the elements making up the human being and the elements making up the cosmos, between the principles of human dynamics and the movements of the cosmos. . . . In the *Athawa Veda* the human being is regarded as the cosmic pillar that keeps heaven and earth from collapsing, the principle of unity that tends to be identified with Brahma. . . . According to the Chinese, the human being is a set of correspondences between its body and the cosmos: the head is the heavens, the hairs are the constellations, the eyes are the sun . . . the limbs are the four seasons, the major joints are the twelve months, and the minor joints the three hundred and sixty days of the year."[10]

In fact, the anthropological system of symbols differs according as the symbols are of the cosmos or Brahma or the gods (as in Greek and Latin pagan culture, each in its own fashion) or spirits (as in African cultures, in their fashion). To symbolize the universal cosmos is to raise visible nature up to the human being who transcends it, or vice versa. To symbolize principles or elements of the unnameable divine is to bring the human being down to the level of forces that do not bear comparison with him. To symbolize a god with a name is to raise the human being up to an otherness that is comparable to him. Symbolization in human terms of the cosmos and symbolization in human terms of a named god are under certain conditions compatible with each other; symbolization of a named god and

[10] M. M. Davy, "Homme," in *Dictionnaire des symboles*, ed. J. Chevalier and J. Gheerbrant (Paris, 1974²) III, 33–35 passim.

207

symbolization of an unnameable divine are incompatible under any conditions; these again are signs of the identity of the human being and are to be recorded as such.

The fact is that in recognizing itself to be a symbol the human being sees itself reflected *in* and *trans:* an otherness proper to the very race, such as occurs in human love, which is the unqualified self-reflection of the real in the ideal (whereas every narcissistic reflection of the self is a pathological negation of the aspiration and project of an all-embracing self-transcendence).[11] Self-reflection in the cosmos or in a god or in the divine or in anything else gives rise to systems of thought and operational attitudes that are inevitably synchronic among themselves. But the eternal return and reincarnationism, annihilation in the source and the pantheisms, the ecologisms and the angelisms, and the disintegrations and the divinizations — all these are cultural variants. Each in its own way is instructive and makes its demands, but all of them follow upon and do not condition the importance of the privileged anthropological constants. This importance, on the contrary, leads directly to the rise of symbolic cultic concatenations.

2. The worship of the human being (subjective genitive):
Worship is anthropological because the human being is ritualis.
As I have pointed out, *symbolicus* and *religiosus* are privileged anthropological predications; *ritualis* and *mythicus,* on the other hand, are anthropological predications which we must analyze in view of our question, while prescinding from any privileged status. The play, then, of *homo ritualis* and *mythicus* is derived from the play of *homo symbolicus;* rites and myths have their place in the chains of symbols proper to meta-immanent intentionality and anthropological symbolization.

At a time when the supposed secularization of everything transcendent and the phenomenological reduction of liturgy to the human sciences have become widespread, it has become difficult, in these demanding postconciliar years, to talk of "rite" because the indiscriminate identification of it with ritualism has forced it back into the narrow confines of an antipathetic romanticism or of one or other kind of formalism, and because the elements of socialization and psychological reassurance to be gained from ritual structures have

[11] M. Nédoncelle, *La réciprocité des consciences* (Paris, 1942); L. Lavelle, *L'erreur de Narcisse* (Paris, 1939).

been confused with the crudely functionalist interpretations given by sociology and psychology. But the disintegration of an uncivilized demythization and the spread of the hermeneutic approach in relating liturgy to anthropology have led to a rethinking and restatement in which the reality of ritual is tackled without the weight of extrinsic hindrances pressing on the intrinsic reality of the phenomenon. In my view, then, I speak of rite, which is a constant cultural product and good, by speaking of *homo ritualis* and adopting the perspective of the human being. This undoubtedly enables us to outline better and more clearly the anthropological interpretation of our question.

A rite is "religion in action."[12] It is an operational translation of the ideas and beliefs of the culture that produces it. It is "an action that is repeated, and whose efficacy is in whole or in part of the extraempirical order."[13] In fact, the very word "ritual," from the Indo-European root *r'tam*, signifies an activity conformed to a universal and transcendent order. Not by chance, then, did one of the ancients say that "custom is the use of something usual, with the consent of two or more; a rite, however, has to do with justice, as the right norm from which piety, equity, and holiness derive."[14] Repetition is not enough to make a rite! (It is the journalists who speak of the merely customary as "ritual.") For a rite it is necessary that many agree on a usage connected with justice and that from this justice as from a norm there flow due respect, a favorable tranquility, a divine stability.

The meaning assigned by Isidore is obviously not a generic one. The others, too, whom I have cited, are not satisfied with the (legitimate) generalization that a rite is a rule for use from which flows an effect that is extraempirical although not absolutely transcending the order of immanence. Isidore is speaking of rite in a strict sense, that is, in the sense of the usual symbolic link between *in* and *trans,* which makes of it a connection due specifically in justice, whose effects are both intraempirical and extraempirical. In other words, "rite" in the strict sense is cultic rite alone, a rite performed by a human being insofar as he is *ritualis-religiosus* (*homo ritualis* also can and does perform noncultic rites).

Since *homo ritualis* has these qualifications, "rite" too has properties that always characterize it, though differently in its actuation in

---

[12] M. Dhavomony, *Phenomenology of Religion* (Rome, 1973) 158.
[13] J. Cazeneuve, *Les rites et la condition humaine* (Paris, 1958) 4.
[14] Isidore of Seville, *Differentiarum liber* 1, 122.

general and in its actuation in worship. We must therefore not lose sight of the fact that the review of these properties marking the influence of anthropological predication is the work of anthropological phenomenology, which moves inductively from *homo basicus* (objective genitive), as the jargon calls that which corresponds to the *homo universalis* deduced by philosophy.

A rite is a programmed dramatic action. It belongs to the order of ἐργ- (ἔργον), of "acting by suffering," comparable to the order of λέγ- (λόγος), of "gathering together by speaking,"[15] although we must not deny its clearly operative form. At its best, it is intense action, that is, action that is psychically "dramatic" (δράω = "I act in a way that is completely absorbing"; from ideas to action via the "visibility" of the most penetrating perceptions and the deepest feelings). Therefore it is action that is not improvised but "programmed" (προγράφω = "I notify with an order to promulgate") for a purpose that is not dilettantish, starting with a plan whose realization is assured, along the lines of the most direct and suitable action, by imposing social responsibility.

A rite in the strict sense is an institution (the Romans, who did not have anthropologico-cultural categories would have called it an *ordo / numerus*), based on a theme, that is, on culturally directed values of the dynamism that leads from immanence to transcendence, and on a model, that is, on the repetition of these values in a cultural exemplar that is feasible for all and each member of a particular culture. A cultic rite is brought into being by an *auctoritas*, that is, a source that is capable of programming human dramas, in the full sense of the word, by making itself a guarantor of the history of individuals and of the collectivity. This authority may be a genius, a hero, tradition, a group, an envoy of the divinity or some god, but in any case someone capable of *augere*, of "increasing, enriching" in their *humanitas* the actors in the instituted ritual action.

The performer of the rite is the collective "we" who are intensely immersed up in the same "symbolic field" (in contrast to the individual "I" — the aspect that has been analyzed, and sometimes greatly exaggerated, by the sociologists). The addressee of the rite is the same cultural group, which sees reflected in it its own "we," but also

---

[15] G. Bertram, "ἔργον," *TDNT* 2, 655; A. Debrunner and H. Kleinknecht, "λέγω," *TDNT* 4, 69–91.

210

each individual whom the rite brings into the presence of his *trans* and at the same time of every other individual in the same culture (the aspect that has been analyzed, and sometimes greatly exaggerated, by the psychologists).

The efficacy of the rite, which has no technical usefulness, is in the line of the integration of the *in* with the *trans* (vertical integration) and in the line of psychological and sociological integration (horizontal integration); it is proved by the certainty which repetition brings. The ritual program is repeated as such every time that this integration is sought; in fact, trust is placed in this repetition as in archetypes that are re-experienced diachronically, generation after generation, age after age, and brought here and now into the synchrony of our present certainty, that is, brought into agreement with the original and successive certainties. The result is a dialectic between the intangibility of the rite and the actualizing growth in institutional certainty, which is highly productive. Should a ritual formalism, a ritualism, develop, the institutional intangibility turns into a "rubrical" formalism; in a culturally correct practice of ritual, however, a rite is eminently historicized; this is nothing more or less than hominization.

In fact, every institution is both a support of and an obstacle to its own themes and models; in our case, the institutionalization of rite, insofar as it is a support, leads to hominization within the cultural history; insofar as it is an obstacle, it leads to a ritualism that militates against the culture's own anthropological dynamisms.

Cultic rite has its counterfeit, namely, the magical rite that consists in attempting an upside-down form of the dynamic involved in immanence and transcendence: instead of rising from the *in* to the *trans* by evoking and invoking, there is an attempt to make the *trans* descend into the *in* by inciting and manipulating. It is a counterfeit, because the attempt proves hopeless and disastrous, both as to the integration of a transcendence that cannot be captured by immanence and as to a certainty that cannot be synchronized with nonexistent original and successive certainties (consequently, since the practice of magic is not a cultural institution, it will be counterfeit not only of the cultic but also of the ritual). Note, however, that this is being said solely of magic; for example, the practice of the ritual institution with a fideistic trust in its efficacy is a distorted use of the cultic rite but the rite does not become magical.

I must not neglect to note the classifications of rites that are usually made for various reasons having to do with their function (psychological, sociological, and so on) or with their structures (more or less integrative, more or less performative, and so on) or/and with other considerations. For our purpose, the classification of rites does not seem to contribute much, and it seems that our interest should be concentrated on their phenomenology rather than on the occasions on which rites develop. Therefore, without assigning importance to classification as such, let me record some observations that are quite interesting.

"Rites of passage"[16] have led to reflections on the liminality between the *in* and the *trans* in the dialectics of I-we, life-death, before-after, inside-outside, and so on, which stamp anthropological existence in relation precisely to immanence-transcendence; these would be the symbolically resolutional rites accompanying the liminal polarities: marriage, burial, initiation, and so on. "Rites of crisis"[17] have led to reflection on the anomaly of the powerlessness of anthropological existence before the impossibility of controlling the cosmic world, and the salutary extraversion which the *in* finds and/or seeks by attaching itself to the *trans;* these would be the religiously therapeutic rites connected with existential deficiencies (prayer in illness, in bad weather, in war, and so on). "Cyclic rites"[18] have led to reflection on temporal and spatial returns in which anthropological existence periodically becomes aware of itself and which seem to restore the harmony of the meeting of immanence and transcendence; these would be rites of festive celebration of the cultic synchrony in life and history (calendrical arrangements, temple buildings, and so on).

The interest of the reflections which I have listed under a few main headings, in my opinion, is that they show in concrete instances how cultic rites are always forms of cultural alienation and therefore have a positive value for the human being, and how they continually reshape anthropological time and space by displaying a hominizing *sobria ebrietas.*

[16] A. Van Gennep, *The Rites of Passage,* trans. M. Vizedom and G. Caffee (Chicago: University of Chicago Press, 1960).

[17] B. Malinowski, *Magic, Science, and Religion* (New York, 1957).

[18] M. Eliade, *Images and Symbols. Studies in Religious Symbolism,* trans. P. Mairet (New York, 1961).

I said earlier that a rite is an institution based on theme and model. A rite is founded on a nucleus of words, on a myth, because the order of ἔργον is correctly to be based on the order of λόγος. The learned debate over whether rite precedes myth or vice versa and whether rite is de jure connected with myth does not concern us because in our phenomenology rite and myth show themselves to be synchronous and because in fact there are myths that are not translated into rites, but no rites that are not traceable to myths. For this reason, in our synchrony rite is related to myth as the verb is linguistically related to the noun and as institutions are culturally related to theme and model.

Taken separately, a myth is a function in search of clarity, while a rite is a structure in search of infallibility; a rite is a "visualization" of what is heard in a myth. Taken in combination, a myth is a theme that gives direction, amid cultural variants, to the constant values of immanence and transcendence, while a rite is the resultant institutionalization of these according to the coherences I have pointed out. Between myth and rite there intervene, in an organized manner, the models that adapt the connections between theme-myth and institution-rite according to cultural variants. Immanence and transcendence, the mythical phenomenon (myth) and the ritual phenomenon (rite) are the cultural constants; the thematization of the myth (in the form of myths), the institutionalization of rite (in the form of rites), and the model for connecting the two (cults) are cultural variants. The autonomous way in which theme-model-institution are organized in a culture "systematize" myth and rite.

Rite mediates symbolically the reality it represents, mediates it in the form of an understanding (not a learning), the meaning of which is provided by the originating myth. A myth is a story (of a special kind) of a rite. What is myth in itself? What is the nature of *homo mythicus?* A μῦθος is "a sententious saying, an entertainment in the form of a story, a rumor that gives an account, a proverb, a parable, a fable. . . ." This description is enough to explain the contrasting (positive) valuations of it and even the depreciation it elicits. It is an archaic cultural constant of archaic cultures, and the cultures that have preserved myths which are extremely fascinating in their quality and number, especially the cultures of India and Greece, attest that this interest is not merely contemporary nor merely romantic and that criticism of myth, whether positive or negative, is not merely contemporary nor merely scientific.

The lessons learned from myths must be used with a broad attention to the varied directions taken by myths; in other words, we must distrust the general term "myth," as if it were simply a genus with a variety of species. Myth is certainly that, but it is also a lexical heap of diverse genres; "analogously" to G. S. Kirk (who makes the statement in combatting the functionalist interpretation of Malinowski and the structuralist interpretation of Lévi-Strauss),[19] I am convinced that theories are condemned to be erroneous if they do not separate myths from one another: for example, proverb and parable are species of the same genus, parable and fable are themselves different species (this is why Kirk distinguishes theoretically, among myths, between a genus of myths that amuse, a genus of myths that provide confirmation, and a genus of myths that are explanatory).

I shall not bother to point out classifications of the genus strictly speaking of myth; I shall, however, point out the anthropological interpretations that are useful for our subject, following a fairly common list. Myth springs from the native orientation of the spirit (F.W.J. Schelling); from the domination of monotheistic patriarchal culture by a polytheistic matriarchal culture (W. Schmidt); from the prelogical mentality of primitive human beings (L. Lévy-Bruhl). Myth is a function that gives rise to every model of religio-ethical behavior (B. Malinowski); a structure that gives rise to every linguistic theme concerned with the cosmos (C. Lévi-Strauss); the universal matrix of psycho-social relationships (E. Durkheim); the universal matrix of cultural forms (M. Mauss). A myth is a "true story" (M. Eliade). All of these are interpretations that condition the link between myth and rite, to say that it exists or does not, to say in what sense it exists.

My attention turns therefore to the effects of myth on the connection with rite or to the effects of the connection. And therefore to the fact that a myth is a story of probability rather than truth; that it is a psycho-social and cultural projection of human existence; that it is a utopian intentionality extending from the origins of the human being to its infinitude. Myth belongs therefore to the order of *logos*: an ascientific, metaphenomenological, potentially presential *logos* of infinite complexity in a germinal limit; not in the manner of scientific, phenomenological, reflective discourse. Myth is thus the transmission

[19] G. S. Kirk and J. E. Raven, *The Presocratic Philosophers* (Cambridge, Mass., 1957).

of experience/anticipation of being/actuality of becoming. Its time is the utterly remote and also the metahistorical end-time of history; its space is the concentrated presence of the metacosmic distances in the cosmos. Myth of its nature "connives" with the symbolic, and it is in this way that it "precedes" rite.

Rite, which has its co-precedent in myth has its con-sequent in celebration. A celebration, which is the carrying out of the ritual program, is always an obedience to ritual as supporting institution, by way of a variant model, starting with the theme of the originating myth.

IV. THE CHRISTIAN HUMAN BEING AND CHRISTIAN WORSHIP

Let me now take my cultural analysis as a starting point and single out the "variants" which Christian culture offers in its worship, that is, in the liturgy; and the "variants" which it offers regarding the human being, both the human being *according to* Christianity, or the human according to Christian anthropology, and the human being *of* Christianity, or the human being according to Christian anthropological experience. In relation to our question, the human being of Christianity concerns us directly; the human being according to Christianity only indirectly. Therefore I shall treat directly of the one and indirectly of the other.

1. The human being of liturgy (objective genitive): The Christian human being produces liturgy insofar as he is homo iconicus (εἰκόν). The anthropological variant that is Christian culture combines the constant predicates: *religiosus* and *symbolicus* (the human being as itself a symbol). Christian culture combines the predicate *religiosus* in its totality and this aspect of the predicate *symbolicus* in *homo iconicus;* that is, in the concept of "icon" by which Christian culture, which is a horizontal culture and therefore a culture co-existing with many vertical cultures, defines its own special constitution. Christian human beings consider themselves makers of symbols, like human beings in every culture; makers of images, analogously; and they consider themselves to be an εἰκόν, an "image" ("in the image of God") insofar as they themselves are symbols. "In the image," but differently for the human being of Christianity and for the human being simply according to Christianity; each therefore, in his or her own way.

This conception,[20] the foundations of which are biblical ideas of Hebrew culture and of the Old Testament, was not, however, brought into awareness in a linear way; the New Testament foundations gave rise to varying emphases in the cultures of the first and second millennium, both eastern and western. The confluence of Hebrew culture as reflected in Genesis and of Pauline Christian culture with Greek Platonic or Aristotelean or any other culture brought with it a clash between a threefold perspective and a dichotomy, between a unified conception of the human being (though with many phenomenological aspects) and a dualistic conception of the human being as internally divided. The syntheses that were attempted brought new anthropological reflection on protology and eschatology by way of a Christology installed in the history of the world (the world has its meaning in the Word of God prior to its existence / the Word of God is in the world prior to his incarnation) and in the history of salvation (through the paschal mystery the human being moves from the Logos-Alpha to the Logos-Omega).

But all these remained syntheses that swung from one extreme to another, and syntheses of a Christian culture thrown off balance and monopolized by pagan Greek culture. When all is said and done, despite the impossibility of refusing to enter into symbioses with the anthropological conceptions of the surrounding cultures, the challenge which Christian culture must accept, and cannot fail to meet successfully, is to trust fully in its own biblical tradition. In other words, the problem is not so much to entrust the image which its own biblical tradition reveals to it to one or another privileged element in the cultures with which it dialogues, as to be able to recover from the image itself the qualities, the freedom, the reciprocity, the grandeur, and so on which one culture finds in reason, another in something else, and so on.

Generally speaking, the Greek Fathers asserted the substantial invisibility of the divine image in the human being, whereas the Latin Fathers, beginning with Augustine of Hippo, set off in the direction of psychological visibility. But this choice, as seen in the medieval and other treatises *De anima*, would lead, repeatedly and unfortu-

[20] See C. Moeller, "Renouveau de la doctrine de l'homme," in *La théologie du renouveau* (Montreal-Paris, 1968) I, 211–47; R. Javelet, *Image et ressemblance au douzième siècle* (Strasbourg, 1967).

nately, to inadmissible and distorting ways of obscuring the image itself. "The reason of the human being is an image of the Supreme reason and grasps the truth interiorly through God's teaching" *(Est hominis ratio Summae Rationis imago / quae capit interius vera docente Deo):*[21] the human being is not "in the image" of God, but human reason is an image (without "in the") of the divine Reason. But in the analysis of Christian culture the real problem of an iconic anthropology has to do with the interaction between who is the image, of whom it is the image, and how it is the image.

According to Thomas Aquinas *(Summa Theologiae* I, 93), the starting point *(terminus a quo)* of true and proper iconicity, that is, not simply of a likeness in genus but of a likeness in species (93, 2 resp.), is the intellectual nature of the human being (93, 4) to the exclusion of his or her corporeity (93, 5, ad 3); the iconic character is defined by this exclusion. The goal *(terminus ad quem)* is God who is one in nature and three in persons (93, 5 resp.), but without it being possible to conclude from the trinity of persons to a detailed description of interpersonal human iconicity, thus excluding the idea that the distinction between the masculine and feminine sexes might found the relationship between the human being and God; the image is "in the mind, in which there is no distinction of the sexes" (93, 6 ad 2). The measure *(modus)* of the iconicity is established by the "in the image" *(ad imaginem)* of the biblical description from Genesis 1:26 on, in which the "in" signifies the approach of distant entities to each other (93, 1 resp.), and by the distinction which the biblical description makes between image and likeness, understanding likeness as a descriptive "preamble" and "subsequent" perfection of the image (93, 9 resp.), with the reference to John Damascene who, summarizing the tradition, gives "likeness" an ethical meaning.

The developmental or evolutionary line taken by Gregory of Nyssa suggests other paths to follow. According to Gregory, it is the human being as such, in its totality, that is in the image of God. Although God is not corporeal, the corporeal element of the human being is not on that account separable from the human person, as having is from being or becoming is from being: the human being is a person who

---

[21] A. Orbe, *Antropología de San Ireneo* (Madrid, 1969); C. Militello, "La categoria di 'immagine' nel *Peri kataskeues anthropou* di Gregorio di Nissa per una antropologia cristiana," *Ho Theologos* 1 (1974, nos. 2–3) 107–22.

is, in his or her makeup, in the image of God. If this raises problems which interact with problems caused by other, subsequent aspects, they will be problems that must lead to a solution; it will not be the iconic constitution that is incapable of including the person in its full amplitude. In fact, it will be precisely the iconic constitution that will solve the question.

The human being is in the image of God one and three, of the divine totality, and the distinction of persons in God, which is the divine way of saying simultaneously and completely what it is in itself and of uttering itself with creative generosity outside itself, grounds the relationship of human persons among themselves. This relationship, though not simultaneous or complete, is one of reciprocity and endless dynamism. Moreover, in the distinction of the sexes, even though this does not exist in God, the distinction of persons in God is reflected symbolically in a relationship in space and time, where and when the interrelatedness after the manner of God is mediated by the divine economy of corporeality. The mode of being proper to iconicity is established by the "in the image" which is the given germ of the utopia-gift, of perfection endlessly perfectible, of becoming further what it already is. It is therefore established by the distinction between image and likeness as a teleological distinction between the given and the gift, the already and the still, of hominization.

The Fourth Lateran Council provided the West with the way of interpreting the root problem and its interactions, when it said that the unlikeness between God and the human being is always greater than any likeness of the human being to God (*DS* 806). Anthropological iconicity is a phenomenon to be gauged by the reflective measure of analogy, both in understanding the closeness and in not forgetting the distance between the *in* and the *trans*.

Christian culture also offers the phenomenon of its theandric conception, the play of mirror facing mirror, for an understanding of its iconicity. The human being, though made in the image of God, does not de jure become the likeness in an uninterrupted way. The Word of God, who is also the A-Ω of every human being and is the divine (and not teleological) Image of God (Col 1:15; 2 Cor 4:4), himself becomes a human being in the likeness of flesh and even of sinful flesh (Rom 8:3) and thereby opens the way to a solution of the riddle which the human being is to itself (see Vatican II's outline of a Christian anthropology in *Gaudium et spes* 12–22). As a result of this added iconicity, there is de facto added to the human being the "in the image and likeness" of the incarnate and paschal Word who brings to the anthropological utopia of hominization the grace of theandric divinization; such is the "wonderful exchange" *(admirabile commercium)* of liturgical sacramentality. All the cultures of Christianity have given abiding expression to this aspect of iconicity that comes "through the Son in the Spirit."

But neither has the connected problem of the relation of nature to supernature been brought to consciousness in a linear way. The East has preserved a dynamic conception of "nature," while in the West the preoccupation with various forms of immanentism has caused an abnormal distrust of any dynamics between the two terms in question, forgetting that the words functionally imply each other: "super/ nature" is the principle of operation proper to the divine persons and is so called to indicate their operational control over persons having a human "nature."

The fate of the approach taken by H. de Lubac in his *Surnaturel* and abruptly ended as a result of *Humani generis* (August 15, 1950) was saddening. It would be necessary to wait for the address of Paul VI at the closing of the fourth period of Vatican II (December 7, 1965) in order to hear once again, after the passage of centuries, the "burning words of Catherine of Siena: 'In your nature, eternal deity, I shall know my nature'" (*Orazione* 24). To hear, that is, a statement of the continuity between nature and supernature which moves beyond static conceptions that define the two as a double, even if analogous, "principle of operation" (according, of course, to the principle of analogy of Lateran IV).

So much, then, on the nature of persons, both divine and human (each in their own way), for the purpose in our case of applying it precisely to the theandric character of liturgical activity. But we must also speak with precision of the "person," in order chiefly to eliminate from our question the juridical concept of the "individual." "Undivided in itself, divided from everyone else" *(indivisum in se, divisum a quolibet alio)* may be a useful model in assigning juridical responsibilities, but the human person — icon of God is not explained by defining the human person as an "individual substance of a rational nature" *(individuum subsistens in rationali natura),* while defining a divine person as "being in relation to" *(esse ad)* (western conceptions derived, as everyone knows, from M. S. Boethius[22] and passed on by the Scholastics).

Furthermore, it is necessary to describe the human person precisely both as "I" (which is not a psychological individual) and as "we" (which is not a sociological collectivity). As for the "I," even Christian anthropology (see the outline in Vatican II, *Gaudium et spes* 23–32) bases it on socialization, which obviously means not only on the interhuman but on the theandric "solidarity" with the incarnate and paschal Word and on the "connaturality" with God who created the human being in his own image and likeness. As for the "we," Christian anthropology has an understanding of "corporate personality," while optimally exemplifying the present-day psycho-social category from Hebrew biblical anthropology (think of Adam, Noah, Abraham, Israel, and so on), also provides, in its revelation of the whole Christ, head and members, a single spousal body, the supreme embodiment among all those observable in human cultures.

These, then, are the extreme forms of *homo* εἰκών, the Christian cultural variant of both *homo religiosus* and *homo* σύμβολον. A sensitive cultural analysis, which asserts a variety of stratified conceptions, works synchronically and therefore does not distract from conclusions to be drawn. And the conclusions lead in turn to the persuasion that if the liturgy, Christian worship, is "sacramental," it is so to the extent that the Christian human being is *religiosus* and *symbolicus*. Therefore the liturgy is revelatory of the Christian human being, and the Christian human being is revelatory of the liturgy. In analyzing the cultural variant that is Christian worship, let us not forget that the two phenomena, *homo* εἰκών and liturgy, are in an osmotic relationship.

2. The liturgy of the human being (subjective genitive): The liturgy is anthropological inasmuch as the Christian human being is liturgicus.
At this point, the addition of *liturgicus* is even tautological. I do not set it down idly, however, but in order to explain several points, without mediating words: that *homo liturgicus* is a particular cultural variant of *homo ritualis*; that *homo ritualis* is a generic cultural constant for the Christian human being; that accordingly, and specifically, in Christian culture the general idea of "cult" is specified as "liturgy"

[22] M. Nédoncelle, "Les variations de Boèce sur la personne," *RSR* 29 (1953) 201–38.

and is characterized anthropologically by the properties of *homo iconicus*/εἰκόν and not of *homo* generically *religiosus* and generically *symbolicus;* that in keeping with the iconic status of Christianity, in virtue of which the human being is theandric, the liturgy has a sacramental status in virtue of which the Christian rite (of Christians) is theandric in an all-embracing sense: always and everywhere divine and human, divine and human in its totality and in the scansions of its themes, models, and institutions, wholly divine (of God) and wholly human (of the human being). This last is our concluding point of interest: because otherwise the understanding of liturgy will lose its specific symbolico-sacramental character and don the garb again of a generic religio-sacrality.

A liturgical rite, like every cultic rite, is based on a nucleus of words; but its λόγος is the Word, the God-man (John 1:1-5, 9-14, 16-18), and its ἔργον therefore is a celebration "in spirit and in truth" (John 4:23). In this respect, Christian culture follows to the end the course adopted by Hebrew culture of giving myths new meanings; like the latter, Christian culture historicizes the myths in the history of the divine economy, bringing about a cultural shift in the symbolic field by giving space-time a new shape, linear instead of cyclical, and it completes the Hebrew process by hypostatizing Word and Action in the persons of the Son of God and the Holy Spirit. The integration into the vertical and the horizontal effected by a ritual institution based on such a theme does not consist, therefore, in a flight from space-time but in making connections with the history of salvation, and the repetition that certifies it is connected with the historical phenomenality of the events, which it celebrates by way of memorial, that is, by an iconically mimetic and participative renewal of saving efficacy, actuated "through" (because of *and* by means of *and* for the purpose of) the phenomenal event itself.[23] From the "at that time" *(in illo tempore)* of a story to the "here, today" *(hodie hic)* of the actuation.

The conscious grasp of this transignification and liturgical transculturation has been pretty much linear; however, it remains latent in certain cultural phases and has at last, in the present phase of our culture, felt the effect of the various demythizations. In fact, in the liturgy (but not only there) the effect has been a confused one, considering that to demythicize the Christian transignification of myth

---

[23] B.-B. De Soos, *Le mystère liturgique d'après Saint Léon le Grand* (Münster, 1985).

amounts to demythicizing it only in the understanding of one who does not analyze or measure or reject the transculturation that has taken place.

The theme of liturgical ritual institution proves therefore to have three aspects: the programmed dramatic action which, as a norm of justice, gives rise to due respect, fostering tranquility, and divine stability, gravitating around the word, the glory, and the mystery as one; one (in addition to their theological unity) with the unity of the foundational anthropological theme. The word, it hardly need be said, is the revealed word, the word written in the Book, the word handed on in the Church, the hypostatic Word that is equivalent to Logos-Theandric-Person; the "celebration" on Easter evening on the road to Emmaus and at the table there (Luke 24:13-35) may be taken as a point of reference.

The glory, which comes between word and mystery, is the visual transposition of the word and is the epiphany of the mystery, it is the face of God; as a point of reference, "the prayer" of Moses and God's answer: "'Show me your glory, I pray.' / 'I will make all of my good-ness pass before you, and will proclaim before you the name, "the Lord" . . . but you cannot see my face, for no one shall see me and live'" (Exod 33:12-23), as compared with the "critical threshold" that is the Prologue of the Fourth Gospel: "We have seen his glory. . . . No one has ever seen God. It is God the only Son, who is close to the Father's heart, who has made him known" (John 1:14, 18) and with Philip's "plea" and Jesus' answer: "'Lord, show us the Father, and we will be satisfied.' / 'Whoever has seen me has seen the Father'" (John 14:8-9).

The mystery, from word to glory, is the mystery in Pauline theology; as a point of reference, the liturgical "hymn": "Without any doubt, the mystery of our religion is great: He was revealed in flesh, vindi-cated in spirit, seen by angels, proclaimed among Gentiles, believed in throughout the world, taken up in glory" (1 Tim 3:16).

Models for the organization of this theme, with its three aspects, in relation to the ritual institution are: the proclamation/hearing of the word, the revelation/vision of the glory, the sapiential taste/experi-ence of the mystery. It is not a question of moving from the cognitive order to the operational order; the theandric composition of proclaim/hear, reveal/see, and give a taste/experience is much more interest-ing than that (we need only note that these same models are used in another concatenation of Christian culture, namely, the anthropological structure of liturgical spirituality — that is, Christian spirituality without declensions and conjugations — and are its foundational theme). All three pairs together are to be analyzed linguistically as an anthropological unity that corresponds to the theological unity of their terms, word-glory-mystery, with the circuminsession of the three. There would be no effective analysis of the cultural variant that is the liturgical ritual model if we allowed the theandric unity to escape us.

Let me take each pair by itself (by agreement, for easier exposition) and indicate only, first, the interpersonal theandric reciprocity present in both the vertical and the horizontal dimensions, a reciprocity to which proclaim/hear refers emblematically, since it is διά/λογία; second, the chiasmus, again theandric, between hearing the glory and seeing the word, to which revelation/vision refers in a way that is again emblematic, for it is the catalyzing code of Christian culture; third, the divinization, likewise theandric, of the human senses, to which sapiential taste/experience refers, once again emblematically, for it is the syntax of the asyntactic. So much for ease of exposition. Returning to the aspect of unity: the scriptures and the Fathers take the transfiguration as point of reference: showing-seeing the Face, uttering-hearing the Voice, leading to-entering into the Cloud of God: bestow/use the eyes, give/acquire the ear, transform/live the very βίος of God.

V. "HOMOLOGIZE"

The term is not one to stir enthusiasm; nevertheless, when it is purified of inappropriate elements and accepted in its meaning of putting things in order through likeness, it will do to express the thought that the analysis of cultural constants and variants is serviceable to the extent that it persuades us operationally about the proximities *and* the distances between them. It is from the balance-sheet of proximities and distances (and not from a simple listing of these) that the interpretation of our question is to be drawn.

A twofold balance-sheet. One is a matter of right; the balance I have tried to show between human being and Christian human being, cult and Christian cult, by hermeneutical reference and by methodological example. The other is of fact: that which is to be drawn up not through a preparatory discussion but contextually, through detailed

223

discussions. The anthropological and cultural component is analyzed in the same way that the "pastoral" or "spiritual" component of liturgical rites in their specificity is brought out. To these two balance-sheets are then added the "rites" of popular piety ("devout practices"), to be analyzed in terms of the liturgical vehicles they use, and the "rites" of popular ("natural") religiosity, to be analyzed as transignificative transculturations of liturgy and/or significations that are not liturgically transcultural. This is Guardini's urgent call as renewed by scientific progress in the philosophy of religion and in the history and phenomenology of the religions, and fostered by postconciliar re-evaluations of the phenomenon "popular."

From the understanding we have acquired we can derive three special warnings for subsequent analyses.

The proposal of a least common denominator, even one that serves for a "human" self-resolution of liturgical problems, is not an anthropological hermeneutic of the liturgical phenomenon; it is not a proposal of meaning, but simply an evasion by way of facile reductions; but "the more difficult reading is to be followed" *(lectio difficilior sequende est)*.

Between liturgy and anthropology there is much more than a juxta-position, however far-reaching. Without (Christian) anthropology there is no (liturgical) worship; the (Christian) human being is the subject (co-subject) who produces the object we call (liturgical) worship. But the liturgy is an object-effect in such a way that it immediately turns around and becomes a cause of the anthropological development of the subject-cause that has produced it. Between liturgy and anthropology runs the anthropogenetic circle of osmotic exchange between the human being and that which hominizes it. This reciprocity is germinal and fruitful. At this point begins the subject of the influence of Christian anthropology, beyond the human being of Christian culture, to every human being, to all human beings. In a manner known only to God, his Holy Spirit associates all of them with the paschal mystery *(Gaudium et spes* 22) that is celebrated in the liturgy.

Bibliography

Benoist, L. *Signes symboles et mythes.* 2nd ed. Paris, 1977.

Bouyer, L. *Rite and Man: Natural Sacredness and Christian Liturgy.* Trans. M. J. Costelloe. Notre Dame, Ind., 1963.

Cassirer, E. *The Philosophy of Symbolic Form*. Trans. R. Manheim. 3 vols. New Haven, Conn., 1953–1957.

Di Nola, A. M. "Mito." *Enciclopedia delle religioni* 4:486–530. Florence, 1972.

Erikson, E. *Le comportament rituel chez l'homme et l'animal*. Paris, 1971.

Isambert, F. *Rite et efficacité symbolique: Essai d'anthropologie sociologique*. Paris, 1979.

Le Gall, R. "Anthropologie et liturgie." *QL* 69 (1988/1) 96–104.

Maggiani, S. "Rito/Riti." *NDL* 1223–31.

Valenziano, C. "Aspetti antropologici dei simboli nell'iniziazione cristiana." In *I simboli dell'iniziazione cristiana*, 243–59. Rome, 1983.

_____. "'Confitemini': Practica culturale della penitenza." *EphLit* 97 (1983/3–4) 362–70.

_____. "Costanti e varianti in celebrazioni coniugali di culture cristiane." In *La celebrazione del matrimonio cristiano*, 299–360. Bologna, 1972.

_____. "Liturgia e religiosità popolare: Interazione ed equivoci." *Presenza pastorale* 50 (1980/5) 111–15.

Silvano Maggiani, O.S.M.

12

The Language of Liturgy

Anyone observing or participating in a Christian liturgical celebration can easily notice that the "experience" of "telling the story of God," the God of Jesus Christ, the "experience" of communicating in the Holy Spirit with the source event of salvation, namely the paschal mystery, the "experience" of living from a historical memory in the density of the present, the "experience" of praising and glorifying the Living One, is effected by putting into play expressive fields of a composite nature. By articulating with one another, they constitute a symbolic fabric that permits genuine communication, with variants according to the historical times and cultures in which the "experience" happens. It belongs to human existence to constitute people in a relation with each other and with the world through words, actions, gestures, movements, things and objects, sounds, music, colors, scents, in which people deposit experiential meanings of different sorts and which they make use of as *languages*. Language allows making reality one's own, making it exist as a possibility of union and of conscious communion with and through subjects and with the world. Language allows, in the diversity of its articulation, for reaching a plurality of levels including the religious. Of these, the liturgical "experience" can be considered one of the loftiest and the most profound. In this case, although not alone, language is not just any language but is qualified as *symbolic language*, since it lives by the polarity proper to every symbol able to unite the human *and* divine experience of Christian celebration. Symbolic language gives us something to think about and allows us to know. But when it is structured into a symbolic fabric, it finds itself unfurled in a context of doing in which saying is doing and acting is expressing meanings, in which language finds its coordination in ritual action, and rituality allows symbolic language in liturgical action to become an experience transforming the subject and communicating the divine. In this perspective we can affirm that liturgical experience lives both from a symbolic language and a ritual action, always in reference to an object (in the Christian experience, the event of Jesus Christ) and to a subject (in the Christian experience, the Church that celebrates and prays) in a determined time and space. That which is experienced in the celebration is confirmed by liturgical science every time it reflects on the celebrative practice with a viewpoint of theological-historical-anthropological nature and with particular attention to the liturgical books, authoritative *Models of Practice,* whether those of the Western and Eastern traditions or the *Ordines* renewed by the Second Vatican Council.

LITURGICAL LANGUAGE IN
SACROSANCTUM CONCILIUM

We can state that *SC* does not appear to be directly concerned with the problem of liturgical language in the sense that we are looking at in this context; nevertheless, the constitution, attentively read, can become a referential *auctoritas* for our subject. It has clearly posed the problem of liturgical "tongue," with relevant norms (*SC* 36, 39, 54, 63, 101). The conciliar and postconciliar discussion has been lively on this area.[1] But if we consider the whole structure and articulation of *SC* in the light of the pastoral currents emerging in the council, which wanted to reconsider the Church's liturgical life and to look at the foundation of liturgical action itself in the light of the theological quest, it is possible to illuminate in depth the problem of liturgical language. For our line of argument, no. 7 of *SC* turns out to be a keystone. In this, it is affirmed that the liturgy is an *exercitatio* of the *muneris sacerdotalis* of Jesus Christ; it belongs to the order of acting, of action that has as its sole and absolute referent the *historia salutis* which it ritualizes in its salvific efficacy. The Church, subject of liturgical action (*SC* 6), performs a work that is an actuation *hic et nunc* of Christ's salvific work, of his paschal mystery.

[1] Cf. G. Venturi, "Evoluzione della problematica relativa alla traduzione liturgica," *Mysterion. Nella Celebrazione del Mistero di Cristo e la vita della Chiesa* (Leumann, Turin, 1981) 307–27; ibid., "Traduzione liturgica," *NDL* 1525–34.

In the actuation of the salvific *opus,* in the liturgical action, we can find three aspects or dimensions that constitute and characterize the liturgical action itself:

— *Per signa sensibilia . . . modo singulis proprio* (Through signs perceptible to the senses . . . in a way suitable to each one): this is the dimension of liturgical MEDIATION, ultimately rooted in the glorious humanity of Christ, the instrument of our salvation, and therefore in our humanity, inspired by the same Holy Spirit by whom Jesus Christ was anointed;

— *significatur et efficitur sanctificatio hominis et integer cultus publicus exercetur* (the sanctification of humans is achieved and complete public worship is carried out): this is the dimension of the SALVIFIC REALITY of the celebration, expressed in the descending (sanctification) and ascending (glorification) movements that every celebration, as a celebration of the paschal mystery, achieves, albeit with different emphases and modalities;

— *a mystico Iesu Christi Corpore, Capite nempe eiusque membris* (by the Mystical Body of Jesus Christ, namely by the Head and by its members): this is the dimension of the SUBJECTS present and acting in the liturgy; it is configured as a synergy between Christ and the Church; here they are simply brought side by side, although in reality they are agents in different ways, with respect to the reality of salvation and to celebrative mediation.

Within the theological foundation the pastoral quest has enabled us to reconsider the whole actuative value of the salvific action through the mediation of the *signs perceptible to the senses.* We consider these signs no longer as "matter" of necessity or as decorative and accessory but as "matter" that in the perspective of divine "condescension" is inserted into the dynamics of the incarnation and paschal mystery. From them the signs find meaning and horizon.[2]

The Operative Quality of the Signa Sensibilia
SC, while not intending to provide a list of the *signa sensibilia,* indicates unsystematically but with clarity of purpose a rather large number of elements considered proper to the context of liturgical

---

[2] Cf. M.-D. Chenu, "Pour une anthropologie sacramentelle," *MD* 119 (1974) 85–100.

mediation and of language: *textus et ritus* (texts and rites) (*SC* 21); *lectiones, psalmi, preces, orationes, carmina liturgica, actiones, signa* (readings, psalms, prayers, orations, liturgical songs, actions, signs) (*SC* 24); *acclamationes, responsiones, psalmodia, antiphonae, cantica, actiones, gestus, corporis habitus, silentium* (acclamations, responses, psalmody, antiphons, canticles, actions, gestures, body postures, silence) (*SC* 30); *canti, oratio, signa visibilia, actiones* (songs, prayer, visible signs, actions) (*SC* 33); *ritus* (rites) (*SC* 34); *ritum et verbum, lectio sacrae scripturae, admonitiones, orationes, canti* (rite and word, reading of sacred scripture, admonitions, orations, songs) (*SC* 36); *musica sacra, artes, processiones* (sacred music, arts, processions) (*SC* 39); *ritus et preces* (rite and prayers) (*SC* 48); *verba et res* (words and things) (*SC* 59); *caerimonia, textus* (ceremony, text) (*SC* 76); *cantus sacer et verba* (sacred chant and words) (*SC* 112). Nevertheless, to be more complete this list should be supplemented by references to the constitutive symbols of the sacraments (e.g., *SC* 70: *aqua baptismalis*) and to the chapters dealing generally with time (*SC* 81–111); music (*SC* 112–21); and space, art, and furnishings (*SC* 122–30). The schematization of this set of elements and components that we can include under the term "liturgical language" finds, according to the specific instance of the *Ordines*, its own distribution, constituting in reality the true "Model of Practice."[3] The *signa sensibilia*, summarized in *textus et ritus* or *ritus et preces*, indeed lead to considering the liturgical celebration under the category of a communication with respect to the whole human person and to his or her experience.[4] Nonetheless, *SC* establishes the value, meaning, and effectiveness of liturgical language; it acknowledges that the efficacy of the celebration passes through the mediation of sensible signs; thus attentive consideration is given to invariability and variability and therefore to revision and reform. Since this is true, reform becomes necessary as well for the Eucharist, or rather, for the eucharistic celebration in particular, since the faithful can participate in it; this reform has been done but still is some-

[3] Cf. S. Maggiani, "Dalla 'Sacrosanctum Concilium' al libro rituale. Analisi e valutazioni," *RL* 69 (1982) 31–83; ibid., "La proposta celebrativa del nuovo 'Rito della Confermazione,'" *RL* 76 (1989) 232–4; ibid., "La proposta celebrativa del 'Rito dell'Unzione degli infermi,'" *RL* 80 (1993) 29–53.

[4] Cf. G. Venturi, "Temi linguistici nella costituzione liturgica," *Costituzione liturgica "Sacrosanctum Concilium,"* ed. Congregazione per il Culto Divino (Rome, 1986) 237–66, esp. 246–65.

thing that always can be carried out, *quapropter . . . etiam rituum forma, plenam pastoralem efficacitatem assegnatur* (so that . . . in ritual forms as well, it might achieve full pastoral effectiveness) (*SC* 49).

The effectiveness of ritual language, in the sense of mediation between the mystery celebrated in a given time and space and the integral subject, is made clear especially in *SC* 21 and *SC* 48, articles that, in parallel synopsis, have the value of considering all of Christian liturgical experience (sacramentality, time, sacramentals: no. 21; eucharistic celebration: no. 48).

SC 21	*SC* 48
1. *textus et ritus* ita ordinari oportet (texts and rites should be so ordered)	1. christifideles [. . .] per *ritus et preces* (Christ's faithful . . . through *rites and prayers*)
2. ut *sancta,* quae significant, clarius exprimant (so that they might more clearly express the holy things that they signify),	2. *id* [= mysterium fidei] (it [= the mystery of faith])
3. eaque populus christianus, in quantum fieri potest, facile *percipere* (and that the Christian people, as far as possible, might easily understand them)	3. bene *intellegentes* (*understanding* it well)
4. atque plena, actuosa et communitatis propria celebratione *participere* possit (and *participate* in full, active celebration as a community).	4. sacram actionem conscie, pie et actuose *participent* (might *participate* consciously, piously and actively in the sacred action). . . .

In these two paragraphs it is explained that, by means of the rites and prayers, the mystery that is celebrated is expressed, and at the same time people participate liturgically in the mystery. The symbolic effectiveness of ritual language is stressed, along with its capacity for mediation, which allows the faithful "to encounter a reality that transcends the celebration but that is given within it, since it is in the ritual form that the efficacy of the liturgy is displayed. This same mediation involves the very act of faith; indeed, the sacraments 'not only presuppose the faith, but with words and ritual elements *(verbis et rebus)* nourish, strengthen and express it' *(SC* 59)."[5]

LANGUAGE AS MEDIATION

Language is the ability of humans to communicate through a tongue, understood as a system of vocal signs specific to members of the same community. A complex physical technique is involved, along with a symbolic function through the genetically specialized nerve centers of the brain.[6] Given its complexity, language is the object of study under the most varied angles and is under observation by many disciplines. For the purposes of our study it seems useful to dwell on a basic anthropological reading of language. With respect to a concept proper to classical philosophy that sets language in an *instrumentalist* perspective (language as instrument), we consider language in its place as *mediation* of the subject to self, to others, to the cosmos, to culture in general. We can summarily state that in the instrumentalist scheme the subject attains and establishes a relation with reality as if it were between their immediacy: from the relation subject-reality direct images arise, concepts that language then allows to be communicated. Thus we have a subject placed before language, and it is instrumental in the subject's operations; therefore an ideal subject is presupposed, outside of language, outside of mediation, outside of one's own body and history, with the inevitable non-appreciation of everything that is language. Language becomes an obstacle to the immediate subject-reality relation. Among researchers the great linguistics expert E. Benveniste helps us to overcome this concept impoverishing human subjectivity and its still-complex situation. He states: "The comparison of language as an instrument — and since the comparison is barely intelligible, it must involve a material instrument — should be employed with caution, like any simplistic statement concerning language. To speak of an instrument means contrasting a human being to nature. The hoe, the arrow, the wheel are not found in nature; they are artifacts.

[5] G. Lukken, "La liturgie comme lieu théologique irremplaçable," ibid., *Per visibilia ad invisibilia* (Kampen, 1994) 256–68; L.-M. Chauvet, "La structuration de la foi dans les célébrations sacramentelles," *MD* 174 (1988) 75–99.

[6] Cf. the entry "Langage," *Dictionnaire de linguistique,* ed. J. Dubois et al. (Paris, 1973) 274–6.

Language is in the nature of the human, who has not crafted it. . . . We can never take the human separated from language and we never see him or her in the act of inventing it."[7]

Preexistence cannot be granted to the subject, and therefore the instrumentality of language that an unreal subject would use cannot be presupposed. By working with language the subject begins to be within his or her subjectivity and relates to self, to others, to the world. In order to be able to "invent" language, it is necessary to think about it; but to be able to think, one must already be in language. It is therefore true that "language dictates the very definition of human beings," and that, as E. Benveniste himself adds, "it is in language and through language that they establish themselves as *subject*."[8] Hence the *mediation* that language performs and that allows it to be effective. The subject, in relating to reality, that is, when it establishes a significant and therefore properly human relation, makes use of the mediation of language and makes culture. While building the real in the sense of cultural foundation, the subject builds the self and becomes; the subject becomes in relation to time, which is such insofar as time is the "time in which one speaks." "Language is therefore the possibility of subjectivity, by the fact that it always contains the forms adequate to its expression, and discourse stimulates the emergence of subjectivity, by the fact that it consists of discrete situations. Language provides some 'empty' forms, so to speak, of which every speaker avails of in the exercise of discourse, which refers to one's 'person,' defining simultaneously oneself as *I* and a partner as *thou*."[9] Reality is, as if it were, called from its "givenness" to a kind of existence of meaning, which in its turn becomes significant for the subject, so that in the "empty" forms the real is instituted that is proper to humans, and the world/culture is built where they can be situated and placed.

The path toward the real thus necessarily passes through the means of sensible and cultural mediations; these also become acquired in the history of a human person, are institutionalized, and can be recognized as such by the very activity of mediation. Liturgical-sacramental

[7] E. Benveniste, *Problemi di linguistica generale* (Milan, 1971) I, 311.

[8] Ibid., 316. The inquiry can be usefully completed with the contribution of psychoanalysis (cf. Lacan) and of Heideggerian philosophy.

[9] L.-M. Chauvet, *Les sacrements. Parole de Dieu au risque du corps* (Paris, 1993) 25; all of this chapter, pp. 21–35, is important.

action as well bases its language on the mediation of language in general. In the mediation of language and in its operative dynamic, the Church places itself in the experience both of sanctification and of glorification (cf. *SC* 7 and 10).

SYMBOLIC LANGUAGE

Even in its universality, language is not univocal. Within it there are differences that allow establishing relations with as many universes of human relations. Thus in order to carry out the reality of the gift of human sanctification and the glorification of God in the sense of *SC* 7 and 10, specifically of religious and markedly Christian reality, mediation takes place through that particular quality of language that is called *symbolic*. As we will see, the peculiarity of liturgical action finds in the peculiarity of symbolic language its own expressive and experiential modality, respectful both of the nature of the object of the action and of the subject that celebrates and prays. Language in general is based and is structurally built on a system of *signs* composed in their turn by a dynamic between matter (the signifier) and conceptual meaning proper to the mind (the signified).[10] It helps to speak of dynamic, since sign is not just the signifier but rather also the signified; this is the basis for its denoting quality or referential function as well as for its direct referral to reality (e.g., a road map). It is a referent, since there are present as a sign in the map both the signifier, for example, of "left turn" and the signified of turning in that direction. It escapes no one, however, that the communicative message in this case becomes communication, if between the sender and the receiver a code exists that enables them to relate to one another. The receiver is informed about the signs of the highway code, to stay within the scope of our example. Diverse human languages, diverse types of signs, derive in large part from the innumerable ways of combining signifiers and things signified. Something curious can happen, however, in which the solidity of the sign is broken. The most surprising case of this breaking is represented by the *symbol*, which broadens the horizon of the *sign* and which, like the sign, regards the wide spectrum of human language, word, objects, and actions.

[10] Cf. F. De Saussure, *Cours de linguistique générale*, new ed. (Lausanne, 1972) and further refinements in U. Eco, *Il segno* (Milan, 1980).

From Sign to Symbol
With P. Ricoeur we can comprehend the type of "infraction" by which one can speak of symbol, when he argues:

"I give to the word 'symbol' a more restricted meaning than do authors, like Cassirer, who call 'symbolic' every apprehension of reality done by means of signs: from perception of myth, of art, over to science; and a wider meaning than authors who, starting with Latin rhetoric or with the neoplatonic tradition, reduce symbol to analogy. *I call 'symbol' every structure of meaning in which a direct, primary, literal sense designates further another indirect, secondary, figured sense that can be apprehended only through the first.* This delimitation of expressions in a double sense constitutes specifically the hermeneutical field."[11]

Symbolic language therefore exists when at least two things signified can be connoted by the same signifier. The infraction occurs just when there is a relation only between a signifier and the thing signified, as by a sign, but not between a signifier and an immediate thing signified that in turn enables connoting something signified of another nature. In the verbal expression or icon or ritual sequence immediately before communicating with the Body and Blood of Christ: "Behold the Lamb of God," we have the signifier "lamb" with everything that it can connote as a sound-image (or even that which immediately does not allow me to elaborate why that signifier is the fruit of some experience of mine). At the same time a further dimension of meaning and of significance is opened by putting the lamb in relation to God. The signifier "lamb," bearing the signified determined in relation to its animal nature and cultural use, is enhanced by another signified that does not invalidate or condition the first one but allows the existence of a further meaning. In the event that I am not aware of what the term "lamb" includes, the fact of relating it to God in a specific referential context starts a process of cognition; the language leads me to reflect and to think on the why of this "loading" the signifier "lamb" with a "divine" signified.

[11] *Il conflitto delle interpretazioni* (Milan, 1977) 26; for E. Cassirer, *Filosofia delle forme simboliche* (Florence, 1965–1966); for other orientations cited cf. G. Manetti, *La teoria del segno nell'antichità classica* (Milan, 1987); T. Todorov, *Théorie du symbole* (Paris, 1977). For some contemporary currents, cf. G. Raio, *Ermeneutica e teoria del simbolo* (Naples, 1988).

It is in this relation that language finds its *humus* in a culture and its specification in a human language, that by its referring to the "divine" we can call it "religious" and, even more identifiably through our reflection, "Christian." From this relation there flows an epiphany of meaning that is both perceptible and not delimitable. It is in the dynamic of language that a person experiences the epiphany of human existence, in which the things that language makes use of allow its manifestation.

"Religious symbolism bears a truth: that of religious discourse that takes shape in things and confers a power revealing the divine. From this perspective, one grasps at the same time the arbitrariness of religious symbolism and the laws of its structures. The ambiguity of religious symbolism lies in its very constitution. It is constituted by a double bond among the three elements that make it up: the discourse on existence, the natural element that it incorporates, and the reference to the original logos. By means of the bond between the human meaning and the religious meaning of the word, the natural elements gain an increase of meaning: in their application of metaphors to human existence, they become the metonymies of the sacred that is absent and rendered present."[12]

There is no mystagogy in symbolic language or in the symbols that language enables to exist. Their power to make seen or to represent aspects of the divine and, in Christian experience, of the paschal event in its whole connotation, consists (1) in the fact that they establish relations of signifiers; (2) they lead into the reality in which they delight, and (3) at the same time they permit a communicative act between subjects, an alliance, a συμβάλλω in the original sense of "placing together"; (4) they give something to reflect on by facilitating a deeper entry into the meaning; (5) they are "intransitive," they do not refer to an idea that could be external to them, and thus they have in themselves the object to be symbolized; (6) they establish communication; they are in the order of act or event, never enunciated but rather are the act of enunciation; (7) they nourish the polysemy toward ambivalences richer in meanings, and all this is possible and comes forth with respect to created reality in which we move and

[12] A. Vergote, *Interprétation du langage religieux* (Paris, 1974) 70.

236

exist and with absolute respect for the Christ-event which, though unattainable, becomes for us a tangible gift.

In the *Ordines*, in particular in the major ritual sequences of a celebration, we find the most pertinent example for what has been stated until now. One can think of the example of the rite of baptism and in particular of the symbolic language inherent in water.[13]

The Body as Arch-symbol

While we should reaffirm the salvific efficaciousness that is rooted in the founding event and is communicated to us through the mediation of the "matter," we should not forget that the use of symbolic language does not involve the subject only in the sphere of pure or mental or psychological knowledge. The subject indeed is in relation not just mentally with the surrounding reality, including the reality of symbolic language (the base of the subject's freedom being thinking awareness), but the sphere of the mental enters into contact with reality through the sensory awareness of the body itself.[14] And it is through and by means of the body that symbolic order acquires its own constitution, so that the subject inscribes in his or her own living body the act of symbolization that the language of symbol in action carries out. Psychoanalytical and philosophical research find a singular accord of views. M. Merleau-Ponty, in his fundamental work, *Phenomenology of Perception*, bases in the spatiality of the body, in its expressive and communicative corporeity, the possibility for the human person to be "a perpetual common sensorium": "My body is the place, or rather the actuality itself, of the phenomenon of expression *(Ausdruck)*; in it the visual experience and the auditory experience, for example, are pregnant with each other; their expressive value establishes the ante-predicative unity of the perceived world and, through it, the verbal expression *(Darstellung)* and the intellectual

---

[13] S. Maggiani, "Il simbolo dell'acqua. Riflessioni su un simbolo primordiale ripreso dal cristianesimo," *Alle origini del Battesimo cristiano*, ed. P.-R. Tragan (Rome, 1991) 49–50; cf. other examples of reading of symbolic language in the *Ordines* in ibid., "La mano e lo Spirito. Per una lettura simbolica della imposizione delle mani," *RL* 78 (1991) 391–401.

[14] M. Bernard, *Le corps* (Paris, 1976); C. Bruaire, *Philosophie du corps* (Paris, 1968); M. Henry, *Philosophie et phénoménologie du corps* (Paris, 1965); V. Melchiorre, *Corpo e persona* (Genoa, 1995) reprint; A. Vergote, "Le corps. Pensée contemporaine et catégorie bibliques," *Revue Théologique Lovaniensis* 10 (1979) 157–79.

meaning *(Bedeutung)*. My body is the common texture of all objects and is, at least with regard to the world, the general instrument of my understanding."[15] Merleau-Ponty, by taking up a meaningful expression of Schopenhauer, can speak of the living body: body understood as a *motor* act, need, tension, hunger, sexual appetite, synthesis of interiority and exteriority, of activity and passivity, as the only means that a human has to get to the heart of things and in which is experienced as well sensibility, image and imagination, meaning. D. Dubarle, in this perspective, incisively defines it "as the arch-symbol of all symbolic order. It is the one that supports and that nourishes all the actuality differentiated from the symbolic commerce of a living soul's active consciousness with its own individuality, with the cosmic environment and other humans, with what a human apprehends as divine."[16]

On these anthropological bases as well, it appears well-founded that the integral subject of liturgical action can only be the *ecclesia* that celebrates and that prays.[17] The *ecclesia*, which emerges from those structural laws that R. Guardini perceived at the foundation of the spirit of the liturgy and of liturgical theology itself, can celebrate and pray if it takes seriously the arch-symbolical quality of its members:

"The subject who carries out the liturgical action of prayer is not the mere total of all the individual participants of the same faith. It is the whole of the faithful, yet insofar as their unity has autonomous value, prescinding from the quantity of believers who form it as *the Church.* . . . Rather, the faithful are bound together by a real common principle of life. This common life is the living Christ. . . . The believers — however they might wish to celebrate the liturgical action with living participation — should make themselves aware that they pray and act as members of the Church, and the Church in them."[18]

[15] *Fenomenologia della percezione*, 3d ed. (Milan, 1980) 31.

[16] "Pratique du symbole et connaissance de Dieu," AA.VV., *Le mythe et le symbole*, 243–4.

[17] Cf. Y. M. J. Congar, "L'Ecclesia' ou communauté chrétienne, sujet integral de l'action liturgique," *La liturgie après Vatican II*, ed. J. P. Jossua and Y. Congar (Paris, 1967) 241–86.

[18] *Lo spirito della liturgia. I santi segni* (Brescia, 1980) 39–41. English editions: *The Spirit of the Liturgy* (New York, 1935) and *Sacred Signs* (St. Louis, 1956).

In the fundamental arch-symbol, which for Christians is Christ who is the body of the incarnation of the Word and the body of the resurrection, the *ecclesia* accepts the sacramentality that has been granted to it within the foundation of its own sacramentality. In the intense reflection conducted in osmosis, it finds the search for symbolic language. We have matured, as it were, the search in liturgical activity, which on God's part is the whole assumption of the human and who, with the gift of the Spirit, made language fit for containing and transmitting the multiple richness of the Word, who gives life, and of the love that saves (*GS* 38).

And all this, because the Word was made flesh (John 1:14ff.). "And he spoke as flesh speaks, he thought as flesh thinks, he communicated as the flesh can and should communicate."[19]

RITUAL ACTION AND ITS LANGUAGES

Symbolic language, including in the religious and Christian field, appears as much more than a simple means of human communication. Its function goes beyond stating and manifesting. We find ourselves before a dimension that constitutes and conditions the people who live in a specific culture. Nonetheless their efficacy is not left to a juxtaposed proliferation of symbols with their dynamism of double meaning. A symbol, while having a complete meaning in itself, normally yields meanings when it is linked to other symbols and constitutes a symbolic fabric. This gathering of liturgical symbols in a given context, a symbolic system, is called "rite."

Rite refers to a universal aspect of humanity taken inclusively, which is action, giving rhythm and order against chaos with a particular coloring, which makes it, even in the ordinary, a singular human expression. Christian ritual action, which is qualified as religious rite and is identified with the relation to the event of Jesus Christ, is a sequence of ritual actions that unfold in an orderly fashion with their own rhythm and with a symbolic language. The attention to ritual action, including in the liturgical ambit, goes beyond the new reexamination of human rituality in general conducted with new horizons in our century; and attention to the necessity for rites, even in modern times, goes beyond the liberation achieved also by the conciliar reform from the pathologies of ritualism, rubricism, and

---

[19] APL, ed., *Celebrare in Spirito e Verità* (Rome, 1992) 33–4.

juridicism, things long combated by the liturgical movement. We do not wish to get lost in the dispute between ethnologists and anthropologists on the *phylogenetic* origins of rituals (as the former maintain) or of the *ontogenetic* origins based on the development of the symbolic faculties of humans (as the latter maintain). Our concern is to observe in the light of anthropological research of social reality and the research inherent in the sphere of psychoanalysis (research that studies people in situation and in relation), that ritual action, with its languages, yields a modality of being that structures people in relation — between themselves, with others, with reality — by means of fundamental but variable elements, some secondary.

It could also be stated that the "qualities" found in symbolic language, entering in orderly rhythm into the experience of a ritual fabric (action), qualify its initial givenness, develop it, characterize it by accepting from it in their turn quality, development, characterization. In reality, as regards religious and Christian quality,

"a religious rite, in the majority of cases, is a repetitive action that presupposes some preceding phenomenon, some original event, in which the sacred is inserted into the profane, the transcendent has broken into immanence; this is much more and, in any case, is 'other' with respect to the actions that it performs. From this point of view, ritual action seems similar to symbolic language. Just as symbol is made beginning with sign, so rite is made beginning with action; and so also symbolic language bears within itself the polarity between action and rite. Rite, however, appears as a succession of actions; this presents itself as a 'process' which we call precisely *ritual process,* in which the polar dynamic of the rite itself can be perceived in a more explicit way."[20]

Codes for "Listening" and "Seeing"
From the careful examination of the liturgical *Ordines,* understood as a program or as ritual models, in the fashioning of symbolic language intended for liturgical-ritual action, a variety of components emerges, as we were able to bring out from *SC* as well. In the linguistic perspective, where we have placed ourselves, we call these components of symbolic-ritual language by the name of *codes:* a system of signals, or of signs or symbols, that by accepted conven-

[20] G. Bonaccorso, *Celebrare la salvezza,* 42–3.

tion are intended to represent or transmit information between a source of communication and the recipients of the same.[21] In liturgical action, because of its aforementioned peculiarity, codes are not just instrumental in the service of expressivity but indeed are reducible to actions that involve communication: the codes *signa sensibilia* allow us to participate in the given gift, in the paschal mystery. As has been fittingly observed, when *SC* 21 expresses some directives on the quality of the announced liturgical reform, it refers to aspects proper to codes: *Qua quidem instauratione, textus et ritus ita ordinari oportet, ut sancta, qua significant, clarius exprimant, eaque populus christianus, in quantum fieri potest, facile percipere atque plena, actuosa et communitatis propria celebratione participare possit* (for this renewal, texts and rites should be so ordered so that they might more clearly express the holy things that they signify and that the Christian people, as far as possible, might easily understand them and participate in full, active celebration as a community). The verbs *exprimere, percipere, participare,* summarize the dynamic proper to language *(exprimere),* which is structured in codes, through which the message can be understood between the sender and the receiver *(percipere)* and is in active relation with the reality that the sender wants to express and communicate *(participare).* The codes are at the service of the "seeing" and the "listening" by each individual and by the assembly, seeing and listening, as it was for the first disciples, in order to have an experience of the Lord, an aesthetic and poietic for sharing in the mystery:

"The theandric *érgon* that is the divine liturgy — the divine work of the people / the work of the divine people — causes language to perform it through the articulated dynamic of hearing the Word, seeing the Glory, experiencing the Mystery. On the divine part, word-glory-mystery; on the human part, listening-seeing-experiencing. It must be carefully noted that God's part is his alone and the human person is only its receiver, and her or his part is synergy with God. The dynamic is complex, given a sort of circular flow of hearing the word and seeing the glory, symbiotically empowering in virtue of experiencing the mystery; and complex because of the recodifying linguistic content that each code has on another and all have on other codes

[21] U. Eco, *Trattato di semiotica generale* (Milan, 1975) 178ff.

of the chain — in the liturgy always in virtue of experiencing the mystery."[22]

As *OL* 6 in particular notes, since the codes can communicate this experience proper to Christian liturgical action, their givenness in process can never be interpreted only in their human origin but in relation to the Word of God and to the economy of salvation.

In this perspective, the codes in their turn can properly and suitably be at the service of the ritual process "in Spirit and in truth," with respect to both the object and the subject of liturgical action. Nonetheless this set of ritual codes, called "system," contains secondary rules that are called "subcodes." This process, proper to the "stylistic maxims" and to the "ceremonial systems" is called "hypercoding" and is an example of particular "hypercodification" both of linguistic codes and of behavioral codes. Before examining these kinds of fundamental codes, it can be useful to have at hand the symbolic fabric (the result of the interweave of general codes with the subcodes) both of liturgical action in general and of the ritual text in particular, referring any further investigation to the relative documentation.

	Liturgical action subcodes	Cultural codes	Ritual text subcodes
	Conventions that regulate gesture, movement, expression	↔ General kinetic codes	↔ Norms for the interpretation of movement according to ministries
S Y S T E M I C	Spatial conventions (regarding the church assembly room, the presbytery, etc.)	↔ Proximity codes	↔ Norms for the reading of spatial configurations in terms of interrelations, places for the celebration
	Rules for liturgical garments and their connotations	↔ Vestiary codes	↔ Rules for assigning garments according to ministries
	Limitations to musical accompaniment, songs, supports, etc.	↔ Musical codes	↔ Norms that regulate the use of music in rite

[22] C. Valenziano, "'Vedere la Parola.' Liturgia e ineffabile," *EO* 9 (1992) 125.

L I N G U I S T I C		Decoding of liturgical action on the basis of constitutive rules	↔ Structural / semantic / syntactic constitutive rules	↔ Interpretation of text on the basis of constitutive rules	
		Conventions that regulate the relations between ministers and assembly	↔ Pragmatic rules (conventional and contextual)	↔ Conventions relating to the interpretations of inter-personal communication	
		Rules of proclamation ↔ Rhetoric		↔ Stylistic and rhetorical conventions in the euchology	
T E X T U A L	**S T R U C T U R A L**	Textual rules that regulate the semantic integration of different messages and the syntactical order of ritual action	↔ General textual competence: acknowledgment of texts as syntactically and semantically consistent structures	↔ Textual rules that govern the consistency of the ritual text and its structure	
E P I S T E M I C		Framework of liturgical action (definition of liturgical reality of such)	↔ Episteme (conceptual organization of the world)	↔ Ritual framework (construction of the possible world of rite as such)	
		Definition of the elements of liturgical action	↔ Encyclopedia (total of reference points, elements of knowl-edge)	↔ Construction of the universe of ritual discourse	
T H E O L O G I C A L		Definition of data underlying liturgical action	↔ Theology (conceptual organization of the human-God relation)	↔ Links to the interpretation of ministerial relations, to the overall decoding of textual meanings	
H I S T O R I C A L		Awareness of the traditional modalities of ritual action, heritage of liturgical history	↔ Knowledge of historical events, notions regarding the characteristics of a period	↔ Authorization for historical differences in ritual sequences, in language, in customs. . . .	

THE PRINCIPAL ACTIVE CODES OF
LITURGICAL ACTION

Silence

The code of silence guides liturgical action. This characteristic, in the alternation of the ritual process among a before, a during, and an after and in the alternation of verbal, non-verbal, and musical-sound codes, enables the individual and the community to enter into the depths of the action and to experience it. R. Guardini indicates, among the functions that derive from the eucharistic liturgy, as a paradigm for every liturgical action, the priority of silence: "It is important to realize that the true Church can emerge only from silence . . . in my view, liturgical life begins with silence. Without it, everything appears useless and vain. This is no unusual claim of an aesthetic nature. Considering silence as an argument that 'goes without saying' would mean nullifying everything. The topic, however, is very serious, very important and unfortunately neglected; it is the first presupposition of every sacred action."[23]

The importance of this code is taken into account by *SC* 30 and is authoritatively emphasized also by the instruction on song and music in the liturgy, *Musicam sacram* (March 5, 1967). The influence of these directives is such that it can be affirmed that the reference to the code of silence has never been as mentioned in the previous liturgical books as it is made explicit in the *Ordines* of the reform of Vatican II. The typological scheme that flows from an organic reading related to the verbal and the gestural (silence of recollection, of appropriation, of meditation, of adoration) confirms that ritual silence is *silence in worship,* silence that gives rhythm to the word in a pragmatic- communicative perspective. From this it derives that the silence-word rhythm should be understood as a pragmatic rhythm, that is, as a sender-receiver rhythm according to the following scheme:

SENDER   word / silence

RECEIVER   silence / word

"Silence allows verbal, and more generically sign, 'movement' of the ritual action. In this, however, the ritual action shares the functional

[23] *Il testamento di Gesù,* 2d ed. (Milan, 1993) 33.

244

status of any communicative (social) action. The peculiarity of rite lies in the fact that this function becomes also an image, something of a religious icon: acknowledgment, that is, of the 'other' by way of negating the pure self-aware positivity of speaking. Thus when not just a part of the ritual community is silent, allowing the other part to speak, but when the whole community is silent, an acknowledgment is made of an 'other,' other with respect to the whole community."[24]

It is the acknowledgment that the subject is in reality an active and passive subject, insofar as he or she can only act by opening the self to the "other" who is the Holy Spirit. Silence is the seal, in terms of ritual (poietic) codes of the christological-trinitarian movement proper to Christian liturgy, and is the (aesthetic) epiphany that "our word, our movement, song and adoration should take form from the silent action of the Spirit, the Spirit of the Word of God. Our finite silence, including ritually expressed silence, also arises from the silence of the Spirit, and only from it does it gain power, meaning, and horizon."[25]

The Verbal Code: The Word in Action
As we have been able to note in *SC* and as is easy to find in the *Ordines* and in their actuation in the celebration, the fundamental and constant structure on which liturgical action is based is the close connection between gestures and words (*SC* 35): the communication of salvation *per ritus et preces* (*SC* 48). The word is given to us, and is proclaimed in sacred Scripture for us, the celebrating subject; it can become a euchological form in the Liturgy of the Hours and is an ideal fabric or horizon of meanings through the euchological texts, various verbal formulas, hymns and songs; it should be the absolute referent in that particular form of speaking known as the homily. In considering the synchronic quality of the presence of the verbal and the non-verbal, we are drawn to refer to "ritual language" our understanding of the verbal and its qualification. The very presence of the verbal code is indeed by its nature an "action" and does not renounce its quality of signifying but demands an acknowledgment that is on the order of gesture, of acting, of the act of saying. In this a certain analogy can be perceived, as Wainwright points out in the biblical concept of *dabar*: "The Hebrew *dabar* means thing, act, event,

[24] G. Bonaccorso, "Il ritmo silenzio-parola nel rito," *RL* 76 (1989) 333–4.
[25] S. Maggiani, "Il silenzio: per celebrare in Spirito Santo," *RL* 76 (1989) 379.

as well as word; God and men 'speak' also through actions, and speech is also an 'act.'"[26]

Beyond the literary genres and the functions of liturgical verbal language, the form that the word in action pursues as a privileged form is that which actuates the communicative event of the *dialogue* between God and humans and between human beings and God: speaking — listening — saying.

This dynamic, which assumes various forms (greeting, acclamation, praise, thanksgiving, petition), indicates that the verbal code is made to become the actual Word of God, or a word addressed to God or a word to a specific people.[27] The information is relative, the cognitive order is secondary. The verbal code of the liturgy is essentially *performative language:* "what is said" is "as it is said."

The ambit that allows the understanding of the use of liturgical verbal language is specifically the ambit of the pragmatic. Within this ambit verbal language rests, indeed, on the general principle designated by the term "performativity." Three modes of performativity are seen in liturgical language: an existential induction, an institution, and a making present. The first mode of performativity is understood to be the opening of the speaking "I" or "We" to a specific reality in an expressive form that arouses affections. One can think of the dialogic dimension I-Thou / We-Thou of all praying, which necessarily involves those praying. For the second mode of performativity, it is understood that the plural form, the We, a plurality of people speaking but acting in a collective way as if they constituted a single speaker, as indeed often it is, establishes the community. In saying "we," the participants praying become responsible for all the acts that are performed, acts that are regulated and codified and that do not depend on their choice.

The third mode is the most fundamental aspect of the performativity of liturgical language: making present.

"This language, through all the acts that it puts into being, makes present for the participants that which it speaks about, not as a spectacle but as a reality, the effectiveness of which they assume into their

---

[26] "The Language of Worship," *The Study of Liturgy,* p. 466–67.

[27] K. Richter, "Die Messe lesen? Gottesdienst in der Spannung von frei gesprochenem und gelesenem Wort," *Glauben durch lesen? Für christliche Lesekultur,* eds. H. T. Khoury and L. Muth (Freiburg-Basel-Vienna, 1990) 39–65.

own lives; it also puts this into being in different ways, namely the mystery of Christ, his life, his death and his resurrection, the revelation that in him has been made to us of the mystery of God, the fulfillment of the eternal plan in virtue of which we are called to become children of God, coheirs of Christ in eternal life. Liturgical language does not make this mystery present in the manner of descriptive language, that may make us see what it is speaking about, but by permitting it to produce itself effectively, by loaning it, so to speak, its own operativity (namely that of the acts that constitute it) to give it the possibility of becoming operative for the community built by the liturgy."[28]

The highest level of making present is something we have in the sacramental aspect of language. In the plausibility of human language, this making present depends in its effectiveness only on the faith.

"Nevertheless faith is not like an experience, mute in itself, that liturgical language would only have the function to describe. Between faith and liturgical language there is a kind of double assumption. On the one side, faith assumes in itself this language and gives it its own efficacy, taking up the specifically linguistic acts that are constitutive of this language in the opening that it itself constitutes, insofar as it is per se a recapitulation of the mystery of Christ, an acceptance of salvation, hope for future goods. On the other side, language gives to faith something of a terrain for structuring that allows it to be articulated according to the requirements proper to the reality to which it is attuned."[29]

The reference to faith thus points us, necessarily, to the contents of the *anamnesis*, to the object of the memorial action. From these contents flow the vital urgings for liturgical and prayerful expressivity.

It is in the perspective of these vital urgings that, once again with respect to the subject and the object, problems arise regarding the question of feminine language. This question emerges at the basis of the operative quality of the performativity of liturgical language: the question bears on the language of and for some groups or communities of persons, such as the non-hearing or the seriously disabled!

[28] A. Meli, ed., *Jean Ladrière*, 153.
[29] Ibid., 157.

A key that should be taken seriously, however, is that the universality of the first question, regarding the "sectoriality" of the second, also involves a difference of hermeneutics, of instruments, and of methods for being addressed.[30]

The historical posing of the questions, the first more recently, the second more reflectedly, involves a diversity of methodological and interpretive investment, even though both in reference to liturgical language can be considered at the beginnings. This research must not neglect the problem of "translation" and especially of adaptation proper to the themes and laws of ritual language of the sacramental and hourly liturgical action.

Sound-Musical Code: Song and Music
By their singularity, musical or sound-musical codes can be suitably classified between verbal (with word, they have in common both sonority and vocality) and non-verbal. Precisely because of their singularity and because of an overall recovery of the expressive capacity of these codes in relation to humans, it seems more correct to speak of sound codes.[31] The category of sound summarizes voice, word, music, and gesture in itself (without immediately relating it to other communication forms such as theater) by which it is a singing or "a telling that is also a doing though also a non-telling."[32] It is a language that is action and is understood with pragmatic codes, and its semantics is to be applied from time to time, without the absence of aspects proper to emotion, even when it is difficult to denote these "energetic" or "emotional" aspects and to name them. The pragmatic aspect that bears the sound code motivates its presence in the ritual action and in the liturgical action of the Christian mystery. SC 112–21, although laced with a concept of music oscillating between a concept of sacrality of the music in itself, as it works, and a concept, matured during reflection in the liturgical movement, of music *for* the liturgy, at the service of and in relation to the celebration, has indicated programmatic principles already present and marked and translated in the conciliar *Ordines* (cf. e.g., IGMR 12, 14–9, 21–2, 25–6, 36–40, 50, 56,

[30] C. Militello, *Donna in questione. Un itinerario di ricerca* (Assisi, 1992) 91–3.
[31] Cf. C. Cibien, "Quale codificazione sonora per celebrare la liturgia," *Musica per la liturgia. Presupposti per una fruttuosa interazione,* ed. A. N. Terrin (Padua, 1996) 139–65.
[32] G. Stefani, *Capire la musica* (Milan, 1985) 14–15.

66–7, 83, 90, 92–3, 100, 119, 121, 131, 147, 324, 328; *IGLO* 14, 16, 33, 94–5, and passim, esp. 267–84; *OE* 10, 12, 21, 35, 37, 39, 40, 45, 47, 50, 52, 57–8 passim). The sound code enters into a global situation that is the ritual one, that is integrated. This is determined by the meaning of the ritual process and contributes to determining its meaning. The multiplicity of dimensions of the musical, since the modes of being and the modes of thinking of the human person are multiple, establishes singular relations with reality or can establish them. "It is certainly people's ways of being and ways of thinking that determine the *horizon of motives* that allow the musical imagination to follow its course, putting in motion that *dialectic* from which its works emerge. *No musical thought could emerge if there were no other thoughts.*"[33] The symbolic function that arises from this function permits it, in its turn, to be placed at the service of ritual action and to enter into the processes of symbolization of all liturgical language. The various ritual sequences as they are linked in a symbolic fabric indicate, in relation both to the subject and to the celebrated object, the relative "liturgical" functions in which to employ the sound code (hymn, acclamation, meditation, lyric proclamation). On this basis one can proceed to make operative choices in relation to the modalities (how), and to what to use of the sound codes.[34] Attention to the aesthetic, finally, is based on the poietic in order to dialogue with it. A sound "poietics" of hearing and manifesting the faith (*auditus, intellectus,* and *affectus fidei,* the living body) is understood and is stated in the deep intrinsic relation with the saving word. "They are capable therefore of employing the many possible forms of people's musical experience today: from 'popular' to 'cultured' ones, from 'common' to more 'singular' ones that celebrate the beauty of the calling together that the Lord issues among us, and of the consecration deriving from it, for our existence."[35]

Non-verbal Codes: Action and Gestures of the Human Person
The archaic relation between the gesture that becomes action to permit the human subject to relate to reality and to work with it, and the gesture that becomes language to express the same reality and to

---

[33] G. Piana, *Filosofia,* 295.
[34] Cf. G. Stefani, "Il canto," *Nelle vostre assemblee* 1, 255–74; see also 275–85.
[35] P. Sequeri, "L'estetico per il sacro. Affectus fidei e ars musica: la questione teologica," *ScC* 123 (1995) 657.

signify its meaning, constitutes what we call the "non-verbal code." In this interactive dynamic of action and expression, and according to the functions that non-verbal communication intends in a given human context, the codes can be schematized, and in relation to the channel used to draw upon them, the purpose for which they are used can be carried out. Some non-verbal codes, or between the verbal and the non-verbal, have already been mentioned; here we present in table form other codes that are available in a ritual and specifically liturgical context, which we will briefly illustrate.[36]

CODE	CHANNEL	DESCRIPTION
Non-verbal vocal	*Vocal - auditory*	Tones of voice, pauses, exclamations
Spatial: proximity	*Visual*	Relations of subjects to a place
Spatial: kinetic	*Visual*	Movements of subjects in a place
Spatial: topographic	*Visual*	Organization of places
Temporal	*[Multiple]*	Chronological sequences
Musical	*Vocal - auditory*	Music and song
Iconic	*Visual*	Symbolic value of objects
Optical	*Visual*	Play of luminous signals and of colors
Tactile	*Tactile*	Physical contact
Olfactory	*Olfactory*	Transmittal of odors
Gustatory	*Gustatory - visual*	Eating and drinking

As can be deduced from this overall scheme, non-verbal code carries in the ritual a knowledge that unveils or communicates more specifically subjective and intense emotional experiences, and it produces effects both of a physical and a psychological nature in addition to effecting possible changes in social relations. And all this more than verbal language.

"Nonetheless, words are used in the ritual, and the rituals in part derive from meanings through verbalized sets of ideas, as in Christian theology. Rituals can be described by words and started by words, but, as Firth says (1970), gestures 'have a significance, a fac-

---

[36] Cf. J. Schermann, *Die Sprache im Gottesdienst* (Innsbruck-Vienna, 1987) 79–94.

ulty, a restorative effect, a kind of creative power that words alone cannot give.' Words are joined to the meanings of non-verbal signals; thus, religious ritual consists typically in a combination of verbal and non-verbal, in which the two types of meaning are combined. This joins the precision of words to the emotive power of non-verbal signals."[37]

Kinetic Code: Movements of the Celebrating Subject
The kinetic code, normally situated between the spatial codes and the perceptive ones (tactile, optical, gustatory, olfactory), connotes movements, gestures, and mimics aspects of the body that during social interaction are intended to communicate something. We distinguish it from posture (erect, sitting, kneeling, lying down) that lies between gestures and spatial behavior, and we identify it in the act: stately walking, bowing, genuflecting, and so on. Either the *Ordines* make explicit the kinetic code (cf. e.g., *OBP* 42, 52–3, 60 . . .; *OP* 41, 47, 48, 54, 55 . . .; *ODEA* I, 10, 14; II, 11, 16, 29, 31–5 . . .) or it is implicit when, for example, indication is made of the postures to be assumed (cf. *IGLH* 23; *OPR* I, 60–2). In this way, "by alternating, even though within limits, one's own spatial positions, the believer-celebrant modifies his or her own perceptive abilities; standing up, kneeling down, lying down, signify grasping (perceiving) in different ways one's own relation with surrounding reality and with God himself."[38]

The perception of this totality in its singularity finds a high point in the ritual experience of dance; dance as an encounter in space of the sound code and the kinetic code. Ritual dance is a response of absolute gratuitousness, fluid as water, in which corporality is involved as an absolute desire to present oneself to the celebrated object without any reservation and at the same time underlines the powerless, yet acting, power of the ritual subject.[39] In the Western liturgical tradition, for reasons of a historical-cultural nature, ritual dance is extremely confined to expression close to folkloric values rather than to genuine liturgical ones. Nonetheless, in the Roman Rite, for a local

[37] M. Argyle, *Il corpo e il suo linguaggio*, 297. For confirmation of these statements, cf. the analysis by S. Maggiani, *La dimensione escatologica del celebrare cristiano*, AA.VV. escatologia e liturgia. Atti XVI. Sett. APL 1987 (Rome, 1988) 145–81.
[38] Cf. M. Argyle, *Il corpo e il suo linguaggio*, 199–209.
[39] P. Bourcier, *Danser devant les Dieux. La notion du divin dans l'orchestique* (Paris, 1989); bibl., 397–410.

church, that of Zaïre,[40] ritual dance has recently gotten its own codification, just as for numerous Oriental liturgical traditions.[41]

Iconic Code: Symbolic-Iconic Ordering
The "representative" function cf objects, which, in a celebration, the topographical code offers and contributes to putting into effect in a specific communicative relation, is what we call "iconic code." In a space-time specific to rituality, nothing is to be provided casually. The ritual site enters into a polysemous play of the ritual to mediate the dynamics between the subject and the object in the celebration in "metaoperative" and "transitional" terms, therefore in the order of the symbolic. Its functionality can only be joined with the symbolicalness that allows responding fully to the meaning of the ritual places and to their destination, and opens to "beauty," the fruit of the truth of things and of elements gathered together with "austerity." Guidance in this direction was given for the Roman Rite in chapter VII of *SC*. The conciliar reading now finds authoritative actuation in the *Ordines*, especially in *IGMR*, chapter V, and in *ODEA* both in the *Praenotanda* and in the model ritual. The iconic code that is required at the base of a real iconographic program should in its manner prolong and describe the mystery celebrated and in relation to the *ecclesia* and to salvation history, or somehow to serve both.

Optical Code: Luminous Signals, Colors
Light in the rhythm of light-darkness or functional-nonfunctional light (quality of light that is the basis of colors) is at the origin of the optical code and at its development in human relations and in religious rituals. Light, a perennial presence in religious ritual, even when it is made to disappear only to reappear, gives life to multiple presences of things and persons and reveals it through means or instruments or sources of light (fire, candle, lamp). The use of this code,

[40] Cf. Conférence Épiscopale du Zaïre, *Missel romain pour les diocèses du Zaïre* (Kinshasa, 1989) *Présentation générale*, 29–30. Cf. *Not* 24 (1988) no. 264, 454–72. Cf. E. E. Uzuku, *Worship as Body Language. Introduction to Christian Worship: An African Orientation* (Collegeville, 1995).

[41] T. Berger, *Liturgie und Tanz. Anthropologische Aspekte, historische Daten, theologische Perspektiven* (St. Ottilien, 1985); L. Debarge, "De la danse sacré aux liturgies dansantes," *Mélanges de Science Religieuse* 49 (192) 143–61; E. Theodorou, "La dance sacrée dans le culte chrétien et plus specialment dans la famille liturgique byzantine," AA.VV., *Gestes et paroles*, 285–300.

however, beyond arousing presences and giving them their emphasis, opens the possibility to interior and emotional experiences that place the celebrant in a "tension" within the self, with things, with persons, and with the object that is celebrated.[42] With respect to colors, *IGMR* 307 sets these codes in relation to the particular characteristic of the mysteries being celebrated and the meaning of Christian life during the liturgical year. Nos. 308–10, with their indications, allow establishing some symbolic relation between the color of the day and the mystery being celebrated.[43] In *CE* there is a chart of the use of colors in reference to particular celebrations (cf. *Indices,* 314). Regarding luminous signals, reference must be made to the celebration of the Easter Vigil and to *ODEA* II, 69–71; it is still useful to compare the same *CE, Indices, luminaria,* p. 339, which in its indicative referential quality helps to understand the use of the code in study.

Tactile Code: Symbolic Interaction
Touch in action suggests the related code and its use. Direct physical contact such as a kiss or an embrace, or indirect through a reality that mediates tactile perception (e.g., anointing with oil), emphasizes in human repetition, or with things in their immediacy, their "resistance." In closeness and proximity experience turns toward their intangibility, and in the symbolic fabric of ritual this aspect can really open the individual subject toward a process of symbolic nature. Christian liturgy frequently, in its liturgical ordering, makes reference to the tactile code (cf. e.g., *OBP* 16, 17, 18, 33, 41, 49, 62 passim; *OICA* 83–7, 109, 130 passim; *DOE* I, 45, 49 . . .; *OCM* 61; *OUI* passim; *ODEA* 63–4 passim). Especially in sacramental celebrations, it is evident that contacts that express and indicate the gift and the specific sacramental quality show at the same time the non-identification between gift and matter that resists. This refers back to the gift by resisting and revealing its nature.

Olfactory Code: Symbolic Perfume
In the olfactory code, the anthropological "mysteriousness" comes in that is linked to the channel that carries it, the *sense of smell,* certainly

---

[42] Cf. AA.VV., "Il sentimento del colore. L'esperienza cromatica come simbolo, cultura e scienza," RED (Como, 1990).

[43] Cf. S. Maggiani, "La proposta celebrativa del 'Rito dell'Unzione degli Infermi,'" *RL* 80 (1993) 45–8. Ibid., *La speranza celebrata,* 298–301.

the most unknown of the senses. The olfactory code, more than the other codes, always produces "reactions" in anyone to whom it is directed. In religious rituality, but not only, it bears the recall in the truest sense of historical memory and covers with newness the one experiencing it, just as prayer has the ability to evoke, call, and provoke. Incense, flowers, perfumed oils, fragrant waters, are at the service of the olfactory code; through these symbols they silently make their entrance in ritual play in the most total perspective. Without forgetting some functional aspects, the olfactory code, referred to normally and constitutively in the Eastern liturgies in a symbolic perspective, is well present also in Western liturgical tradition (cf. the indications in *CE Indices: Chrisma*, p. 312, *Turificatio*, p. 370).

Gustatory Code: The Symbolic Bread
The gustatory perception arises in its optimal phase from the encounter of the visual and the gustatory channels, from seeing and tasting. The "beauty" of creatureliness arouses such an attraction to communicate with it through taste so that the "beautiful" might become "good": for me, for us. From contemplated "life" to assimilated "life." Ritual foods, even in their basic form, stimulate the desire for ingestion in order to assimilate the vital energies: the pleasure of tasting life, of communicating with it. The summit and the source of Christian sacramental experience uses the gustatory code to express the greatest ritual communion with the Body and Blood of Christ. Eucharistic worship itself, developed in great part around the visual code, has as its primary purpose the arousal of the desire to taste what is being shown. The desire to participate in the sacramental banquet, the "presence" of the glorious Body of Christ, contains in itself the desire for another banquet, definitive and eternal, of which his word is the pledge (John 6:53ff.). Moreover in *DB* some "blessings" are ritualized in reference to some fruits of the earth that are then consumed out of devotion, often in harmony with the liturgical year (1139–61).

CONCLUSION: THE SPIRIT, WATER, AND BLOOD
The complexity and the richness and, at the same time, the fragility proper to the elements of a Christian ritual process increase the wonder through the dynamics underlying *per ritus et preces,* dynamics through which one experiences the gift of Christian salvation. At the same time they caution about the rigor required in pursuing a reflection and an inquiry on behalf of a liturgical science of which the cele-

brative practice remains the point of departure and the point of arrival for an authentic life in the Spirit.

Moreover, at the same source of faith there are three that give witness: the Spirit, water, and blood (1 John 5:5ff.). In the very act of faith or in faith in act, none of this triad can be forgotten: liturgical language is crossed and takes meaning and becomes operative precisely because, although proper to the human person and to his or her life (water), it attains its ultimate meaning and the efficacy of the redemptive work of the Lord Jesus (blood), who communicates himself to us through human languages. These are used in a ritual-symbolic dynamic with perennial reference to the Holy Spirit, in whom alone is it possible to celebrate and pray "in spirit and truth," in the spirit of Christ (John 4:23-24).

Bibliography

Argyle, M. *Bodily Communication*. 2nd ed. London, 1988.

Bernard, M. *L'expressivité du corps*. Paris, 1986.

Bertelli, S., and M. Centanni. *Il gesto nel rito e nel cerimoniale dal mondo antico ad oggi*. Florence, 1995.

Grillo, A. *Teologia fondamentale e liturgia: Il rapporto tra immediatezza e mediazione nella riflessione teologica*. Padua, 1995.

Hameline, J. Y. "Eléments d'anthropologies de sociologie historique et de musicologie du culte chrétien." *RSR* 78 (1990) 397–424.

Hinde, R. A., ed. *Non-verbal Communication*. Cambridge, 1972.

Isambert, F.-A. *Rite et efficacité symbolique: Essai d'anthropologie sociologique*. Paris, 1979.

Lacoste, J.-Y. *Expérience et absolu: Questions disputés sur l'humanité de l'homme*. Paris, 1994.

Merleau-Ponty, M. *Phenomenology of Perception*. Trans. C. Smith. New York, 1962.

Meslin, M. *L'expérience humaine du divin: Fondements d'une anthropologie*. Cogitatio fidei. Paris, 1988.

Rapallo, V. *La ricerca in linguistica*. Rome, 1994.

Ricoeur, P. *La sémantique de l'action*. Paris, 1977.

Rouvillois, S. *Corps et sagesse: Philosophie de la liturgie*. Paris, 1995.

Zadra, D. *Il tempo simbolico: La liturgia della vita*. Brescia, 1985.

1. LITURGICAL LANGUAGE IN SACROSANCTUM CONCILIUM

Maggiani, S. "La riforma liturgica dalla Sacrosanctum Concilium alla IV Istruzione 'La liturgia romana e l'inculturazione." In *I trent'anni dal Concilio: Memoria e profezia*, 39–83. Ed. C. Ghidelli. Rome, 1995.

Pistoia, A. "Linguaggio e liturgia: Rassegna bibliografica." *EphLit* 92 (1978) 214–37.

Schermann, J. *Die Sprache im Gottesdienst.* Innsbruck-Vienna, 1987.

Sodi, M. "Vent'anni di studi e commenti sulla 'Sacrosanctum Concilium.'" In *Costituzione liturgica 'Sacrosanctum Concilium,'* 525–70. Ed. Congregation for Divine Worship. Rome, 1986.

Thiselton, A. C. *Language, Liturgy and Meaning.* Bramcote, 1975.

Wainwright, G. "The Language of Worship." In *The Study of Liturgy*, ed. C. Jones, G. Wainwright, E. Yarnold, P. Bradshaw, 519–28. London–New York, 1992.[2]

2. LANGUAGE AS MEDIATION

Benveniste, E. *Problems in General Linguistics.* Trans. M. E. Meek. Coral Gables, Fla., 1971.

Breton, S. *Écriture et révélation.* Cogitatio fidei 97. Paris, 1979.

Ducrot, O., and T. Todorov. *Encyclopedic Dictionary of the Sciences of Language.* Baltimore, 1994.

Evans, D. D. *The Logic of Self-Involvement: A Philosophical Study of Everyday Language with Special Reference to the Christian Use of Language About God as Creator.* New York, 1969.

Flahaut, F. *La parole intermédiaire.* Paris, 1978.

Heidegger, M. *On the Way to Language.* Trans. P. Hertz. San Francisco, 1982.

Jakobson, R. *Essais de linguistique generale.* Paris, 1963.

Ortigues, E. *Le discours et le symbole.* Paris, 1962.

Ricoeur, P. *The Conflict of Interpretations: Essays in Hermeneutics.* Ed. D. Ihde. Northwestern University Studies in Phenomenology and Existential Philosophy. Evanston, Ill., 1992.

____. *Filosofia e linguaggio.* Milan, 1994.

____, and E. Jüngel. *Dire Dio: Per una ermeneutica del linguaggio religioso.* 3rd ed. Brescia, 1993.

Smith, F., and G. A. Miller, eds. *The Genesis of Language: A Psycholinguistic Approach.* Cambridge, Mass., 1969.

3. SYMBOLIC LANGUAGE

AA.VV. *Symbolisme et théologie.* SA 64. Rome, 1974.

Benoist, L. *Signes, symboles et mythes.* 2nd ed. Paris, 1977.

Biedermann, H. *Dictionary of Symbolism.* Trans. J. Hulbert. New York, 1992.

Breton, S., D. Dubarle, J. Greisch, et al. *Le mythe e le symbole.* Paris, 1977.

Charbonneau-Lassay, L. *The Bestiary of Christ.* New York, 1991.

_____. *Il Giardino del Cristo ferito.* Rome, 1996.

Chevalier, J., and A. Gheerbrant. *A Dictionary of Symbols.* Cambridge, Mass., 1994.

Crespi, F. *Mediazione simbolica e società.* Milan, 1984.

Dillistone, F. W. *Traditional Symbols and the Contemporary World.* London, 1973.

_____, ed. *Myth and Symbol.* London, 1966.

Eliade, M. *Traite d'histoire des religions.* Paris, 1948.

Farnedi, G., ed. *I simboli dell'iniziazione cristiana.* Rome, 1983.

Guénon, R. *Symboles fondamentaux de la science sacrée.* Collection Tradition 11. Paris, 1962.

Maggiani, S. "Nella foresta dei simboli: Signifcato e prospettiva di una ricerca. *RL* 67 (1980) 291–316.

Sini, C. *Il simbolo e l'uomo.* Milan, 1991.

Sperber, D. *Rethinking Symbolism.* Trans. A. Morton. Cambridge Studies in Social Anthropology 11. Cambridge, 1975.

Todorov, T. *Symbolism and Interpretation.* Trans. C. Porter. Ithaca, N.Y., 1982.

Turner, V. *The Forest of Symbols.* Ithaca, N.Y., 1970.

Urech, E. *Dictionnaire des symboles chrétiens.* Neuchâtel, 1972.

Van der Leeuw, G. *Religion in Essence and Manifestation.* Trans. J. E. Turner. Gloucester, 1967.

4. RITUAL ACTION AND ITS LANGUAGES

AA.VV. "La celebrazione cristiana: Dimensioni costitutive dell'azione liturgica." In *Atti della XIV. Sett. APL 1985.* Genoa, 1986.

Bell, C. *Ritual Theory, Ritual Practice.* New York–Oxford, 1992.

Cazeneuve, J. *Sociologia del rito.* Milan, 1996.

Eliade, M., ed. *The Encyclopedia of Religion.* New York, 1995.

Geertz, C. *The Interpretation of Cultures: Selected Essays.* London, 1975.

Grimes, R. L. *Beginnings in Ritual Studies.* Studies in Comparative Religion. Columbia, S.C., 1995.

____. *Research in Ritual Studies: A Programmatic Essay and Bibliography.* Metuchen, N.J., 1985.

____. *Ritual Criticism: Case Studies in Its Practice. Essays on Its Theory.* Columbia, S.C., 1990.

De Heusch, L. "Introduction à une ritologie générale." In *L'unité de l'homme, invariants biologiques et universaux culturels,* 679–713. Paris, 1974.

Maggiani, S. "Rito/riti." *NDL* 1141–50.

Maisonneuve, J. *Les rituels.* Paris, 1988.

Symbols and Society: Essays on Belief Systems in Action. Ed. C. E. Hill. Southern Anthropological Society Proceedings, no. 9. Athens, Ga., 1975.

Terrin, A. N. *Leitourgia: Dimensioni fenomenologiche e aspetti semiotici.* Brescia, 1988.

Tagliaferri, R. "La violazione del mundo." In *Ricerche di epistemologia liturgica.* Rome, 1996.

Turner, V. *The Anthropology of Performance.* New York, 1986.

Vergote, A. "Le rite: expression opérante." In *Interprétation du langage,* 199–215.

5. THE PRINCIPAL ACTIVE CODES OF LITURGICAL ACTION

a) Silence

AA.VV. *Parola e silenzio di Dio.* Rome, 1991.

AA.VV. *Chi è come te fra i muti?* Milan, 1993.

Baldini, M. *Le parole del silenzio.* 2nd ed. Cinisello Balsamo, 1986.

____. *Le dimensioni del silenzio.* Rome, 1988.

Carmelus 23 (1976).

Communautés et liturgie 63 (1981).

Dauenhauer B. P. *Silence: The Phenomenon and Its Ontological Significance.* Bloomington, Ind., 1980.

Dougherty, I. "Silence in the Liturgy." In *Wor* 69 (1995) 142–54.

Downey, M. "Silence, Liturgical Role of." In *The New Dictionary of Sacramental Worship.* Ed. P. Fink. Collegeville, Minn., 1990.

Philosophy Today 27 (Summer 1983).

RL 76 (1989).

Sartore, D. "Silenzio." *NDL.*

b) The verbal code: the word in action

Bach, K., and R. M. Harnish. *Linguistic Communication and Speech Acts.* Cambridge–London, 1979.

Green, G. M. *Pragmatics and Natural Language Understanding.* Tutorial Essays in Cognitive Science. Mahwah, N.J., 1996.

Hornig, G. "Analyse und Problematik der religiösen Performative." In *Neue Zeitschrift für systematische Theologie und Religionsphilosophie* 24 (1982) 53–70.

Ladrière, J. "La performatività del linguaggio liturgico." *Conc* 9 (1973) 276–92.

____. *Language and Belief.* Trans. G. Barden. Notre Dame, Ind., 1972.

Lukken, G. *Per visibilia ad invisibilia: Anthropological, Theological and Semiotic Studies on the Liturgy and the Sacraments.* Ed. L. van Tongeren and C. Caspers. Liturgia condenda 2. Kampen, 1994.

Renaud-Chamska, I. "La lettre et la voix." *MD* 190 (1992) 25–49.

____. "Les actes de langage dans la prière." *MD* 196 (1993) 87–110.

Ricoeur, P. *The Rule of Metaphor: Multi-Disciplinary Studies of the Creation of Meaning in Language.* Trans. R. Czerny. University of Toronto Romance Series 37. Toronto, 1977.

Sbisa, M., ed. *Gli atti linguistici: Aspetti e problemi di filosofia del linguaggio.* 3rd ed. Milan, 1991.

Schaller, J. J. "Performative Language Theory: An Exercise in the Analysis of Ritual." *Wor* 62 (1988) 415–32.

Van Duk, T. A. *Testo e contesto: Studi di semantica e pragmatica del discorso.* Bologna, 1980.

Ware, J. H. *Not with Words of Wisdom: Performative Language and Liturgy.* Washington, 1981.

c) Sound-musical code: song and music

Joncas, J. M. *Hymnum tuae gloriae canimus. Toward an Analysis of the Vocal and Musical Expression of the Eucharistic Prayer in the Roman Rite: Tradition, Principles, Method.* Diss. Rome, 1991 (bibliography 558–600).

Piana, G. *Filosofia della musica.* Milan, 1991.

Rainoldi, R. *Sentieri della musica sacra. Dall'Ottocento al Concilio Vaticano II: Documentazione su ideologie e prassi.* Rome, 1996.

d) Non-verbal codes: action and gestures of the man/woman

AA.VV. *I gesti: Origini e diffusione.* Milan, 1983.

Davis, M. *Understanding Body Movement: An Annotated Bibliography*. New York, 1972.

———, and J. Skupien, eds. *Body Movement and Nonverbal Communication: An Annotated Bibliography 1971–1981*. Bloomington, Ind., 1982.

Key, M. R. *Nonverbal Communication: A Research Guide and Bibliography*. Metuchen, N.J., 1977.

1. Kinetic code: movements of the celebrating subject

Birdwhistell, R. L. *Kinetics and Context: Essays on Body Motion Communication*. Philadelphia, 1970.

Dubuc, J. *Le langage corporel dans la liturgie*. Montreal, 1986.

Le Boulch, J. *Verso una scienza del movimento umano: Introduzione alla psicocinetica*. Rome, 1985.

Ricci Bitti, P. E., ed. *Comunicazione e gestualità*. Milan, 1987.

2. Iconic code: symbolic-iconic ordering

Maggiani, S. "L'arredo liturgico." *Spazio e rito: Atti della XIII. Sett. di Studio APL 1994*. Rome, 1996.

Menozzi, D. *La chiesa e le immagini: I testi fondamentali sulle arti figurative dalle origini ai giorni nostri* (bibliography 305–21). Cinisello Balsamo, 1995.

Valenziano, C. *Architetti di Chiese*, 128–52. Palermo, 1995.

3. Optical code: luminous signals, colors

Holz, H. H. *Le strutture della visualità: Corpo, superficie, movimento, luce*. Milan, 1984.

Indergrand, M. *Cromatologue*. Paris, 1984.

Pastoureau, M. *Dictionnaire des couleurs de notre temps: Symbolique e societé* (bibliography 216–21). Paris, 1992.

4. Tactile code: symbolic interaction

Dellantonio, A. *Il tatto: Aspetti fisiologici e pricologici*. Padua, 1993.

Goffman, E. *Behavior in Public Places: Notes on the Social Organization of Gatherings*. New York, 1966.

Montagu, A. *Touching: The Human Significance of the Skin*. New York, 1986.

Shiff, W., and E. Foulke, eds. *Tactual Perception*. Cambridge, 1982.

5. Olfactory code: symbolic perfume

Classen, C., D. Howes, A. Synnott. *Aroma: The Cultural History of Smell*. New York, 1994.

Ferrara Pignatelli, M. *Viaggio nel mondo delle essenze.* Padua, 1991.

Valenziano, C. "Per una mistagogia dei simboli rituali 3. 'Chrismatis hostia.'" *RL* 76 (1989) 277–91.

6. Gustatory code: the symbolic bread

Accademia Italiana della Cucina, ed. *Il cibo e la Bibbia. Atti Conv. Nat. Biblia 1992.* Rome, 1992.

Valenziano, C. "Aspetti antropologici dei simboli sulla iniziazione cristiana." In G. Farnedi, ed., *I simboli dell'iniziazione,* 243–57.

Vogel, C. "Simboli cultuali cristiani: cibi e bevande." *Conc* 16 (1980) 309–18.

Silvano Maggiani, O.S.M.

13

Liturgy and Aesthetic

The singular dialogical act that we find in every Eucharistic Prayer of the Roman[1] and Ambrosian[2] missals, edited in the light of the conciliar reform of Vatican II, is contained in the syntagma *mysterium fidei* and in the variable response of the assembly. It is an action inspired by the anaphoral models of the Eastern Christian liturgies. It leads to the heart of ritual action (*SC* 2, 10; *LG* 11; *PO* 5; *UR* 15; *AA* 3), to the conscious wonder that seizes the praying person when the *splendor of truth* assumes the form most suitable for that person and expresses itself singularly in that form.[3] This ritual sequence now seals the section of the thanksgiving for the institution of the Supper in the great prayer of the Church. From the linguistic point of view, taking into account the context in which it is done, it can be classified as a dialogical act that has the property of causing specific awareness with the intention of affirming something. In other words, after having begun to give thanks, to invoke the Holy Spirit, and to fulfill what the Lord Jesus did with regard to the bread and the wine in the farewell supper, which he commanded his disciples to do also, the eyes of faith open like those of the disciples of Emmaus (Luke 24:30-31). Following the Pauline reading (1 Tim 3:16a) we confess, astonished, between affirmation and acclamation, that the Eucharist, that which is being celebrated, is that which recapitulates all of salvific reality, the event that is identified in the Lord Jesus. *Mysterium fidei* as

---

[1] *MR* 1975, passim.

[2] *MA* 1981, passim.

[3] For the history of the syntagma and its original collocation, but with the same function, cf. J. A. Jungmann, *The Mass of the Roman Rite*, II (Dublin, 1986) 194–217.

263

mysterium pietatis: "He [or "It," i.e., the mystery of Christ][4] who became manifest in the flesh, was justified in the Spirit, appeared to the angels, was announced to the pagans, was believed in the world, was assumed into glory" (1 Tim 3:16); otherwise, as the variable acclamations are normally expressed, it is an event that is identified with the paschal mystery and that the tradition has synthesized in the events of death, resurrection, and glorious advent of the Lord Jesus.[5]

As we will see by the example of the other ritual sequences, the liturgical action expresses the wonder that arises from the experience, the synthesis of *aesthetic* and *poietic;* the Church makes that wonder its own in the whole range of celebrative experience. However, in the eucharistic context, the sequence assumes an emblematic character regarding how one should consider all liturgical experience of the sacraments and of the Hours: it is acting, doing, performing realities given to us (τά ποιητά), in the perception or mediation of sensible realities (τά αἰσθητά).

The conciliar Constitution on the Sacred Liturgy *Sacrosanctum concilium (SC)* clearly and authoritatively has set the foundation of liturgical action and its purpose, the glorification of God and the sanctification of humans (SC 7), through the sole salvific action performed by Christ in the paschal mystery. It is the same action or work of salvation that, in its effects through proclamation and living, continues in the mission of the Church and that is done in a singular way in the liturgical celebration (SC 6). The celebration, a human-divine work, a poietic experience, performs the *opus salutis*. Not, however, in imaginary abstract or in theory. In harmony with the dynamics put into play by the founder Jesus Christ for performing the *opus salutis,* in its turn an aesthetic experience, the liturgical action makes use of sensible signs "to signify invisible realities" (SC 33). Thus the liturgical celebration, "the work of Christ the priest and of his Body, which is the Church" (SC 7), is based on this particular polarity: a poietic fundamental that is expressed aesthetically.

In the light of the more properly liturgical sources, with the help of theological science and of some so-called human sciences, we are

---

[4] This pronoun can, according to the reading that the codices make of it, refer to Christ or to the Mystery, without altering the meaning.

[5] Cf. S. Maggiani, "La celebrazione cristiana: celebrare 'in Spirito e verità per mezzo dei riti e delle preghiere,'" *Celebriamo il Signore,* eds. M. Dosio and A. Meneghetti (Rome, 1995) 91–119.

attempting to study thoroughly what is understood by aesthetic and poietic in liturgical action; why the event of Jesus Christ, in order to be given to us in its salvific efficacy, communicates itself through these two singular aspects; how the aesthetic and the poietic are articulated and structured so as to correspond adequately to their fundamental and dynamic purpose.

THE AESTHETIC IN THE CELEBRATION OF SALVATION
When we observe the unfolding of liturgical-sacramental celebrations spanning the liturgical year, but also when we observe the celebration of the sacramentals, it appears evident that each believer and the assembly stand in total openness before the "mystery of piety." At the same time *per ritus et preces* (through the rites and prayers) (*SC* 7, 21, 24, 33, 48, 59) in the awareness of acting "in the Holy Spirit," they welcome the salvific efficacy of the event of Jesus Christ, which happened one time for all. In this mysterious exchange the *per ritus et preces*, the "form," allows in accordance with structurally human dynamics to manifest and to make accepted what the Lord Jesus, in relation to the Father and in the Holy Spirit, has gained "for us and for our salvation."[6]

This manifestation, this epiphany, which for us is authentic "revelation" effecting the gift, is at the same time, indissolubly, the sacramental presence of the salvific mystery and the gift. The liturgical action, theandric action, becomes a mediation of the immediateness of the mystery in dynamic ritual terms. It makes present the source event without exhausting its efficacy and without being able to possess it. Thus, the liturgical action is placed in perennial tension of having to refer to the same event.[7]

All those things that permit "formally" the symbolic-sacramental presence of the gift and the entrance into the depth of the gift are

[6] Concerning the anthropological aspect of rite, cf. the term "Rito/Riti," *NDL* 1983 (later editions), 1223–32. Concerning the christological-trinitarian activity in the liturgy, cf. C. Vagaggini, *Theological Dimensions of the Liturgy* (Collegeville, 1976) 192–246. For the meaning of liturgical action "in the Holy Spirit," cf. S. Maggiani, "Celebrare il mistero alla luce della riflessione pneumatologica," AA.VV., *Spirito santo e liturgia*, Atti della XII Settimana di studio APL 1983 (Casale Monferrato, 1984) 59–84.

[7] For thorough examination of this topic, see A. Grillo, *Teologia fondamentale e liturgia*. Il rapporto tra immediatezza e mediazione nella riflessione teologica (Padua, 1995).

inseparable realities that constitute the epiphany of the "mystery of piety." When the form, ritually speaking, is manifested to us who are celebrating the liturgical action, and in this epiphany the depth of the gift is shown to us, our participation becomes wonder over the splendor and the glory of the event we see being manifested and explained. This wonder cannot be identified with devotionalistic sentimentalism but rather is guided by the same ritual sequences toward a gratitude that can be released in acclamations, praise, glorification, and pleasure in the most authentic and profound sense.[8]

Some general examples can help in understanding better what we aim to summarize. We can recall the structure of the Eucharistic Prayer, enriched in the Roman and Ambrosian tradition by movable prefaces, the whole prayer being related to the bread and the chalice of wine on the table-altar. We recall the dynamic structure of each sacrament constituted by an epiclectic blessing as a symbolic or natural or human element and by the ascending and descending blessings of the sacramentals in reference to persons, places, things.[9] We recall too the ritual structure that flows into and out of the adoration of the Cross on Good Friday;[10] the progressive rhythm of the Easter Vigil fire-light-water-bread and wine experienced by the proclamation of the resurrection, the transformation of enlightened catechumens, and thanksgiving.[11] The keystone of this epiphany, its very possibility, is based, as *SC* notes, on the very presence of Christ:

"'Having offered himself one time on the cross, he still offers himself through the ministry of priests,' and is present in the Sacrifice of the Mass both in the person of the minister and especially under the eu-

[8] The recovery of the dimension of the senses in liturgical-sacramental experience and reflection appears also with methodological interest in the monographic numbers of *MD* 187 (1991); 188 (1991); *RL* 82 (1995) 195–332.

[9] For the *Benedizionale* see *DB* 1984 (Italian ed., *Ben* 1992).

[10] Cf. the documentation in A. Catella and G. Remondi, eds., *Celebrare l'unità del triduo pasquale. 2. Venerdì Santo: la luce del Trafitto e il perdono del Messia* (Turin, 1995) esp. 143–75. Cf. as well the communication of D. Sartor, "L'Adoratio Crucis' come esempio di progressiva drammatizzazione nell'ambito della liturgia," Centro di Studi sul Teatro Medievale e Rinascimentale (ed.), *Dimensione drammatica della liturgia medievale*, Atti I Convegno di Studio 1976 (Viterbo, 1977) 119–25.

[11] Cf. H. A. Schmidt, ed., *Hebdomada sancta* (Rome, 1956) 117–74; 211–21; *Hebdomada sancta, II/2*, ibid., 1957. In addition, H. Auf der Maur, *La liturgia della Chiesa, 5. Le celebrazioni nel ritmo del tempo* (Turin, 1990) 93–122; 133–53; 193–207.

charistic species. He is present with his power in the sacraments, so that when anyone baptizes it is Christ who is baptizing. He is present in his Word, since he is the one who is speaking when Sacred Scripture is read in the Church. Finally, he is present when the Church prays and praises, he who has promised: 'Where two or three are gathered in my name, I am there in their midst' (Matt 18:20)."[12]

The presence of Christ and, beyond individual examples, its obediential and historical "formalization" in every ritual action, is the basis of liturgical aesthetics.

THE LORD JESUS, KEYSTONE OF LITURGICAL AESTHETIC

As can be readily seen, this manner of reading the "forms" of the beautiful that flow from the Truth has one of its roots in the reflection of aesthetic philosophy.[13] Indeed,

"the influence of beautiful forms on the soul can be described, from a psychological point of view, in a variety of ways, but an approach to them is impossible without going back to the concepts of logic and ethics, of truth and value, in short, to a comprehensive doctrine of being. The form that manifests itself is beautiful only insofar as the pleasure that it arouses is based on the self-manifestation and self-giving of the deep truth and goodness of the reality itself. This reality therefore reveals in this gift and manifestation of itself the inexhaustibility and infinity of its fascination and of its value. The appearance, as a revelation of depth, is indissolubly and simultaneously the real presence of the depth of the whole and a real reference, beyond itself, to this depth. It is possible that, in the various epochs of the history of spirit, the first aspect is emphasized one time and the second another, the classical completion (of the form that grasps the depth) one

---

[12] Cf. the study by A. Cuva, *La presenza di Cristo nella liturgia* (Rome, 1973).

[13] A more thorough study will find useful: S. Zecchi and E. Franzini, eds., *Storia dell'estetica*. Antologia di testi. I. *Dai presocratici a Hegel*. II. *Dalla crisi dei grandi sistemi alla ricerca contemporanea* (Bologna, 1995), extensive international bibliography, 519–80; 1069–126. In particular, S. Givone, *Storia dell'estetica* (Rome–Bari, 1988); F. von Kutschera, *Aesthetik*, Berlin–New York, 1989; F. Rella, *Bellezza e verità* (Milan, 1990); F. Perniola, *Del sentire* (Turin, 1991); E. Garroni, *Estetica. Uno sguardo attraverso* (Milan, 1992); R. Bodei, *Le forme del bello* (Bologna, 1995); S. Kofman, *L'imposture de la beauté* (Paris, 1995).

time and the romantic infinity (of the form that transcends toward the depth) another time. Both the one and the other are inseparable nonetheless and together constitute the fundamental figure of being. We 'descry' the form, but when we really descry it, not only as a dissolved form, but rather as a depth that is manifest in it, then we see it as splendor and glory of being. By gazing at this depth we are 'enchanted' by it and 'captivated' in it, but (insofar as the beautiful is concerned) never in such a way as to leave behind us the (horizontal) form to immerse ourselves (vertically) in the naked depth."[14]

In the realm of Christian theology in general and of liturgical theology in particular, univocal applications or translations cannot be accepted under pain of the liturgical-sacramental action itself becoming incomprehensible.[15] The God of Jesus Christ is not reducible to an *ens* under the category being, nor to the "being" itself that takes form in the manifestation. The begetting before all ages of the Word in the *in principio* of God, thus well before the Word took flesh by the work of the Holy Spirit, leads to referring to the living God as a closer activity of the utterable "One" than to the fundamentality and manifestation of being.[16]

Nevertheless, between the revelation of God in the world and people and the *historia salutis,* from the creation to the redemptive salvation worked by Jesus Christ, we discern the goodness and the wisdom of God that reveals itself and manifests the mystery of the divine will (cf. Eph 1:9). This divine "condescension" does not harm the truth and the holiness of God but makes explicit the divine wisdom that allows us to know and love God. "The words of God, therefore, expressed with human languages, became like human speech, just as the Word of the Eternal Father, having assumed the weakness of human nature, became like man" (*DV* 13). In the Christmas liturgy, in the classic text of the embolism of the old Preface I, we find lyri-

---

[14] H. Urs von Balthasar, *Gloria. I. La percezione della forma* (Milan, 1975) 104. The other volumes of *Gloria,* seven in all, are also important for the purposes of our reflection.

[15] Cf. the contributions of P. Sequeri, *Estetica e teologia* (Milan, 1993); the term "Estetica," *Dizionario delle religioni* (Cinisello Balsamo, 1993); *Il Dio affidabile. Saggio di teologia fondamentale* (Brescia, 1996) passim, and relevant biographical references.

[16] Cf. K.-J. Kuschel, *Generato prima di tutti i secoli? La controversia sull'origine di Cristo* (Brescia, 1996).

cally described the why and the how of the divine epiphany, of the aesthetic experience of the ritual action: *Quia per incarnati Verbi mysterium nova mentis nostrae oculis lux tuae claritatis infulsit: ut dum visibiliter Deum cognoscimus, per hunc in invisibilium amorem rapiamur* (For through the mystery of the incarnate Word the new light of your clarity shined in the eyes of our mind, so that, by knowing God visibly, we might thereby be seized by the love of things invisible).[17] We are helped again by the fine analysis of von Balthasar. He points out that the accent is placed upon *seeing* and that in reality *listening* is implicit (referring to the incarnate Word), as is *faith* (the mystery of the invisible God). He explains:

"But the comprehensive act, which contains in itself listening and faith, is a perception, in the strong sense of the term: as an acceptance of something true that presents itself. Indeed, for this particular perception, there is an express need for a 'new light' which, as it illuminates this particular form, bursts at the same time from it and is thus contemporaneously the co-object of the vision and a condition that makes it possible. The *splendor* of this *mysterium* that presents itself cannot therefore be equated to any other aesthetic splendor found in the world, without, however, any comparison being impossible for this under any aspect. Since here seeing becomes a word (both not exclusively and from the beginning of listening), this shows that, despite all veiling, there is still something to see and to grasp *(cognoscimus)*; it therefore is not spoken to us only in a mysterious manner, by which we are required to accept in obedience, in a naked faith that sees nothing, something that remains hidden to us. Rather, here it is said that something is 'offered' to him by God and in such a way that we are capable of seeing it, understanding it, making it our own and experiencing it humanly."[18]

The active and conscious experience emerges of a person seized by the invisible God, seen in a human mode.

"'To be seized' should be taken here in a rigorously theological sense; therefore, not as a purely psychological response to the visual encounter with a worldly beauty, but rather as a movement of the

[17] MR 1975, p. 395; for the sources, cf. E. Moeller, *Corpus Praefationum* (Tournai, 1981) 1322; *Not* 24 (1987), nos. 252–4, pp. 455–9.
[18] *Gloria*, I., 105–6.

person's whole being (thanks to the motion of the light of divine grace in the mystery of Christ) from himself, through Christ, in God. It must simply be specified that this movement that God (the object that is contemplated in Christ and that seizes the person) performs in man (a sinner, reluctant and indignant) becomes, in the Christian *éros*, voluntarily performed by us as well, rather, by us in-spired (by the Divine Spirit)."[19]

The true epiphany is Christ. In his resurrection we are enabled to continue to *see* his glory (cf. John 1:14) and therefore the glory of the Father (John 14:9) in the aesthetic experience of the celebration, in the absolute respect of the work of Christ which, gratuitously offered, can — in the freedom of human act — be gratuitously accepted in its wholeness by a human person. We can conclude with R. Guardini in saying: "The contemplation of what shines from the hidden reality; the perception of that which resounds from the eternal silence; the tactile reception even to the intensity of eating and drinking, are operative facts also in the liturgy."[20] The living God's work of creation, transfigured by the work of the Son, continues to manifest in the Holy Spirit with the forms proper to creation, the glory of the living God, so that the *ecclesia* might live by this glory.

In this sense the aesthetic dimension that flows is of a symbolic nature. In the dynamic of symbols, symbolic language permits by its polarity, at its two levels of meanings that coexist in the same signifier,[21] the organizing of a referential dimension. A communicative dimension is guaranteed, respectful of humans, of created reality and of the event to which it refers. The symbolicalness of sensible things, in the given context, such as the celebrative one, establishes relations not only with the event but, in order to express it better and to perceive its meaning better, between the human person and the world, between the human and the self, and between one person and another. Thus

"the possibility is given to humans to open themselves to their own origins, and to the unsurpassable Origin proper to the religious expe-

---

[19] Ibid., 106.

[20] "La funzione della sensibilità nella conoscenza religiosa," *Scritti filosofici*. II (Milan, 1964) 165.

[21] Cf. P. Ricoeur, *Il conflitto delle interpretazioni* (Milan, 1977) 26, quoted by G. Bonaccorso, *Celebrare la salvezza* (Padua, 1996), which can serve for further study, pp. 13–37 with relevant bibliography.

rience of the Christian faith. The liturgical celebration reaches, or rather is reached by, the Pasch of Christ, precisely because it creates the spaces in which humans can turn their gaze toward their own deepest and most authentic origins. This celebration, however, implies a context in which the symbols that open these spaces 'are performed.' The symbolic language of the faith is not scattered to the four winds, but lives gathered in that context that we call *rite*. The symbolic language is thus joined with the *ritual action*."[22]

The aesthetic harmonizes with the poietic.

THE POIETIC IN THE CELEBRATION OF SALVATION

The poietic dimension of the celebrated liturgy also finds its source and meaning in the keystone that we have identified in the Lord Jesus Christ. As we have already noted, in citing the teaching of *SC*, the dynamic of salvation history is made up of events, signs, and actions, which we find again in Christian celebration.

"Just as Christ was sent by the Father, so also he has sent the apostles, filled with the Holy Spirit, not only so that, by preaching the Gospel to all people, they might proclaim that the Son of God by his death and resurrection has freed us from the power of Satan and from death, and has brought us into the Kingdom of the Father, but also so that they might put into effect, by means of the sacrifice and of the sacraments, on which the whole of the liturgical life hinges, the work of salvation they were proclaiming" (*SC* 6).

In reality, the sacramental liturgical action contains in the action and in the word, harmonized, the intrinsic relation of the Event and the Word in the salvific history that is communicated to us by sacred Scripture.

The poietic experience, not to be undervalued, is a singular yet partial feature of human experience. With regard to the Christian faith, the proclamation of the event of Jesus Christ, the Lord, is an aspect that runs the risk of not involving all of life with its relative choices. More than a mere enunciation of doctrine, the κήρυγμα is addressed to every person in relation to God, to his or her fellow humans, to history, and to creation. The very nature of the κήρυγμα is based on the dynamic of the incarnation of the Word and on his death and resurrection:

[22] G. Bonaccorso, p. 36.

"Paul, a servant of Christ Jesus, called to be an apostle, chosen to proclaim the gospel of God, which he had promised through his prophets in the Sacred Scriptures, regarding his Son, born of the line of David according to the flesh, made Son of God with power according to the Spirit of holiness through the resurrection of the dead, Jesus Christ, our Lord" (Rom 1:1-4).

The κήρυγμα looks at the encounter with a Living One, an intense, personal, involving encounter, a "knowledge" of biblical lineage, a bond of relationships. Suffice it here to remember the fruit of the paschal mystery in its pentecostal synthesis and the relative dynamic expressed in the Acts of the Apostles: "God has raised this Jesus, and we are all witnesses of it. Raised up to the right hand of the Father, and after having received from the Father the Holy Spirit whom he had promised, he poured him out, as you yourselves can see and hear" (2:32-33).

The experiential proclamation is matched by an experiential awareness: "Upon hearing all this, they felt pierced in their hearts and said to Peter and the other apostles: 'What should we do, brothers?'" (2:37). But the pentecostal dynamic cannot be stopped. The interior process becomes personalized only when it issues from deep desire and takes form out of confused images. Belief has to be articulated, not only in the need for action and ἔθος (attitudes and values); it also has to find its historical and, we may say, its primary and source expression: "And Peter said: 'Repent, and let each of you be baptized in the name of Jesus Christ, for the remission of your sins; then receive the gift of the Holy Spirit'" (2:38). An experience is not truly human unless the experience itself takes on a corporeal power of its own in which sentiments, interior dispositions, notions, and knowledge, through a symbolic weave take the form that allows a human person to recognize them, to actualize them, to manifest them to others, and therefore transform them in relationships.[23]

"This is also true for the act of believing: so that it might be part of every person who enters into contact with the God of salvation, it must be expressed in words, symbols, and symbolic actions. And that

[23] To study more thoroughly these aspects from an anthropological viewpoint, cf. E. Ortigues, *Le Discours et le Symbole* (Paris, 1962); F. Flahault, *La parole intermédiaire* (Paris, 1978).

is just what happens in the liturgy . . . faith, indeed, is more than a condition for the liturgy, and the liturgy is more than a confirmation of faith already present, since faith is not fully realized unless it is expressed in a symbolic mode. Only in words, in symbols, and in symbolic actions of the liturgy can faith be realized as *my* faith. The expression of faith in the liturgy is therefore not something added on, something utterly accidental. On the contrary: it is of essential importance that the faith be translated 'into action.'"[24]

In this sense the Christian liturgy is in the category of *urgia;* it is poietic, and it is ritual action. As an action it is relevant to the universality of human behavior; as a ritual it is an action that is the vehicle for a behavior, which in our case opens to the salvific event, to the paschal mystery, which, as has been noted, involves the aesthetic dimension. "The agreement between religious experience and ritual action is expressed completely in celebration, given that this is precisely the 'act' of turning to the sacred or historical-salvific event through a ritual mode of performing that act."[25]

WORD OF GOD AND POIETIC FUNCTION:
SOURCES OF THE AESTHETIC AND THE POIETIC

Our reflection up until now has led us to establish the bases concerning *what* are the aesthetic and the poietic in liturgy, and *why* these two dimensions are constitutive of the communication of salvation. Also addressed is *how* the aesthetic and the poietic in their articulation can respond to their operative significance: not just the dynamics underlying the two dimensions, nor underlying the constitutive elements whether of historical or theological origin, but rather underlying their roots of meaning and their source bases.

The Word of God
Reference is constantly made to the paschal event to signify the ultimate origin of every possible consideration of ours in the liturgical-

---

[24] G. Lukken, "Nella liturgia la fede si realizza in modo insostituibile," in *Conc* 9/2 (1973) 27–8; by the same author, also see "La liturgie comme lieu théologique irremplaçable, méthodes d'analyse et de vérification théologiques," *QL* 56 (1975) 97–112. For further inquiry see A. Vergote, *Interprétation du langage religieux* (Paris, 1974); L.-M. Chauvet, *Linguaggio e simbolo* . . . (Torino, 1982) (original French ed. 1979); ibid., *Simbolo e sacramento* . . . (Turin, 1990) (original French ed. 1987).
[25] G. Bonaccorso, op. cit., 44.

sacramental field, and that has meant referring to sacred Scripture. It is important to remember specifically that one of the fundamentals of the aesthetic and poietic dimensions is the Word of God. It is normative and constitutive of every sequence or ritual structure, directly or indirectly, and with its own characteristics involves the whole Christian ritual action.[26]

Account is taken of this in *OLM* 6, which is appropriately furnished with relative references to liturgical books: ranging from *IGMR* 21, 23, 95, 131, 146, 234, 235, to the celebrations of the Word of God in the Pontifical, in the Roman Ritual, and in the Liturgy of the Hours reformed according to the decrees of the Second Vatican Council, though it could also properly refer to every ritual family both of the East and of the West: "The attitude of the body, the gestures, and the words by which the liturgical action is expressed and the participation of the faithful is manifested, receive their meaning not only from human experience from which such forms are drawn, but also from the Word of God and from the economy of salvation to which they refer."

In reality, the ritual action that in its codification is transmitted to us from the *Ordines* proves to be a "precipitate" of the Scriptures. This is particularly true for the sacramental *Ordines*. They give reason and testify to the passage from letter-sacrament to body-sacrament in the expressive mediation of the rites.

"As the baptismal formula well expresses it, the sacrament is *the precipitate of Christian Scriptures.* The formula 'In the name of the Father, of the Son and of the Holy Spirit' is indeed, for the Church, a kind of concentrate of all of Scripture. Joined with the sign of the

---

[26] There are numerous studies on the link "liturgy and Bible" both in its understanding of "Sacred Scripture in the liturgy" and "Sacred Scripture and liturgy." Cf. e.g. the term with ample bibliography by A. M. Triacca, "Bibbia e liturgia," *NDL,* pp. 175–97; Spanish ed., pp. 230–57; French ed., pp. 129–44. Cf. also: various authors, *La Bibbia nella liturgia.* Atti della XV Settimana di studio APL 1986 (Genoa, 1987); the trilogy: various authors, *Dall'esegesi all'ermeneutica attraverso la celebrazione - Bibbia e liturgia.* I (Padua, 1991); various authors, *Scriptura crescit cum orante - Bibbia e liturgia.* II (Padua, 1993); various authors, *Dove rinasce la parola - Bibbia e liturgia.* III (Padua, 1993). Cf. also the Atti del XXXI Convegno liturgico-pastorale dell'OR, ed. R. Falsini, *Fondamento biblico del linguaggio liturgico* (Milan, 1991); the contributions of the monographic issue of *MD* 189 (1992) and D. Huerre, "Une liturgie imprégnée par l'Ecriture," in *MD* 190 (1992) 7–24.

cross as a distinctive characteristic of a Christian, this formula functions as the symbol par excellence of Christian identity, a symbol that seeks to be inscribed on the body, that is, on experience. Joined with water or with bread, the Word precipitates into sacrament. St. Augustine is saying nothing else in his celebrated formula: *'Accedit verbum ad elementum, et fit sacramentum'* (The word approaches the element, and becomes sacrament). The *Verbum* indicated here can be understood on the threefold level of *Christ-Word* (he, rather than the minister, is the operative subject of the sacrament), of the *Scriptures* which are read in the celebration, and finally of the *sacramental formula* itself, pronounced *in persona Christi.*"[27]

This singular dynamic relation of sacred Scripture, "by whose inspiration and spirit the liturgical prayers, orations and hymns are imbued" and "from which the liturgical orations and gestures take their meaning," (*SC* 24) does not come about by discourse and only in part didactically. This can be taken as a source for every structure of the text or at least as a fundamental source, continually in its perspective. In virtue of this perspective, every time that I celebrate I am referred directly or indirectly, explicitly or implicitly, echoing or resounding the event that has become embodied in the Scripture and that the Scripture passes on to me normatively. The image of Emmaus possesses in this regard a fullness of special meaning.[28] Yet, undoubtedly, this scriptural perspective consolidates the meaning; truly, in the tradition of the Church, *scriptura crescit cum orante* (the Scripture grows with the one praying it).[29] Thus, as far as we are concerned, we cannot fail to read the *Ordines* as a precipitate, a perspective, an intense semantic rendering of the Scriptures that establish a basic relation between Christ and the sacraments: the Scriptures are for the *Ordines* the source, even an arch-text, just as there is talk of an arch-symbol in reference

---

[27] L.-M. Chauvet, *Simbolo e sacramento*, 155.

[28] This simple allusion is enough for our purposes. For further study, see L.-M. Chauvet, *Simbolo e sacramento*, 115ff. It can finish with the reflection by P. Pretot, "Les yeux ouverts des pélèrins d'Emmaüs," *MD* 195 (1993) 7–48.

[29] I am borrowing the singular expression of Gregory the Great: *Scriptura crescit cum legente* (scripture grows with the one reading it) interpreted in the sense cited by I. Gargano, "'Scriptura cum legente crescit.' Dal testo scritto al momento celebrativo," various authors, *Bibbia e liturgia*, I, 152–82, and selected, in the cited interpretation, as the title for *Bibbia e liturgia*, II.

to the living body.[30] By way of example: the celebration of Christian penance is "informed" in its sealing of the path of conversion to God in the Church by the *summula* [little summa] that the arch-text contains of the relation between the redemptive death-resurrection of the Lord Jesus and the person who converts in order to live; of the salvific and merciful attitudes of Jesus toward the sinner and community, attitudes involving God's merciful "fulfillment" expressed in the first revelation, without excluding the power to remit sins (John 20:22; Matt 16:19ff.; 18:18ff.) and the practice of mutual confession (James 5:16). And all this, without the still binding Tridentine doctrine; or else with its last interpretive mediation as ungenerated consciousness.[31] The Church celebrates on the basis of the arch-text. In this sense no intrinsic difficulty is raised in the ancient anaphora said to be of *Addai and Mari,* where the narration of institution is absent. The question of its presence or absence in the original text from the critical viewpoint or however allusively present it is in the memorial is moot.[32] The anaphora is situated in the eucharistic celebration, at the base of which we find everything that the Church has received from the arch-text in the *summula* on the sacrament of the sacrifice of Christ, theologically speaking.

The Poetic Function
An exhaustive reflection on the poetic function of the Christian sacramental liturgical action would demand ample space. In this setting it will be enough to summarize some essential points.

[30] The living body "as the arch-symbol of all symbolic order. The one that supports and that nourishes every actuality differentiated from the symbolic commerce of the awareness in act of a living soul with its own individuality, with the cosmic environment and other humans beings, with what a human person apprehends as the divine. Arch-symbol precisely because it is mediation, effectiveness and value of exchange between the constitutive ipseity of a conscious subject and all that which, unavoidably, is other for the conscious subject: the universe, the collectivity of human beings, God, if God is acknowledged": D. Dubarle, "Pratique du symbole et connaissance de Dieu," AA.VV., *Le mythe et le symbole* (Paris, 1977) 243–4.

[31] In this regard, truly valuable are the particular notes by A. Duval in "La confession," in his two-volume study *Des sacrements au Concile de Trente* (Paris, 1985) 151–222.

[32] Cf. the critical edition with notes and translation by A. Elston, *The Eucharistic Prayer of Addai and Mari* (Oxford, 1992). On the narrative of the institution see pp. 72–6.

276

The arch-text is accepted together with other, additional human words, with other signs of various sorts in a harmonic discourse, a harmonized action, all structured in a globally poetic way, even in pragmatic terms. The aesthetic in the poietic is not said and acted in systematic terms appropriate for theologizing; it acquires the rigor proper to poetry.[33] Poetry manifests, is word-action that builds, does not just designate things, does not describe them, but names them, and establishes a process of *vocation*. R. Jakobson states:

"[Poetic quality is manifest] in this, that the word is heard as word and not just as a simple substitute of the named object nor as an explosion of emotion. The words and their syntax, their meaning, their external and internal form are not indifferent signs of reality, but possess their weight and their own worth. Why is all this necessary? Why must it be underscored that the sign should not be confused with the object? Because along with the immediate awareness of the identity between the sign and the object (A is A1), the immediate awareness is needed of the absence of this identity (A is not A1); this antinomy is inevitable because, lacking contradiction, there is not a play of concepts, there is not a play of signs, the relation between concept and sign becomes automatic, and the course of events stops, the awareness of reality dies."[34]

In the *Ordines* and in the ritual action, the verbal and non-verbal language is organized and thought out in poetic function so as to speak of the event without exhausting it, circumscribing it, or denoting it: it speaks of the calling of the event into being, the calling of God.

"Calling God: a clear possibility, since he has spoken first, he is veiled and he has addressed us while respecting the human dialogic structure. Calling God: in the poetic functionality of language that aims at being such, so that in responding by speaking to us of the Absent-Present One the fathomless absence of the God of Jesus Christ might not be exhausted. Calling God: freed from regressive images, we are opened here to the Other, to the Living One, not ceasing to be subjects, but rather becoming in a constant maturation ever more

[33] S. Maggiani, "La Parola che diventa canto e inno," ed. R. Falsini, *Fondamento biblico*, 106–20; cf. in addition L.-M. Chauvet, *Simbolo e sacramento*, 36–78.
[34] *Questions de poétique* (Paris, 1972) 124.

creatures, ever more children in the Son of the only Father. Calling God: the ability to say the essential about both life and death and afterlife; the ability to say what is most original in order to respond to the Originator, with the consequence that the language becomes a means that mediates the truth by opening the infinite in the finite and the finite in the infinite."[35]

CONCLUSION

In his little volume *Liturgische Bildung*, R. Guardini, as in other of his writings, insists deliberately on the fact that liturgical experience should cultivate the sense of the objective. He states: "Only in starting from this does expressive behavior gain its full significance, insofar as it is inserted into the totality of the relationships of the being. Even more so because this objectivity should not be borne outside in an expressive process that is totally subjective, but should spring from within the process itself, required by its very nature."[36] A wise principle that can guide every further approach to the aesthetic and poietic dimension of Christian celebration. It is not just a matter of identity to be safeguarded, nor of possible pathologies. It is certain that the passage, whether in action or in inculturation, from the aesthetic to aestheticism, or from the poietic to babbling, is easy and possible. Here it is urgent that the *ecclesia* that celebrates in the Holy Spirit receive and live the totality of the "divine glory."

[35] S. Maggiani, "La parola che diventa canto," p. 112.
[36] Cf. the ed. OR (Milan, 1988) 77; there is no English translation of this work.

Bibliography

AA.VV. *Liturgia soglia dell'experienza di Dio?* Padua, 1982.

AA.VV. *Celebrare il mistero di Cristo. Manuale di liturgia.* Vol. 1, *La celebrazione: Introduzione alla liturgia cristiana.* BELS 73. Studi di liturgia, n.s., 25. Rome, 1993.

Balthasar, H. Urs von. *Gloria.* Vol. 1, *La percezione della forma.* Milan, 1975.

Bonaccorso, G. *Celebrare la salvezza: Lineamenti di liturgia.* Padua, 1996.

Chauvet, L.-M. *Linguaggio e simbolo: Saggio sui sacramenti.* Turin, 1988.

Dalbesio, A. *Quello che abbiamo udito e veduto: L'esperienza cristiana nella prima lettera di Giovanni.* Bologna, 1990.

Dubac, J. *Il linguaggio del corpo nella liturgia.* Cinisello Balsamo, 1989.

Fagerberg, D. W. *What Is Liturgical Theology? A Study in Methodology.* Collegeville, Minn., 1992.

Guardini, R. "La funzione della sensibilità nella conoscenza religiosa." *Scritti filosofici* 2:135–190. Milan, 1964.

____. "Fenomenologia e teoria della religione." *Scritti filosofici* 2:191–329. Milan, 1964.

Irwin, K. *Context and Text: Method in Liturgical Theology.* Collegeville, Minn., 1994.

Nicolaci, G., ed. *Segno ad evento nel pensiero contemporaneo.* Milan, 1990.

Nocke, F. J. *Parola e gesto: Per comprendere i sacramenti.* Brescia, 1988.

Ricoeur, P. *Semantica dell'azione: Discorso e azione.* Milan, 1986.

Sequeri, P. *Estetica e teologia.* Milan, 1993.

Valenziano, C. "'Vedere la parola': Liturgia e ineffabile." *EO* 9 (1992) 121–40.

Wainwright, G. *Doxology: The Praise of God in Worship, Doctrine, and Life: A Systematic Theology.* New York, 1984.

Jan Michael Joncas

14

Liturgy and Music

TERMINOLOGY

Before undertaking our investigation we should offer some clarification on the terminology employed. Different terms have arisen in different eras to designate the music employed in Catholic Christian worship. Each term suggests a particular perspective through which worship music can be viewed.

Religious music *(musica religiosa)* labels any music perceived to have a connection to religion or spirituality, explicitly or implicitly understood. Thus a Tibetan Buddhist chant or Richard Wagner's *Parsifal* might both be called "religious music." In Joseph Gelineau's taxonomy of definitions, religious music denotes "all music which expresses religious sentiment but which is not designated for use in the liturgy."[1] Although religious music may be imported into Roman-rite worship (as when an organist plays a concert piece during preparation of the gifts), it is usually performed and experienced outside of a liturgical context.

Sacred music *(musica sacra)* is a term frequently employed by official Catholic documents in the last two centuries to refer to music used during the liturgy and in popular devotions. In Gelineau's taxonomy, sacred music is that which "by its inspiration, purpose and destination, or manner of use has a connection with [Catholic Christian] faith." In popular usage, however, "sacred music" and "religious music" frequently overlap. For example, Edward Elgar's *The Kingdom*, although an oratorio intended for the concert hall and not

---

[1] J. Gelineau, *Voices and Instruments in Christian Worship: Principles, Laws, Applications* (Collegeville, 1964) 59–65.

intended for use in Catholic liturgy or popular devotions, is categorized as "sacred music."

Church music *(musica ecclesiastica)* designates music employed by the Christian churches. It tends to be the preferred term for musicological and academic treatments of this repertoire's history. However since "church music" may include catechetical songs intended for classroom education, prayers sung as blessings before and after eating a meal at home, biblical texts sung during work, or folk hymns sung during processions and popular devotions, it should be clear that "church music" includes more than the music specifically associated with liturgical rites.

Liturgical music *(musica liturgica)*, although infrequently used before the twentieth century, has taken on prominence after the Second Vatican Council as a specific term for the music integral to (Catholic Christian) liturgy. In Gelineau's taxonomy, liturgical music is defined as that "which the Church admits, both in law and in practice, to the celebration of her official and public worship." Liturgical music is *of* the liturgy, rather than simply *in* or occurring *during* the liturgy. Thus Edward Foley defines liturgical music as that "which weds itself to the liturgical action, serves to reveal the full significance of the rites and, in turn, derives its full meaning from the liturgy."[2]

Some contemporary theorists, emphasizing the role music plays in enacting liturgical celebrations, employ the term "Christian ritual music." For example, "Point of Reference 1.4" of the Universa Laus document *Music in Christian Celebration* states: "We understand 'ritual music' to mean any vocal or instrumental practice which, in the context of celebration, diverges from the usual forms of the spoken word on the one hand and ordinary sounds on the other. The domain of sound we have just defined can go beyond what certain cultural contexts would currently describe as 'music' or 'singing.'" While in some ways "liturgical music" and "Christian ritual music" can be considered synonymous, the former more clearly accents the total submission of music to the liturgical *rite* and not simply to the liturgical *texts*.

We will use the term "worship music" with appropriate qualifiers, since at various times the investigation will treat music employed in non-Christian religious traditions as well as music produced and used by Christians in worship contexts that are liturgical (in celebrations

---

[2] E. Foley, "Liturgical Music," *A New Dictionary of Sacramental Worship*, 855.

of the sacraments, sacramentals, and the Liturgy of the Hours) and non-liturgical (in popular devotions, pilgrimages, and instruction).

Fundamentally the human sciences provide descriptions of musical events and explanatory frameworks for how these events function. They do not provide normative statements of the adequacy and appropriateness, the congruence and coherence, of musical events for Christian ritual worship. Establishing such criteria is the task of historical, philosophical, and theological disciplines, whose treatment of music we will now sketch.

HISTORICAL SKETCH OF CHRISTIAN WORSHIP MUSIC
Historical musicologists identify a variety of sources for constructing the history of Christian worship music: artifacts, visual representations, written remains, and audible recordings. To these basic categories should be added the evidence of acoustic environments and contemporary performances.

More data can be gained from written records, which can in turn be divided into two subcategories: writing about music and music written for use. Christian writing about music ranges from incidental remarks or images (e.g., "Your most renowned presbytery . . . is attuned to the bishop as strings to a cithara")[3] through theoretical treatises (e.g., Boethius' *De institutione musica libri quinque*) to technical manuals (e.g., Aurelian of Reóme's *Musica disciplina*). The interpretation of these musical references demands sensitivity to literary forms, identification of the competence and intent of the author(s), and attention to shifting semantic fields for technical terms.

Christian worship music written for use subdivides into two main groups: non-notated (vocal) and notated (vocal, instrumental, and combined vocal-with-instrumental) documents. Before the invention of printing from movable type in western Europe in the fifteenth century, manuscripts provided all records of Christian worship music written for use; these manuscripts exhibit a plethora of notational systems. Except for a fragment of a trinitarian hymn stemming from the third century, texts intended to be sung at Christian worship appear without any notation until about A.D. 800, worship texts with precise pitch notation appear in manuscripts about A.D. 1000, and definite rhythmic notation appears in manuscripts from A.D. 1200 on.

---

[3] Ignatius of Antioch, *To the Ephesians* 4:1.

Only with the rise of recording technologies in the nineteenth century do audible reproductions of musical performances appear. Field recordings of worship-music performances are now being supplemented with film and videotapes correlating musical activity and ritual behavior. But these recordings also betray a particular point of view/audition that may or may not correlate with others' experiences of the worship event. A peculiar difficulty arises in performances of worship music created only for the recording medium in contrast to recordings of musical worship events in practice.

Architectural environments provide their own evidence of Christian worship music practices. The echoes, delay, reverberance, and dead spots of a barrel-vaulted stone Romanesque church crypt encourage particular types of worship music practices, while a carpeted wooden meeting-house environment demands others. Careful attention to the architecture in which a worship event takes place provides clues about the sonic environment.

The Greek, Roman, and Jewish Matrix for Christian Worship Music
Culturally the Christian movement took shape in a complex interaction of Hellenistic culture, Roman politics, and Jewish traditions. The religious and musical practices of these civilizations made their own contributions to primitive Christian worship music. Some attention must be paid to each of these factors in order to understand the fusion of earlier traditions and new endeavors in Christianity's ritual activity.

That Greek music was bound to influence early Christian music is clear from the fact that the New Testament itself is written in Greek. But actual evidence for this influence is scarce. Notions of scale and mode as well as certain aesthetic judgments seem to be taken from Greek thought, but this may also represent later Christian authors retrojecting Greek influence back into primitive Christian practice.[4]

In order to understand the role of music in ancient Roman religious ritual we must examine the religious institutions of the Etruscans, from whom the Romans derived the most important elements. The original purpose of music in the Roman cult was to chase away demons and malevolent spirits through loud noises as the sacrifices and divinations took place. Thus brass and percussion instruments held pride of place. No sacrifice could take place without the sound-

---

[4] W. D. Anderson, *Music and Musicians in Ancient Greece* (Ithaca, N.Y., 1994).

ing of the aerophone *tibia*. After Greek customs were incorporated in the Roman cult, stringed instruments also took their place. Religious functionaries honored the war gods Mars and Quirinius with war dances and appropriate songs. Each year in March and October they held armed processions in the city led by a dancer *(praesul)* and a singer *(vates)* performing archaic songs and ancient war dances. The texts sung were so archaic that in the imperial period they could no longer be understood. Contrast the Christian emphasis upon "rational sacrifice" (λογικὴ θυσία) with a corresponding emphasis on logogenic worship music. The influence of Roman worship-music practice on those of Christians thus appears mostly negative: some Christian rituals and songs may have been chosen to contrast with those of Roman paganism.

Ancient Jewish musical practice can to a certain extent be recovered from literature in Hebrew, Aramaic, and Greek, supplemented by archaeological relics of musical instruments, iconographic representations of musical scenes, and comparative material from neighboring cultures.[5]

The Old Testament mentions a wide variety of musical instruments used in Jewish life and worship, although some of the terms in Hebrew, Aramaic, and Greek remain obscure. Chordophones include the *kinnor* (lyre), *sabbeka* (trigon), *asor* (ten-stringed zither), and *nebel* (harp). Aerophones include the *hatsotsrah* or *taqoa* (trumpet), *khalil* ([double] pipe), *ugab* (flute), *yobel* (coronet), *mashroqi* (whistle), and *keren* (horn); the *shophar* (ram's horn), still in use in the synagogue, produces only two or three notes and was used mostly for signals in times of war or national celebration. The *toph* was probably a small membranophone: a hand drum or possibly a tambourine. Idiophones include *tseltselim* and *metsiltayim* (cymbals) and *menanim* (sistrums); bells attached to the high priest's robes whose sound was intended to ward off demonic influences should also be mentioned in this category.

[5] H. Avenary, *Studies in the Hebrew, Syrian, and Greek Liturgical Recitative* (Tel Aviv, 1963); idem, "Contacts between Church and Synagogue Music," *Proceedings of the World Jewish Congress on Jewish Music* (Jerusalem 1978) (Tel Aviv, 1982) 89–107; J. W. McKinnon, "On the Question of Psalmody in the Ancient Synagogue," *Early Music History* 6 (1986) 159–91; E. Werner, "Jewish Music, I: Liturgical," *The New Grove Dictionary of Music and Musicians*, 20 vols., ed. Stanley Sadie (London, 1980) 9:614–34.

The Old Testament, especially in the psalm superscriptions, provides many terms for genres of vocal music, although some of the terminology remains obscure. *Shir* appears to be the general term for "song," with *shir hamma'alot* ("song of the ascents") meaning "song sung in a series," "song employing step parallelism," "song created when going back up to Jerusalem from Exile," "song sung on the steps of the Temple," or "song sung during the pilgrimage festivals." A *mizmor* appears to be a song with plucked string accompaniment, but it is frequently interchanged with *shir*. Both *maskil* and *miktam* remain obscure, though the former may suggest an artistic didactic song and the latter a secret atonement song. *Tehillim* and *tephillim* are hymns or songs of praise and laments or bidding prayers respectively. Various passages provide musical directions (e.g., "upon the eighth," Psalms 6, 12) or indicate tune titles (e.g., "hind of the dawn," Psalm 21). The mysterious *selah* has been interpreted as an inserted stereotyped doxology, a cue for an instrumental interlude, a directive to increase volume or repeat a section, a signal to bow, or a time to pause in silence.

Music was associated with a variety of social functions in Jewish life. Warfare produced ballads recounting the exploits of heroes (possibly the content of the lost "Book of the Wars of the Lord" [Num 21:14] and the "Book of Jashar" [Josh 10:13; 2 Sam 1:18]), victory chants (Exod 15:20-21; Judg 6; 15:16; 1 Sam 18:6-7), and laments for the fallen (2 Sam 1:19-27). Both farewells (Gen 31:27) and homecomings (Judg 11:34) were marked by music, as well as the feasts of the idle rich (Isa 5:12) and wedding ceremonies. Songs alleviated the monotony of work (Num 21:17-18; Isa 21:12; Jer 25:30; 48:33), elicited prophecy (2 Kgs 3:15), and soothed disturbed psyches (1 Sam 16:23).

We have the most information about the use of music at court and Temple in Jerusalem from the time of the monarchy on. According to 2 Sam 6:5 and 1 Chr 13:8, the transport of the ark of the covenant to Jerusalem is accompanied by the playing of lyres, drums, rattles, and cymbals, perhaps an indication of popular festival music making rather than strictly cultic practice. 1 Kgs 1:38-40 describes musical practices at Solomon's accession as successor to David. Scattered references during the period of the divided monarchy suggest that music at court, in cult, and among commoners continued much as under the united monarchy (e.g., 2 Kgs 11:12-14; 2 Chr 13:13-15; 35:25); prophetic literature likewise makes passing references to Jewish musical practices (e.g., Isa 5:11-12; 16:10-11; 23:15-16; 24:8-9; Jer 31:45).

After the Babylonian Exile music flourished in three central institutions of emerging Judaism: the Jerusalem Temple, local synagogues, and Jewish homes. By the first century Temple music was performed by hereditarily designated professionals (Levites). This music was primarily vocal and choral in character and followed the offering of sacrifices. Instrumental music accompanied these Levitical chants; priests signaled the sacrificial acts with trumpet blasts. As far as we know the choirs and instruments associated with Temple worship did not appear in the synagogue (except for the blowing of the *shophar,* which served more a signaling than a musical purpose and was never used to accompany song). Thus the musical aspects of synagogue worship were not the responsibilities of cultic professionals. Rather, a prayer leader (*sheliach tsibbur:* "emissary of the people") was responsible for chanting various texts in unison or alternation with the worship assembly. This suggests that the style of music employed may have been less ornate than that of the Temple. It was clearly logogenic ("word-born") music, connected to the proclamation of ritual texts: the *Shema Yisrael* with its surrounding benedictions, the *Shemoneh Esreh,* the scriptural readings with their surrounding benedictions, and (possibly) psalmody. Presumably domestic music making also occured in a religious context (e.g., the singing of Hallel psalms during the Passover Seder), but concrete data about such practices are few in number.

In summary, primitive Christian worship music may have been influenced by Greek music theory and philosophical understandings, negatively by Roman ritual music practices, and positively by Jewish musical practices in Temple, synagogue, and home. We now turn to an investigation of the New Testament to explore primitive Christian worship music itself.

Christian Worship Music in the New Testament Era
Describing primitive Christian worship music practices is quite difficult due to the scarcity of sources. No surviving musical artifacts, visual representations, or acoustic environments unassailably dated to the first century of the Christian movement survive. Only the twenty-seven documents that make up the New Testament and a handful of other "subapostolic" writings (e.g., the *Didache,* the *First Letter of Clement of Rome,* the *Letter of Barnabas*) allow us to reconstruct in some way the liturgical life of the first generations of Christians. It

should be remembered that musical topics are not the primary concern of the authors of these documents. The documents are marked by an intensely local character: worship music performed in the Corinthian community is not necessarily that performed in Jerusalemite, Antiochene, Ephesian, or Colossian communities, let alone those represented in the Johannine epistles, the letter to the Hebrews, or the book of Revelation.

A clearer picture of New Testament worship-music practices is gained with the help of form criticism, which has identified various musico-poetic genres embedded in the New Testament's documents and confirmed the logogenic character of its worship music. The genres include short praise formulae (including doxologies, eulogies, and thanksgivings), ejaculations and interventions (e.g., *Amen, Hallelujah, Hosanna, Marana tha, Abba* — seemingly technical terms retained in Hebrew/Aramaic), infancy canticles, God-hymns, Christ-hymns, psalms, readings, and table prayers. There is also reference to ecstatic speech (glossolalia) which may have had a musical character. Presumably these texts would have been performed by worshipers in various settings and formats with diverse melodies and rhythms, but in the absence of rubrical directives and notation, reconstruction remains conjectural.[6]

Christian Worship Music in the Early Patristic Period (ca. 100–ca. 313)
The fragmentary information we have about Christian worship in the post–New Testament period allows only the broadest sketch of Christian worship-music practices prior to the Edict of Milan. There seems to be scholarly agreement that Christians did not employ instrumental music at their worship during this era. According to Clement of Alexandria in *The Tutor,* Christians shunned instrumental music because the instruments had unsavory connotations and the music they produced led to irrational sensuality. But if Christians did not play instruments at their worship, they did sing.

As in synagogal practice, Christian prayer leaders most probably "improvised" public prayers (such as primitive Eucharistic Prayers)

---

[6] E. Foley, *Foundations of Christian Music: The Music of Pre-Constantinian Christianity,* (Alcuin/GROW Liturgical Study, 1992); J. Sanders, *The New Testament Christological Hymns* (Cambridge, 1971); J. A. Smith, "First Century Christian Singing and Its Relationship to Contemporary Jewish Religious Song," *Music and Letters* 75 (1994) 1–15.

on certain fixed themes. Perhaps certain recitation formulae were associated with the cantillation of these texts as in Jewish practice, but since we have no notational evidence from this era, it is difficult to be certain. It is clear that these cantillated texts had to be constructed and chanted in such a way as to lead to vocal affirmations by the assembly, such as *Amen* or *Marana tha*. It is possible that as the Christian public prayer-texts were increasingly standardized and differentiated from those of Judaism, the cantillation patterns were likewise standardized and differentiated.

In addition to public prayers offered by a prayer leader and affirmed by a congregational intervention, early Christian worship also included proclamation of the Scriptures. Presumably the biblical texts were cantillated to particular tonal formulae as in Jewish practice, though notational evidence is lacking. In the later part of the era, designated officials (lectors) increasingly took responsibility for reading the Scriptures during Christian worship; as a guild they may have handed on cantillation traditions to their successors.

Contrary to popular opinion there is little direct evidence that canonical psalms formed a regular part of primitive Christian worship, although they were sung during banquets and to mark table fellowship. While citations from the psalms formed a significant part of early Christian apologetic, it appears that singing portions of the Psalter only began in Christian worship at the beginning of the third century as an antidote to unorthodox but popular chants. *Acts of Paul* 7:10, written around 190, is the first indisputable reference to singing "David's psalms" at a Christian feast. Tertullian's *On the Soul* 9:4, written between 208 and 212, describes a Montanist liturgy of the word in which "scriptures are read, psalms are sung, sermons are delivered and prayers offered"; presumably members of the great church in North Africa would have shared similar contents and structure in their worship.

If Christians rarely used canonical psalms in their worship during this period, they did produce non-canonical psalmody in great profusion, some of it of questionable orthodoxy: for example, the *Odes of Solomon; Acts of Thomas* 3–6, 108; *Acts of John* 94–7; the "Ophite Hymn" (Hippolytus, *Refutatio* V.9.8–9); the "Naassenians' Psalm" (Hippolytus, *Refutatio* V.10.2); the "Valentinians' Psalm" (Hippolytus, *Refutatio* VI.37.7); Ignatius of Antioch's *Letter to the Ephesians* 7:2, 19:2–3, and *Letter to Polycarp* 3:2; and *Fragment 13* of Melito of Sardis.

Perhaps the most famous of these is the so-called "Evening Hymn of the Greeks," the Φῶς ἱλαρόν still used in Eastern evening prayer.

Clement of Alexandria's Greek poem in *The Tutor* addressed to Christ as Savior ("Bridle of untamed colts") may be the earliest version of Christian metrical hymnody extant, but there is some doubt that Clement ever intended it for actual use in worship. Oxyrhynchus Papyrus 1786 preserves a fragment of a Christian hymn written in Greek anapaestic meter set to a diatonic melody. It is the only notated piece of Christian worship music extant prior to the 800s, but it is unclear whether or not the hymn was intended for public worship.[7]

Christian Worship Music in the East and Non-Roman West
From the time of Constantine until the rise of Islamic political control changed the character of the city, Jerusalem (and Palestine in general) was a center of Christian pilgrimage. Visitors to Jerusalem witnessed a liturgy of intensely local character, related to the holy places marked by the great churches built under imperial patronage.

As pilgrims returned home with reports of the worship engaged in at the very places where the earthly Christ had walked (and even more importantly, when Jerusalemite Christians fled the city after Islamic control was asserted), the liturgical customs of Jerusalem greatly influenced other liturgical families both Eastern and Western, especially in three areas: the structure and organization of the daily offices (Liturgy of the Hours), the celebration of annual seasons and festivals (liturgical year), and the practices associated with Christian initiation (catechumenate, initiation, mystagogy).

Although the sources make reference to musical elements in Jerusalemite worship (hymns, responses, antiphons, litanies, invocations), they do not give us precise information about how these elements were performed, although mention is made of soloists, monastic choirs, and singing by the assembly.[8]

---

[7] C. Hannick, "Christian Church, Music of the Early," *New Grove Dictionary of Music and Musicians*, 4:363–71; A.W.J. Holleman, "Early Christian Liturgical Music," *SL* 8 (1972) 185–92; J. Lamb, "The Psalms in the Early Church," *The Psalms in Christian Worship* (London, 1962) 23–45; J. W. McKinnon, *Music in Early Christian Literature* (Cambridge, 1987); J. Quasten, *Music and Worship in Pagan and Christian Antiquity*, trans. B. Ramsey from the 2d German ed. (Washington, D.C., 1983).

[8] Peter Jeffery, "The Sunday Office of Seventh-Century Jerusalem in the Georgian Chantbook (Iadgari): A Preliminary Report," *SL* 21 (1991) 52–75.

The fundamental worship-music tradition for the Byzantine rite is Greek, although other languages (especially Russian) have produced their own worship-music repertoires. For our purposes "Byzantine chant" refers to the unaccompanied modal monophonic vocal music in use in the Greek church through the middle of the fifteenth century, though historical musicologists identify two further stages of development in the Greek Byzantine worship-music tradition: "Neo-Byzantine" from the mid-fifteenth through the eighteenth centuries and "Chrysanthine" from the reforms undertaken by Archbishop Chrysanthos in the early nineteenth century.[9]

In addition to various forms of cantillation developed for the proclamation of scriptural passages and liturgical prayers, Byzantine worship music developed three characteristic musico-poetic forms. The κοντάκιον entered Byzantine liturgical use in the early sixth century with the compositions of Romanus the Melodos (sixth century), who presumably transformed the *sogitha* of his native Syrian liturgical tradition into a Greek poetic sermon-paraphrase; more than eighty of Romanos' authentic κοντάκια survive in Byzantine liturgical use. The κανών with its nine odes (the second of which is frequently omitted in practice) developed under the initiative of Andrew of Crete (c. 660–c. 740) and possibly Germanos I, who served as patriarch of Constantinople from 715 to 730, as a set of poetic paraphrases for nine biblical canticles (Exod 15:1-9; Deut 32:1-43; 1 Sam 2:1-10; Heb 3:2-19; Isa 26:9-19; Jonah 2:29; Dan 3:26-45, 52-56; Dan 3:57-88; Luke 1:46-55, 68-79). Each ode consisted of a model stanza (τρόπος) with three to four additional stanzas (τροπάρια) employing the same poetic structure and melody. The στίχηρον is a single-stanza hymn chanted at Eucharist or during the Liturgy of the Hours and usually intended to venerate an individual saint. As new saints are canonized, new hymns are created, though today usually to preexisting poetic models and melodies.

Syria is the site of another of the four ancient patriarchates, Antioch. With Ephrem the Syrian (306?–373), Narsai of Nisibis (ca. 410–503), and Jacob of Sarug (ca. 450–521), an extensive hymnographical tradi-

[9] D. Conomos, *Byzantine Hymnography and Byzantine Chant* (Brookline, Mass., 1984); J. Szövérffy, *A Guide to Byzantine Hymnography: A Classified Bibliography of Texts and Studies,* 2 vols. (Brookline, Mass., 1978–1979); E. Wellesz, *A History of Byzantine Music and Hymnography,* 2d ed. (Oxford, 1971).

tion enriched Syrian worship. Writing in Syriac, these authors employed three basic poetic forms: *memra* (a metrical homily), *madrasha* (an "instruction" or didactic song), and *sogitha* (an acrostic); a long-standing tradition claims that the "antiphonal" method of hymn singing came into existence under Ephrem's guidance. In the sixth century Simeon the Potter, deacon of Ghezir, introduced a new genre, the *qala/qolo* (a "tone"/"tune" alternating long and short verses with interspersed doxologies). Other hymnographers, including Severus of Sozopolis (460–538?) and Romanos the Melodos (a sixth century Syrian who moved to Constantinople and enriched Byzantine worship there), employed Greek as their language of composition. Reconstruction of the original melodies associated with these texts is extremely difficult because no consistent system of notation was ever developed that could treat the variants of the same texts appearing in the different rites, although a few Melkite manuscripts employing Greek neumes survive. French Benedictines (especially J. Jeannin) collected and transcribed Syrian liturgical chants beginning in the second half of the nineteenth century, but the systematic collection and analysis of these chants in the second half of the twentieth century by Heinrich Husmann has revolutionized understanding of Syrian worship-music practices.[10]

Sometimes classified as an offshoot of the Syrian Rites, the Maronite liturgical family represents an independent synthesis of East and West Syrian traditions. Proud of a traditional union between Maronite Christians and the See of Rome, the Maronite liturgy became heavily Latinized from the medieval period on. An attempt to restore the Maronite Rite's Syrian roots has been occurring since the Second Vatican Council, although Maronite worship music has never lost its special emphasis on the popular pietistic hymns and versified *sedro*. Various texts of the liturgy are performed in Aramaic, Syriac, and Arabic (and/or the vernacular of the worshiping group), each with characteristic musical settings.[11]

Deriving from yet another of the ancient Eastern patriarchates, Alexandria, the Coptic Rite represents the liturgical worship of the

---

[10] H. Husmann, "Syrian church music," *New Grove Dictionary of Music and Musicians*, 18:473–81; M. Velimirovic, "Christian Chant in Syria, Armenia, Egypt, and Ethiopia," *The Early Middle Ages to 1300*. (Oxford–New York, 1990) 3–25.

[11] L. Hage, *Maronite Music* (London, 1978).

Christians native to Egypt. In contemporary practice the Coptic Orthodox (Monophysite) church is presumed to be the most faithful to ancient worship-music practices; many melodies employed in the Coptic Catholic church appear to be abbreviations and simplifications of those used among the Coptic Orthodox.

Solo, choral, responsorial, and antiphonal singing appear in Coptic liturgical practice, as well as the use of certain percussion instruments (cymbals and triangles) to accompany the chants in strict rhythm. Melismatic improvisations by cantors are highly prized. Coptic eucharistic services, lasting between three and six hours, employ lengthy interchanges sung between priest, deacon, and congregation/choir. Copts preserve a variety of hymn forms in a special office called the *Psalmodeya,* sung between Compline and the Office of Evening Incense and also between Lauds and the Office of Morning Incense: *hos* (ancient Egyptian term for "sing"/"praise," a type of biblical canticle corresponding to a Byzantine ode), *theotokion* (a Greek term for a hymn to the Virgin, each day of the week having its own set ranging from seven to eighteen), *psali* (paraphrases of biblical psalms or canticles, longer ecclesiastical hymns frequently exhibiting Coptic or Greek alphabetic acrostics), *lobsh* (Coptic for "roof," "house-top," or "crown," inserted after the various sets of *hos* and *theotokia*), and *turuhat* (hymns to the saints, doxologies). Coptic chants are normally sung in alternation between two sections of a choir positioned on the right-hand *(bahari)* or left-hand *(qibli)* side of the sanctuary door. Much work still needs to be done in separating the Byzantine elements of Coptic hymnody from its native flowering.[12]

Ethiopian ecclesiastical and liturgical history represents a fascinating blend of Alexandrian Hellenistic traditions and Byzantine and Syrian missionary activities with underlying Hebraic roots.

The three basic modes of Ethiopian chanting are *ge'ez* (a technical term not to be confused with the language), *'ezl,* and *araraye.* The *dabtara,* liturgical singers and dancers, take up to fifteen years to collect, memorize, and perform these chants in special schools under the personal direction of renowned teachers. Although the process of

---

[12] I. Borsai, "Coptic Rite, music of the," *New Grove Dictionary of Music and Musicians,* 4:730–4; E. O'Leary de Lacy, *The Daily Office and the Theotokia of the Coptic Church* (London, 1911).

transmission is primarily oral/aural, each *dabtara* learns *meleket* musical notation and is expected to create a personal book of all the chants needed in Ethiopian services. In addition to transmitting the traditional chants, the *dabtara* are expected to create new poetry and hymns, especially in the form of *qene* (a single stanza of two to twelve lines of text with a single rhyme). The *dabtara* must also learn how to perform a sacred dance *(aquaquam)* and play at least the most prominent musical instruments used in worship: the *kebero/kabaro* (a large drum suspended from the player's neck), the *snansel / tsenatsel* (a sistrum-like instrument consisting of a rattle of small bells), and the *meqomia / maqwamia* (a long conducting stick that can also be used as a bodily support during the lengthy services).[13]

In addition to the gradual differentiation of the Eastern liturgical families and their respective worship-music practices, Western liturgical families also developed in this era. Although all shared a common Latin liturgical language, the non-Roman Western rites exhibited distinctive liturgical texts, structures, spirituality, and ethos. Chant scholars identify subgroupings such as Beneventan, Central Italian (Ravenna, Aquileia), Celtic, and Anglo-Saxon chant traditions, but here we will only treat the church music traditions of the major liturgical families: Ambrosian, Gallican, and Old Spanish.[14]

The Ambrosian liturgical family represents the practices of Milanese Lombardy. Although an independent rite, it has adapted some materials from Roman, Byzantine, and Gallican traditions. Its chant repertoire is the only non-Roman Western tradition to survive relatively completely in decipherable notation. The earliest chant manuscripts date to the eleventh century, with a significant number of manuscripts in fully diastemic notation containing chants for Mass and the Divine Office dating from the twelfth century.

Ambrosian chants are not classified in the eight-mode system employed for Gregorian chant. While the melodies do exhibit four finals on D, E, F, and G, authentic and plagal forms of the modes are not easily established; a variety of recitation tones are possible for a

---

[13] M. Powne, *Ethiopian Music: An Introduction. A Survey of Ecclesiastical and Secular Ethiopian Music and Instruments* (Westport, 1980); K. K. Shelemay, and P. Jeffery, *Ethiopian Christian Liturgical Chant: An Anthology,* 2 vols. and cassette tape, Recent Researches in Oral Traditions of Music 1 (Madison: Wis., 1991).

[14] K. Levy, "Latin Chant Outside the Roman Tradition," *Early Middle Ages to 1300,* 69–110.

single final. The range of Ambrosian chant may be quite wide, with a twelfth not uncommon; the tessitura often centers on the upper half of the melodic register. While psalmodic, syllabic, neumatic, and melismatic chants are all represented in the Ambrosian repertoire, its ornate forms are unmatched by any other Western chant tradition. (Alleluia V, for example, is about 110 notes long, its *melodiae primae* [for an extended repeat after the verse] about 240, and its *melodiae secundae* [for another repeat] over 320.)

Ambrosian chants for the Proper of the Mass include (1) *ingressa* (an opening chant parallel to the Roman introit but sung without psalmody); (2) *psalmellus* and *cantus* (florid chants corresponding to the Roman gradual and tract respectively); (3) *post-epistolam* alleluia and verse (a melismatic chant preceding the proclamation of the Gospel); (4) an antiphon *ante-Evangelium* (neumatic chants sung at Christmas, Epiphany, and during Easter Week before the Gospel); (5) an antiphon *post-Evangelium* (syllabic to moderately melismatic chants sung after the Gospel); (6) *offerenda* (melismatic chants corresponding to the Roman offertorium); (7) *confractatorium* (variable antiphons corresponding in function to the Roman *Agnus Dei*); and (8) *transitorium* (relatively simple chants to accompany the Communion procession).

As in the Roman Rite, the liturgical books of the Ambrosian Rite have undergone extensive revision (including translation into Italian) since the Second Vatican Council. What impact these textual and ceremonial revisions will have on the chant repertoire remains to be seen.[15]

The Gallican liturgical family refers to a variety of local practices in use in the area of southern Gaul before they fused with the Roman Rite under Carolingian impetus in the late eighth and early ninth centuries. No purely Gallican antiphonary for Mass or the Office has survived, although Gallican material may appear in Celtic, Old Spanish, or Ambrosian liturgical books. Most of the notated chant pieces are preserved in the Franco-Roman tradition, which probably edited them to conform to the Gregorian style.[16]

[15] G. B. Baroffio, "Ambrosian rite, music of the," *New Grove Dictionary of Music and Musicians*, 1:315–20; T. Bailey, and P. Merkeley, *The Melodic Tradition of the Ambrosian Office-Antiphons* (Ottawa, 1990).

[16] M. Huglo, "Gallican rite, music of the," *New Grove Dictionary of Music and Musicians*, 6:113–25.

Also known as "Visigothic" or "Mozarabic," the Spanish liturgical family represents the worship practices of communities on the Iberian peninsula until the imposition of the Roman Rite in the eleventh century.

Chants for the Spanish Mass include (1) *praelegenda* (antiphonal psalmody to accompany the entrance procession); (2) *Gloria in excelsis Deo* (rarely appearing in the manuscript tradition); (3) *trisagion* (melismatic settings in transliterated Greek, Latin, or both languages); (4) *benedictiones* (neumatic to melismatic settings of the *Canticle of the Three Young Men* from the book of Daniel); (5) *psalmi [pulpitales]* (neumatic or melismatic chants corresponding to the Roman gradual); (6) *clamores* (only about twenty feasts are assigned this two-part chant surrounding the acclamation *Deo gratias* and concluded by the refrain of the preceding *psalmo*); (7) *threni* (melismatic chants drawn from Job, Jeremiah, and Lamentations that substitute for the *psalmi* on certain days of Lent); (8) *laudes* (correlates of the Roman-Rite pre-Gospel alleluia chants, although there are *laudes* sung without the alleluia during Lent); (9) *sacrificia* (long and melismatic chants corresponding to the Roman-Rite offertories); (10) *ad pacem* (antiphons sung during the exchange of the kiss of peace); (11) *ad Sanctus* (texts related to the Roman-Rite *Sanctus* appearing on only a few important feasts); (12) *ad confractionem panis* (sung at the breaking of the bread); (13) *ad accedentes* (chants corresponding to the Roman-Rite Communion antiphons).

Chants for the Spanish Office include (1) *antiphons* (about three thousand survive in the manuscripts, moderate in length and syllabic or moderately neumatic in style); (2) *alleluiatici* (alleluiatic antiphons occurring as the third item in the *missae* at Matins and the second antiphon at Vespers); (3) *responsories* (about five hundred survive in the manuscripts, generally neumatic in style); (4) *matutinaria* (antiphons treating early-morning themes sung only at Matins); (5) *benedictiones* (antiphons associated with the canticle beginning at Dan 3:52); (6) *soni* (melismatic chants possibly sung by a soloist with refrain at Matins and Vespers); (7) *laudes* (except during Lent, the chanting of Alleluia is featured in this form, sung at Matins, some of the minor Hours, and Mass); (8) *psallendi* (sung at Matins and Vespers and concluded by a doxology); (9) *vespertini* (neumatic chants corresponding to the Ambrosian *lucernarium*); (10) *preces* (rhythmic poetry in short strophes separated by a brief refrain and sung to syllabic or moderately neumatic chant); (11) *hymns* (assigned to Matins, Vespers, and some of the minor Hours).[17]

During the late patristic era patterns of cantillating fixed prayers and biblical readings continue in all liturgical traditions, although with increasing differentiation by language and region. Canonical psalmody takes over the role of foundational texts for liturgical song. Various styles of executing this psalmody (responsorial, antiphonal, *in directum*) appear for sacramental worship and in the Liturgy of the Hours. Some psalms are sung for their own sake (psalm during the Liturgy of the Word, psalmody in the Divine Office), while other psalms accompany ritual action (processionals, vigils). Probably as a reaction to non-orthodox *psalmi idiotici,* the creation and use of non-canonical psalmody wanes, although such examples as the *Te Deum* and the *Gloria in excelsis* find widespread acceptance. The most intense development occurs in metrical hymnody. We have already noted the profusion of Syriac and Greek hymnography; a parallel explosion of Latin hymn writing likewise takes place. Although Hilary of Poitiers (ca. 300–368) wrote a *Liber hymnorum* of which only three fragments are extant *(Ante saecula qui manens, Fefellit saeuam uerbum factum te caro,* and *Adae carnis gloriosae et caduci corporis),* the father of popular Latin hymnody is Ambrose of Milan (340–397). His compositions created models for Latin hymnody for the next millennium: the so-called Ambrosian hymn-form (eight stanzas with four lines of iambic dimeters, divided into two equal units [1–4 and 5–8]). Thirteen or fourteen hymns are usually attributed to him but only four of them can be identified as his from contemporary or very early sources *(Aeterne rerum conditor, Iam surgit hora tertia, Intende qui regis Israel,* and *Grates tibi Iesu novas).* These hymns are made up of three basic thematic categories: hymns for the canonical hours, hymns for the feasts of the ecclesiastical year, and hymns on saints' feasts, especially martyrs. Latin hymns in other meters and with different themes appear in the poems contained in the *Cathemerinon, Apotheosis, Psychomachia,* and *Peristephanon* of Aurelius Prudentius Clemens (348–413); the *Carmen Paschale* and *A solis ortus cardine* of Caelius

---

[17] H. Allinger, *The Mozarabic Hymnal and Chant with Special Emphasis on the Hymns of Prudentius* (New York, 1953); C. W. Brockett, Jr., *Antiphons, Responsories, and Other Chants of the Mozarabic Rite* (Brooklyn, 1968); D. M. Randel, "Mozarabic rite, music of the," *New Grove Dictionary of Music and Musicians,* 11:667–75.

Sedulius (fifth century); the anonymous *Hymnum turba dicat fratrum* (late fifth century); the hymns for the canonical hours of Magnus Felix Ennodius (late fifth century) and those contained in the monastic rules of Caesarius and Aurelianus of Arles (sixth century); the *Deus mirande, uirtus alma* of the Frankish king Chilperich (sixth century); the foot-washing hymn *Tellus ac aethra iubilent* of Bishop Flavius of Châlon-sur-Saône (sixth century); and the Holy Cross processional hymns *(Crux benedicta nitet; Pange, lingua, gloriosi proelium certaminis; Vexilla regis prodeunt)* of Venantius Honorius Clementianus Fortunatus (530–609). It should be noted that these hymns were usually not employed in Roman-Rite Eucharist.

From this point on our historical sketch will only consider the development of church music for the Roman Rite with some glances at the church music practices developed by the churches of the sixteenth-century Reformation.

Roman-Rite Worship Music in the Early Medieval Period
The development of the so-called Gregorian chant repertoire for the Roman Rite parallels the creation of the hybrid Franco-Roman liturgy in the Carolingian era. Just as Charlemagne attempted to unify the eucharistic liturgy throughout his empire by means of a standardized Gregorian Sacramentary (a Roman textual exemplar that was in fact supplemented by Frankish formularies), so he decreed in the *Admonitio generalis* of 789 that Roman chant in its entirety should be used when chanting the Mass and the Divine Office. Cantors were imported from the Roman *schola cantorum* to teach this chant under imperial patronage in an attempt to eradicate native chant practices, but a generation after Charlemagne's decree went into effect Walahfrid Strabo declared that one could still recognize the old Gallican melodies in the reconstituted chants.

Gregorian chant melodies occupy a relatively narrow range (usually not more than an octave and frequently less) and progress usually by intervals of seconds and thirds, although fourths and fifths also appear. Between phrases longer intervals might be used. Types of melodies tend to associate themselves with particular liturgical functions: scriptural readings, prayers, Office psalmody and antiphons, doxologies, and short responses are primarily psalmodic; litanies, salutations, *Glorias*, *Credos*, sequences, and most hymns are syllabic; tropes, introits, and *Sanctus* and *Agnus Dei* melodies tend to be neu-

matic; graduals, *Kyries*, alleluias, tracts, offertories, great responsories, and preces are fundamentally neumatic with frequent
melismatic passages. Those in major orders executed particular
psalmodic chants by reason of office, while the clerical and/or
monastic choir performed the more complex melodies. It is unclear to
what extent the non-clerical members of the assembly joined in the
singing, especially those who might not know the languages in
which the texts were sung. Evidence for popular vernacular
devotional songs *(Ruf, Leise)* in the Frankish kingdom dates from the
ninth century.

Three manuscripts, all from Rome itself and produced between
1050 and 1300, record texts and melodies for chants associated with
Roman-Rite Eucharist distinct from but related to the Gregorian
chants for the same liturgy; a fourth manuscript from central Italy
also witnesses to this tradition. Two manuscripts from the thirteenth
century provide sources for the Roman-Rite Office chants distinct
from but related to the Gregorian chants for the Liturgy of the Hours.
These are the manuscript sources for a chant tradition labeled "Old
(or 'Urban') Roman."

Old Roman chant exhibits many of the same formal, structural,
and tonal elements as Gregorian chant; Old Roman chant, however,
tends to be more ornate. Some scholars have claimed that the Gregorian tradition simplified Old Roman chant because of the difficulty
the Franks found in reproducing it; others have claimed that it em-
bellishes Gregorian material.

Both textual and musical embellishments of the fundamental
Gregorian chant repertoire occurred in the latter part of the early
medieval period. *Proses* and *prosulas* set new texts to the established
melismas of responsories and alleluias. *Tropes,* new creations of (possibly vernacular) text or text-and-melody, were inserted into liturgical
formulae: as introductions to the introit; as interpolations in *Kyrie,
Gloria,* lessons, Office responsories, *Ite missa est;* and as additions to
the processional antiphons. *Versus* provided recurring invariant refrains after each strophe of a hymn. *Planctus* and *conductus* constituted new paraliturgical genres, the former for the funeral procession
of a notable, the latter to accompany extraordinary events such as a
royal crowning.

The monodic Gregorian chant repertoire was musically enriched
by the development of organum. Examples of two-voice polyphony

appear in the ninth-century anonymous treatise *Musica enchiriadis* and Guido of Arezzo's *Micrologus* (ca. 1040), but the most valuable source is the eleventh-century *Winchester Troper,* containing about 164 organa. Historical musicologists presume that organum was produced and performed in more sophisticated centers such as larger monasteries and courts, where there would be both interest and opportunity to use such music. For the vast majority of liturgies monody remained the norm.[18]

Roman-Rite Worship Music in the Late Medieval Period
Textual and musical transformation of the early medieval worship-music repertoire continued in the late medieval period. *Sequences,* syllabic chants consisting of a series of rhymed couplets each having two isosyllabic lines sung to the same melody, with each couplet differing from the preceding in melody (and usually in length), appear to be a development of the earlier proses. They came to be sung at Masses of particular seasons, feasts, or saint's days after the Alleluia; they provided an outlet for local creativity and piety. Of the thousands of medieval tropes generated, only four were retained in the *Missale Romanum* 1570: *Victimae paschali laudes, Veni Sancte Spiritus, Lauda Sion* and *Dies irae;* the *Stabat Mater* was inserted in the Roman Missal as a sequence in 1727. The *Missale Romanum* 1970–1975 retains all but the *Dies irae. Rhymed offices,* in which the antiphons and refrain sections of responsories in the Liturgy of the Hours were provided with new metrical texts and melodies, also stimulated local creativity during this period, although a rhymed office in honor of the Holy Trinity was widely disseminated.

In the late twelfth and early thirteenth centuries composers associated with Notre Dame cathedral in Paris took the lead in worship-

[18] W. Apel, *Gregorian Chant* (Bloomington, 1958); P. Bernard, "L'origine des chants de la messe selon la tradition musicale du chant romain ancien impropre-ment dit «chant vieux-romain»," *L'Eucharistie: célébrations, rites, piétés. Conférence Saint-Serge XLIe semaine d'études liturgiques. Paris, 28 Juin–1 Juillet 1994.* EphLit Susidia, 79 (Rome, 1995) 19–97; S. Fuller, "Early Polyphony," *Early Middle Ages to 1300,* 485–556; D. Hiley, *Western Plainchant: A Handbook* (Oxford, 1993); M. Huglo, *Les Livres de Chant Liturgique,* Typologie des Sources du Moyen Âge Occidental, 52 (Turnhout, 1988); H. Hucke, "Gregorian and Old Roman Chant," *New Grove Dictionary of Music and Musicians,* 7:693–7; A. Planchart, *The Repertory of Tropes at Winchester* (Princeton, 1977).

music composition for the Roman Rite with a polyphonic style later theorists termed the *Ars antiqua*. Leoninus (twelfth century) and Perotinus (ca. 1160–ca. 1240) were considered the greatest composers of *organa* and of *discant* (two-, three-, or four-voice compositions in measured rhythm) respectively.

Just as the composers of the *Ars antiqua* period freed melodies from the constraints of single-note counterpoint, so the composers of the so-called *Ars nova* period (fourteenth century) freed rhythms from the constraints of the six rhythmic modes employed in the earlier period. Melodic and rhythmic independence in the voices was so highly prized in the *motetus* form that each voice might intone a different text, possibly in different languages. For example, in one composition the *tenor* voice carries in Greek the liturgical text *Kyrie eleison,* while the *motetus* voice in Latin chants, "A love which wounds the heart, which springs from a human source, can never be without flaw," and the *triplum* voice sings in French, "Many there are who often by their envy speak against love. But there is not a better life than to love loyally, because from love comes all courtesy, all honor, and all good instruction."[19] Many of the innovations developed by the *Ars nova* were condemned in 1324–5 by Pope John XXII in his bull *Docta Sanctorum Patrum.*[20]

In summary, by the late medieval period Roman-Rite worship music exhibited itself in cantillation formulae for readings and prayers executed by priests, deacons, and lectors with the more complex Gregorian repertoire and various forms of polyphony chanted by the clerical and/or monastic choir. It appears that the non-clerical and non-monastic members of the worshiping assembly did not usually sing at worship except possibly for a few simple responses. A repertoire of songs in various vernaculars *(cantigas, cantiques,* carols, *Gleisslerleider, laude spirituali)* evolved for popular devotional singing outside of the liturgy (pilgrimage, instruction); on occasion such songs may have been sung during community worship (e.g., after a sermon, after the consecration of the eucharistic elements), though never as a formally approved component of the liturgy.

[19] Cf. J. Nisard, *L'Archéologie musicale, et la vrai chant grégorien* (Paris, 1890) 273.
[20] R. F. Hayburn, *Papal Legislation on Sacred Music: 95 A.D. to 1977 A.D.* (Collegeville, 1979) 20–1.

Christian Worship Music in the Renaissance, Reformation,
and Counter-Reformation

Five "generations" can be distinguished in the worship music composed during the Renaissance. In the first, John Dunstable's works (1380/90–1453) signal a transition between late medieval compositional patterns and those of the Renaissance.[21] In the second, Guillaume Dufay (ca. 1400–1474) continued to employ paraphrased chant melodies in some of his liturgical compositions (e.g., his settings of the Marian antiphons *Alma Redemptoris Mater* and *Ave Regina Coelorum*), but frequently the chant was so profoundly transformed as to be unrecognizable aurally.[22]

In the third period, Johannes Ockeghem (ca. 1430–1495) is noted as the first composer of a surviving polyphonic setting of the Requiem (introit, *Kyrie*, gradual, tract, and offertory). Josquin Deprez (ca. 1450–1521) dominates the fourth period of Renaissance church-music composition. He employs with great technical skill all of the compositional devices (isorhythm, paraphrase, cantus firmus, parody) developed by his predecessors. Perhaps Desprez' greatest contribution appeared in his motet writing, where a wide range of texts produced an equally wide range of emotional effects (cf. *Planxit autem David*, where Josquin paraphrases in all four parts the plainsong Lamentations performed in Holy Week).[23]

In the fifth period, Nicolas Gombert (ca. 1490–1560) brought the technique of extensive imitation among polyphonic voices to a higher level of development; for example, one of his Marian motets quotes the plainchants *Alma Redemptoris Mater, Salve Regina, Ave Regina, Ave Maria, Beata Maria, Inviolata,* and *Hortus Conclusus* with elements of at least four chants usually being sung simultaneously.

It is in the context of the church-music practices of the Renaissance that those of the sixteenth-century Reformation must be situated. To varying degrees all the Reformed church-music traditions sought to

[21] M. Bent, *Dunstable,* Oxford Studies of Composers, 17 (London–New York, 1981).

[22] R. Bockholdt, *Die frühen Meßkompositionen von Guillaume Dufay,* Münchner Veröffentlichungen zur Musikgeschichte, 5 (Tutzing, 1960); L. Sampaoli, *Guillaume Dufay: un musicista alla corte dei Malatesti* (Rimini, 1985).

[23] C. Dalhaus, *Studien zu den Messen Josquin der Pres* (Göttingen, 1952).

simplify the complexities of Renaissance compositional technique and to assert again the primacy of the scriptural texts.[24]

Martin Luther's esteem for music is well-expressed in his Preface to George Rhau's *Symphoniae Iucundae*, where he declares that "next to the Word of God, the noble art of music is the greatest treasure in the world." Luther seems to have been an accomplished amateur singer, player, and composer, with a special appreciation for the works of Josquin. Thus it is not surprising to observe a concern for worship-music reform as well as liturgical and evangelical reform in his writings and activity. In accordance with his principle that worship should be intelligible to the worshipers, he replaced some of the traditional sung elements of the Mass with German songs but also permitted chant and polyphony in Latin in "learned" worship settings such as schools and religious communities. Sources for the new vernacular Lutheran worship music are quite varied. Some are German translations of plainchant hymns and sequences set to the original or slightly adapted melodies. Some adapt the popular unison hymns known as *cantios*. Still others rework vernacular devotional (*Geisserlieder*) and secular (*Minnesäng*) songs, while others are based on Latin or German part-songs. Published in 1524, the *Geystliche Gesangk Buchleyn* ("Booklet of Spiritual Songs") produced by Luther's friend and colleague Johann Walter (1496–1570) can be considered the first in a long line of Protestant hymnbooks.

Jean Calvin, convinced that true Christian worship could only be structured on what is revealed in the Scriptures, demanded a more radical break than Luther did with Roman-Rite church-music practice. He eventually reduced the worship music of Reformed Genevan churches to metrical psalmody sung in unison without instrumental accompaniment by the assembly.

Taking the principle of rejection of Roman-Rite worship to a logical conclusion, Ulrich Zwingli, although an accomplished musician himself, had by 1523 banned all music — congregational singing as well as choir and organ music — from the Reformed church services in Zurich; he argued that music's appeal to the emotions could only

---

[24] F. Blume, *Protestant Music: A History* (New York, 1974); C. Schalk, *Luther on Music: Paradigms of Praise* (St. Louis, 1988); L. A. Voshi, *Martin Luther: Reformer and Musician*, Morris Moore Series in Musicology, 3 (Silver Spring, 1988); P. Le Huray, *Music and the Reformation in England, 1549–1660* (Cambridge–New York, 1978).

disturb genuine worship. Interestingly, removing music making from the Zwinglian church service led to its greater employment in household devotions.

Anglican church-music practices vacillated with the shifts in the monarchy and the various editions of the *Book of Common Prayer*. Thomas Tallis (ca. 1510–1585), along with a host of lesser composers, set both Latin and English worship texts in a wide variety of genres: in addition to Masses and motets, "services" for the Church of England (including music for Matins, Vespers, and the Eucharist), hymns, anthems, psalms. Eventually a distinctive form of harmonized chant-formulae (so-called Anglican chant) was developed for the choral declamation of psalms and canticles.

The so-called radical reformers produced a distinctive body of church music in Anabaptist hymnody. These lengthy compositions (sometimes running to thirty or more stanzas) had some use during worship but more frequently lauded the courage and commitment of Anabaptist martyrs.

In reaction to the theology and practice of the sixteenth-century Reformers, the Council of Trent (1545–1563) convened to clarify and strengthen Catholic theology and polity. Although church music was not a topic of major interest at the council, four issues concerning Roman-Rite worship music were treated: musical settings that truncated liturgical texts, compositions that made the sacred words unintelligible, inappropriate secular vocal music during worship, and lengthy secular organ pieces played during liturgy. On August 8, 1562, when a compendium of abuses in the Mass was discussed, the council decreed: "The type of music in divine services . . . should be sung so that the words are more intelligible than the modulations of the music." The council recognized polyphonic worship music as appropriate to the Roman Rite as long as it faithfully and intelligibly enshrined the liturgical texts and avoided all secular resonances in melody or rhythm.[25]

The Roman-Rite worship music developed in the immediate aftermath of the Council of Trent during the so-called Counter-Reformation continued the practices of the late Renaissance with appropriate

[25] R. F. Hayburn, *Papal Legislation on Sacred Music: 95 A.D. to 1977 A.D.*, 27–9; K. G. Fellerer, "Church Music and the Council of Trent," *Musical Quarterly* 39 (October 1953) 576–94; H. Leichtentritt, "The Reform of Trent and Its Effect on Music," *Musical Quarterly* 30 (1944) 319–28.

adjustments to the conciliar decrees and aims. A variety of national "schools" can be identified, although all set the reformed liturgical texts contained in the *Missale Romanum* of 1570 and similar products of the post-Tridentine promulgation of revised liturgical books.[26]

Associated with the early Roman school are Costanza Festa († 1545), whose *Te Deum* was frequently sung at papal elections, and Giovanni Animuccia († 1570), credited with the invention of the "oratorio" from the *Laudi Spirituali* he wrote for Philip Neri's Oratory (1563– 1570). But the dominant figure is Giovanni Pierluigi da Palestrina (1525– 1594), director of the Sistine Choir in 1555 and again from 1571 until his death. He composed 105 Masses (parody, paraphrase, *cantus firmus*, and free) and between four and five hundred motets in a style marked by careful attention to the intelligibility of the text, balanced phrases, conjunct melodic motion, highly sonorous chords, and discreet word painting.

Associated with the early Spanish school are Cristóbal de Morales (ca. 1500–1553) and Francisco Guerrero (1528–1599). But the dominant figure is Tomás Luis de Victoria (1548–1611). Composing exclusively sacred music, Victoria wrote Masses for four to twelve voices, a Requiem, an Office of the Dead, an Office for Holy Week *(Tenebrae)*, motets for four to eight voices, hymns for the entire liturgical year, canticles, psalms, litanies, and miscellaneous other works.

Although frequently identified as the last great representative of the Netherlands polyphonic tradition, Roland de Lassus/Orlando di Lasso (1532–1594) was a cosmopolitan European. His sacred music includes Masses for four to eight voices, *Magnificats*, Passion, psalms (including a unified setting of the Seven Penitential Psalms), lamentations, vigils, and more than a thousand motets for two to twelve voices. In employing more chromaticism, wider vocal intervals, and new forms of declamation, Lassus anticipated some of the compositional ideals and techniques of the baroque period.

Roman-Rite Worship Music in the Baroque Period
Musical style in the baroque, heavily influenced by the development of opera, exhibits five major characteristics: (1) reliance on figured-bass technique leading to an emphasis on melody and bass with improvised harmony occupying the middle ground; (2) extension and

---

[26] A. Harmon and A. Milner, *Late Renaissance and Baroque Music* (London, 1988); M. T. Levey, *Sacred Music of the Counter Reformation* (Sydney, 1988).

perfection of earlier polyphonic forms and techniques; (3) establishment of equal temperament in tuning with tonic and dominant chords situated as the principal foundations of harmony (i.e., the replacement of the modal system by major and minor keys); (4) emphasis upon improvisation and ornamentation in performance; and (5) the *stile concertante* with its love of contrast effects (abrupt changes, solo-tutti alternations, echo-effects).

In Italy, Roman-Rite worship-music composers wrote both in the *stile antico* based in sixteenth-century choral practices and the new *stile moderno* exemplified in Giovanni Gabrieli's (1557–1612) polychoral motets for St. Mark's Cathedral in Venice and Claudio Monteverdi's (1567–1643) *Vespers of the Blessed Virgin Mary*. In the new style expressive setting of text became the overriding compositional principle. Solo singing was contrasted with multivoiced choirs, simple figured-bass accompaniment alternated with full orchestral settings, vocal lines were paired with instrumental melodies to great effect. The *cantata,* on both sacred and secular subjects, arose as a new form in which these strongly contrasted movements would find unity.

Roman-Rite worship-music composers in France adopted many of the ideals and techniques of the Italian baroque. Jean Baptiste Lully (1632–1687) brought the full resources of his operatic experiments into his worship-music compositions. Instrumental overtures and interludes contrasted with solo vocal recitative and aria punctuated by double choir effects in works such as his *Miserere* and *Te Deum*.

With the growing importance of instrumental accompaniment and interludes, non-texted non-vocal music for the first time began to have a major place in Roman-Rite worship-music practice. The *sonata da chiesa* consisting of four contrasting slow/fast movements accompanied ritual action and on occasion substituted for the sung liturgical texts.

Karl Gustav Fellerer summarizes the situation of Roman-Rite worship music during the baroque era as follows:

"Church music was considered as an ornament of worship, and a means for providing artistic display; no longer was it looked upon as a liturgical unit. The notion that church music is an integral part of the liturgy was lost. Baroque worship and musical conception had overstepped the balance of form and setting of the sixteenth century by this external embellishment and thus transferred the center of gravity. No longer was the liturgical action itself the focal point; instead it was man, and music was conceived of in terms of its effects on man, and in reference to man's taste. Temporal and spatial distinctions came to the fore and the objective communal attitude of a music *of* worship was replaced by music *at* worship that unfolded freely and without restraint."[27]

Roman-Rite Worship Music in the Classical Period
Responding to the intellectual currents of the Enlightenment, composers produced worship music of clear formal structure, balanced contrast, and theatricality during the classical period. The Mannheim school of the mid-eighteenth century applied classical ideals of intense expressiveness and formal constraint to Roman-Rite worship music in the works of Franz X. Richter (1709–1789), Ignaz Holzbauer (1711–1783), and George Vogler (1749–1814). The worship music of Italian composers such as Niccolò Jomelli (1714–1774), Baldassare Galuppi (1706–1785), and Giovanni Paisiello (1741–1816) employed operatic and cantata conventions such as highly decorated vocal lines sung in *bel canto* style, division of single liturgical texts into contrasting movements, and theatrical orchestrations. In the so-called number Masses, sections of the liturgical text were composed symphonically as separate movements; at an extreme was the *Kyrie-Gloria* Mass in which the first two elements of the Mass Ordinary were set to such lengthy music that the other elements were omitted.

The most powerful reconciliation of operatic convention and symphonic orchestral writing applied to Roman-Rite worship music occurred in the Viennese masters. Franz Joseph Haydn (1732–1809) wrote Masses, Offertories, *Te Deums*, a *Stabat Mater,* and miscellaneous other church music. Rather than contrasting solo arioso passages with those of the full choir, Haydn preferred to alternate solo vocal quartet writing with choral sections. His delight in orchestral effects, however, led him to produce "military" music before the *Dona nobis pacem* of the *Agnus Dei* in some compositions. Haydn's two highly successful oratorios, *The Creation* and *The Seasons*, displayed his skill at word painting and programmatic effects. Wolfgang

[27] K. G. Fallerer, *The History of Catholic Church Music* (Baltimore, 1961) 134; M. Bukofzer, *Music in the Baroque Era* (New York, 1947); Gino Stefani, *Musica e religione nell'Italia barocca* (Palermo, 1975).

Amadeus Mozart (1756–1791) composed Masses, *Kyries*, Offertories, litanies, a *Te Deum,* and various motet and vesper settings in an arioso-cantata style, many during his time of service for the archbishop of Salzburg. In later works such as the unfinished *Mass in C minor* (1782–1783), the *Ave verum Corpus* (1791), and the unfinished *Requiem* (1791) he yoked his classical techniques with some of the religious expression of Bach and Handel. Ludwig von Beethoven (1770–1827) brought the compositional techniques of Haydn and Mozart to new levels of expressiveness. While his *Mass in C* (1807) remained within a framework of liturgical utility, the *Missa Solemnis* (1818–1823), commissioned for the installation of Archduke Rudolph as bishop of Olmütz in 1820, disregards liturgical requirements for the sake of personal expression. Franz Schubert (1797–1828) brought a delicate lyricism to the Mass form developed by his Viennese predecessors. His early *Mass in G major* (1815) and *German Singmesse* beguile the listener with their tenderness, while the *Mass in A flat major* (1822) and the *Mass in E flat major* (1828) are more profoundly expressive. Schubert's settings sometimes distort the liturgical text; he omits clauses from the *Credo* and adds the phrase "of the dead" *(mortuorum)* to the clause "I confess one baptism unto the remission of sins" *(Confiteor unum baptisma in remissionem peccatorum mortuorum).* Karl Maria von Weber (1786–1826) produced Mass settings influenced by incipient Romanticism: his *Mass in E flat major* (1818) alternates solo and chorus sections (expanding to eight voices in the *Sanctus*) richly accompanied by varied orchestral effects, while his *Jubilee Mass in G major* (1819) uses the leitmotiv technique as a means of illustrating particular texts and unifying the composition.

Joseph Jungmann's judgment about the church music developed during this period may seem polemic but does identify most of these compositions as music *at* the liturgy rather than music *of* the liturgy: "Music spread its gorgeous mantle over the whole Mass, so that the other details of the rite had scarcely any significance. . . . [T]he liturgy was not only submerged under this ever-growing art but actually suppressed, so that even at this time there are festive occasions which might best be described as 'church concerts with liturgical accompaniments.'"[28]

[28] J. A. Jungmann, *The Mass of the Roman Rite (Missarum Sollemnia)* (New York, 1951) 1:148; M. Holl, *Messen* (Kassel, 1992); R. G. Pauly, "The Reforms of Church

Roman-Rite Worship Music in the Romantic Period

The romantic period's emphasis on the individual, the subjective, and the emotional, in contrast to the Enlightenment's idolization of reason, had mixed impact upon Roman-Rite worship music. On the one hand, interest in the Middle Ages led to a new appreciation of chant and polyphony, although they were frequently treated as exotic effects in theatrical pieces; on the other, much music composed for the liturgy simply attempted to create a religious aura for personal devotion rather than illustrate the texts (as in the baroque) or enable the liturgical act (as in plainchant). Many romantic composers intended their works for the concert hall rather than the church (cf. Rossini's *Stabat Mater* and *Petite Messe Solennelle*, Dvorak's *Stabat Mater* and *Requiem*, and Verdi's *Stabat Mater* and *Requiem*).

Concerted worship music continued to be produced in France by, among others, Charles Gounod (1818–1893), Charles Ambroise Thomas (1811–1896), César Franck (1822–1890), and Camille Saint-Saëns (1835–1921). Scholars criticize many of these works for their sentimentality. Composers from German-speaking areas such as Joseph Rheinberger (1839–1901), Franz Liszt (1811–1866), and Anton Bruckner (1824–1896) both developed and purified the concerted Mass tradition of the Viennese masters.

Two "restoration" movements appearing in the nineteenth century had great impact on Roman-Rite worship music. Scholarly investigation of the plainchant heritage conjoined to daily worship in plainchant made the Benedictine Abbaye Saint-Pierre de Solesmes a center for Roman-Rite liturgical and musical restoration. Important musicological monuments and studies such as the volumes of the *Paléographie Musicale* and the *Études grégoriens* laid the foundations for the Vatican editions of the chant in the early twentieth century, with a concommitant commitment to teaching congregations to sing the actual liturgical chants of Catholic worship (rather than devotional hymnody during worship). In 1867 Francis Xavier Will (1834–1888) founded the so-called Caecilian movement with the dual aim of combatting orchestral Masses for their liturgical impropriety and of restoring sixteenth-century style sacred polyphony.

Music Under Joseph II," *Musical Quarterly* 43 (1957) 372–82; W. Senn, *Messen* (Kassel, 1978).

The romantic era witnessed a profound disjunction between musical progress and liturgical need. The individualism of the romantic composer conflicted with the reemerging ecclesial doctrine of the Mystical Body with its emphasis on the objective communal liturgical act. Leading composers preferred not to write for the limited resources of parochial communities and identified worship music not with the musical avant-garde but with nostalgic re-creation of earlier eras.[29]

Roman-Rite Worship Music in the Twentieth Century
Roman-Rite worship music was profoundly changed in the twentieth century by magisterial pronouncements, theological developments, liturgical revisions, societal influences, and artistic trends.

Pius X's *Tra le sollecitudini (TLS)*, issued *motu proprio* on November 22, 1903, set the agenda for magisterial treatment of Roman-Rite worship music in the twentieth century until *Sacrosanctum concilium (SC)*, Vatican II's Constitution on the Sacred Liturgy, appeared on December 4, 1963. Profoundly influenced by both the Solesmes chant restoration and the Caecilian movement, *TLS* posits a complete divorce between sacred (represented by chant and polyphony) and profane (represented by the secular and theatrical) texts, compositions, styles, and instruments. While all twentieth-century magisterial documents agree that the purpose of Roman-Rite worship music shares in the purpose of the liturgy itself (i.e., the glorification of God and the sanctification of humanity), later documents offer quite different directives about what is encouraged and forbidden in the repertoire, what qualities worship music must exhibit, and who should sing and play it. *SC*'s permission to use vernacular texts and a variety of musical styles, its lifting of restrictions on which instruments could be played and its encouragement of "full, conscious and active" participation of the worshiping assembly in song during Roman-Rite worship set the agenda for composition and programming in the last quarter of the twentieth century.

Theological developments also had implications for church-music practice. The scholarly renaissance in Roman Catholic biblical studies, given the highest official approval in Pius XII's *Divino afflante*

---

[29] C. Donakowski, *A Muse for the Masses: Ritual and Music in an Age of Democratic Revolution* (Chicago, 1977); A. Hutchings, *Church Music in the Nineteenth Century* (London, 1977).

Spiritu (1947), led to a plethora of new Scripture translations, commentaries, and pastoral applications, engendering a new appreciation of biblical song. (For example, the techniques of "Gelineau psalmody" arose in conjunction with a French project to translate the Psalter.) The renewal of patristic studies *(ressourcement)* evidenced in the work of such scholars as Henri de Lubac and Jean Danielou proposed ecclesial and liturgical models unconstricted by post-Reformation polemics. The patristic works cited often included evocative hymn texts and descriptions of church-music practices, set and popularized by such composer-scholars as Lucien Deiss. Missionary activities in the Third World and reevangelization initiatives aimed at an increasingly secularized First World challenged theologians to rethink the relation of Catholic Christianity to other world religions and to diverse cultures. Multicultural and multilinguistic worshiping assemblies and compositions such as the *Missa Luba* encouraged church musicians to consider the religious and cultural values contained and conveyed in their repertoires and performance practices. Catholic counterparts to the Protestant "social gospel" movement — Catholic Action, the worker-priest experiment, the Young Christian Student/ Young Christian Worker initiatives, etc. — linked liturgical worship with impulses for societal transformation and impacted upon music sung and played at worship.

A new musical repertoire is being created in the wake of the revision of the liturgical books after Vatican II. The *editiones typicae* of the new rites have contained notated ministerial chants for when the rites are celebrated in Latin. New editions of the chant books have gradually appeared under the direction of the monks of Solesmes. But most compositional energy has been devoted to creating a new vernacular repertoire sung not only by the ordained and choirs but by the worshiping assembly itself. Settings of the official texts in a wide variety of styles have appeared for many cultures and language groups. Since regulations for what may be sung during Roman-Rite worship are now often facultative rather than prescriptive, texts taken from biblical, devotional, and even secular sources have made their appearance. As *editiones typicae alterae* appear and as the first sets of vernacular texts are further revised, additional compositions will be needed. Problems and opportunities created by the revision of the liturgical books include (1) how the chants developed for the pre-Vatican II repertoire will be maintained not as museum-piece curiosities but as the sung prayer of living communities; (2) how the heritage of sacred polyphony, generated without concern for vocal congregational participation, will be preserved; (3) how a common worship-music repertoire can be developed for multinational and multilingual gatherings; (4) how a common worship-music repertoire can be developed within language and cultural groups; (5) how to determine which styles and genres of musical composition genuinely support the liturgical action of a given assembly; (6) how development, distribution, and regulation of church music will take place and under whose auspices.[30]

THEOLOGICAL REFLECTIONS

Theological Reflections on Sound

In "Toward a Sound Theology" Edward Foley explores five aspects of the human experience of sound that make it especially appropriate as a vehicle for revealing the God of biblical religion.[31]

First, sound is an experience of *impermanence*; it makes time audible and renders its form and continuity sensible. This aspect of the experience of sound appropriately reveals the nature of God as profoundly involved in human history; it also has the ability to engage worshipers in the present reality of worship, signaling that union with God is an existential possibility in the here and now.

Second, sound is an experience of the *intangible*; unlike art forms (sculpture, painting), which perdure over time and are perceivable by more than one sense (sight, touch, even taste), sound is usually only perceived by hearing (although it may on occasion be felt). The intangible character of the experience of sound fittingly discloses God as an elusive presence, a powerful symbol of a God who is both present and hidden; the mysterious and wholly other character of the holy is powerfully communicated by the insubstantial nature of sound.

---

[30] J. M. Joncas, "Re-Reading *Musicam Sacram*: Twenty-Five Years of Development in Roman Rite Liturgical Music," *Wor* 66/2 (May 1992) 212–31; E. Routley, *Twentieth Century Church Music* (New York, 1964).

[31] E. Foley, "Toward a Sound Theology," *SL* 23/2 (1993) 121–39; P. W. Hoon, "The Relation of Theology and Music in Worship," *Union Theological Seminary Quarterly Review* 11/2 (1956) 33–43; A. Pike, *A Theology of Music* (Toledo, 1953); E. Routley, *Church Music and Theology* (Philadelphia, 1965); M. T. Winter, *Why Sing? Toward a Theology of Catholic Church Music* (Washington, D.C., 1984).

Third, sound is an experience of *activity*, since sound events perdure only as long as the sound is being generated and because human hearing discriminates between sound events with more precision than human sight. The dynamic character of the experience of sound suitably divulges the dialogic character of God's interaction with humanity; sound not only announces presence but engages others in dialogue and communion, resonating within diverse individuals at the same time, eliciting sympathetic vibrations: a fitting image of the encounter between God and humanity.

Fourth, sound is an experience of *invitation to engagement,* a fundamentally unitive act connecting the sound producer with the sound, the sound perceiver with the sound, the sound producer with the sound receiver, the sound receiver with other sound receivers, and the sound producer in a new way with him- or herself. The ear is a metaphor for human beings open to reality, to engagement with sounds and the people and things that produce them. The engaging character of the experience of sound harmoniously presents the unitive character of God's interaction with humanity; the experience of revelation not only unites an individual with God but forges a common identity and network of relationships among a people who share the experience and commit themselves to it.

Fifth, sound can be an experience of the *personal*, not only of *the* other but of *an*other; it is in the acoustic arena that genuinely reciprocal "I-Thou" relationships (in Martin Buber's terminology) become possible through shared interiority manifested sensibly. The personal character of the experience of sound profoundly images a God who is not simply a force in nature and history but a person. Music, as a distinctively human sound creation, even more powerfully symbolizes the God who chooses to reveal Godself in personal terms.

Magisterial Reflections on Worship Music
Twentieth-century magisterial teaching has considered worship music as a particular form of musical art intended for liturgical use. It has treated such topics as the nature, purpose, and qualities of Roman Catholic worship music and the people who and instruments that produce it. Exploring these magisterial documents reveals how their teaching on these topics has developed and changed. We will consider here only those documents issued for universal Roman

Catholic consideration; magisterial documents generated by local authorities (e.g., bishops' conferences, Ordinaries) apply these universal insights to local conditions.

TLS lists three categories for Roman-Rite worship music: Gregorian chant, "classical" (Roman school) polyphony, and "more modern music," sung in the non-vernacular languages of the approved liturgical books. Its purpose is yoked to that of the liturgy itself: glorifying God and sanctifying and edifying the faithful by increasing ceremonial splendor and by rendering liturgical texts more efficacious. It exhibits three qualities: holiness, beauty, and universality. *TLS* teaches that, since singing at the liturgy fulfills a genuine liturgical office, only men and boys (preferably clerics) can compose a liturgical choir. It further states that, although church music is properly only vocal, an organ may accompany the singing; "noisy and irreverent instruments" such as pianoforte, drums, timpani, cymbals, and triangles may not be played in liturgical worship.

Musicae Sacrae disciplina of 1955 *(MSD)* adds "popular religious hymns" to the three categories of Roman-Rite worship music identified in *TLS*. It reaffirms the purpose and functions of worship music articulated in *TLS* and nuances its treatment of the qualities demanded in worship music. *MSD* concedes that women may form (part of) a liturgical choir as long as they are located outside of the sanctuary, are separated from men singers, and avoid unbecoming behavior. In addition to the organ, *MSD* encourages bowed string instruments as appropriate supports for worship music.

On September 3, 1958, the Sacred Congregation of Rites issued *De musica sacra et sacra liturgia ad mentem litterarum Pii Papae XII "Musicae sacrae disciplina" et "Mediator Dei"* [1958Inst], a set of exhortations and directives applying magisterial teaching to the celebration of Roman-Rite worship. 1958Inst recognizes six categories of Roman-Rite worship music: Gregorian chant, sacred polyphony, modern sacred music, sacred organ music, popular religious singing, and religious music; only the first five may be admitted to liturgical worship. It asserts that worship music should promote the interior and exterior liturgical participation of the faithful, ordered toward their sacramental participation. It clarifies the worship-music responsibilities of priest-celebrants, clerics, the worshiping assembly, and the choir during the liturgy and offers guidance to authors and composers of sacred music, organists and choir directors, singers and instrumental musicians. While continuing the ban on employing "profane instruments" at worship, 1958Inst singles out "automatic instruments" (e.g., automatic organ, phonograph, radio, dictaphone, tape recorders) as especially forbidden.

SC devotes an entire chapter to worship music. In addition to Gregorian chant and other types of sacred music in the ancient liturgical languages, *SC* permits song in the vernacular as genuine liturgical music in Roman-Rite worship. *SC* modifies the *TLS* teaching on the purpose of worship music by deleting its edifying role and describing its *munus ministeriale* as adding delight to prayer, fostering oneness of spirit, and solemnizing the rites. While promoting the continued activity of choirs, *SC* emphasizes the sung participation of the entire assembly at worship. It permits instruments in addition to the organ at worship as long as they are fitting for sacred use, congruent with the space and pastorally appropriate.

Musicam sacram (MuS), issued by the Sacred Congregation for Divine Worship on March 5, 1967, applies the magisterial teaching of *SC* to the celebration of Roman-Rite worship (much as 1958Inst implemented *MSD*). *MuS* recognizes four categories of music fitting for Roman-Rite worship: Gregorian chant, ancient and modern polyphony, sacred music for organ and other permitted instruments, and popular sacred music; both ancient liturgical languages and approved vernacular texts may be sung. While quoting *SC*'s modification of the *TLS* teaching on the purpose of sacred music, *MuS* provides a new fivefold taxonomy of the functions exercised by worship music: alluring or decorative, differentiating, unifying, transcendental, eschatological. While not denying the qualities of holiness, beauty, and universality listed in earlier magisterial teaching, *MuS* prefers more functional categories: "The Church does not exclude any type of sacred music from liturgical services so long as the music matches the spirit of the service itself and the character of the individual parts and is not a hindrance to the required active participation of the people" (9). *MuS* clarifies the worship-music responsibilities of priest-celebrant, choir, and assembly oriented toward complete, conscious, and active participation, both internal and external. It notes two functions for the use of instruments in Roman-Rite worship (accompanying singing, played for its own sake) and nuances *SC*'s statement of the criteria for judging which instruments are suitable for use in worship.

CONCLUSION

We conclude this examination of music and liturgy with ten theses drawn from our investigation, summarizing the results of our study of liturgy and music.

Sound, as a component of the created order, is a divine gift. The vibrational capacities of the material universe can be perceived by human hearing, granting access to elements of its intelligibility. God, as the source and guarantor of the created order, establishes sound as *creatura*. Reflection on the nature of an effect (in this case, sound) gives insight into the nature of the cause(s)/Cause (proximately, various sounding media; ultimately, God). Thus theological insight into the nature of God and God's creation correlates with philosophical reflection on the nature of sound and the intersection of time and eternity.

Humans structure sound in a variety of ways according to differing cultural codings for specific purposes. Humans both produce and perceive sound within various social contexts. Spoken language and performed music are fundamental examples of such production and perception, although the structurings of and boundaries between the two vary from culture to culture. No single language and/or music exhausts the potentiality of human sound-structuring, so no single language and/or music must be considered a priori the only one appropriate for divine communication and human response. Biblical religion will prize, however, the languages and/or music of its inspired Scriptures, believing that these enshrine in some fashion the originating revelatory experience that brought it into existence. Thus it would not be surprising to discover worship events employing both hieratic and vernacular languages, dialects, and styles. Like other aspects of the created order, sound may be employed by humans in ways consistent or inconsistent with the divine intention.

Biblical writings emphasize the linguistic sound event as a root metaphor for God's self-revelation and human response to that revelation. Narratives of divine manifestations in the Old Testament privilege auditory over visual, tactile, oral, or olfactory imagery: the proclamation of God's word *(dabar)* orients and completes theophanies. A *dabar* is a thing of dynamic power, an event creating and manifesting reality. While distinct from the speaker, it mysteriously makes the personal reality of

316

the speaker manifest and establishes the speaker's intention and will. God brings the created order into being (Gen 1:3, 6, 9, 11, 20, 24, 26) and decrees the covenant stipulations (Exod 20:1) by means of *dabar*. The prophetic charism is fundamentally to receive and transmit God's *dabar*. In the New Testament this auditory image is further developed. Jesus preaches God's word (Mark 2:2), and the gospel from/concerning him is termed God's word (Acts 4:31). Ultimately Jesus himself is declared God's Word (λόγος) (John 1:1, 14; Heb 1:2).

Catholic Christian worship music shares in the sacramentality of the liturgy, symbolizing and actualizing the saving encounter between God and humankind in Christ Jesus. A sacramental theology inspired by the biblical understanding of Jesus as the incarnate Word of God would assert that: the humanity of Jesus is the sacrament (efficacious sign) of the saving encounter with God in the divinity of Jesus. The Church, in turn, embodies and extends the saving presence of God-in-Christ through space and time: the Church is the sacrament (efficacious sign) of Christ in human history. What have traditionally been termed sacraments are privileged communal actions ultimately grounded in Jesus' activity by which the Church actualizes the redemption won by Christ for the sake of the world. Sacramental activities disclose and actualize the spiritual density of humanly transformed material goods. In a similar way, it is not raw vibration that is the proper matter of Christian worship but sound transformed by human activity and cultural coding as language and music that can provide an effective disclosure of and encounter with God's mysterious presence and purpose. From this perspective music is not a decorative addition to liturgical worship but one of the means by which it is accomplished.

Catholic Christian worship music serves a dual purpose: the glorification of God and the sanctification of humankind. Catholic Christian liturgy, and therefore its worship music, is simultaneously "anaphoric" (God- oriented) and "katabatic" (humanity-oriented). Human beings declare God's glory *(kabod/δόξα)* whenever they acknowledge God's importance manifest in natural phenomena and the movements of history. For Christians the ultimate revelation of God's glory occurs in the life and deeds, mission and ministry, death and destiny, of Jesus the Christ. Catholic Christian worship music glorifies God when it faithfully acknowledges who God is and what God does, when it recognizes and celebrates what God has done, is doing, and will do through Christ in the power of the Holy Spirit, when it commits worshipers to a proclamation of God's presence and true significance in the scheme of reality. Human beings are sanctified insofar as they participate by grace in the very holiness of God. Catholic Christian worship music sanctifies human beings when it becomes a vehicle by which they encounter transforming grace. Any attempt to divorce the glorification of God from the sanctification of humanity in the theory and practice of Catholic Christian worship music distorts its purpose.

Catholic Christian worship music fulfills a variety of functions within the liturgy. In service of its fundamental glorifying and sanctifying purpose, Catholic Christian worship music serves a variety of functions. It provides a vehicle by which scriptural and liturgical texts more effectively fulfill their revelatory and sacramental character. It supports the proper deployment of ritual activity. It unifies worshipers in common action and differentiates roles within that assembly. It yokes present-day worshipers with those who have gone before them in faith. It symbolizes human and heavenly harmony. However, using catechetical, therapeutic, or ambient music in Catholic Christian worship is problematic, as is programming pieces for the sake of nostalgia, entertainment, consciousness raising, or inculcating ideology.

Catholic Christian worship music is fundamentally logogenic. Curt Sachs distinguishes between music as a medium conveying a linguistic message ("logogenic") and music as an expression of states of feeling ("pathogenic"). Both in theory and practice over the centuries Catholic Christianity has viewed its worship music primarily as a vehicle for evoking and conveying the power of the divine Word and the human response to it. Though glossolalia has marked some Catholic charismatic worship in recent years, texts sung in Catholic worship have traditionally been rationally communicative rather than ecstatic vocalizations. For the greater part of its history these texts have been directly biblical, biblical paraphrases, or anonymous ecclesiastical compositions. More recently the texts of individual authors have been employed, though usually permissively rather than prescriptively. Theoretical justification for the use of instrumental music in Catholic Christian worship needs further development. In addition to supporting sung texts and accompanying ritual action, instrumental music may provide experiences of beauty leading to religious insight and engagement. Catholic Christian worship music can be distinguished from some other religions' worship-music traditions in that it does not seek to induce altered consciousness in participants (e.g., trance states, hallucinogenic frenzy), manipulate the divine will (e.g., incantations, spells), or ward off demonic forces.

Catholic Christian worship music is constitutionally communal. Like the liturgy itself, understood as an action of the whole Mystical Body of Christ, head and members, music sung and played at the liturgy is communal. While individual members of the worshiping assembly may chant some elements of the liturgy solo by reason of office (bishop, presbyter, deacon) or deputation (reader, psalmist, cantor), the assembly as a whole most frequently gives voice to its common prayer in acclamations, responses, refrains, antiphons, and hymns. Theoretical justification for the musical activity of schola or choir in Catholic Christian worship needs further development. In addition to provoking and supporting the assembly's sung participation and offering experiences of beauty beyond the capabilities of the assembly, the schola or choir may have a symbolic function of mirroring unity in diversity for the ecclesial body. Taking seriously the *munus ministeriale* of worship music poses questions about its choice (e.g., employing music intended by its composer for the concert hall, theater, or mass media; employing music generated by other Christian ecclesial bodies or religions) and performance (e.g., musicians seeking social prestige or emotional gratification from their work at worship; singers or instrumentalists leading worship music who are members of other Christian ecclesial bodies, religions, agnostics, or atheists).

The Church can and has developed criteria for employing music in its liturgy. Some criteria, reflected in the Church music practices of concrete worshiping assemblies, are informal and implicit. Other criteria, the product of scholarly reflection and magisterial teaching, are explicitly articulated. Determining which music is appropriate for a concrete worshiping assembly involves a complex decision-making process involving judgments of musical value and beauty, liturgical structure and propriety, and pastoral appropriateness and utility informed by a knowledge of the tradition, present legislation, and theological insight into the liturgical act.

Catholic Christian worship music heralds, enshrines, and finds fulfillment in the reign of God. Catholic Christian liturgy, and therefore its worship music, is not an end in itself. Though lauded as "source and summit of the Christian life" (*SC* 10), it demands evangelization, faith, penitence, and conversion in its participants and issues in works of charity, justice, and devotion. Biblical teaching images heavenly worship in terms of the songs of angels and saints rapturously lauding God throughout eternity in perfect harmony. Catholic Christian worship music is the "pre-echo" of the sound of God's reign and finds its fulfillment in the sonorous silence of eternity where and when God is "all in all."

Bibliography

Cardine, E. *Gregorian Semiology.* Sablé-sur-Sarthe, 1982.

Carroll, J. R. *Compendium of Liturgical Musical Terms.* Toledo, 1964.

Duchesneau, C., and M. Veuthey. *Music and Liturgy: The Universa Laus Document and Commentary.* Washington, 1992.

The Early Middle Ages to 1300. Ed. R. Crocker and D. Hiley. New Oxford History of Music 2. 2nd ed. Oxford–New York, 1990.

Fellerer, K. G., ed. *The History of Catholic Church Music.* Trans. F. A. Brunner. Baltimore, 1961.

Foley, E. "Liturgical Music." In *A New Dictionary of Sacramental Worship.* Ed. P. Fink, 854–70. Collegeville, Minn., 1990.

_____. "Liturgical Music: A Bibliographic Introduction to the Field." *Liturgical Ministry* 3 (Fall 1994) 130–43.

Gelineau, J. *Voices and Instruments in Christian Worship: Principles, Laws, Applications.* Collegeville, Minn., 1964.

Joncas, J. M. "Liturgical Musicology and Musical Semiotics: Theoretical Foundations and Analytic Techniques." *EO* 8/2 (1991) 181–206.

_____. *From Sacred Song to Ritual Music: Twentieth-Century Understandings of Roman Catholic Worship Music.* Collegeville, Minn., 1996.

_____. *Hymnum Tuae Gloriae Canimus. Toward an Analysis of the Vocal and Musical Expression of the Eucharistic Prayer in the Roman Rite: Tradition, Principles, Method.* Rome, 1991.

The New Grove Dictionary of Music and Musicians. 20 vols. Ed. S. Sadie. London, 1980.

Stefani, G. *L'espressione vocale e musicale nella liturgia: gesti–riti–repertori*. Liturgia e cultura 3. Turin, 1967.

____. "Bibliographie fondamentale de musicologie liturgique." *MD* 108 (1971) 175–89.

15

Liturgy and Iconology

Iconology, that discipline which considers the way in which images convey meaning, allows those who understand and use it properly to identify art which is both Christian and liturgical.

In this century,[1] the terms "iconology" and "iconography" have generally been treated as though they were somehow opposite[2] in meaning. Iconography, for example, has been held to be a merely descriptive process, which reduces meaning to content. On the other

---

[1] C. Ripa, *Iconologia. Opera nella quale si descrivono diverse immagini di Virtù Vitii Affetti Passioni humane, Arti Descipline, Humori Elementi Corpi celesti, Provincie d'Italia Fiumi Parti del Mondo, et altreinfiniti materie* (Rome, 1613) (final ed.); J. Baudoin, *Iconologie, ou la Science des Emblèmes, Devises, etc. qui apprend à les expliquer, dessiner et inventer. Ouvrage très utile aux orateurs, poètes, peintres, sculpteurs, graveurs, et généralement à toutes sortes de curieux des Beaux Artes et des Sciences* (Amsterdam, 1698).

[2] A. Warburg, "Italienische Kunst und Internationale Astrologie im Palazzo Schifanoia zu Ferrara," *Atti del X Congresso Internazionale di Storia dell'Arte* (Rome, 1922) 179–93 (the term is used here for the first time in the new sense); G. J. Hoogewerff, "L'Iconologie et son importance pour l'étude systématique de l'art chrétien" (expansion of a conference given before the special section for Iconography at the International Historical Congress in Oslo, August 1928), *Rivista di archeologia cristiana* 8 (1931) 53–82 (the new method is mentioned); E. Panofsky, "Zum Problem der Beschreibung und Inhaltsdeutung von Werken der bildenden Kunst," *Logos* 21 (1932) 102–19; idem, *Studies in Iconology* (New York, 1939) (a theory is proposed for the methodological procedure). See also W. S. Heckscher, "The Genesis of Iconology," *Akten des XXI International Kongresses für Kunstgeschichte* (Bonn, 1964) t. 3 (Berlin, 1967) 239–62; G. Hermerén, *Representation and Meaning in the Visual Arts: A Study in the Methodology of Iconography and Iconology* (Stockholm, 1969); J. Bialostocki, "Iconografia e Iconologia," *Enciclopedia Universale dell'Arte*, t. 7 (Venice-Rome, 1971) 163–77; E. Kaemmerling, *Ikonographie und Ikonologie: Theorien, Entwicklung, Probleme* (Cologne, 1979).

hand, iconology has been regarded as an attempt to delve more deeply into the meaning of the signs of which the work of art is composed. However, according to Panofsky the dichotomy is a false one: "the difference between iconography and iconology is not so much the subject with which they are concerned, as it is with the process, albeit this difference may result in a different sort of subject."[3] In short, the two are different methods with which one may approach works of art.

Until now art has been studied from three perspectives. One is a historical approach which situates a particular work within the context of broader historical developments. A second focuses on the externals of the work of art, paying special attention to its technical characteristics. A third is more speculative, devoting its attention to criteria for the aesthetic appreciation of works of art. To these three, there must be added a fourth if one is really to achieve a complete understanding of works of art. This fourth is the iconological approach outlined in this essay. Although this fourth approach is still in its early stages of development, the terminology used may strike some as obsolete. Nonetheless, this paper will show how, when precisely understood and situated in our own period, this approach remains useful in the study of art.

The term fell into disuse after the French Revolution, as the study of art became increasingly content with a mere description of subject matter, i.e., with iconography, while the spirit which underlay the work was neglected, being regarded as peripheral in importance. This, the attempt to penetrate into the very nature of art itself, is the stuff of iconology.

An outstanding example of what can be achieved by this method is the famous three-volume work of M. Mâle on the religious art of medieval France. The original was subtitled *A Study of the Origins of the Iconography of the Middle Ages*. While this was clear it was also misleading because the book was not so much about iconography, i.e., description, as it was with the very origin of the image depicted. This was rectified in subsequent editions by the insertion of the new subtitle: *A Study of the Iconography of the Middle Ages and Its Sources of Inspiration*. While this is better, *A Study of the Iconology . . .* would have been more accurate still.[4]

[3] Heckscher, "The Genesis . . .," 260–1, no. 52 passim.
[4] Hoogewerff, *L'Iconologie . . .*, 53–9 passim.

Two criticisms are leveled against what I am calling the "iconological method." The first is that the artistic form is neglected in favor of the abstract meaning of the work, while the second is that the iconological method may become mired in a web of symbols and allegories which, however attractive, are nonetheless wrongly imputed both to the artist and to the work in question.

However, our concern is not with this debate in the world of art in general. Our concern is more narrow, considering these issues within a Christian context. In this context, the consideration of the way in which images convey meaning, i.e., iconology, is not some abstract theoretical musing. Rather it is the foundation of the way in which we create images, i.e., iconography. So we are attempting first to come to some global understanding of the way in which meaning is communicated in art. We do so in order to arrive at a more precise formulation of the way in which art which is consciously Christian and liturgical may be made, i.e., a more precise formulation of the poietics of Christian and liturgical art. In other words, Christians make images because images convey meaning. And iconology, whatever its methodological limitations may have been, is the hermeneutic we bring to this study.

Our authority for this assertion is that of the Seventh Ecumenical Council, the Second Council of Nicea,[5] which clarified these issues in a definitive way. As Pope John Paul II has written:

"The twelve-hundredth anniversary of the Second Council of Nicaea, has given rise to numerous ecclesiastical and academic commemorations in which the Holy See has desired to take part and to share. The event has also been worthily memorialized in the encyclical letter of His Holiness, the Patriarch of Constantinople, and his Synod, in which the theological importance and ecumenical meaning of this seventh Council, the last to be recognized both by the Catholic Church in the West and the Orthodox Church in the East, has been extolled."

"But it is the doctrine concerning the veneration of icons (images) in the Church of which special mention ought to be made, both because of the spiritual riches which have it has borne as well as the postulates it provides for sacred art in general. . . ."[6]

[5] Mansi 12, 951–13, 496.

[6] *Duodecimum saeculum,* apostolic letter of John Paul II, December 4, 1987, in the liturgical remembrance of St. John Damascene, 1.

The Second Council of Nicaea teaches that all sensation, including what we see and hear, is to be caught up in God.

In the first quarter of the ninth century, two of the seminal thinkers of the post-Nicene era, while working on a number of philosophical and theological questions related to sense perception, also posited a psychological argument which held for a certain predominance of the visual over the aural.

According to Patriarch Nicephorus, what is seen is sensed more immediately and in a more penetrating fashion than what is heard.[7] The monk Theodore, while agreeing that the eye is more important and more trustworthy than the ear,[8] extends the argument to say that language itself is a result of some prior visual imagery. The prophets, according to Theodore, are visionaries before all else, and the disciples and the evangelists spoke of Christ only after having seen him. "One cannot form an idea of any reality which is not currently present without first having seen it."[9] Both are aware that their psychological and physiological observations are suggestions *ad abundantiam*.

The conciliar teaching on the use and adoration of images by orthodox Christians reflects both a liturgical faith and liturgical actions. For example, Theodore regards icons as necessary for all Christians, imperfect or perfect, because this is the manner of the divine economy and asserts that problems regarding icons are only related to their "spiritual understanding."[10] If by this formulation he dissents from the justification for the use of images offered by Bishop Hypatius (who tolerates them only as instructional material for the disadvantaged in imitation of God's condescension toward the "non-spiritual.")[11] it is because such a minimalist and didactic view falls well outside of theological assertions about the Christian and images in general.

The attitude adopted by Hypatius in the ninth century is nearer to that of Bernard of Clairvaux[12] in the twelfth century than to that of

---

[7] Nicephorus of Constantinople, *Against Heretics* 3, 3. See also *Apologeticum* 61; *Against Epiphany* 2.

[8] Theodore of Studion, *Against Heretics* 3, 1. See also *Letter to Nicholas*.

[9] Idem, *Against Heretics* 3, 4.

[10] Idem, *Letter to Nicetas*.

[11] Hypatius of Ephesus, *Letter to Julian of Atramizia*.

[12] Bernard of Clairvaux, *Apology to William* 112, 28–9.

Gregory the Great[13] in the sixth. The latter says that even if icons are acceptable only for the instruction of the disadvantaged, for that reason alone they ought not to be destroyed. This seems to affirm the catechetical utility of icons while denying their role in celebration. Were that the case, John Damascene, the great inspirer of the theology of icons found in the seventh ecumenical council, would have been sadly mistaken in affirming both.[14] What is more, Canon 3 of the Fourth Council of Constantinople (870) would declare: "Just as all find salvation through the meaning of the words written in the gospels, so too, all, whether the learned or the disadvantaged, may take advantage of the very colors which are used to depict sacred images."

The ultimate justification for the use of images among Christians is found in the liturgical Profession of Faith in "That which was from the beginning, which we have heard, which we have seen with our own eyes, which we have looked upon and touched with our hands, concerning the Word of Life, — the Life was made manifest and we saw it and testify to it and we proclaim to you the eternal life which with the Father was made manifest to us — that which we have seen and heard . . ." (1 John 1:1-3).

Theodore of Studion's "spiritual understanding" is a function of the visible economy of God in which both sight and hearing are caught up in the human experience of God.

The fundamental importance of the signs of Jesus (John 12:37) is not merely that they are visible. Rather, what is celebrated in the liturgy is that he is himself the Word of Life, the Logos, which he himself cries out (John 12:44-50). In him the Word is made visible, which allows us to see the unseen and to hear the unheard. The trinitarian theophany which took place at the transfiguration, witnessed by the apostles as well as by the Law and the prophets, transformed the very essence of what it means to hear the Word of God. Although mention had been made of a thunder-like voice and a dark cloud at the covenant with Moses at Sinai and to Elijah's hearing of a still, small voice as he stood at the entrance of the cave (1 Kgs 19:12-13), when one speaks of God's visible and audible manifestation at Sinai one uses expressions like "vision of his glory" and "God's voice

---

[13] Gregory the Great, *Letter to Serenus of Marseille.*
[14] John Damascene, *Defense of Icons* 1, 17.

coming down out of heaven" to express the immediate knowledge of "the coming of the power of our Lord Jesus Christ (2 Pet 1:16-19).

This making visible of all things is the fundamental principle of the Christian liturgy and aesthetics. This is why *Sacrosanctum Concilium* insists on visibility. Elsewhere I have made a synopsis of the essential passages:[15]

SC 7	*SC 33*
1. *in qua [Liturgia]* (*in which [the Liturgy]*)	
2. *per signa* sensibilia (*through sensible signs*)	2. *signa* visibilia (visible *signs*)
	1. *quibus utitur sacra Liturgia (which the sacred Liturgy uses)*
3. *significatur* (*is signified*)	3. *ad res divinas invisibiles significandas (for signifying invisible divine things)*
4. *et efficitur sanctificatio hominis (and the sanctification of humans is effected)*	
5. *et a Jesu Christi corpore (and by the body of Jesus Christ)*	5. *dum Ecclesia (while the Church)*
6. *capite nempe eiusque membris (namely the head and its members)*	6. *vel orat vel canit vel agit . . . (either prays or sings or acts . . .)*
7. *integer cultus publicus exercetur (complete public worship is practiced)*	7. *ut rationabile obsequium ei praestent (so that they might offer to him proper homage)*
	4. *gratiamque eius [Dei] recipiant (and might receive his [God's] grace)*

The important contrast here is between #6 of *SC* 7 and #66 of *SC* 33. In *SC* 7 the subject of the liturgical action is "the head" of Christ's body, both head and members. In *SC* 33 this is explicitly identified with visible behaviors; specifically, prayer, singing, and movement.

[15] C. Valenziano, *L'anello della Sposa* (Magnano, 1993) 44.

Christian aesthetics is necessarily rooted in the visible because of the connection between God and humanity, as is made clear in the Nicene iconology of *Duodecimum saeculum:*

"According to St. Germanus, patriarch of Constantinople and one of the most well-known victims of the iconoclast heresy, the whole economy of the Incarnation is involved in the dispute over images. . . . The Church is convinced that God, in Jesus Christ, has truly redeemed and sanctified the flesh as well as the entire visible universe. That is, Christ has redeemed the whole of the human person, with all five senses, so that this renewed person might become, with full knowledge, the image of the Creator" (Col 3:10).[16]

Special note should be taken of the identification of the entire visible universe with the human person, including all the human senses. The Carolingian refusal to accept the Second Council of Nicaea, whatever the intentions behind it,[17] has impoverished the West in a way difficult to fathom. It has also led to a secularization of Christian and liturgical art. Patriarch Demetrius I was correct when he wrote:

"In iconoclasm there came back to life a number of past heresies, Manichean, Gnostic, Docetist, Nestorian and Monophysite as well as more recent heretical teaching such as the Paulician heresy. There were also Jewish and Islamic elements which revived traditions of the non-Christian East. . . . In this way, iconoclasm worked to deny the Incarnation, the sanctification of human life and matter, of a passage from earthly things to a divine heavenly reality. John Damascene put it bluntly: "Iconoclasm has declared war, not on icons, but on the Saints. [Defense of Icons 1, 19] . . . and on all that on which Orthodoxy bases its theology of icons . . . the teaching of the Church on matter and spirit, essence and energy, that which was created and uncreated, the heavens and the earth, the eternal and the finite. . . ."[18]

HAGIOGRAPHICITY
Since the Second Council of Nicaea the normative understanding of iconicity in a Christian and liturgical context is that iconography

---

[16] *Duodecimum saeculum*, 9.

[17] C. Valenziano, "Iconismo e aniconismo occidentale post niceno," *EO* 13 (1996).

[18] Ἐπὶ Τῃ 1200 ῆ, encyclical letter of Dimitrios I and his synod, September 14, 1987, on the feast of the Exaltation of the Cross, 6. 8. 11.

mediates iconology. The tragic histories of both East and West have caused there to be a multiplicity of norms for Christian and liturgical art. It would be a good thing if all, both East and West, would accept the words of the Council Fathers who spoke in 787. They spoke of icons with the words of Psalm 47:9 "As we have heard, so we have seen in the city of our God." When they spoke of the painter of icons they did so in terms similar to those used for the authors of Scripture itself, speaking of the artist (ζωηγράφος) as one who wrote holy things (ἁγιόγραφος). Iconology is the way in which biblical revelation is made visible in the Church:

"Icons have been handed down to the Church just as the Gospels have been. It is by hearing reading and by seeing images that the mind is illuminated. So I say that both in listening to Scripture and in looking at an image we grasp the same history. It is about this unity of hearing and sight of which the Song of Songs speaks: 'Show me your face and let me hear your voice, for your voice is sweet and your face is comely.' Psalm 47:9 agrees when it says 'As we have seen and we have heard in the city of our God.' . . . The insight and the tradition are from the fathers, not the artist. From the artist comes the art."[19]

In other words, just as there is a synergy between the artist and the Word, so too there is a synergy between the artist and the author of Scripture. So a Christian and liturgical artist has as a task not merely to produce art, even religious art, but also to be a writer of sacred things, one who renders sacramental Christian revelation. In 1987 *Duodecimum saeculum* declared:

"The Greek and Slavic Churches especially, having been taught by the eminent theologians and reveres of icons such as St. Nicephorus of Constantinople and St. Theodore of Studion, have maintained the icon as an integral part of the sacred liturgy no less than the celebration of the Word. Just as the reading of physical books allows us to perceive the living Word of the Law, a painted image allows the one who contemplates it to come to the mystery of salvation by means of sight. . . . Works of art which are of a truly ecclesial quality should be produced in greater numbers . . . works which truly aim at telling the mystery rather than hiding it. Today, just as in the past, it is faith

[19] Nicene Council II, *Actio* VI; Mansi 13, 220–2, 253–4.

itself which must be the indispensable inspiration of ecclesial art. Art for art's sake, which refers only to the artist and establishes no relationship with the heavenly reality, is foreign to what is meant by the Christian icon. Whatever style is adopted, all sacred art must proclaim the faith and hope of the Church.

"The unbroken tradition of sacred art confirms that the artist must be aware of performing a ministry for the Church. Art is authentically Christian when it enables one to understand by means of sight that the Lord himself is present in the Church, that salvation history gives a meaning and direction for our lives and that the glory promised to us already transforms our existence. Sacred art must offer us a comprehensive view of all aspects and logic of our faith. The Church's art works should try, as it were, to speak the *language* of the incarnation and to show through the elements of matter him who, as stated in the beautiful formulation of St. John Damascene, 'chose to dwell in matter in order to achieve my salvation through matter'" [Defense of Icons, 1, 16].[20]

The Latin original: "imaginem reputaverunt veluti complentem aliquam liturgiae sacrae partem haud secus atque verbi celebrationem," corresponds to the conciliar text: "In the churches, the reading (of the Scriptures) is proclaimed at intervals while the icons, always available, speak to us and evangelize us about the truth of the events, evening, morning and at midday. . . ."[21] The icon is, in essence, another form of liturgical proclamation, in this case, not an auditory proclamation, but a making visible of the Word.

In the work of this artist-hagiographer, the activity is sacramental and the end is revelatory. This is what makes art authentically Christian: that it enables one visibly to realize that glory which awaits, and is indeed already present among us, but which is not yet fully available. Working together with the Body of Jesus Christ, both head and members, the artist is based within a particular tradition of the making of images, but is otherwise boundlessly free to speak the language of the Incarnation, as the history of Christian art, full as it is of masterpieces, demonstrates. At the same time, we must be aware that there will be a wide variation among artists of the degree to which

---

[20] *Duodecimum saeculum*, 10, 11 (the italics are in the original; on John Damascene, see the more extensive quote of the same passage in *Epí tῃ 1200 e*, 22).

[21] Nicene Council II, *Actio* VI; Mansi 13, 220–2, 253–4.

they are conscious of carrying out a ministry for the Church. On the one hand, paradoxical as it may seem, there will be the non-believer who succeeds nevertheless in depicting the faith and hope of the Church (even an atheist can baptize, after all) while at the other end of the spectrum there is the tradition of the Evangelist Luke as painter of the incarnation and so painter of the ineffable Motherhood of Mary.

ICONICITY

In the post-Carolingian era, East and West, with their different theologies, spiritualities, and styles of pastoral ministry, diverged in the way they came to understand how images convey meaning. The question is a fundamentally hermeneutical one upon which *Duodecimum saeculum* did not touch but to which *Epí tῃ 1200 e* dedicated its central part:

"The visible humanity of the Lord is the image of his indivisible divinity. . . . The two natures united in the single person of the Lord offer us a unitary image of the God-Man Jesus as a way of imaging the absolutely ineffable and inconceivable person of God. The Lord is the image of every image, the archetype that comprises the totality of the divine essence . . . and we see God only through his divine-human hypostasis: His Son and his [visible] Word. This is a theological idea which seems to be contradictory, but which Gregory Palamas justifies in this way: God, unknowable and inconceivable, absolutely transcendent according to His essence, becomes a person who takes part in this empirical world, and in whom all those who will see the Lord in his second coming may take part as well. Then will we truly contemplate the face of the divine self-revelation. When we are transfigured into the glory of the Lord, all the justified will see God face to face . . . (1 Cor 13:14) the very face of the Word made human, the very face of the Son who is the image of the invisible God, begotten before all creatures (Col 1:15). . . . Nor should we forget that the human person, created in the divine image and likeness, is an icon of God. Although this image was obscured by the Fall and sin, this person is still able to be transfigured in the light and in the glory of the divine hypostasis. This is made known above all in the presence of the hypostasis of the Lord in the icon, with the saints next to him, because those whom he has known he has predestined to be conformed to the image of his son (Rom 8:29). Just as we bore the image of the earthly man, so too we will bear the image of the heavenly man

(1 Cor 15:49). The believer who contemplates the light of the Presence, the hypostasis, might also become the shining likeness of the model. According to Gregory of Nyssa, 'By approaching the light, the soul itself becomes light'" (Commentary on the Song of Songs 5).[22]

In other words, the theory of the making of icons consists in the fact that in itself it:

"contains the hypostasis of the transcendent categories of glory and of light. . . . Therefore the icon presents the holy person . . . in his glorious and luminous situation. . . . In the Western tradition, the image shows how far apart matter and spirit are. In the Eastern tradition, on the other hand, spirit and matter harmonize, in an understanding that is reflective of our spirituality."[23]

While this difference between East and West surely exists, the true problem, the solution of which will revitalize Christian art both East and West, is to arrive at a clear understanding of the philosophy of the making of images. All Christians, East and West, can learn from St. John Damascene:

"Only when you see the incorporeal become man for you will you be able to portray the image of the human form; only when the invisible becomes visible in the flesh will you be able to see the resemblance with what you have not seen. . . . In earlier times God, who is incorporeal, was not able to be imaged in any way; now that he has revealed himself in the flesh and has entered into visible contact with humanity, I can form an image of what I see of God. [And by venerating the icon] I venerate not the matter but the creator of the matter, he who has become matter for me, deigned to dwell in matter and saved me through matter; I will not cease to respect matter, through which my salvation has been achieved."[24]

In short, the purpose of the making of Christian images is this: to make visible, until the Lord's Second Coming, the glory of the Incarnation of God in the flesh and the glory awaiting the saints. No truly liturgical art can do otherwise.

[22] Ἐπὶ Τῇ 1200 ῇ, 15.

[23] Ibid., 28, 14.

[24] John Damascene, *Defense*, 1:10, 16 (quoted in Ἐπὶ Τῇ 1200 ῇ, 18, 22; and see the assonance with *GS* 22).

"One correctly insists on the fact that the Word of God in whom all the fullness of divinity dwells bodily (Col 2:9), the promised Word, revealed and revealer, who has been touched and heard, is contained entirely within the holy Scriptures. Yet he is the same Word who assumes architectonic form in the construction of the holy edifice within which the Synaxis takes place. He is the same Word who, sung and represented in the eucharistic Synaxis, composes the holy Liturgy. He is the same Word who offers himself both to mystical contemplation and to the theology of sight in the one image of Christ, whose memory is conserved in the Church."[25]

The entirety of Christian liturgy and art, whether figurative or musical or even architectural, must be understood to be iconic of the reality which is Christ.

In conclusion:

1. Iconology and liturgy must collaborate. Just as liturgical spirituality is the benchmark for all Christian spirituality, so too liturgical art must serve as the benchmark for all Christian art.

2. "For some decades now a growing interest in the theology and spirituality of Eastern icons has been noted. This is an index of the growing need for something of a spiritual language which authentically Christian art might make use of. . . . The rediscovery of the Christian image will also help to gain awareness of the great necessity of reacting against the depersonalizing and often degrading effects of the various images that condition our life with advertising and the tools of social communication. Indeed, this image turns toward us the face of the invisible author and discloses to us the access to spiritual realities. . . . Our most authentic tradition, fully in common with our (Eastern) Orthodox brethren, teaches us that the language of beauty employed in the ministry of faith is capable of moving the human heart toward the inner knowledge of the One whom we dare to depict outwardly, Jesus Christ the Son of God made Man."[26]

It seems to us that the reason for this growing appreciation, both inside and outside of their liturgical use, for Eastern icons is that one expects liturgical art to center on the mysteries of the faith, not

[25] Επι Τη 1200 η, 15.
[26] *Duodecimum saeculum,* 11, 12.

peripheral matters. This has been noted throughout the liturgical reforms of the twentieth century.[27] However, simply to adopt in the West the liturgical use of the icons of the East would be healthy neither for East nor West. It is rather our task to find a language for the incarnation appropriate to our time and culture. Above all, however, one must learn the gratuitousness of art in liturgy. It is neither for evangelization nor simply for its own sake. Above all one must seek liturgical art, a celebration in itself, and the rest will follow. For finally it is a question of a pastoral theology which includes liturgical theology.

[27] A. Cingria, *La décadence de l'art sacré* (Paris, 1930); P.-R. Régamey, *Art sacré au XXe. siècle?* (Paris, 1952); F. Débuyst, *L'art chrétien contemporain de 1962 à nos jours* (Paris, 1988); S. de Lavergne, *Art sacré et modernité. Les grandes donnés de la revue Art Sacré* (Namur, 1992).

Bibliography

Débuyst, F. *L'art chrétien contemporain de 1962 à nos jours.* Paris, 1988.

Hermerén, G. *Representation and Meaning in the Visual Arts: A Study in the Methodology of Iconography and Iconology.* Stockholm, 1969.

Kaemmerling, E. *Ikonographie und Ikonologie: Theorien, Entwicklung, Probleme.* Cologne, 1979.

Mitchell, W.J.T. *Iconology: Image, Text, Ideology.* Chicago-London, 1986.

Panofsky, E. "Zum Problem der Beschreibung und Inhaltsdeutung von Werken der bildenden Kunst." *Logos* 21 (1932) 103–19.

_____. *Studies in Iconology: Humanistic Themes in the Art of the Renaissance.* New York, 1972.

Valenziano, C. "6 Tesi per l'Arte Cristiana." In *Profezia di bellezza.* Rome, 1996.

_____. "Iconismo e aniconismo occidentale post niceno." *EO* 13 (1996).

Anscar J. Chupungco, O.S.B.

16

Liturgy and Inculturation

A DEFINITION OF LITURGICAL INCULTURATION

The Concept of Inculturation
The word "inculturation" was coined in 1962 by the French theologian J. Masson when he called attention to the "need for a Catholicism that is *inculturated* in a pluriform manner."[1] In 1973 it was used by G. L. Barney, who wrote that the "supracultural components" of Christianity "should neither be lost nor distorted but rather secured and interpreted clearly through the guidance of the Holy Spirit in *'inculturating'* them into the new culture."[2] In 1979 the word was introduced into the official Church documents by Pope John Paul II, who admitted that the word, though a neologism, "expresses one of the elements of the great mystery of the incarnation."[3]

---

[1] J. Masson, "L'Eglise ouverte sur le monde," *NRT* 84 (1962) 1038.

[2] G. L. Barney, "The Supracultural and the Cultural: Implications for Frontier Missions," *The Gospel and Frontier Peoples* (Pasadena, 1973). See G. De Napoli, "Inculturation as Communication," *Inculturation* 9 (1987) 71–98. The Latin *inculturatio* was adopted by the delegates to the 32d General Congregation of the Society of Jesus in 1975. See A. Crollius, "What is So New about Inculturation?" *Gregorianum* 59 (1978) 721–38. It was probably intended to be the Latin equivalent of enculturation (Latin does not have the particle *en*), which is an anthropological jargon for "socialization," or the learning process "by which a person is inserted into his or her culture." See A. Shorter, *Toward a Theology of Inculturation* (London, 1988) 5–6.

[3] "Address to the Pontifical Biblical Commission," *Fede e cultura alla luce della Bibbia* (Torino, 1981) 5. See idem, Apostolic exhortation *Catechesi tradendae,* 53, *AAS* 71 (1979) 1319.

In the context of theology, A. Shorter defines inculturation as "the creative and dynamic relationship between the Christian message and a culture or cultures."[4] He notes three traits of inculturation: first, it is an ongoing process that is relevant to every country or region where the faith has been sown; second, Christian faith cannot exist except in a cultural form; and third, between Christian faith and culture there should be reciprocal interaction and integration.

In its concluding declaration the Extraordinary Synod of Bishops in 1985 offered the following definition of inculturation: "Since the Church is a communion, which is present throughout the world and joins diversity and unity, it takes up whatever it finds positive in all cultures. Inculturation, however, is different from mere external adaptation, as it signifies an interior transformation of authentic cultural values through their integration into Christianity and the rooting of Christianity in various human cultures."[5] The Synod's definition contains the basic concept of inculturation, namely the reciprocal integration of pertinent elements between Christianity and culture.

On several occasions Pope John Paul II used the word "inculturation" to express "the incarnation of the Gospel in autonomous cultures and at the same time the introduction of these cultures into the life of the Church." Echoing the Synod of 1985, he defines inculturation as the "intimate transformation of the authentic cultural values by their integration into Christianity and the implantation of Christianity into different human cultures."[6] The instruction *The Roman Liturgy and Inculturation (RLI)*, issued in 1994 by the Congregation for Divine Worship and the Discipline of the Sacraments, prefers inculturation to adaptation, since this word could lead one to think of modifications of a somewhat transitory and external nature. Its definition of "inculturation" is borrowed from Pope John Paul II.[7]

---

[4] *Toward a Theology of Inculturation*, 11. See "L'inculturation," *MD* 189 (1989); "Inculturazione e liturgia oggi," *RL* (Luglio-agosto, 1995) n. 4; A. Chupungco, *Liturgies of the Future: The Process and Methods of Inculturation* (New York, 1989) 23–40; idem, *Liturgical Inculturation: Sacramentals, Religiosity, Catechesis* (Collegeville, 1992) 13–31.

[5] Final Report *Exeunte coetu secundo* (December 7, 1984) Declaration 4.

[6] Encyclical letter *Slavorum Apostoli*, 21, *AAS* 77 (1985) 802–3; Discourse to the Plenary Assembly of the Pontifical Council for Culture, 5, *AAS* 79 (1987) 1204–5; encyclical letter *Redemptoris Missio*, 52, *AAS* 83 (1991) 300.

[7] *The Roman Liturgy and Inculturation*. IVth Instruction for the Right Application of the Conciliar Constitution on the Liturgy, (nn. 37–40), (Rome, 1994) no. 4, p. 4.

The concept of inculturation is made up of three principal elements. The first is interaction, whereby Christianity and culture enter into dialogue. Inculturation is not one-sided: both parties have something to offer and something to take. It is in the course of this dialogue that Christianity critiques cultural values, patterns, and institutions. It is the stage when, in the light of the gospel, the components of culture such as values, rites, and symbols are examined for their suitability and usefulness. Though mutual respect governs this dialogue, it is clear that not everything in the possession of a given culture is suitable or useful for Christian purposes. Some cultural components might even be incompatible with the Christian tenets. Apropos it is important to note that inculturation does not eliminate the countercultural character of Christianity. The second element is integration of pertinent cultural elements. These are entered into the scheme of Christian values, practices, and institutions. Often the cultural elements will need to be adjusted or modified in order to be integrated. Sometimes integration into the corpus of Christian doctrine and practices may even involve a change in the meaning of the cultural components while keeping intact their external shape. The third is the dynamic of transculturation, whereby the parties involved retain their identity in the process of interaction and integration. Inculturation enriches Christianity without prejudice to its nature as a divine-human institution. In other words, an inculturated Christianity will not be reduced to a mere component of culture.

Applying this concept of inculturation to the liturgy, one may define liturgical inculturation as the process whereby pertinent elements of a local culture are integrated into the texts, rites, symbols, and institutions employed by a local church for its worship. Integration means that the cultural components influence the liturgical pattern of composing formularies, proclaiming them, performing ritual actions, and symbolizing the liturgical message in art forms. In some cases integration can also mean that local rites, symbols, and festivals, after due critique and Christian reinterpretation, become part of the liturgical worship of the local church. The history of Christian liturgy attests to this. One result of inculturation is that the people are able to identify with the liturgy and claim it as their own. This is because the liturgical texts, symbols, gestures, and feasts evoke something from the people's history, traditions, cultural patterns, and artistic genius. The power of the liturgy to evoke local culture is a sign that inculturation has taken place.

The immediate aim of inculturation is to create a form of worship that is culturally suited to local people. Inculturation brings about a liturgy for the local church. In this sense the ultimate aim of inculturation is active and intelligent participation, which springs from both the people's conviction of faith and their ability to claim the liturgy as their own.

No historical model illustrates liturgical inculturation better than the classical Roman liturgy. This type of liturgy flourished in Rome between the fifth and eighth centuries through the work of such popes as Gelasius, Vigilius, Leo the Great, and Gregory the Great. They belonged to the elite class of Roman society, to that group of *homines classici* celebrated for their noble simplicity and sobriety, mastery of rhetorics, and practical sense. It is for such a group of people that these popes developed the classical Roman liturgy. Its texts and rites, even when translated into other languages, still betray the thought, language, and ritual pattern of the people for whom they were fashioned.[8]

Inculturation means reciprocal enrichment. The Roman liturgy absorbed the wealth of classical culture. What did culture gain from its union with the liturgy? J. Jungmann gives the following answer: "Society, political life, the lives of the people, family life, the position of women, the appreciation of human dignity, whether slave, child, or infant yet unborn — all this was transformed in a slow but sure process of fermentation: out of a pagan society a Christian society was born." History affirms that inculturation is an effective means of evangelization.[9]

Some Related Terms
It might be helpful at this point to define other terms that at some point were used to express the relationship between liturgy and cul-

---

[8] See E. Bishop, *Liturgica Historica* (Oxford, 1962) 2–9, where the author describes "The Genius of the Roman Rite"; G. Dix: *The Shape of the Liturgy* (London, 1964) 103–40, which deals with the classical shape of the eucharistic liturgy; Th. Klauser, *A Short History of the Western Liturgy* (Oxford, 1969) 59–68, which speaks of the traits of the Roman euchology.

[9] J. Jungmann, *The Early Liturgy to the Time of Gregory the Great* (London, 1966) 165.

ture.[10] These are indigenization, contextualization, adaptation, and acculturation.

Indigenization, which was coined from the word "indigenous," indicates the process of conferring on the liturgy a cultural form that is native to the local church. In the seventies D. S. Amalorpavadass used the word to mean liturgical adaptation in the context of the Indian culture or, as he puts it, "to give to our liturgy a more Indian setting and complexion."[11] The problem with this word is that both etymologically and literally it represents an impossibility. Nothing can be made native or indigenous in a foreign land. To be indigenous it is necessary to be born or to be produced in one's native land. An indigenized Christian liturgy is thus an impossibility, because as John Paul II explains in *Catechesi tradendae* 7, no. 53, the message of the gospel does not spontaneously grow from a cultural ground: it is always transmitted through apostolic dialogue. Another difficulty presented by the word "indigenization" is the question of defining, for some countries, what is truly indigenous, that is, without admixture of other cultures. Furthermore, a return to the indigenous seems to savor romanticism and archaeology.

Contextualization was introduced into the active ecclesiastical vocabulary by the World Council of Churches in 1972. Derived from the word "context," it fittingly expresses the need for the Church to be relevant to contemporary society. The term distinctly echoes Vatican II's constitution *Gaudium et spes,* which calls for the Church's relevance in today's world. Local culture and environment are the concrete contexts in which local churches live, operate, and worship. The liturgy should thus take into consideration the concrete context of a given assembly: its urban or rural setting, its work and product, its geographic and temporal conditions, and its socioeconomic and political situation. Unfortunately, because of its agricultural beginnings the liturgy seems to give little attention to the industrial world with its life-style, the factory conditions, the strikes that are as regular as the seasons of the year, and the bargaining tables.[12]

---

[10] A. Chupungco, *Liturgical Inculturation: Sacramentals, Religiosity, and Catechesis,* 13–54.

[11] D. S. Amalorpavadass, *Towards Indigenisation in the Liturgy* (Bangalore, 1971) 26–53.

[12] See P. Hiebert, "Critical Contextualization," *Missiology* 12 (1984) 287–96; R. Costa, *One Faith, Many Cultures: Inculturation, Indigenization, and Contextualization*

Since in some parts of the world oppression is the dominant feature of daily life, the context in which the local church lives and worships is deeply affected by struggle for political, economic, and cultural freedom. In such places contextualization has been used to signify efforts toward liberation. Thus it gained popularity in those places where the theology of liberation has taken root because of concern for progress, political liberty, and social justice. The Church has the duty to review and update its institutions in the context of the human aspirations for freedom and progress.[13]

Adaptation is the official word used by the Constitution on the Sacred Liturgy *(SC)*, especially in articles 37–40. In *SC aptatio* and *accomodatio* are synonymous, though in chapter 3 *aptatio* was systematically replaced by *accomodatio,* seemingly as a *via media,* or compromise. At some point during the council discussion on the liturgical reform, *aptatio* began to give the threatening impression of radical reform of the sacraments.[14] *SC* 1 states that one of the aims of the council is "to adapt more suitably to the needs of our times those institutions that are subject to change." Taking its lead we may assume that *SC*'s *aptatio* (or *accomodatio*) refers to the general program of Church renewal or updating. In other words, it seems that adaptation used in a broad sense has the same meaning as Pope John XXIII's *aggiornamento. SC* itself proposes two principal ways to bring about the updating of the liturgy: through revision of existing rites and cultural adaptation.

The distinction between *aptatio* and *accomodatio* began to take shape only with the publication of the *editio typica* of the conciliar liturgical books. In their introductory part there is a section on *De aptationibus,* which belongs to the competence of the conferences of bishops, and *De accomodationibus,* which is the right and duty of the minister. Because the word "adaptation," taken in a missiological context, could lead one to think of changes that are transitory and external in na-

---

(New York, 1988); L. Luzbetak, *The Church and Cultures: New Perspectives in Missiological Anthropology* (New York, 1993).

[13] D. Power, "Alternative 1: Ordination of a Presbyter in a Church Constituted by Basic Christian Communities," *Alternative Futures for Worship* (Collegeville, 1987) 157–64.

[14] A. Chupungco, *Cultural Adaptation of the Liturgy,* 42–57; see R. Gonzalez, "Adaptación, inculturación, creatividad. Planteamiento, problematica y perspectivas de profundización," *Phase* 158 (1987) 129–52.

ture, *RLI* has opted to employ the word "inculturation."[15] The articles of *SC* that deal with the adaptation of the shape of the liturgy should be reread in the light of this instruction.

Acculturation, which consists of the juxtaposition of two cultures, operates according to a dynamic of interaction without the benefit of mutual integration. Though the relationship between the two is defined in terms of mutual respect or tolerance, the components of one is not assimilated by the other. Nonetheless, because acculturation favors interaction between two cultures, it is a necessary condition of inculturation.[16]

In the liturgy a good example of acculturation took place during the baroque period. Unable to penetrate through the canonical and rubrical barriers that guarded the Tridentine liturgy against any external intrusion, baroque culture stayed on the periphery of the liturgy. The baroque manifestations of festivity, drama, and exuberance were not absorbed by either the texts or the rites of the Tridentine liturgy. As J. Jungmann aptly observed, "At this time there were festive occasions which might best be described as church concerts with liturgical accompaniment."[17] But acculturation is not a thing of the past. It still exists in such juxtapositions as the recitation of the *Angelus* during Mass.

A THEOLOGY OF LITURGICAL INCULTURATION

The Theological Starting Point
The starting point for a theology of inculturation is the incarnation of Jesus Christ insofar as it involves the Church.[18] In other words, the theology of inculturation is not premised on the incarnation as such, that is, as the initial event of the New Testament history of salvation. Rather, it is based on the incarnation as a mystery that continues to be realized in the life and mission of the Church. One may speak here

[15] Instruction *The Roman Liturgy and Inculturation*, no. 4, p. 4; G. Arbuckle, "Inculturation Not Adaptation: Time to Change Terminology," *Wor* 60/6 (1986) 512–20.

[16] A. Shorter, *Toward a Theology of Inculturation*, 6–8.

[17] J. Jungmann, *The Mass of the Roman Rite* (New York, 1961) 111–7; idem., *Pastoral Liturgy* (London, 1962) 80–9.

[18] G. Brambilla, "Ermeneutica teologica dell'adattamento liturgico," *Liturgia e adattamento* (Rome, 1990) 39–83, especially 54–71; D. S. Amalorpavadass, "Theological Reflections on Inculturation," *SL* 20/1 (1990) 36–54.

of the incarnation in its ecclesiological dimension. When Vatican II's decree *Ad gentes (AG)* speaks of Christ's incarnation, it presents it as the paradigm of the Church's own "incarnation." *AG* 10 declares that "if the Church is to be in a position to offer all peoples the mystery of salvation and the life brought by God, it must implant itself among them in the same way that Christ by his incarnation bound himself to the particular social and cultural circumstances of the people among whom he lived." The principle is applied in article 22 to the young churches: "So too indeed, just as happened in the economy of the incarnation, the young Churches, which are rooted in Christ and built on the foundations of the Apostles, take over all the riches of the nations which have been given to Christ as an inheritance."

These two statements present Christ's incarnation as the model for the Church: *ad instar oeconomiae incarnationis.* The incarnation, whereby the Son of God became a member of the Jewish people and a sharer of their faith, culture, and traditions, is in this sense not exclusive to Christ. The mystery of the incarnation pertains to both the head and the body. The mystery of the incarnation should find extension in the Church if the saving purpose for which Christ assumed a human nature is to be achieved through its ministry. In imitation of Christ the Church should share the history, culture, and traditions of the people among whom it dwells. This means that the Church should integrate into its worship and institutions the pertinent elements of a people's life and activities. The Church should not only speak the language of the people but also think in the way the people think; it should not only perform the people's rites but also adopt the cultural patterns that run through their celebrations. The measure in which the Church is "incarnated" among a particular people becomes the measure in which Christ and his gospel are made present there. As Christ became a Jew in all things save sin, so the Church must identify itself historically and culturally with its people and become not merely a Church *in* but the Church *of* a particular place.

Thus inculturation is premised on a christological and ecclesiological principle, namely the incarnation of the Son of God as a historical paradigm and the "incarnation" of the Church as the continuing realization of that paradigm. With reason Pope John Paul II said that inculturation "expresses one of the elements of the great mystery of the incarnation." *RLI* sums up this theological principle in these words: "On coming to the earth the Son of God 'born of a woman, born under the law' (*Gal.* 4:4), associated himself with social and cultural conditions of the people of the Alliance with whom he lived and prayed. In becoming a man he became a member of a people, a country and an epoch 'and in a certain way, he thereby united himself to the whole human race.'" This means that "faith in Christ offers to all nations the possibility of being beneficiaries of the promise and of sharing in the heritage of the people of the covenant (cf. *Eph. 3:6*), without renouncing their culture."[19]

Obviously the principle of critical evaluation is part of the process of ecclesial incarnation. While utmost understanding should be exercised in regard to a people's culture and traditions, not everything can be integrated into the rites and institutions of Christians. Indeed, there can be instances when Christians have to turn their backs on some components of their tradition because they are irremediably incompatible with the gospel. *SC* 37 refers to them as elements in a people's way of life that are "indissolubly bound up with superstition and error." The word "indissolubly" implies that there are superstitious and erroneous elements that can still be salvaged through the process of critical evaluation. Such process requires a reinterpretation of the elements in the light of salvation history. Patristic writers often employed biblical typology to achieve it. Apropos *RLI* notes that "the challenge which faced the first Christians, whether they came from the chosen people or from a pagan background was to reconcile the renunciations demanded by faith in Christ with fidelity to the culture and traditions of the people to which they belonged."[20]

Inculturation brings about a degree of pluralism in the shape of the liturgy on the basis of cultural diversity. Pluralism implies that each cultural group is able to claim the liturgy as properly its own, that is, as a celebration that resonates and evokes the people's history, culture, and traditions. Inculturation, however, safeguards those basic tenets of Christian faith and tradition that unite local churches throughout the world. Pluralism in cultural expressions may not be pursued at the expense of unity in essentials. In this sense inculturation does not produce a liturgy that is so localized that it becomes unrecognizable to other local churches. An inculturated liturgy is the liturgy of a local church, but it will always maintain a universal

[19] Ibid., no. 10; 14, pp. 7; 8.
[20] Instruction *The Roman Liturgy and Inculturation*, no. 20, p. 11.

dimension because of its essential content or meaning. Every local liturgy belongs to the entire Church. That is why it needs to be recognized and claimed by the other churches as an authentic form of Christian worship. In short, liturgical inculturation means diversity in cultural expressions and unity in Christian faith and tradition.

RLI expresses the foregoing considerations in these words: "The liturgy of the Church must not be foreign to any country, people, or individual, and at the same time it should transcend the particularity of race and nation. It must be capable of expressing itself in every human culture, all the while maintaining its identity, through fidelity to the tradition which comes to it from the Lord."[21]

The principle of the incarnation is sometimes invoked for introducing the use of eucharistic elements other than wheat bread and grape wine in places where these are not staple food and drink. The argument often runs thus: had Christ been incarnated in China, he would have used rice and tea for the Eucharist. The syllogism is, of course, based on mere hypothesis. Historically Christ was a Jew and nothing can change it. That he made use of the Jewish ritual food and drink at the Last Supper is therefore to be expected. Yet the law of the incarnation is such that, granted the hypothesis, there is no doubt that Christ would have chosen the ritual food and drink of the place. To do otherwise would deny the very essence of the mystery.

But the point at issue here is not the value of the hypothesis regarding Christ's incarnation outside Judaism. We are not dealing with a christological question. Rather, the issue is an ecclesiological one: the Church is called to live *ad instar oeconomiae incarnationis*. This means that the Church has the duty to be "incarnated," in imitation of Christ, in the culture and traditions of the local people. By virtue of this ecclesiological principle it would seem that in theory the Church could permit another foodstuff and drink for the Eucharist provided they express the meaning and intention of Christ's institution at the Last Supper. In practice, however, the Church has the prerogative to require wheat bread and grape wine for a valid sacramental celebration. It would be a gravely irresponsible act of audacity to use other foodstuff and drink.

That the Church can in fact modify to some extent the matter for the celebration of the Eucharist gets support from the discipline

---

[21] Ibid., no. 18, p. 10.

allowing low-gluten altar bread and *mustum* on behalf respectively of persons affected by celiac disease and of priests affected by alcoholism.[22] Low-gluten bread should of course be made of wheat, but it does not have the consistency and cohesiveness of normal bread. On the other hand, "by *mustum* is understood fresh juice from grapes, or juice preserved by suspending its fermentation." Thus under special circumstances the Church can dispense with the tradition of using wine for the Eucharist. Will the Church permit other types of bread and wine that are not made of wheat and grapes in response to a cultural and pastoral necessity?

At a time when the paschal mystery is uppermost in both theological and liturgical thinking, it is important to note that the paschal mystery is not a paradigm of inculturation. Christ's death and resurrection are not the starting point for inculturation. Rather, they are the goal toward which liturgical inculturation should tend. If elements of a people's history, culture, and traditions are integrated into the celebration of Christ's paschal mystery, it is in order to allow the people to experience in ways that are proper to them the presence and power of that mystery. Just as the incarnation of Christ pointed to the paschal mystery as its goal, so does the inculturation of the liturgy aim to render the paschal mystery culturally accessible to the people.

Theological Liturgical Principles

The mystery of the incarnation is the premise for liturgical inculturation. How is this premise expressed in concrete theological liturgical principles? A. Bugnini, echoing the Constitution on the Sacred Liturgy, names them as the guiding and operational principles of Vatican II's liturgical reform.[23] These same principles apply to inculturation. It is to be expected that in the process of inculturation the liturgy will eventually acquire a diversity of forms based on the culture of each local church. The process, however, should be guided and influenced by certain liturgical principles in order to preserve the fundamental elements of Christian and, to some extent Roman, liturgy. Though inculturation tends toward cultural diversification, it protects the essential unity of the liturgy.

[22] See Letter from the Congregation for the Doctrine of Faith, Prot. N. 89/78 (June 19, 1995).

[23] A. Bugnini, *The Reform of the Liturgy 1948–1975* (Collegeville, 1990) 39–48.

The first principle, which is derived from *SC* 7, defines the liturgy as "an exercise of the priestly office of Jesus Christ." The definition implies that the person of Christ and what he did for humankind, especially when he died, rose again, and sent the Holy Spirit, is at the center of every liturgical celebration. The liturgy is always an anamnesis of the paschal mystery and an epicletic prayer for the bestowal of the Holy Spirit. Anamnesis, which focuses on the Easter mystery, and epiclesis, which refers to the mystery of Pentecost, are the two basic theological principles that should guide the work of inculturation. One may say that ultimately the aim of inculturation is to render these two mysteries of Christ accessible to the local community so that it can relive and experience them in the context of its own culture.

To the exercise of his priestly office Christ always associates the Church. For this reason the liturgy is the Church's "sacred action surpassing all others; no other action of the Church can equal its effectiveness by the same title and to the same degree." Consequently the work of inculturation should in no way reduce the liturgy to one of the local community's cultural activities. Liturgy will always be an act of worship, even if its external form is deeply influenced by culture. Furthermore, inculturation will seek to underline not only the sacred character of liturgical celebrations but also their efficacious role in building up the Christian community.

The second principle deals with the hierarchic and communal nature of the liturgy. *SC* devotes articles 26 to 31 to this principle. A. Bugnini sums them up in these words: "Communal celebrations show forth the nature of the Church as a hierarchically organized community; all play a part, but each member has his or her task, depending on the ministry received, the nature of the rite, and the principles of liturgy."[24] In liturgical celebrations there is always one who presides and ministers who assist the presider and serve the assembly. Furthermore, liturgical celebrations are communal in structure rather than private. The work of inculturation should not lose sight of these two dimensions. When integrating into the liturgy the local pattern of leadership, service, and people's role in community gatherings, one should examine whether such pattern corresponds to the hierarchic and communal nature of the liturgy. The process of incul-

---

[24] Ibid., 42.

turation should always produce a liturgy that is clearly premised on the Church's hierarchical structure and communal celebrations.

The principle also implies that every liturgical celebration by the local community belongs to the entire Church. The emergence of local liturgies, especially in situations that are multiethnic and multicultural, should not obscure the universal character of the Church's liturgy.[25] Across the diversity of languages, musical forms, and symbols one should be able to recognize a particular celebration as the action of the universal Church gathered here and now. Thus the holy Eucharist celebrated in the cultural tradition of an ethnic group should possess all the necessary conditions in order to belong to the Catholic Church. Provided therefore that the nature and purpose of the eucharistic celebration as defined by the authority of the Church are kept, we should consider it an action of the entire Church. A caution is apropos: the liturgy should not be so localized that it does not even evoke the universal and unifying elements of Christian worship.

The third principle comes from *SC* 10. It states that "the liturgy is the summit toward which the activity of the Church is directed; at the same time it is the fount from which all the Church's power flows." A. Bugnini writes that "evangelization and catechetical instruction are not ends in themselves."[26] Their aim is to "help human beings attain to full communion with God and participation in the salvation which Christ has accomplished and which is made present in liturgical celebrations." The local church will be able to realize this aim more fully if its apostolic works are embodied in the culture and traditions of the people. Now, if the liturgy is to be in effect the summit and fount of apostolic works, it should likewise be embodied in culture and traditions. A liturgy whose language, rites, and symbols do not match with those of the local church's structures and pastoral activities is hardly recognizable as their summit and fount. In this sense, when inculturating the liturgy one should be attentive to the cultural forms that have been integrated into the structure and apostolic works of the local church. Liturgy, for instance, should not speak one language while catechesis another.

The fourth principle is conscious, active participation of the faithful. *SC* 14 says that "in the reform and promotion of the liturgy, this

---

[25] M. Francis, *Liturgy in a Multicultural Community* (Collegeville, 1991).
[26] Ibid., 41.

full and active participation by all the people is the aim to be considered before all else."[27] Hence the principal aim assigned to inculturation is to bring about this kind of liturgical participation in the context of the people's culture. The style of presiding and ministering, the manner of greeting and responding, the opportune moment of breaking into song, reciting prayers, and observing silence, the type of acclamations, the forms of bodily gestures, and the assigned places for the presider, ministers, and assembly — all these have a cultural overtone. Presiding, ministering, and participating are basic components of a liturgical action, but they also belong to the realm of cultural institutions. The important thing to consider here is that the liturgy, which distinguishes these three roles, does not suffer them to be confused with one another. The work of inculturation should respect the distinction while it develops a form of liturgical presidency, ministry, and active participation that is evocative of the local people's cultural patterns.

The fifth principle is provided by SC 23: "That sound tradition may be retained and yet the way remain open to legitimate progress, a careful investigation is always to be made into each part of the liturgy to be revised. This investigation should be theological, historical, and pastoral." This principle should be read in the light of SC 21: "The liturgy is made up of immutable elements, divinely instituted, and of elements subject to change. These not only may but ought to be changed with the passage of time if they have suffered from the intrusion of anything out of harmony with the inner nature of the liturgy or have become pointless."[28]

Since the work of inculturation necessarily involves changes and modifications in the shape of the liturgy, it is of utmost importance to distinguish elements that may be changed from elements that may not without impinging on the nature and purpose of Christian worship. For example, to divorce the Eucharist from the Last Supper and the sacrifice of the cross is to empty it of its meaning. Careful research into the theology and history of the liturgical components is a preliminary condition of inculturation.

---

[27] G. Shirilla, *The Principle of Active Participation of the Faithful in Sacrosanctum Concilium* (Rome, 1990).

[28] See also SC 50 and 62.

It needs to be said at this point that inculturation preserves not only what is essential to the nature and purpose of the liturgy but also what is part of sound tradition. A great part of that tradition comes from the Jewish and Greco-Roman worlds. According to *RLI*, every local Church is united with the universal Church not only in faith and sacraments but also in "those practices received through the Church as part of the uninterrupted apostolic tradition," such as the observance of Sunday, daily prayer, and the practice of penance.[29] In the course of centuries the liturgy has integrated into its plan, language, rites, and symbols elements from other cultures and traditions. They have since become traditional. One who works on inculturation will examine them closely in the light of Vatican II's higher principles, like active participation, in order to evaluate their relevance to the local church. Inculturation translates and transmits faithfully what is essential while it makes effort to adjust and update what is traditional in the liturgy though not essential to it.

The sixth principle is stated by *SC* 33: "In the liturgy God is speaking to his people and Christ is still proclaiming his Gospel." This is supported by *SC* 7, which teaches that Christ "is present in his word, since it is he himself who speaks when the holy Scriptures are read in the Church." That is why *SC* 24 rightly claims that "Sacred Scripture is of the greatest importance in the celebration of the liturgy. For it is from Scripture that the readings are given and explained in the homily and that psalms are sung; the prayers, collects, and liturgical songs are scriptural in their inspiration; it is from the Scriptures that actions and signs derive their meaning." Since "the Church is nourished on the word of God written in the Old and New Testament," *RLI* 23 reminds all that it "must not be replaced by any other text, no matter how venerable it may be."[30]

Some religions possess sacred scriptures. Because their content is often similar to what is written in the Old and New Testament, there is a temptation to insert them into the liturgy as an added, if not as an alternative, reading. The work of inculturation should primarily be based on the sacred Scriptures for its language, symbols, and

[29] Instruction *The Roman Liturgy and Inculturation*, no. 26, p. 14.
[30] Ibid., no. 23, p. 13. See Introduction to the *Ordo Lectionum Missae*, no. 12: "It is absolutely forbidden to replace these readings [from sacred Scriptures] by other non-biblical readings."

texts. But history tells us that Christian liturgy uses also non-biblical compositions, though biblically inspired, which are known today as *psalmi idiotici*. Some of them are venerable, like the *Gloria* and *Te Deum*. History furthermore tells us that the Church, especially in the age of the early Christian writers, adopted rites and symbols from the culture of local communities. Examples are the foot washing of neophytes, their vesting in white garments, and the giving of a cup of milk and honey to them. Though these belonged to the culture of the Greco-Romans, they were interpreted in the light of Scriptures through the use of typology.

SOME HISTORICAL MODELS

This part examines a number of historical models of liturgical inculturation that can give insight on what local churches can imitate or avoid on the basis of past experiences. The models also present the different principles, criteria, and methods that have been employed in the past.[31]

The New Testament offers basic models. Jesus, who was brought up in the culture and religion of his own people, chose the elements suited to express the worship of the new people of God. He did this by predicating a new meaning to some of the Jewish traditions. Without radically changing their external form, he reinterpreted them in the light of his paschal mystery.

Thus Christian baptism retains the Jewish form of washing in water. But now it means the forgiveness that flowed from the cross of Christ, initiation into the life of the Trinity, and incorporation into the Church of Christ (Matt 28:19; Rom 6:3-11; Eph 5:25-26). The Eucharist too had its origin in the paschal meal of the Jewish people commemorating their Exodus from Egypt. On the night before his own exodus from this world to the Father, Jesus celebrated the paschal meal in sacramental anticipation of his death and resurrection (John 13:1). The Last Supper retained the principal elements of the paschal meal (bread, wine, prayer of thanks), but the bread signified the pierced body of Jesus, the wine his blood, and the meal itself the anamnesis of his sacrifice (1 Cor 11:23-26). Likewise, the books of the Old Testament

---

[31] For general reference see G. Dix, *The Shape of the Liturgy* (London, 1965); J. Jungmann, *The Early Liturgy to the Time of Gregory the Great* (London, 1966); T. Klauser, *A Short History of the Western Liturgy* (Oxford, 1969).

received from Jesus a new interpretation: "Everything written about me in the law of Moses and the prophets and the psalms must be fulfilled" (Luke 24:44). Jesus saw in them prophetic references to himself.

The disciples of Jesus followed his example in regards to Jewish rites that gave rise to Christian ordination, reconciliation, and anointing of the sick. A good example is the anointing of the sick, as explained in Jas 5:14-15: the practice is Jewish, but now it is performed by the Christian presbyters in the name of the Lord.

Jewish feasts of Passover and Pentecost obtained a new meaning after the death of Jesus and the coming of the Holy Spirit. These were events that took place during these feasts. Sunday, on the other hand, which was also observed by the community of the Essenes, was kept by the disciples as the day when their risen Lord appeared to them in the reading of the word and the breaking of bread (Luke 24:1-35).

The period from the third to the seventh century is marked by a rapid development in the shape of sacramental celebrations, especially the rites of Christian initiation. The development was greatly influenced by the culture of the Greco-Roman world, whose language, rites, feasts, art forms, architecture, and so on were integrated into the liturgy. Often the Church Fathers used biblical types to express their new Christian meaning.

Tertullian, for example, mentions the rite of anointing neophytes in his book *On Baptism*.[32] He records that they were anointed, it would seem, on the crown of their head, "as Moses anointed Aaron unto priesthood."[33] He describes the rite as a generous pouring of oil: "The oil flows down our bodies." The point of interest here is the origin of this rite. Baptismal anointing is nowhere to be found in the New Testament. In fact, it is not mentioned even by patristic literature prior to Tertullian.[34] We know that the practice was observed in certain mystery rites, and so it is possible that Christians borrowed it from them. But what makes the practice Christian is the meaning that was attached to it: the priesthood of the baptized. To bring this out,

[32] *De baptismo*, in *CCL* I/1 (1954) 277–95; B. Botte, "Le symbolisme de l'huile et de l'onction," *QL* 62 (1981) 196–208.

[33] *De baptismo* 7, 282.

[34] B. Botte thinks that the following statement of Tertullian in *De corona* (ch. 3) refers to baptismal anointing: "Hanc si nulla scriptura determinavit, certa consuetudo corroboravit, quae sine dubio de traditione manavit." The text seems, however, to refer to *linea serra*.

Tertullian employs a biblical type, the anointing of Aaron. Later authors like Ambrose of Milan and Cyril of Jerusalem explained the meaning of this postbaptismal anointing in the same way as Tertullian. For instance, Ambrose in his work *The Mysteries* tells the neophytes: "You were anointed that you may become a chosen race, priestly, precious; for we are all anointed unto the kingdom of God and unto priesthood with spiritual grace."[35]

Biblical typology, both from the Old and the New Testaments, was a favorite method among the Fathers for reorienting cultural elements to the Christian mystery. Tertullian applies this method also to the baptismal water when in connection with it he recalls the water of creation, the great deluge, the Red Sea, and the Jordan River. Biblical typology was probably the best method at hand to insert culture into the framework of salvation history and thus make it a bearer of the Christian mystery.

Besides the postbaptismal anointing there existed another, which was made before the baptismal bath. Ambrose of Milan in his mystagogical catechesis *The Sacraments* delivers the following instruction to neophytes regarding the meaning of this rite: "You were anointed as an athlete of Christ, as one who will fight the battle of this world."[36] It is difficult to miss the allusion to 1 Cor 9:24-27, which describes Christian life in the context of athletes in the arena, though it is unlikely that the rite was introduced with this biblical passage in mind. Yet this allusion to athletes allows us to detect the entry of a secular ritual into the rite of Christian baptism. It is possible that anointing, whether it was done before or after the sacramental bath, was in some way influenced by the practice of anointing and massaging the body of athletes with oil before the combat.

Another example of cultural influence is the cup of milk and honey at the Communion of neophytes, though it did not survive the test of time. The *Apostolic Tradition* attributed to Hippolytus of Rome mentions that it is offered to neophytes between the reception of the consecrated bread and wine.[37] The positioning of this rite could give a

---

[35] *De sacramentis/De mysteriis*, ed. B. Botte, in *SCh* 25 bis (1961) 6, p. 117.

[36] *De sacramentis* I, 4, p. 55.

[37] *La Tradition Apostolique de Saint Hippolyte*, ed. B. Botte (Münster, 1989); *Lac et melle mixta simul ad plenitudinem promissionis quae ad patres fuit, quam dixit terram fluentem lac et mel.*, no. 21, p. 56.

sharp impression of recklessness. There was doctrinally much at stake as far as the possible popular interpretation of the cup was concerned. But the author takes the necessary precautions. He urges the bishop to explain diligently to the neophytes the meaning of the cup.[38] According to him, the mixed drink symbolizes the "fulfillment of God's promise to our ancestors that he would lead them to a land flowing with milk and honey." The symbol fits perfectly the meaning of baptism as *pascha,* or the passage of God's people to the Church through the sacramental water of baptism. Having crossed the new Jordan, they enter the new promised land flowing with the eucharistic milk and honey. Ritually the place of the mixed cup in the order of Communion seems to strengthen the meaning of the Eucharist as the fulfillment of God's promise.

Tertullian alludes to the same practice of offering the cup of milk and honey to neophytes. In his work, *The Crown,* he writes: "After we have been welcomed [by the bishop], we taste the cup of milk and honey which signifies concord."[39] The word "welcome" roughly translates the Latin *susceptio* or *munus susceptionis,* which was the Roman legal term for the father's official claim that the newborn infant was his.[40]

Can we trace the source for the cup of milk and honey in the Roman cultural milieu? The ancient Romans had the custom of giving milk mixed with honey to newborn infants. The drink was expected to strengthen the infants against sickness and the influence of evil spirits. It was considered to possess an apotropaic quality. But together with the *susceptio* it could also signify the act of welcoming the infant to the family. Tertullian probably had this in mind when he described the mixed cup as *lactis et mellis concordiam.*

Could the early Church have been inspired by 1 Pet 2:2's baptismal discourse: "Like the new-born infants you are, you must crave for pure milk"? History seems to tell us that outside the core of apostolic tradition liturgical forms, especially the explanatory rites, developed not by the process of incorporating biblical elements into the liturgy

[38] *De universis vero his rationem reddat episcopus eis qui percipiunt,* ibid.

[39] *De corona* in CCL II/2 (1954) pp. 1042–3: *Inde suscepti lactis et mellis concordiam praegustamus.*

[40] *Susceptio* in this legal context is echoed by *The Rule of St. Benedict,* ch. 58, which carries the title *De disciplina suscipiendorum fratrum* (Collegeville, 1981) 266.

but by admitting suitable elements of contemporary culture and investing them with biblical meaning. Direct borrowing of elements from Scripture seems unlikely. On the other hand, it is not farfetched to imagine that the Roman custom had its share in the introduction of the said cup into the Christian rite of initiation. Nor should we lightly dismiss the possible influence of the Eleusinian mystery rite, which included the offering of a cup of honeyed drink to the initiates.[41]

Another example, this time particular to the church of Milan, is the washing of the feet of neophytes as they ascended from the baptismal pool. Ambrose of Milan attests to this in his work *The Sacraments*.[42] He defends it against Roman critics, who felt that it was too secular an act to be incorporated into the sacred celebration of baptism. In response he notes that the church of Rome itself used to observe it in the past, but "perhaps on account of the multitude [of neophytes] the practice declined." Considering the proverbial Roman sense for practicality, Ambrose's guess might not be far from the truth. Even today the rite of baptism for children permits the omission of anointing with chrism if there are many children who are baptized.[43]

As biblical basis for his church's practice, Ambrose used John 13's Last Supper washing of feet. Was this the source of the practice, or did it serve merely as biblical type? This New Testament narrative was inserted in the context of a meal, not of baptism. But for Ambrose it gave scriptural force to a local tradition. We may note in passing that chapter 53 of the sixth-century *Rule of St. Benedict* directs the abbot and the entire community to wash the feet of guests who come to the monastery. At a time when most people traveled on foot, nothing could have been more soothing than water for one's tired and dusty feet. Washing the feet of guests was a sign of welcome and hospitality. Could this have been the original meaning of this Milanese baptismal rite? The washing of feet upon coming up from a pool of water has little sense outside this cultural setting.

Pagan mystery rites influenced the rites and language used for Christian initiation. Φωτισμός or enlightenment, λουτρόν or bath, and

---

[41] E. Yarnold, "Baptism and the Pagan Mysteries in the Fourth Century," *HJ* 13 (1972) 247–67.

[42] *De sacramentis* III, 1, pp. 72–4.

[43] *Ordo baptismi parvulorum*, ed. *typica altera* (Vatican City, 1986) no. 24, p. 20.

μυσταγογία or the initiatory instruction were words the pagans shared with Christians. These were words whose meaning an average Christian would have easily grasped and probably used with a certain awareness that pagans had entered them even earlier into their religious lexicon.

Other factors also influenced the shape of the liturgy. In the writings of Tertullian dealing with baptism we come across words that have legal character. Tertullian, it will be remembered, was a jurist. In his book, *The Crown*, he calls the rite of baptismal renunciation *eieratio*. This legal term was used to indicate cessation of contractual service. Applied to baptism it implies that the Christian has disclaimed all further obligation to serve the devil. In another book, *The Spectacles*, Tertullian calls the baptismal profession of faith *sacramenti testatio* and *signaculum fidei*.[44] These terms had likewise a legal force. They were used in reference to the oath of allegiance soldiers swore to the emperor. Used for baptism, they reminded the Christians that they had solemnly vowed to serve Christ alone and with absolute loyalty. By employing such legal terms Tertullian impressed a certain juridical character on the neophytes' act of renunciation and profession of faith. He seems to tell them that these were serious things that should not be taken lightly.

Turning to the period between the fifth and eighth centuries, we see the development in Rome of a liturgy whose shape came to be known as classical, that is, in the style of Rome's *homo classicus:* noble, dignified, cultured.[45] It was a liturgy for the Roman people, whose cultural genius was marked by noble simplicity, brevity, sobriety, and practicality. It is a perfect example of an inculturated liturgy: its language and ritual expressions absorbed the cultural traits of classical Rome. Later liturgical reforms, in an effort to recapture this classical shape, would look back to it as model: the reform of Gregory VII, the Tridentine reform, the Catholic illuminism, the classical liturgical movement, and the reform of Vatican II. The liturgy of Vatican II as described in *SC* 34, 50, and 62 cannot be fully appreciated except in the context of the classical Roman liturgy.

[44] *De spectaculis* in CCL I/1 (1954) 24, p. 248.

[45] E. Bishop, "The Genius of the Roman Rite," *Liturgica historica* (Oxford, 1918) 2–9; G. Dix, *The Shape of the Liturgy*, 103–40. See also A. M. Triacca, "Tra idealizzazione e realtà: liturgia romana pura," *RL* 1993/4–5, pp. 413–42.

It was after the fourth century that the ritual shape of the Eucharist began to be increasingly bound up with the culture of the period, thanks largely to the conversion of Emperor Constantine and the Edict of Milan in the year 313. For Rome and the other metropolitan cities, especially in the East, culture meant, concretely, the culture of the imperial court. Under the patronage of the emperor himself the Church quite understandably integrated into the liturgy the ceremonials of the "ruling class." Unfortunately, our chief document, the *Roman Ordo I,* dates from the seventh century or the end of the sixth at the earliest and hence is a rather late record of what transpired between the fourth and the seventh centuries.[46] However, historical studies supply us with helpful information regarding this time gap.[47] We may reckon that what the *Roman Ordo* describes originated in the time of Constantine or at least during the Constantinian era.

The so-called *Donatio Constantini,* which is quoted by the *Liber Pontificalis,*[48] reports that Constantine gave to Pope Sylvester the Lateran palace as a gift and authorized him to use the imperial insignia, including the throne, and the privilege to have his portrait hung in public halls. We know that in the year 318 Constantine conferred on the bishops the power of jurisdiction in civil proceedings involving Christians. In the process they received titles, insignia, and privileges that belonged to the office of state dignitaries. The *Constitutio Constantini,* forged around the year 750 under Pope Stephen II, tried to establish the legal basis for the papacy's temporal claims against Byzantium.[49]

The eucharistic liturgy described by *Roman Ordo I* was the solemn papal Mass celebrated in the Basilica of St. Mary Major on the Esquiline Hill on Easter Sunday morning before the year 700. It is not possible nor is it necessary to describe here the entire procedure, which was long and quite complicated. Our interest is in several of its elements that are strikingly imperial in character. The historian T. Klauser has identified them for us.[50] The pope rode on horseback

---

[46] *Les Ordines Romani du haut moyen âge* II, ed. M. Andrieu (Louvain, 1971) 67–108.

[47] A. Chavasse, *La liturgie de la ville de Rome du Ve au VIIIe siècle* (Rome, 1993).

[48] L. Duchesne, *Le Liber Pontificalis: Texte, Introduction et Commentaire* (Paris, 1955) 170–202.

[49] *Constitutio Constanti,* ed. C. Mirbt, *Quellen zur Geschichte des Papstums und des römischen Katholizismus* (Tübingen, 1924) no. 228, pp. 107–12.

[50] Th. Klauser, *Short History of the Western Liturgy,* 59–72.

from the Lateran palace to the stational basilica. He was accompanied by the mayor and other dignitaries of the city. He wore the *cappa magna,* a cloak that reached to the feet of the horse. This was a garb worn by the emperor for solemn processions. As the pope walked to the sacristy, two deacons supported him ritually on either side. This was a court ceremonial known as *sustentatio.* In the sacristy his ministers surrounded him, as demanded by the Byzantine court ceremonial, in order to assist him as he vested for the liturgy. He put on an insignia called *pallium* over the chasuble, which is a white woolen band with pendants in front and at the back. This is originally another imperial insignia of authority. Today it is worn by the pope and metropolitan bishops. Although the *Roman Ordo* does not mention the ring, the special shoes, and the *camelaucum,* which later developed into the miter, we may presume that he wore these imperial insignia as well.[51]

As the pope processed to the sanctuary he was preceded by acolytes bearing seven lighted torches and a censer, while the *schola cantorum* of men and boys sang the introit. We note that candles and incense were used in solemn processions to honor the emperor and that he was greeted by a choir of singers when he entered an assembly hall for public audiences. Before proclaiming the Gospel, the deacon genuflected before the pope to kiss his shoes and to receive his blessing. This curious gesture of kissing the feet was required by the Byzantine court ceremonial. Ministers who served the pope waited on him at the throne and the altar with covered hands, again as demanded by imperial ceremonial. He took Communion not at the table but at his throne.

Strangely, the splendor of the imperial court was confined mostly to the entrance rite. Thus the Liturgy of the Word was celebrated with less pomp, and the Liturgy of the Eucharist with the *romana sobrietas* verging on austerity and gravity. Some have expressed reservations about the elite character of the celebration and the political overtones of the insignia used during the liturgy. Surely this type of inculturation need not become a paradigm for local churches today. Though the liturgical insignia of bishops no longer suggest political power but only ecclesiastical leadership, one wonders if there are no

[51] R. Berger, "Liturgische Gewänder und Insignien," *Gottesdienst der Kirche* 3 (Regensburg, 1987) 309–406; T. Klauser, *Short History of the Western Liturgy,* 32–7.

viable contemporary alternatives. A missionary bishop considered substituting the miter with the plumed headdress worn by tribal chieftains, but alas, this form of inculturation does not free the Church and the liturgy from the entanglement with the Constantinian court ceremonials. The miter and the plumed headdress send the same signal: Church authority patterned after the imperial system rather than the earlier concept of shepherding.

This period, however, seems to tell us that when the church in Rome, and the same must be said of Constantinople, decided to inculturate the shape of the Eucharist, it chose what was noble, beautiful, and significant in the culture of the people. The period under discussion should not in any way be so idealized as to suggest to the churches of today to assimilate only what is elite and exclusive in their culture. What it suggests is that, regardless of the socioeconomic condition of the people, the eucharistic celebration should be noble, dignified, and beautiful. And nobility of spirit, dignity, and beauty are not an exclusive possession of the elite and the powerful.

One other example of inculturation is the period known as Franco-Germanic.[52] In the eighth century the classical Roman liturgy was looked upon as model for the young churches in the Franco-Germanic empire of Pepin the Short and his son Charlemagne. Thus the Roman sacramentaries were imported for use in the empire. The problem was that their classical form did not culturally fit the mentality of the Franco-Germanic people. These people had a penchant for dramatic, flamboyant, and sentimental expressions, hence, the need to inculturate the classical Roman liturgy in the culture of the Franco-Germanic people. The simple, sober, and practical character of the Roman liturgy gave way to the new culture.[53]

Through the process of inculturation the Franco-Germanic churches enriched the shape of the Roman liturgy and set thereby a model for other local churches. The reform of Vatican II diminished the Franco-Germanic elements in the liturgy and reinstated its classical form. In

---

[52] E. Cattaneo, "L'Età franco-carolingia," *Il culto cristiano in occidente* (Rome, 1984) 184–219; Th. Klauser, "The Franco-German Contribution," *Short History of the Western Liturgy,* 77–93; B. Neunheuser, "La Liturgia romana nelle riforme franco-germaniche," *Anamnesis* 2, pp. 229–33; AA.VV.: *Culto cristiano. Politica imperiale carolingia* (Todi, 1979).

[53] Examples are given in volume 1, section 2.

doing this the council actually invited the local churches of today to repeat the process of inculturating the classical form of Vatican II's Roman liturgy in much the same way as the Franco-Germanic churches did in the eighth century. Today the starting point for the process of inculturation must begin with the reformed liturgy of Vatican II.

THE PROCESS OF INCULTURATION

Inculturation operates according to a given process and methodology. Process refers to well-defined steps or procedures. We are dealing here with what takes place between the *terminus a quo* and the *terminus ad quem*, or the point of departure and the point of arrival, which is the emergence of an inculturated liturgy. The *terminus a quo* is twofold: the typical edition of Vatican II's liturgical books and the components of culture.

Inculturation is basically a type of translation, even if the translation being referred to here is dynamic rather than formal. Hence it works on the existing liturgical texts and rites as well as on the contemporary components of local culture. Inculturation should not be mistaken for the process of creativity, which can dispense with pre-existing material.

The Typical Edition

The mind of *SC* 37–40 and 63b on this matter is clear: the work of inculturation must be based on the revised typical edition of the liturgical books of Vatican II. For this reason *SC* 38 decrees that "provisions shall be made, even in the revision of liturgical books, for legitimate variations and adaptations to different groups, regions, and peoples, especially in mission lands, provided the substantial unity of the Roman rite is preserved." This is elaborated by *SC* 39: "Within the limits set by the typical editions of the liturgical books, it shall be for the competent, territorial ecclesiastical authority to specify adaptations, especially in the case of the administration of the sacraments, the sacramentals, processions, liturgical language, sacred music, and the arts." Or in the words of *SC* 63b: "Particular rituals in harmony with the new edition of the Roman Ritual shall be prepared without delay by the competent, territorial ecclesiastical authority."

RLI sums up the foregoing principles in its reminder that "the work of inculturation does not foresee the creation of new families of rites; inculturation responds to the needs of a particular culture and leads to adaptations which still remain part of the Roman rite."[54] This explains why *SC* 38 carries the proviso regarding the preservation of the substantial unity of the Roman rite. *RLI* interprets substantial unity as the unity that "is currently expressed in the typical editions of liturgical books, published by authority of the Supreme Pontiff, and in liturgical books approved by the Episcopal Conferences for their areas and confirmed by the Apostolic See."[55]

The typical edition has to be examined under various aspects. These are the historical background of the rite, the theology it contains, the pastoral concern it embodies, and the possibilities for inculturation it envisages. In the words of *SC* 23: "That sound tradition may be retained and yet the way remain open to legitimate progress, a careful investigation is always to be made into each part of the liturgy to be revised. This investigation should be theological, historical, and pastoral."

SC 23 speaks of a "careful investigation." This involves an exegesis of the original Latin text and a historical research on the meaning of gestures and symbols originally intended by the rite. The exegesis of the liturgical rite should include semiotics, which examines what the various signs and symbols present in liturgical text mean and how they are interrelated in the same celebration.[56]

Careful investigation requires also hermeneutics of the official documents on the liturgy, both conciliar and postconciliar. The aim of hermeneutics is to read the mind of the lawgiver, to explicitate the provisions that are only implicitly stated in the document. An example of this is the one short sentence that *SC* 72 devotes to the sacrament of penance: "The rites and formularies for the sacrament of penance are to be revised so that they more clearly express both the nature and effect of the sacrament." Through the art of

[54] *The Roman Liturgy and Inculturation*, no. 36, p. 18.

[55] Ibid.

[56] A. Terrin, *Leitourgia. Dimensione fenomeonologica e aspetti semiotici* (Brescia, 1988); M. Amaladoss, "Ermeneutica antropologico-culturale dell'adattamento," *Liturgia e adattamento. Dimensioni culturali e teologico-pastorali* (Rome, 1990) 23–38; F. Brambilla, "Ermeneutica teologica dell'adattamento liturgico," ibid., 39–83; for liturgical exegesis of texts see A. Echiegu, *Translating the Collects of the "Sollemnitates Domini" of the "Missale Romanum" of Paul VI in the Language of the African* (Münster, 1984) 123–227.

hermeneutics we discover that by the word "nature" of the sacrament the council meant its social and ecclesial character, and by the word "effect" it intended to restore the laying on of hands to signify reconciliation.[57]

The Components of Culture

One of the problems liturgists encounter in the process of inculturation is how to define the culture of a local church. It is not possible here to enter into a thorough discussion of the concept of culture. A working definition, however, is useful. Although cultural anthropology is more immediately related to the liturgy, the other branches of anthropology, namely biological, archaeological, and linguistic, should not be overlooked.[58]

Lumen gentium (LG) 53 offers the following definition: "The word 'culture' in the general sense refers to all those things which go to the refining and developing of the diverse mental and physical human endowments." The definition encompasses human knowledge and work for the improvement of the earth and its environment; of social life, customs, and institutions of families and larger communities; and of spiritual experiences and human aspirations through arts. *LG* 53 adds that "culture necessarily has historical and social overtones, and the word 'culture' often carries with it sociological and ethnological connotations; in this sense one can speak about a plurality of cultures."

In the humanistic tradition of the past culture was synonymous with the vastness of human knowledge. And knowledge referred to ideas and notions, in short, to rational understanding. One was considered "cultured" depending on the amount of such knowledge one had acquired. With the advent of cultural anthropology the concept of culture has evolved into something much broader. For a working definition of culture the following points might be helpful.

---

[57] A. Chupungco, *Liturgies of the Future* (New York, 1989) 113–5.

[58] See L. Luzbetak, *The Church and Cultures: New Perspectives in Missiological Anthropology* (New York, 1988/1993) 133–222; M. Chomsky, *Syntactic Structures* (The Hague, 1964); F. Keesing, *Cultural Anthropology: The Science of Custom* (New York, 1958); T. Tentori, *Antropologia culturale* (Rome, 1980); A. Triacca and A. Pistoia, (eds.), *Liturgie et anthropologie.* Conférence Saint-Serge. XXXVIe Semaine d'études liturgiques (Rome, 1990); V. Turner, *The Ritual Process* (Chicago, 1969).

First, culture embraces not only rational thought but also the practical realities of life, like the pattern of constructing homes, of cooking and eating, of planting and harvesting, of paying worship to God. The liturgy possesses divinely instituted elements, but these are embodied in culture. Second, culture is anthropo-genetic. Applying this principle to the liturgy, we can say that while we shape the liturgical *ordo*, it shapes us by its values and leads us into communion with its divine component. Third, culture is pluralistic. Cultural pluralism means that there are as many cultures as there are culturally differentiated social groups. If we consider the cultural dimension of the liturgy, we should be able to conclude that there should be as many liturgical *ordines* as there are patterns of thought, language, and rites. Fourth, culture is structured: it does not come about casually or by chance. Rather it is governed by set structures, even if such structures undergo evolution. The liturgy is also structured or governed by norms. Liturgical tradition calls structure *ordo*, which implies a set of normative patterns.[59]

To make the foregoing definition work, it is helpful to review the components of culture. These are values, patterns, and institutions.

Values are principles that influence and give direction to the life and activities of a community. They are formative of the community's attitude or behavior toward social, religious, political, and ethical realities. The value of hospitality, for example, shapes the active vocabulary of a community and creates pertinent rites to welcome, entertain, and send off guests. The value of family ties brings members back to parental homes for family meetings and annual celebrations. The value of leadership is extolled by titles of honor and the pledge of loyalty on the part of the community and by the corresponding promise of active service by the leader.

The liturgy has also its set of values. These are parallel to human values, although they are obviously seen from a Christian perspective. Hospitality, for example, acquires a distinctly Christian meaning in the baptismal celebration, when the community receives the newly baptized. It is expressed by the openness with which visitors are welcomed by the community into its eucharistic table. The Sunday ministers of hospitality welcome back members of the parish community and see them off at the door of the church.

[59] C. Di Sante, "Cultura e liturgia," *NDL* 341–51.

Another liturgical value is community spirit, which is a broader version of family ties. When the liturgy is regarded merely as a vertical relationship in which the horizontal can be dispensed with, this value suffers. But if the liturgy is viewed as a cultural reality possessing the value of community spirit, coming together every Sunday in order to celebrate as a Christian community becomes a cultural exigency.

Finally, the value of leadership is a basic ingredient of the concept of liturgical assembly. The liturgy is essentially the worship of an assembled community, that particular image of Christ's Church that is organically structured, or we may also say structurally organized. We refer here to the relationship between the presider and the assembly and in the final analysis to the office of Church leadership. This is a value that is inherent in the very nature of community worship. We cannot conceive of acephalous liturgical celebrations. Even in those liturgies where the hierarchical representative does not preside, there is always a lay leader, a *primus inter pares*, yet *primus*.

The second component of culture are cultural *patterns*. These are the typical way members of a society think or form concepts, express their thoughts through language, ritualize aspects of their life, and create art forms. The areas covered by cultural patterns are thus thought, language, rites and symbols, literature, music, architecture, and all other expressions of fine arts.

We call them cultural patterns because they are rather predictable in the sense that they follow an established course. Things are thought out, spoken of, and done according to certain patterns. Thus every cultural group has its typical way of thinking about things, verbalizing concepts, expressing values, and so on. Cultural patterns are so named also because they are society's norms of life into which a person is born and reared. Through the process of *enculturation* a person is so trained to behave according to such patterns that these become like second nature to her or him. Although cultural patterns do not eliminate individuality, they shape members of society within the established bounds of social acceptability. For this reason we should have no scruples distinguishing one society from another or one racial group from another. Generalizations, which should be avoided, express nonetheless the perception that cultural patterns have the power to shape the life of an individual and the entire society to which he or she belongs.

Though we can ultimately trace our liturgical origins to the Jewish tradition, we have to accept the fact that in the West the Christian liturgy has been ulteriorly influenced by Roman cultural patterns. And even after other European cultural patterns, like the Franco-Germanic, had modified the Western liturgy, its style of formulary and rituality continued to be identified as basically Roman: sober, concise, direct, and practical. The Roman cultural patterns have by and large shaped the patterns of the Roman liturgy. It is in this context that we examine the cultural patterns in the Roman liturgy.

A strikingly Roman pattern inherited by the Roman liturgy is the abruptness with which the assembly is sent off. In concise and direct words the Roman assembly was told: *Ite, missa est.* In modern English we would simply announce, "meeting adjourned." Under the influence of this Roman pattern the liturgical assembly is quickly blessed and sent away in three words. Some even call this rite of leave-taking "the rite of dismissal," which can be quite offensive and is absolutely lacking in social refinements. That people do not find offense at being dismissed is a sure sign that they do not take the words they hear seriously or they have formed the habit of not regarding the liturgy as a cultural reality. The Roman genius for brevity applied to the leave-taking in the liturgy can cause uneasiness among societies where it takes considerable time and art to say good-bye.

The rite of Communion may be reviewed in the context of hospitality. That the presider takes Communion ahead of the assembly can be explained by the office of leadership. But the kind of imagery it creates can be quite culturally strange. The presider in the sight of all eats and drinks first, and only then distributes Communion to the rest. In some Roman Catholic churches the assembly not only receive Communion after the presider, they also have the misfortune of receiving from the reserved hosts in the tabernacle. Here the imagery is that of a host who eats from the freshly cooked dishes and then offers to the guests the leftovers in the refrigerator! Although this curious practice has been criticized time and again (indeed *SC* 55 strongly endorses Communion from the table, not from the tabernacle), the sense of practicality seems to override the value of hospitality.

Perhaps the most significant expression of liturgical hospitality is in the greetings "The Lord be with you" and "Peace be with you." These greetings, which are said at various moments in the celebration, serve as words of welcome, as reassurance of Christ's presence, and as parting words. Some presiders replace them with more contemporary formulas or else juxtapose them, thereby giving the wrong impression that these christological greetings do not have the same value of hospitality that contemporary greetings such as "Good morning" or "Good evening" have.

Similar considerations can be made regarding the value of community spirit. We perceive this liturgical value in words like "family" and "household of God," which are used time and again to describe the assembly gathered together. The biblical imagery of sharing in one bread and one cup heightens the value of family, even though out of practical sense the bread might be pre-broken in very large gatherings. The very name of the church building, *domus Ecclesiae,* or the house of the Church, suggests a pattern of thought and language. The architectural disposition of the building as well as the order of the gathered community, with the presider and the ministers in the sanctuary and the assembly in the nave, seem to be patterned, however, on the arrangement observed among Roman families when they were at meetings. In a cultural ambit wherein the *paterfamilias* reigned supreme, such an arrangement loudly affirmed a cultural pattern regarding the Roman family.

As regards the value of leadership, the liturgy observes a clear thought, language, and ritual pattern. The image of the bishop in the writings of Ignatius of Antioch is that of God, while the presbyters surrounding him depict the college of apostles. In the liturgy the office of leader is traditionally symbolized by the president's chair, probably influenced by the Roman *cathedra,* or seat of authority. The liturgy also reserves certain functions to the leader of the assembly. Traditionally these are the presidential prayers, especially the Eucharistic Prayer, and the homily. We have seen that from the time of Emperor Constantine bishops, and to a degree also the presbyters and deacons, acquired political offices and with them the corresponding imperial court ceremonials. Bishops could use the throne, be greeted with a choral song as they entered the basilica, have their feet kissed, and so on. Thus the liturgy's pattern of leadership, which had previously been focused on shepherding, as we read in the third-century *Apostolic Tradition,* gradually shifted to a pattern of leadership, which was more sociopolitical in expression.

THE METHODS OF INCULTURATION

Correct method is the key to correct inculturation. An examination of historical and contemporary models of inculturation shows that the Church used several methods in the course of centuries. Three of these are creative assimilation, dynamic equivalence, and organic progression.

Different factors are at play in the application of the above-mentioned methods, namely: the theological reflection of a given period in answer to doctrinal controversies; the evolving cultural expressions, especially in the missions; and the pastoral needs of a particular worshiping community.

The Method of Creative Assimilation

During the age of patristic creativity, especially by Church Fathers like Tertullian, Hippolytus, and Ambrose, inculturation came about through the integration of pertinent rites and linguistic expressions, religious or otherwise, used by contemporary society. The examples we have seen are the baptismal anointing, the giving of the cup of milk and honey, and the foot washing of neophytes. Words like *eieratio* for baptismal renunciation, *fidei testatio* for profession of faith, μυσταγογία, and *initiatio* were entered into the liturgical vocabulary.[60]

These rites, after being reinterpreted through the system of biblical typology, often served as explanatory rites of the sacraments. They elaborated the core of the liturgical rite; they developed the shape of the liturgy. Thus the rite of baptism developed from the apostolic "washing in water with the word" to a full liturgical celebration that included prebaptismal anointing, act of renunciation (toward the West) and profession of faith (toward the East), blessing of baptismal water, and postbaptismal rites like washing of the feet, anointing with chrism, clothing, and the giving of a lighted candle.

This method has undoubtedly enriched the shape of the liturgy. It can be a useful reference when one intends to develop or expand the shape of the typical edition into a particular ritual for use in a local church. The rite of marriage, as presented by the typical edition, is in need of such ritual and linguistic elaboration.[61] The institution for a

---

[60] P.-M. Gy, "The Inculturation of the Christian Liturgy in the West," *SL* 20/1 (1990) 8–18. Gy gives other linguistic examples such as *confessio, absolutio,* and *paenitentia.*

[61] R. Serrano, *Towards a Cultural Adaptation of the Rite of Marriage* (Rome, 1987).

local church of new liturgical feasts inspired by contemporary socio-cultural or civil festivities is another area where the method of creative assimilation can be useful.[62] Through this form of inculturation the liturgical year is grafted on the seasons of the year, traditional feasts of peoples, the cycle of human work, and political systems of nations. The Church should not isolate itself from what goes on in the world. Its liturgy should interplay with the academic year, the business year, the political year, the cause-oriented years, the years of struggles and hopes, and the years of war and peace. The liturgical year should interplay with these other years in order to imbue them with the mystery of Christ.

The Method of Dynamic Equivalence
Dynamic equivalence consists of replacing elements of the Roman liturgy with something that has an equal meaning or value in the culture of the people and hence can suitably transmit the message intended by the Roman liturgy. Through dynamic equivalence the linguistic, ritual, and symbolic elements of the Roman liturgy are re-expressed according to the local church's pattern of thought, speech, and ritualization. Dynamic equivalence allows the liturgy to evoke life experience and to paint vivid images drawn from the people's history, traditions, and values.

C. Kraft points out the following traits of dynamic equivalence: (1) each language — the same can be said of the other components of culture — has its own genius and special character; (2) to communicate effectively in another language one must respect this uniqueness and work in terms of it. He notes that attempts to "remake" languages to conform to other languages have been monumentally unsuccessful; (3) to preserve the content of the message the form must be changed. Different languages express quite similar concepts in very different ways, and no concepts are expressed in exactly the same ways. Kraft concludes that "the faithful translator, in attempting to convey an equivalent message in terms of the genius of the receptor language, must alter the form in which the message was expressed in the original language."[63]

---

[62] A. Adam, *The Liturgical Year* (New York, 1981).
[63] C. Kraft, *Christianity in Culture: A Study in Dynamic Biblical Theologizing in Cross-cultural Perspective* (New York, 1979/1994) 272–3; see entire chapters 13–5, 261–312.

The opposite of dynamic equivalence is formal equivalence or correspondence, which does not take into consideration the cultural patterns, history, and life experience of the local church. According to Kraft, formal equivalence "aims to be faithful to the original documents. But this 'faithfulness' centers almost exclusively on the surface-level forms of the linguistic encoding in the source language and their literal transference into corresponding linguistic forms in the receptor language."[64]

Examples of formal equivalence in the liturgy are those translations that try to account for every word found in the original Latin formulary. Some translations are no more than mere transliteration, as for example, mystery for *mysterium;* sacrament for *sacramentum;* "in memory of" for *anamnesis.* Often such formal equivalents, though they are doctrinally safe, do not enrich the assembly's understanding of what the liturgy is saying.

The concept of dynamic equivalence will become clearer with examples of how to translate technical terms. The two basic terms in liturgy, namely *anamnesis* and *epiclesis,* are probably also the basic problems of liturgical inculturation. *Anamnesis* is commonly defined as the ritual memorial of Christ's paschal mystery; by virtue of this ritual memorial the paschal mystery becomes present to the worshiping assembly. To express *anamnesis* the Latin Eucharistic Prayers use *memores* (Eucharistic Prayers 1, 2, and 3) or *memoriale celebrantes* (Eucharistic Prayer 4).

An attempt to use dynamic equivalence for *anamnesis* was made in 1975 by the proposed *Misa ng Bayang Pilipino,* which was submitted to Rome the following year.[65] The narration of the Last Supper begins with the Tagalog phrase *tandang-tanda pa namin* (literally, "how clearly we remember"). It is the phrase used to start the narration of a historical event. By it the narrator claims to have been present when the event happened and witnessed it in person; that is why one can recount it vividly and to the last detail. Is this not perhaps what the Church wishes to say at the narration of the Last Supper? The Church was there, remembers what took place as Jesus sat with his disciples, and now passes on the experience from one generation to the next.

[64] Ibid., 265.
[65] Text in A. Chupungco, *Towards a Filipino Liturgy* (Quezon City, 1976) 96–118.

The other concept is *epiclesis*, which may be defined as the prayer to invoke God to send the Holy Spirit on the sacramental elements and on the people, who receive the sacraments in order that they may be sanctified or consecrated to God. The *Misa ng Bayang Pilipino* uses a graphic expression for *epiclesis: lukuban ng Espiritu Santo*. The verb *lukuban* means "to protect," "to gather under the wings," "to brood." Used for *epiclesis*, it calls to mind the action of the bird brooding its eggs; thereby it conveys the idea of the vivifying and transforming action of the Holy Spirit on the bread and wine and on the assembly.

Idiomatic expressions, which often defy translation, are some of the best material for dynamic equivalence. For example, the Latin word *dignitas* is normally translated as dignity, and people have a notion of what the word means. But we are dealing here with inculturation. An attempt to use an idiomatic expression for *dignitas* is made by a proposed translation of the Christmas collect *Deus, qui humanae substantiae dignitatem* of Pope Leo the Great. Although Igbo, the language of Nigeria, has the equivalent word for dignity, the proposed Igbo translation prefers the idiomatic expression "to wear an eagle's feather." The eagle's feather stuck on one's hair shows the dignity and the position a person holds in society. The proposed Igbo prayer praises God, who gifts every man and woman with the eagle's feather.[66]

The method of dynamic equivalence works also through textual and ritual elaboration. The stress here is on the word "dynamic." The Tagalog rite of marriage, *Pagdiriwang ng Pag-iisang Dibdib*, approved by Rome in 1983, expands the exchange of consent: "Before God and his church I enter into a covenant with you to be my wife/husband. You alone shall I love and cherish as the extension of my life now and for ever." The key word and phrase that expand the exchange of consent are covenant *(tipan)* and extension of life *(karugtong ng buhay)*; the first refers to the covenant between Christ and his Church and alludes to the eucharistic new and everlasting covenant, while the second is an idiomatic expression for the biblical concept of one body in marriage. The formula for the giving of rings, which expands the original text, is a solemn promise of fidelity: "I shall never betray

---

[66] A. Echiegu, *Translating the Collects of the "Sollemnitates Domini" of the "Missale Romanum" of Paul VI in the Language of the African*, 313.

your love! Wear this ring and prize it, for it is the pledge of my love and faithfulness." The Tagalog *pagtaksilan* (to betray) refers to marital infidelity, while *sangla* (pledge) signifies the sacrifice or deprivation the espoused must endure in exchange for love: what is pledged must be redeemed with something that is equal in value.[67]

Examples of ritual elaboration are given by the twelve points approved by the *Consilium ad exsequendam* in 1970 for India. The entrance rite incorporates the presentation of gifts, the Indian rite of welcome, the ceremony of lighting the lamps, and the rite of peace. At the conclusion of the Eucharistic Prayer the assembly performs the *panchanga pranam* (kneeling and touching the floor with the forehead) as sign of adoration. These ritual elaborations are meant to illustrate in a religious cultural way the meaning of the various parts of the eucharistic celebration.[68]

As regards ritual elements, a fine example is the Zairean sign of peace at Mass. In the Zairean Order of Mass the sign of peace takes place after the penitential rite, which concludes the Liturgy of the Word. The sign may consist of washing hands in the same bowl of water that is passed around in the congregation. The gesture is a cultural way of saying "I wash away anything I have against you."[69]

The Method of Organic Progression

The method of organic progression may be described as the work of supplementing and completing, when necessary, the shape of the liturgy established by *SC* and the *editio typica* of the liturgical books. It accomplishes this by rereading these documents with the purpose of supplying what they lack or putting to completion what they only partially and imperfectly state. It is progressive because it operates through two dynamics that develop the shape of the liturgy. These are (1) supplementation, whereby new elements are inserted into the liturgy, and (2) continuance, because it is a sequel to the work begun by the council and the Holy See. The method is organic because it re-

[67] *Pagdiriwang ng Pag-iisang Dibdib* (Manila, 1983) 20 and 23; see R. Serrano, *Cultural Adaptation of the Rite of Marriage.*

[68] *New Orders of the Mass for India* (Bangalore, 1974); see D. S. Amalorpavadass, *Towards Indigenisation in the Liturgy* (Bangalore, 1971).

[69] Text in Conférence épiscopale du Zaïre, *Rite zaïrois de la célébration eucharistique* (Kinshasa, 1985). The decree of approval by the Holy See, "Zairensium Dioecesium," is in *Not* 264 (1988) 457.

sults in a new shape that is coherent with the basic intention of the liturgical documents and, on a wider breadth, with the nature and tradition of Christian worship.

SC 23 contains the concept of organic progression: "Care must be taken that any new forms adopted should in some way grow organically from forms already existing." The key words in this statement are "new forms" *(novae formae)*, "grow" *(crescere)*, "organically" *(organice)*, and "existing forms" *(formae iam exstantes)*. The conciliar commission explained that the text, "using the words, innovations and new forms, suggests that new rites can be produced; it closes no doors, but instills the need to preserve continuity in the process of evolution and puts us on guard against impertinent innovations."[70]

When we compare the present state of the liturgical reform with the provisions of *SC*, we realize that there are lacunae in the conciliar reform. Nowhere in chapter 2 of *SC* is inculturation of the Order of Mass by the local churches addressed. *SC* 50 confines itself to the principles and criteria of revision on the part of the Holy See. There are also lacunae in the *editio typica* of the postconciliar liturgical books. *SC* 77, recognizing the textual and ritual poverty of the current rite of marriage, has ordained that it "be revised and enriched *(ditior fiat)* in such a way that it more clearly signifies the grace of the sacrament and imparts a knowledge of the obligations of spouses." The rite was revised, but there is a consciousness that lacunae still remain. Thus the introduction to the new rite allows that the formularies "be adapted, or as the case may be, supplemented (including the questions before the consent and the actual words of consent)." Furthermore, "when the Roman ritual has several optional formularies, local rituals may add others of the same type."[71]

It is useful to note at this point that organic progression does not consist of emending or modifying what has been established by superior authority. The text of the liturgical provision must remain intact. The Holy See does not rewrite *SC*, and the conferences of bishops do not reedit the *editio typica*. But the former supplements or completes what is lacking in the conciliar document and the latter what is lacking in the *editio typica*.

[70] *Schema Constitutionis de Sacra Liturgia,* Caput I, Emendationes 4 (Vatican City, 1967) 8.

[71] *Ordo celebrandi matrimonium, Editio typica altera,* no. 40 (Vatican City, 1991) 9. See R. Serrano, *Cultural Adaptation of the Rite of Marriage,* 4–112.

No one should put the Holy See to task for having revised all the liturgical books after the council. But neither should anyone be disturbed if in some particular instances the work of postconciliar revision went beyond the limits set by the text of *SC*. The use of the vernacular in all liturgical celebrations, the incorporation into the *editio typica* of new elements like general absolution, the introduction of new Eucharistic Prayers, the faculty to repeat anointing in the course of the same illness, the permission to use another kind of plant oil in the sacrament of the sick, and the possibility to draw up particular Orders of Mass are some examples where the process of organic progression has been clearly at work.

The process of organic progression should continue on the level of local churches. For them the process of organic progression may be laid out in several steps. The first step calls for a close examination of the *editio typica*. Besides the necessary historical, theological, and linguistic study of the document, there should be an examination of the various options of inculturation offered by the *editio typica*.

The second step deals with singling out the cultural and pastoral needs of the local church as a worshiping community and the areas that require the process of organic progression but were not addressed by the *editio typica*.

The third step is an inquiry on whether the new form to be introduced responds to a legitimate need of the local church. As *SC* 23 cautions, "There must be no innovations unless the good of the Church genuinely and certainly requires them." Furthermore, it should be ascertained whether the new form is not alien to the authentic spirit of the liturgy, whether it is coherent with the general program of renewal initiated by Vatican II, and whether it fits with the rest of the rite.

Bibliography

Chupungco, A. *Cultural Adaptation of the Liturgy.* New York, 1982.

____. *Liturgies of the Future: The Process and Methods of Inculturation.* New York, 1989.

____. *Liturgical Inculturation: Sacramentals, Religiosity, Catechesis.* Collegeville, Minn., 1992.

____. *Worship: Progress and Tradition.* Washington, 1995.

374

Congregation for Divine Worship and the Discipline of the Sacraments. *The Roman Liturgy and Inculturation.* Fourth Instruction for the Right Application of the Conciliar Constitution on the Liturgy (nn. 37–40). Rome, 1994.

Francis, M. *Liturgy in a Multicultural Community.* Collegeville, Minn., 1991.

"Inculturazione e liturgia oggi." *RL* (July–August 1995, n. 4).

"L'inculturation." *MD* 189 (1989).

Shorter, A. *Toward a Theology of Inculturation.* New York, 1988.

Subject Index

The following pages list the chief or more commonly treated subjects that are pertinent to the study of fundamental liturgy. This index does not contain the names of persons, events, and places recorded in this volume.